The Ethics of Nature

NEW DIMENSIONS TO RELIGIOUS ETHICS

Series Editors: Frank G. Kirkpatrick and Susan Frank Parsons
Trinity College, Hartford, US, and Margaret Beaufort Institute of Theology, Cambridge, UK

The aim of this series is to offer high-quality materials for use in the study of ethics at the undergraduate or seminary level, by means of engagement in the interdisciplinary debate about significant moral questions with a distinctive theological voice. Each volume investigates a dimension of religious ethics that has become problematic, not least due to the wider climate of reappraisal of Enlightenment thought. More especially, it is understood that these are dimensions which run through a number of contemporary moral dilemmas that trouble the postmodern world. It is hoped that an analysis of basic assumptions will provide students with a good grounding in ethical thought, and will open windows onto new features of the moral landscape that require further attention. The series thus looks forward to a most challenging renewal of thinking in religious ethics and to the serious engagement of theologians in what are the most poignant questions of our time.

Published

1. *The Ethics of Community*
Frank G. Kirkpatrick

2. *The Ethics of Gender*
Susan Frank Parsons

3. *The Ethics of Sex*
Mark D. Jordan

4. *The Ethics of Nature*
Celia E. Deane-Drummond

The Ethics of Nature

Celia E. Deane-Drummond

Chester College of Higher Education

Blackwell
Publishing

350 Main Street, Malden, MA 02148-5020, USA
108 Cowley Road, Oxford OX4 1JF, UK
550 Swanston Street, Carlton, Victoria 3053, Australia

First published 2004 by Blackwell Publishing Ltd

Library of Congress Cataloging-in-Publication Data

Deane-Drummond, Celia.
The ethics of nature / by Celia E. Deane-Drummond.
p. cm. — (New dimensions to religious ethics)
Includes bibliographical references.
ISBN 978-0-631-22938-4
1. Human ecology—Religious aspects—Christianity.
2. Nature—Religious aspects—Christianity.   3. Environmental responsibility.   4. Environmental ethics.   5. Christian ethics.
6. Christianity—Social aspects.   I. Title.   II. Series.
BT695.5.D373 2003
261.8′8—dc22   2003014808

A catalogue record for this title is available from the British Library.

Set in 10.5 on 12.5pt M. Bembo
by Graphicraft Ltd, Hong Kong

For further information on
Blackwell Publishing, visit our website:
http://www.blackwellpublishing.com

In loving memory of my mother:
Mary Evangeline Deane-Drummond
9 November 1916 to 3 July 2002

and my spiritual guide and friend:
Philomena O'Higgins (SSL)
20 July 1932 to 16 November 2002

and my friend Susan Rattenbury
26 February 1963 to 28 May 2003

Contents

Preface

In consideration of how are we to treat the natural world, we are faced with a number of possibilities. The first is that the context in which we live is one dominated by scientific knowledge. There is no escaping the rise of all kinds of modern biological techniques that become currency for popular debates via the media. At the same time, this new biology has precedents in Darwinian evolutionary science that has come to be accepted almost as uncontroversial fact, rather than hypothesis. Yet Darwinian science has also yielded the concept of ecology, one that has overgrown its biological limitations and become a political concept, but one ironically now turned against the perceived environmental damage wrought by science and technology.

The ethics of 'nature' has commonly been interpreted narrowly in terms of environmental concern, with a shift towards endearing value not just to the human species, but also to non-human nature. Indeed, what 'nature' is has been defined variously as either that over and against humans, or inclusive of human beings, with a variety of perceptions emerging at different stages in history.[1] Important though these discussions are, they rarely integrate a scientific understanding of biology with philosophical and ethical demands of the natural world. The paucity of the scientific discussion may arise from a common hostility towards science by those interested in environmental ethics, it becomes a source of blame for current problems, so its discoveries in and of themselves are barely worth detailed consideration. On the other hand, those engaging in debates in science and religion have sought to revise their understanding of God to fit into current scientific evolutionary theories, where this time ethical concern moves to the background. The challenge of a Christian ethics of nature is not just how to delineate the nature and task of what is an appropriate Christian ethic, but also how to take into account the scientific understanding of what nature might be. Of course, a full account of all the various biological sciences is beyond the scope of this book, yet it is my contention that ethical reconstruction that ignores relevant aspects of science runs the risk of evacuating any means of challenging the way science might progress in the future. For the power of science needs to be met on its own terms, rather than dismissed as irrelevant.

The scope of an ethics of nature depends partly on what is understood by the term 'natural'. Does it mean that which is of instrumental use for human culture? Or is nature simply everything that exists, including human beings? Or again is nature that which is opposed to artefact, products of human imagination and ingenuity? Ever since Darwin the continuity between humanity and the natural world has received a much greater emphasis, though modern scientific methodology requires human detachment from its objects, in this case the natural world. Yet, ironically perhaps, overall the tension implicit in Darwin's theory has not necessarily encouraged a more inclusive view of the natural, but rather an instrumental understanding of the natural, its particular usefulness for humanity. Such an instrumental view finds its expression in the most recent development in biology, genetic engineering. On the other hand, the implicitly inclusive view finds its expression in subjects such as ecology and ethology, though such inclusion is thwarted by the specialization of the sciences whereby human ecology is split off from the ecology of plant and animal communities. I suggest that the idea that we are apart from nature needs to be set in the context of awareness that we are part of nature as well. One cannot be considered without the other. Hence an ethics of nature needs to include not just how we treat the natural world around us, our particular environment, but also who we are as persons, our human nature. Furthermore, contrary to much popular thought, I suggest that it is in consideration of our human nature, particularly the virtues, that clues about relating to the natural world in an appropriate and responsible way can be sought.

From the perspective of Christian theology one of the most popular models for envisioning such a relationship with the natural order is not virtue, but stewardship. One of the difficulties of this idea is that stewardship is often associated with an impersonal attitude to nature; it becomes 'resources' to be managed for human good. While it is possible to counter this claim by situating the idea of stewardship in less anthropocentric terms, the difficulty remains that our basic attitudes to the natural world still go unchallenged. Stewardship implies an active verb, a doing, but where it does point to the character of the agents it too easily implies condescension towards non-human nature.[2] It is my suggestion that a refocusing on agents first is concomitant with right action, while still affirming the necessity to act. I also suggest that the combination of stillness and action, of appropriate reflection and concerted judgement, find their most cogent expression in the theology of Aquinas, in particular his understanding of the virtues and practical wisdom or prudence. Prudence was, for Aquinas, a reasoning activity. However, reason meant a 'passage to reality', not narrowly conceived as a form of scepticism characteristic of Descartes and his followers.[3]

A return to the classics and a recovery of virtue might seem strange to modern ears, especially in the light of the breakdown of the classical model of cosmology following the discoveries of modern science. Is the classical notion of goodness tenable in the light of the pessimism or even pointlessness implicit in scientific understandings of the future? In fact, those who seek to reclaim theology in the light of the sciences normally do so by modifying their understanding of God so that it fits in with the latest scientific discoveries, or at least is commensurate with them. But classical theism was the presupposition of the early scientists, including key players such as Isaac Newton, as John Brooke has adeptly reminded us.[4] Hence, to assume that we necessarily need to modify our understanding of God seems to me to rest on a false premise. Of course, some of the ways in which creation is understood need to be updated in the light of modern knowledge and more contemporary understanding of the social and political structures of society. However, I suggest in this book that a classical model of God and creation does not need to be discarded in its entirety, even though it may need some revision. Rather, the strength of the classic is in its ability to withstand the test of time in a way that other modern renderings of the relationship between God and the world, such as we find in process thought, cannot. This does not mean that theology is alien to science; instead, it insists that it does have a contribution to make, and in this sense it can recover its voice, rather than being marginalized as irrelevant.[5]

Of course, the sciences themselves are beginning to accept that their work does not just have practical significance, but also raises areas of ethical concern and consideration. It has grown into a field known as 'bioethics'. Such attempts to find ethical principles, mostly by medical practitioners and scientists, have been summarily dismissed by Michael Banner. He is sharp in his critique that such 'bioethics' is completely new in its insights; moreover, he believes that any attempt to relate ethics to pseudoscientific principles is bound to fail. For:

> According to this picture, the scientist generates a prediction by combining the facts (or initial conditions) with a theory. Here, in the case of ethics, if we believe this model, a similar procedure can be followed, with values doing the work of the theory, and the result being not a prediction but a prescription.[6]

Moreover, the problem is deeper than this in that there is a misconception of the facts on which values are supposed to work. Ideas, such as stewardship, are paraded in the literature, but how can we assume a sense of responsibility:

> unless we have some account of, say, human flourishing, and furthermore, an account of the boundaries of human being? The ritual incantation of 'beneficence, non-maleficence, justice, confidentiality and autonomy' serves no purpose at this point. What we need in order to apply these values, let alone to understand why we should apply them, is an understanding of the reality which demands and constrains their application. Moral practice, in other words, presupposes metaphysics.[7]

Yet despite Banner's critique of the 'rich variety of intellectual confusion, unintelligibility and inadequacy, which, taken as a whole, is known as "bioethics"',[8] the fact that scientists are at least willing to consider ethical issues is surely a positive development. If those trained in the humanities were to attempt to undertake scientific research, equally stinging critiques could be levelled at their early efforts.

I suggest that an ethics of nature that is divorced from all scientific knowledge is as problematic as the caricature of ethics undertaken by those biologists subject to Banner's critique outlined above.[9] Furthermore, ethically such studies may not be as far off the mark as Banner suggests. For the incantation of 'beneficence, non-maleficence, justice, confidentiality and autonomy' is simply a secularized version of much older concepts of virtue that have their roots in the classical tradition. Of course, Banner does recognize this as characteristic of fragments of what was once a coherent moral discourse. I suggest that rather than criticism of the bearers of these fragments for their failure to recognize the roots of their moral concern, what is needed is a *reminder* of the source and fullness from which these fragments originated. It is, then, a recovery of the sense of history, but one that can also be shown to be thoroughly relevant to the contemporary moral problems that we face today.

One might ask: is such a return to a classical view possible in a post-Enlightened world? It is my suggestion in this book that not only is such a return possible, it is also feasible to realign such a view with an acknowledgement of the biological processes inherent in Darwin's theory of evolution. I choose these words carefully, for while Darwin's theory is the best available theory yet found to account for the variety of biological organisms, it is not necessarily the exclusive theory in a way that some biologists would have us believe. Indeed, I would strongly resist attempts to break the scope of Darwinianism beyond the boundaries of biological variation in order to account for differences in human culture in the way that sociobiology has attempted in more recent years.[10] This book does not include a detailed discussion of human evolutionary origins in relation to ethics, though I do touch on Darwinian theory, since this is an inevitable context in which contemporary science has developed. A close examination of historical and contemporary factors implicit in Darwinian theory in relation to ethics would be the subject of a complete volume.[11] Instead, I explore different areas of concern for those interested in developing an ethic of nature.

In the first chapter I set out the ethical framework for the following discussion. I argue specifically for a recovery of a primacy of virtue ethics within a Christian framework, rather than other alternatives that rely exclusively on either deontology or consequentialism. I suggest that virtue ethics is consistent with Christian theology and that an understanding of the classical cardinal virtue of prudence, rooted in the theological virtues of charity, hope and faith and set in the context of the three other cardinal virtues of justice, fortitude and temperance, is relevant for ethical consideration of the natural world. I draw particularly on virtues as discussed in Thomas Aquinas, while recognizing the importance of natural law. In particular, I spell out his understanding of practical wisdom or prudence and show how it is of particular importance to an ethics of nature. Prudence, broadly speaking, is the means through which the good can be achieved, understood in terms of goodness as given by God. Prudence is practical wisdom in human affairs, but wisdom properly speaking is also right judgement about God. Indeed, an ethic of wisdom does not need to deny natural law, but sees its proper place as the framework in which the virtues can grow and develop. I also suggest that the theological category that we need to recover in order to ground any ethical discussion is the idea of the world as *created*. Such a recovery might seem obvious, though rather than simply referring to the idea of fixed order and forms, the more common stereotypical rendering of scholastic thought, the idea of creation by contemplating God as Creator also opens up a deeper sense of the mystery of God and our ability to understand God's creation.

None the less, the search for wisdom has practical consequences for ethical deliberation on all aspects of the natural world. In the chapter 2 I deal specifically with the problems encountered by environmental issues. The somewhat stale philosophical debate between anthropocentric and biocentric views can be by-passed by asking another question altogether, namely what does it mean to act prudently and with justice in the context of environmental issues? Furthermore, I suggest that those who are more inclined to a biocentric view have read into ecological science their own particular political and social constructs. The view of ecology as stable systems needs to take account of more recent research that suggests the opposite. Once we remove the idea of an ordered stable system from ecology, the premise of much of the philosophical secular debate seems to evaporate. Yet this need not deny that ordering is in principle possible, but it is an ordering against a backcloth of fragility and instability.

In chapter 3 I consider the question of justice further by offering a critique of current thinking in animal ethics. I critique the work of Singer, Regan, Clark and Linzey. Christian reflection on animal ethics has been dominated particularly by the work of Andrew Linzey.[12] Of course, our understanding of animal ethics is dependent on our particular view of human persons, who we are *vis-à-vis* the animal world. I consider the clash between Aquinas's own instrumental ethical stance towards animals and his ontology, which seems to suggest the opposite, namely that animals and humans are closely related forms in a hierarchy of being. While Aquinas's understanding of the chain of being needs to be revised in the light of evolutionary biology, his affirmation of the worth of all creatures through a strong sense of the goodness of God manifest in creation softens this stance and allows a rather different animal ethics to emerge. I also suggest that consideration of the virtues is particularly relevant in the light of difficulties associated with current discussion in animal ethics.

In chapter 4 I examine issues associated with the ethics of biotechnology, in particular how far technology as such has served to shape the way we think about nature and the natural, in particular that associated with agricultural biotechnology. Are there alternative ways of reflecting on biotechnology that take into account the ethical difficulties associated with technological culture?

Next I explore the issue of cloning, but with a particular emphasis on the ethical issues related to animal cloning. Theological discussion of cloning has alighted on reproductive cloning in a way that by-passes other important questions for an ethics of nature, namely the ethics of cloning animals. I also include a discussion of the uses of human cloning for therapeutic purposes and stem cell research, since it illustrates clearly trends in our perception of human nature. How might a virtue ethic inform such discussions?

Cloning raises broader questions about the nature of our involvement with the technological world, who we are as persons and in particular whether psychology and associated neurobiology has challenged the possibility of moral agency that a virtue ethics, and indeed all ethics, assumes. I make such a move not because I wish to redefine what biology means, but because once we focus on the nature of human personhood in a way that is inevitable in the construction of a virtue ethics, some account of what science is saying in relation to who we are as persons becomes significant. Furthermore, it seems to me that it helps to shed light on the dilemma that surfaces throughout the book, namely how far can we be said to be distinctive from other life forms? Given this understanding of human persons, what might be the Christian interpretation of ethics?

Are there alternative models of science that we could consider in the light of such developments? I discuss the possibilities inherent in Gaia in the light of earlier discussion. I then move to a chapter on feminist ethics of nature. Are there insights from feminist theology that need to be taken into account in any revision of an ethics of nature? How far does the feminist critique, especially that which develops an ethic of care, cohere with the proposed emphasis on charity and wisdom? Indeed, could such an emphasis be reconceived according to a feminist narrative? Finally, I conclude by drawing together the themes of the book in a chapter that highlights the thread of wisdom alluded to throughout the text. It is my hope that this book will be the start of an ongoing conversation between humanity and the natural world understood through wisdom, yet it is inherent in any approach that draws on wisdom that the task is always one that is partly unfinished, it is a start of a process that is yet to be completed in conversation with others. Aquinas was well aware that his dialectical method inevitably left further areas for development. In this sense I am conscious that this book is an unfinished conversation. I invite the reader to take up that conversation and take it further in whatever context might be relevant for thinking through the dynamics of how humanity relates to the natural world.

Notes

1 For a useful discussion of these see J. Habgood, *The Concept of Nature* (London: Darton, Longman and Todd, 2002), pp. 1–22.

2 Jennifer Welchman has suggested that stewardship can be connected with particular virtues, namely benevolence and loyalty, but the way such virtues are framed reinforces the anthropocentric orientation of the term stewardship. J. Welchman, 'The virtues of stewardship', *Environmental Ethics*, 21 (1999), pp. 411–23.

3 For discussion see S. Hauerwas and C. Pinches, *Christians among the Virtues: Theological Conversations with Ancient and Modern Ethics* (Notre Dame, IN: University of Notre Dame Press, 1997).

4 J. Brooke, *Science and Religion: Some Historical Perspectives* (Cambridge: Cambridge University Press, 1991); J. Brooke and G. Cantor, *Reconstructing Nature: The Engagement of Science with Religion* (Edinburgh: T & T Clark, 1998).

5 See C. Deane-Drummond, 'Wisdom, a voice for theology at the boundary with science', *Ecotheology*, 10 (2001), pp. 23–39.

6 M. Banner, 'The taboos of ethics', *Minerva*, 34 (1996), pp. 199–204, esp. p. 201.

7 Banner, 'The taboos of ethics', p. 202.

8 M. Banner, *Christian Ethics and Contemporary Moral Problems* (Cambridge: Cambridge University Press, 1999), p. x.

9 For a more positive theological interpretation of bioethics that includes a discussion of environmental values see N. Messer (ed.), *Theological Issues in Bioethics: An Introduction with Readings* (London: Darton, Longman and Todd, 2002).

10 There is an important distinction between cultural traits as having some biological precedents, which I accept, and more extreme versions that suggest that genes or even 'memes' account for variation in human culture.

11 Stephen Clark's excellent book, *Biology and Christian Ethics* (Cambridge: Cambridge University Press, 2000) is a good example of this.

12 See, for example, A. Linsey, *Animal Theology* (London: SCM Press, 1994).

Acknowledgements

Those embarking on writing a book need companions and friends to help them on their way. In the three years or so during which this book has taken shape I have been struck by the generosity and kindness of others who have helped me to clarify my thinking, served to encourage me when dispirited and generally supported me in this task. I owe particular thanks to Susan Parsons, whose wisdom, encouragement and helpful feedback went beyond the call of duty as series editor. I would also like to thank the following who, with generosity and sharpness of insight, read different sections of the book and commented on it accordingly, namely William Phillips, Peter Scott, Clare Palmer, Chris Southgate, Michael Northcott, Fraser Watts, Jacqui Stewart and Andrew Hunt. I would also like to thank those anonymous reviewers who, at both at the beginning and end of the project, provided me with such thought provoking comments and questions. Finally, thanks are due to Laura Barry and Lucy Judkins, of Blackwell Publishing, for their willingness to take on this book and offer helpful advice.

The time needed to devote to writing a book is considerable, and the task would have been impossible were it not for the financial assistance of the Christendom Trust, whose support for the Centre for Religion and the Biosciences at Chester College freed me to some extent from my teaching and administrative duties so that I could pursue research. This book emerges as a work of the Centre, dedicated to pursuing areas of conversation between religious traditions and the biological sciences. Some of the material in this book has been delivered in modified versions for lectures at various venues, including the postgraduate seminar in science and religion at Leeds University in January 2002, the Symposium on Religion and Science entitled 'Self and Earth' at University College, Cork, in March 2002, the short paper section of the Society for the Study of Theology at Lancaster University in April 2002, the Windsor Consultation at St George's House on 'Environmental Decision Making in an Age of Technology' in April 2002, the advanced workshop on 'Life on a Threatened Planet: Genetic Controversy and Environmental Ethics' at the Center for Theology and the Natural Sciences, the University of Berkeley, USA, in June 2002, the annual meeting of The British Ecological Society in December 2002 and the science, religion and ethics seminar at Edinburgh University in February 2003. I have benefited considerably from questions and comments arising out of these presentations. The Windsor Consultation lecture has been published in a revised format in the following paper: C. Deane-Drummond, 'Wisdom with Justice', *Ethics in Science and Environmental Politics* (ESEP) (2002), pp. 65–74, available on the journal's web page, and also, in a slightly revised form, in the December 2003 issue of *Ecotheology: The Journal of Religion, Nature and the Environment*, still in press at the time of writing.

In addition, I would like to thank my colleagues at Chester College for agreeing to times of absence during sabbatical leave, in particular for supporting my AHRB grant from September 2002 through to February 2003, during which time this book was completed. I have also benefited considerably from having easy access to St Deiniol's library in Hawarden throughout the time of writing this book. The library is a welcome retreat for those wishing to engage more fully in study and 'divine learning', as Gladstone would have said. I would also like to thank my husband Henry for his patience and my little daughter Sara, whose zest for life keeps me alert to the possibilities inherent in nature.

This book is dedicated to my wonderful mother, whose life of constant cheerfulness and love was a constant inspiration to me, to my perceptive spiritual guide, whose depth of wisdom and insight served to deepen my own faith, and finally to my friend Susan Rattenbury, whose sharpness of mind helped to steer my own thinking as a postgraduate student of theology at Manchester University. My gratitude to them is beyond what words can say.

Chapter 1

Introduction: The Recovery of Virtue for an Ethics of Nature

In the opening chapter of *After Virtue*, Alasdair MacIntyre asks us to imagine that the natural sciences suffered a serious catastrophe. Scientists are blamed directly for environmental damage, riots occur, laboratories are burnt and books and instruments are destroyed.[1] Later there is an attempt to revive science, but all that are left are fragments, experiments detached from the theoretical and practical context that gave them significance. He suggests that a similar malaise is now part of the moral sphere as well, the legacy of modernity is that we have lost a sense of narrative, of being part of the community in which moral concern took shape and developed. Yet his analysis does not stop here; instead he enjoins us to return to an Aristotelian view, one that encourages a search after goodness through the virtues. Ironically, perhaps, he suggests that this particular view is not limited to its historical time; rather we are rationally entitled to have confidence in its epistemological and moral resources.

MacIntyre's book has been highly influential in fostering a stream of thought in philosophy known as virtue ethics.[2] Such a recovery of virtue entails a focus on the agent, rather than action; the character of persons, rather than the particular rules or principles to be followed. But why should Christian ethicists follow this trend in secular philosophy? In particular, why is it particularly suggestive for an ethics of nature, concerned as it is primarily with our treatment of the non-human world? Furthermore, how does it cohere with a scientific understanding of reality? In this chapter I argue that a case can be made for a reappropriation of virtue ethics, drawing particularly on the insights of Thomas Aquinas. I begin with a survey of different possible approaches to ethics from a Christian perspective in order to show points of convergence and divergence with the position I adopt. I explore a spectrum of possible starting points between kerygmatic statements of Christian faith and those that are more closely aligned with natural theology. A further question to consider in this context is the extent to which biological understanding of reality might or should inform ethical analysis. While some ethicists seeking a more deontological approach – that is, one based on particular principles – have taken up the idea of natural law, those concerned with the ethics of nature have generally ignored Aquinas.[3] This may be because he has been branded as one who advocated a particularly negative and instrumental view of animals as brute beasts, useful only so far as they serve the interests of humans.[4] However, I argue that such a stereotypical view ignores the richness of his theological vision, rooted as it is in a theology of creation, one that is possible to cohere with evolutionary ideas about nature, rather than being hostile to it. Moreover, I suggest that not only is this fruitful for thinking about the different dimensions of biological being, but Aquinas's theology situates humanity in creation in a way that marries virtue ethics to theological reflection. A weaker kind of criticism is that Aquinas is too systematic to be taken seriously in ecological discourse about virtues.[5] I argue, instead, that Aquinas's approach, drawing as it does on Aristotelian thinking, offers a philosophical theology that engages with contemporary discourse on virtue ethics, but also expresses such terms in language that can be appropriated within the Christian tradition. I also suggest that the primacy he gives to the four cardinal virtues of prudence (practical wisdom), justice, fortitude (courage) and temperance is an entirely appropriate focus for the virtues in order to develop an ethics of nature. In addition, I argue that wisdom has a priority in such considerations and that the teleological nature of a wisdom ethic developed along these lines not only gives an appropriate place for consequentialism, but also relativizes alternative consequentialist approaches that have been found wanting.

Christian Approaches to Ethics

It is the premise of this book that a Christian approach to ethics is justifiable and offers a distinctive contribution to moral reflection. How far the content of theology impinges on ethical reflection has been the subject of much heated debate, for both Catholic moral theologians and Protestant counterparts.[6] On the one hand, there are those who argue that we need to begin with the kerygma of Christian faith, then move on to reflect on various secular alternatives in the light of such beliefs. Michael Banner is a good example of this method, drawing particularly on the theology of Karl Barth for his inspiration. He suggests that:

> the task of Christian ethics is to understand the world and humankind in the light of the knowledge of God revealed in Jesus Christ, witnessed to by the Scriptures, and proclaimed by the Creeds, and that Christian ethics may and must explicate this understanding in its significance for human action through a critical engagement with the concerns, claims and problems of other ethics.[7]

For him, we need to 'turn the world upside down' by referring first to the law of God, in other words, a standing apart from general conceptions about good and evil.[8] Hence his approach evokes the rejection of natural theology, which understands reflection on the natural world as a valid starting point, while seeking to relate to concerns of theology. Yet when one considers Banner's discussion of biotechnology, he is less consistent than one might expect, for he refers primarily to particular principles that are scattered in the legislation of the United Kingdom, rather than any specific language about God.[9] His theological reasons for resisting an alternative secular ethical framework appear to take inspiration from the idea of the sabbath, a concept that he takes up and develops elsewhere.[10] His idea of the sabbath is suggestive, rather than specific to his earlier premise of conducting all Christian ethics in a Christological key. It seems to me that this reflects a more general difficulty in translating a Barthian ideal of ethics into practical concern for the natural world. While Banner is critical of the shift towards biocentric value, he offers little on the theological challenge of environmental concern and seems more inclined to urge us simply to reconsider a version of Christian humanism.[11] This would be entirely consistent with the relative lack of attention to creation in Barthian theology, though it is fair to say that the distance between Barthian and natural law accounts of creation has been exaggerated.[12]

A rather different, but equally dogmatic, approach to Christian ethics is Esther Reed's *The Genesis of Ethics*.[13] Her book allows for and indeed is built on the idea of the authority of God, expressed as divine grace. It differs from Banner's approach in that greater primacy is given to understanding God as author of all creation, locating Christian ethics in the context of the relationship between creator and created. She is therefore able to give greater priority to an ethics of nature compared with Banner's theology, which seems to render such consideration difficult. Reed urges us to consider not just the challenge of who Christ is in relation to ethics, but also the work of the Holy Spirit in the church, transforming our understanding of what it is to be persons. However, she does not develop the idea of virtue ethics in the way I am suggesting here. She recognizes, accurately in my view, the ethical difficulty of the classical Eastern tradition that views God's grace as infusing all living creatures. The questions that she raises are pertinent. For example, how far should there be a radical discontinuity between Christian ethics and other forms of ethics? Is the Eastern view still credible to the contemporary world? In other words, is it pretence to say that the entire world is restored in Christ when clearly it is not?

James Gustafson's approach is of interest in that, while he rejects dogmatic ethics as 'sectarian', he argues for a greater concern for nature in ethical reflection.[14] He sees himself as following in the tradition of Thomas Aquinas, namely to draw on a *contemporary* understanding of the world as indications of how God is related to and ordering the world.[15] Gustafson strongly objects to what he terms Aquinas's anthropocentrism, namely Aquinas is concerned to reflect on the well being of humanity first, in the context of the good of the whole universe. Gustafson sets out what he calls a *theocentric* ethic, whereby we are obliged to relate to all things in so far as they relate to God.[16] This, he believes, corrects the anthropocentrism characteristic of traditional (including Thomistic) thought. It is understandable, given his particular goals, that he neither specifically uses the notion of human virtue that

Aquinas develops, nor sets his theology in the context of natural law or a teleological search for goodness. Yet Gustafson's ethic does not adequately clarify what relations of creatures to God are possible in Aquinas's understanding of the human good ordered to a universal good, which is integral to Aquinas's understanding of the human to which Gustafson objects. In this sense Aquinas's theory of goodness presents a challenge to Gustafson's moral theory, for Aquinas, unlike Gustafson, has found a persuasive way of ordering creatures to God and one another.[17] How far Gustafson's ethics is really in the tradition of Aquinas seems to be somewhat tenuous, though in as much as he wants to take into account the discoveries of science it is to be welcomed.[18]

Other Catholic moral philosophers, particularly in the Grisez–Finnis school, have drawn on Aquinas's understanding of natural law as a basis for their ethics.[19] Grisez developed his theology in response to the inadequacies of classical scholastic natural law theory, which viewed ethics simply as conformity to a built in pattern. Such an ethic stressed what we as humans should not do, based on the following of rigid rules, rather than what we need to do in order to flourish. His theory attempts to get round the difficulty of the so-called naturalistic fallacy, namely that we cannot philosophically derive an 'ought', what we should do, from an 'is', who we are.[20] He suggests that we can overcome this by arriving at basic human goods, which explain why we act in certain ways. Such goods are substantive, such as life itself, knowledge and aesthetic experience and excellence in work; or reflexive, such as harmony among individuals or within self. The goods *correspond to* different dimensions of human nature, rather than are *derivative from* them, and hence the naturalistic fallacy is avoided. They are *pre-moral* in that they give explanations for acting rather than a judgement on whether such action is right or not. The charge by Hauerwas that Grisez's ethics is not really Christian follows from his understanding that Christianity provides no new moral principles over and above philosophy.[21] While the Christian commitment of Grisez is not really in doubt, even those commentators favourably disposed to Grisez admit to a 'creeping de-Christianization' of his ethics.[22] Grisez's argument is that if human nature is not changed substantially by Christianity, then how can there be new principles? Yet the human condition is clearly challenged in a new way by Christianity, which leads to a distinctive Christian ethic. In any event, the Grisez–Finnis school argues that there are some actions that are never justified. An alternative is to adopt what is known as the proportionalist position, and urge Christian ethics to be more sensitive to circumstances than the Grisez school suggests, for sometimes action may be justified if it prevents greater evil. Yet the question then remains, against proportionalists: by what standard do we assess whether an action is good or not?

What are we to make of these different appropriations of Thomistic thought? Jean Porter believes that contemporary ethicists have 'seized on fragments of what was once a unified moral tradition as the basis for their interpretation of Christian ethics'.[23] Furthermore, the debate between the Grisez school and the proportionalists seems 'interminable'. Instead she urges that we need to return to a unified theory of the past, but one that is rethought in our own contexts. Such a return is bold in the sense that our current context of postmodernity resists any 'grand narrative' accounts of how to do ethics. Yet the splitting up of Aquinas's thought so that it loses its theological base distorts his basic intentions.[24] Certainly Hauerwas rejects the new natural law theory on the basis that it does not take sufficient account of the virtues.[25] While the idea that Grisez theory is unrelated to virtue ethics is contestable, it is fair to say that philosophical parameters, rather than theological ones, seem to set his understanding of the good. This may be one reason why Banner is able to contrast in a stark way those Christian ethicists who align themselves to natural law and those who align themselves to Barth. For if natural law becomes just a secular vision of reality, 'what results is not dialogue at all but the absurd (and finally rather patronising) attempt to echo in advance the views of the other'.[26] However, Banner's critique relies on a *secularized* interpretation of natural law and a Protestant suspicion of its credibility as a starting point for theological reflection.

Christian ethics has drawn on the Bible itself as a basis for moral reflection. While this may be mediated through dogmatics, some theologians argue for a more direct relationship between biblical scholarship and ethical frameworks.[27] Certainly, debates about the way we treat the natural world have focused on the particular interpretation of the command to have dominion over the earth in Genesis 1.28. The much-cited work of Lynn White challenged Christians to reconsider whether they had been in some way responsible for the ecological crisis by fostering notions of human dominion understood as domination of the earth.[28] While biblical scholars have sharply refuted his interpretation of the Genesis text as domination, the issue remains as to how far Christian ethics can use biblical sources for particular ethical reflection outside the particular context intended for the passages to hand. In other words, the issue hinges on the question of hermeneutics.[29] The dilemma for Christian moral theologians is that the specific ethical requirements, such as we find in Pauline letters, are commonly rooted in particular cultural contexts. Yet is there another way that we can draw on biblical sources, while at the same time being sensitive to the historical and cultural distance? I suggest that one way that this is possible is through consideration of virtue ethics, for a focus on the character of human being has a timeless quality that transcends the specific and often outdated ethical demands that we find in the biblical witness. Such a consideration of virtue not only links with contemporary philosophy, it is also highly suggestive of a way to think about our place in the natural world.

Developing a Christian Virtue Ethic

In what sense is virtue ethics distinctive from other approaches? From a purely secular perspective it is possible to classify the most dominant forms of ethics as being either rule based, or deontological, following in the stream of philosophy inspired by Kant; or based on consideration of consequences, or utilitarianism, following in the stream of philosophy inspired by J. S. Mill and Jeremy Bentham. I have discussed the debates within particular Christian deontological approaches above. In consideration of how to treat the natural world the consequentialist approach has been the most dominant, in terms of both environmental concern and consideration of new developments in genetics.[30] Virtue language may, of course, become sprinkled into the discussion, so that 'ecological virtue language seems to turn up especially when authors assume a hortatory, personal and reflection-filled mode of writing. This most often happens in their concluding statements.'[31] While there has been a strong tendency for Christian theologians to follow the secular debate and adjure consequentialist approaches, more recently theologians have questioned the fruitfulness of such an approach in consideration of new advances in biology.[32] An alternative to deontological or consequentialist approaches is to consider the basis of ethics as having a prime focus on the virtues, even though, as I indicated at the start of this chapter, an interest in such an approach has only become fashionable relatively recently in current debates in philosophy. Virtue ethics, unlike the other approaches, asks us to consider not just the actions of the agent, but the agent himself or herself. It focuses on what sort of person we are, rather than what sorts of action we should perform. Actions, where they are considered, are in the light of who we are as persons, rather than detached from human character. The basic premise of a virtue ethic is that goodness is a fundamental consideration, rather than rights, duties or obligations. Furthermore, virtue ethicists also reject the idea that ethical conduct can be codified in particular rules.

There are, of course, difficulties that virtue ethicists encounter and that have to be overcome in arguing a case for a virtue ethic approach. Different virtues may be highlighted by different authors; indeed, MacIntyre insists that given virtues are situated in particular practices of particular communities in particular narratives.[33] How do we choose which virtues to select when virtues conflict? This is not a problem specific to virtue ethics, since it is possible for there to be mixed consequences to an action, or a clash between two rules in a rule-based ethic. For virtue ethicists, what is called for in a conflict of virtues is moral wisdom or discernment, so that with Rosalind Hursthouse, 'the only virtue term we have which is guaranteed to operate as a virtue term – that is, to pick out something that always makes its possessor good – is "wisdom"'.[34] Hence we can be too clever, or too courageous, but never too wise. Wisdom, understood here as practical wisdom or prudence, also highlights the rational element in virtue ethics, though virtue ethicists argue that their approach also gives an appropriate place to the emotions in a way that deontological or consequentialist positions do not. None the less, one of the key ideas in virtue ethics is that it is not just about particular character traits or virtues as opposed to vices in the narrow sense; rather it is to do with developing a life that is centred on *flourishing* or living well. Human choices are involved in such decisions for the good; hence it is not simply a form of naturalism, or a grounding of human nature in who we are as biological beings. This needs to be qualified by the fact that Aristotelian concern for our biological nature is also an important constituent in considering the virtues. For:

no account of the goods, rules and virtues that are definitive of our moral life can be adequate that does not explain – or at least point us towards an explanation – how that form of life is possible for beings who are biologically constituted as we are, by providing us with an account of our development towards and into that form of life. That development has as its starting point our animal condition.[35]

Hence, while a virtue ethic is not necessarily grounded in naturalism, it takes our biological nature sufficiently seriously to warrant close attention. MacIntyre also admits that while Thomas Aquinas draws heavily on Aristotle's account of the virtues, he develops it in particular ways and lays much more emphasis on human vulnerability and dependence.[36] There seems to be some debate among philosophers as to the status of virtue ethics *vis-à-vis* naturalism. Often virtue ethics is taken to be a form of ethical naturalism, as it is based on a human nature that has shared characteristics with the animals.[37] Yet virtue ethics cannot be a strict form of naturalism, since if so it would limit free choice and yield a falsely deterministic picture of human virtue. While some virtues may have a biological *component*, the criteria for an agent acting for the good cannot come simply from consideration of animal behaviour.

Virtue ethics is also generally characterized by a move away from a focus on particular ethical dilemmas or quandaries that highlight the difficulties in coming to a correct decision. Such quandaries, where they are considered, are qualified by a focus on the character of the agent. For example, in some circumstances it may be entirely appropriate for an agent to take either one or another course of action, where both actions are expressions of the good. More difficult scenarios are where either course of action is wrong, so the agent can hardly be said to acting out of virtue. What is the appropriate action to take, for example, when there is a population explosion in rabbits that threatens to upset ecological diversity of an ecosystem? Doing nothing or culling the population could both be seen as regrettable.[38] In these circumstances a virtuous agent will act in pain and regret, rather than indifferently; though it is impossible to avoid the conclusion that the agent is marred in some way by the situation that is forced upon them.[39]

Such a secular analysis cries out for a theological interpretation of the virtues, for how do we deal with the brokenness that is the inevitable part of searching to gain virtue? Stephen Clark's provocative book *Biology and Christian Ethics* hints at such a development. While his book is not specifically couched in terms of virtue ethics, he develops strands that cohere with such an alternative. One of his concerns, for example, is the elimination of beauty from the moral sense when the theory of evolution becomes rarefied into a basis for ethics. In this scenario, 'values are projection, terrestrial life a cosmic accident, and all attempts to deny these claims are priestcraft'.[40] He challenges the idea that humanity is necessarily progressing towards the good, or the end of history, and, he suggests wryly, 'it may be that our civilisation has been a long detour, and supermen will be a lot like savages'.[41] Yet he does suggest that the best life for humanity is one lived in accordance with virtue and, against those who argue for a pluralistic interpretation of value, that most perfect virtue, in the end, is *wisdom*, and Aristotle is as convinced as any Platonist that there is one single strategy for life, by which we may transcend humanity. He did not applaud plurality: on the contrary, it is wicked people who are plural in themselves, and virtue is defined by having a single goal – the beautiful.[42]

He suggests, significantly, that Darwinian theory of evolution alone does not give us a coherent theory of value, since 'If there really are no forms of beauty, no constraints at all on what can happen or the way it grows, then there are no real values.'[43] I endorse such a critique of using Darwinian theory as a basis for ethics, and in this I part company with writers such as John Haught, who come perilously close to this position.[44] Clark also suggests that science itself is dependent on a prior conviction that there is a rational order that can be discerned in the universe, and such a belief is historically dependent on orthodox theism. I am closer to Haught than Clark in believing that contemporary evolutionary science is as much concerned with contingency as with order, though I suggest that a virtue approach is flexible enough to deal with this contingency without falling into the trap that Clark seems to highlight, namely a diffuse relativism.

While Stephen Clark has suggested that 'orthodox theism' can be set alongside philosophical reflection, how might Christian ethics become more *specifically* associated with virtue ethics? Is there any basis at all for suggesting that consideration of the virtues is commensurate with Christian theology? Is it possible that the divine law concept of ethics has been more prevalent than a virtue ethic approach in the Judaeo-Christian tradition?[45] More extreme is the view that Christianity is to blame for replacing an ethic centred on the virtues with one focused on an ethics of duty.[46] Self-denial, rather than self-fulfilment, seems, for some, to be the central kerygma of Christian ethical teaching. Other theologians, following Stanley Hauerwas, simply assume that virtue ethics is Christian.[47]

Joseph Kotva argues that virtue theory is not necessarily *required* by Christian theology, but 'makes good sense from a Christian perspective'.[48] I agree with his suggestion that virtue theory requires some modification in order to be compatible with Christian thought. For example, concepts such as forgiveness, reconciliation and the need for God's grace are essential components of a Christian ethic. Kotva argues that Christian ethicists have tended to view Christ in an abstract way, reducing a rich understanding of his humanity to a rule or principle, such as the law of love.[49] How do we know what love really means without setting it in the context of the story of Christ's life and work?[50] Christian anthropology calls for a deeper understanding of what it is to be human, one not simply conditioned by external forces, which governs a rule-based ethic. I will argue later that rules have their place, as in the discussion of natural law, but they need to be thought of as a means to gaining greater freedom, one that is only possible through the development of virtues. A Christian life is one that is transformed by relationship with God and in fellowship with Christ, so that the self is transformed through observation and imitation of the life of Christ viewed as a whole.

Furthermore, both virtue theory and Christian theology situate decisions in a community context. From a biblical perspective the beatitudes depict the good life as a life lived out of correct internal dispositions of character. Those who are humble before God, who desire God's justice and who live from a position of integrity receive special praise.[51] The idea that external action flows from internal dispositions of character is a thread running through Matthew's gospel; for example, Matt. 3.8, 10; 7.15–20, 12.33. The blessings and warnings are designed to encourage certain behaviour, rather than set out a fixed set of rules to follow. Moreover, like virtue ethics, perfection is the goal of the Christian life, and like virtue ethics, Jesus is the master who displays the kind of character towards which his disciples are called to aspire.[52] The interest in narrative in virtue ethics is also thoroughly consistent with the Bible understood in narrative form.[53] While Kotva admits that Pauline ethics cannot be considered a virtue ethic in the strict sense, there are lines of continuity; for example, 'the appeal to models or examples, an interest in internal qualities, an outlook that is both individual and communal, and the need for quality or skill of discernment'.[54] Particularly significant is his identification of Paul's advocacy of a shared search for wisdom:

> Paul continually exhibits and calls for a kind of discriminatory wisdom or skilful judgement that seeks in a particular situation to 'discern the will of God – what is good and acceptable and perfect' (Rom. 12.2). This discerning judgement is not limited to individuals, but involves the community's shared search.[55]

Another common thread to virtue ethics and Paul's epistles is that of transformation of the character: the need for admonition derives from the discrepancy between what we are and what we are called to become. Christian virtues are not as much a narcissistic concentration on the self, as a way of developing the capacity to reach out to God and others in love.[56]

The Primacy of Prudence (Practical Wisdom) in the Four Cardinal Virtues

Given that we can argue a case for Christian ethics to be a (albeit) modified version of virtue ethics, what particular virtues are appropriate to consider? While many ethicists have resisted any hierarchy of the virtues, I suggest that the four cardinal virtues of prudence, justice, fortitude and temperance developed by Thomas Aquinas give a good starting point for reflection on the ethics of nature.[57] The theological virtues of love, faith and hope are the foundation of the other virtues, though in the moral virtues prudence takes priority, in that like love it can also be described as the 'mother' of other virtues. Prudence, in particular, is at the heart of Aquinas's reflection on moral virtue, for it is implicit in his own method of dialectical questioning, considering all the options available before arriving at a reasoned decision that informs a particular way of life, a life of virtue. While drawing on

Aristotle, Aquinas's view that corruption of reason is impossible to avoid without an act of God's grace runs counter to his position, and indeed that of secular philosophical inquiry. Details of theological debates about the relationship between nature and grace in Thomistic theology need not concern us here. It is sufficient to note that Thomas recognized the reality of original sin but refused to endorse the idea that human nature is *eradicated* by sin; this would amount to Manicheanism. Instead, something of the *goodness* of creation remains, even while restricting its capacity for the good. Following Augustine, Aquinas argued for the *healing* of a disordered nature by grace, but following the Greek tradition, he also argued for the possibility of *divinization* by grace.[58] Keeping such strands together is important in discussions about the virtues as learned and the virtues received by divine gift of grace.

Prudence

Prudence, or practical wisdom, for Aquinas is the 'mother' of all the other cardinal virtues. In the occidental Christian view Being precedes Truth and Truth precedes Goodness. It might be hard to imagine that prudence is in any sense a prerequisite to goodness, since prudence in colloquial use 'carries the connotation of timorous, small minded self-preservation, of a rather selfish concern about oneself'; hence those who shun danger do so by an appeal to 'prudence'.[59] In contrast, the classical approach that Aquinas adopts links prudence specifically with goodness, and moreover there is no justice or fortitude without the virtue of prudence. Instinctive inclinations towards goodness become transformed through prudence, so that prudence gives rise to a perfected ability to make choices as related to practical matters of human reasoning.[60] Hence the free activity of humanity is good in so far as it corresponds to the pattern of prudence. As such prudence is the 'cause, root, mother, measure, precept, guide and prototype of all ethical virtues, it acts in all of them, perfecting them to their true nature, all participate in it, and by virtue of this participation they are virtues'.[61] Truly human action is the inward shaping of volition and action by reason perfected in truth. However, reason is not understood in a narrow sense, it is 'regard for and openness to reality'.[62] Reality includes both supernatural and natural reality, so that realization of goodness presupposes knowledge of reality – simply good intentions are not sufficient. Prudent decisions have universal and particular/singular components. Universal principles are given by synderesis, which relates to the naturally apprehended principles of ethical conduct, or innate conscience. The love of the good is the message of natural conscience, relating directly to natural law.[63] Deliberation and judgement are characteristic of the cognitive stage of prudence, while decision, volition and action demonstrate its practical nature.

Given these different facets of prudence, is it possible to define more closely what prudence means? For Thomas prudence is 'wisdom in human affairs', rather than absolute wisdom; hence phronesis is also called *practical wisdom*.[64] Its orientation is practical, rather than simply theoretical. Drawing on memory and experience, prudence has the facets of taking counsel, judging correctly and then moving to act in a certain way. Prudence does not define what the good is, rather it *facilitates what makes for right choices* by so acting in different virtues in accordance with the ultimate orientation towards the good.[65] It is like, then, a virtue within virtues, showing both *the means* through which an end can be achieved and what is appropriate or *'mean'* of a given virtue in given circumstances.[66] The particular end of moral virtues is set through *synderesis*, which is an instinctive understanding of what the natural law requires. Hence prudence informs the virtuous life, but also is grounded, initially at least, in the requirements of natural law. Yet Aquinas points out that the instinctive reasoning according to innate *synderesis* is not sufficient for correct decision-making, but 'requires to be complemented by the reasoning of prudence'.[67] It is for this reason that MacIntyre suggests that 'it is prudence (phronesis) which is the virtue without which judgment and action in particular occasions are resourceless beyond the bare level of what synderesis provides'.[68] Is prudence then simply a reasoning activity? Aquinas argues against this, for while reasoning is involved in deliberation and judgement, prudence includes *practical execution* of what has been decided upon. While art is the art of judging in a rational way, prudence moves beyond this to specify an action. It seems to me that the holistic task of prudence that serves to inform moral behaviour is vitally important, for it challenges self-reflection *at every stage* in the overall process from deliberation through to action.[69] It also demand an openness to others in a way that prevents prudence from being individualistic, for taking counsel is the first part in the overall process of prudential activity. In addition, the kind of certainty that might be possible to achieve within prudential understanding is not one of a fixed order; intead the contingent incidents upon which it bases its judgement lead to a similar level of contingency, so 'the certitude of prudence is not such so as to remove entirely all uneasiness of mind'.[70] The inclusion of some ambiguity here is also significant, for it avoids a rigid approach based simply on following of rules. While the natural law is implicit in serving to shape the good that is the target of prudence, it recognizes that the kind of certainty that is possible is not the same as statements of theological faith.

Aquinas argues that it is possible to distinguish between well advisedness as a secondary or 'eliciting' virtue and prudence, which is the 'commanding virtue'.[71] This is easier to understand if we envisage acts of justice as rooted primarily in charity; so, in an analogous way, well advisedness is *rooted* in the virtue of prudence. In other words, prudence is *required* for well advisedness to flower in prudential decisions and actions. In a similar way, Aquinas believes that sound judgement is a subsidiary or 'allied' virtue to prudence, which is the 'crown' of good judgement as it leads to concrete action.[72] While the stress here seems to be on action, the different facets of prudential decision-making (taking counsel, judgement and action) are an integral part of the whole. In addition, another significant allied virtue to prudence is what Aquinas terms *gnome*, which is the ability to recognize exceptional circumstances and so act 'by certain principles higher than the ordinary rules followed by sound judgement'.[73] Are such distinctions still helpful in a contemporary context? I suggest that they are, for it is possible to be well advised without being prudent, so it serves to emphasize the multifaceted nature of prudential decision-making. Each allied virtue can serve to highlight the way prudential activity works in practice through such virtues. If the allied virtue is missing, then there is no prudence. On the other hand, these virtues can be present without a person being prudent, since she or her may be lacking in some other facet of prudence.

Accurate cognition at the first stage of prudential activity is not easily acquired, but comes through a patient effort in experience, one that cannot be short-circuited by an appeal simply to 'faith' or a 'philosophical' view that confines itself to the universal and general. This silent contemplation of reality that takes counsel in all kinds of ways also includes the ability to be true to memory, meaning not just the recollection of the past, but one that is true to the nature of things or being itself. Aquinas lists the various components of prudence as memory, insight or intelligence, teachableness, acumen (*solertia*), reasoned judgement, foresight, circum-spection and caution.[74] In addition, given the multiple facets of prudence it cannot be simply an individual task, but includes the ability to take advice from others. Beyond this Aquinas distinguishes between individual prudence, aimed at the good of the individual, domestic prudence for family life and political prudence, aimed at the common good.[75] Relating the three aspects of prudence – individual, domestic and political – is particularly significant in an ethics of nature that includes decision-making at all levels. While the form of politics adopted by Aquinas, namely a monarchical society, is inappropriate in a democracy, the distinction between the way prudential activity needs to be shaped depending on context is significant.

Aquinas distinguishes between imprudence, negligence and sham prudence. Dif-ferent types of imprudence are a result of imperfections at any stage in the process of deliberation, judgement and action. If there is a failure to take counsel this leads to foolish haste, if there is a failure in judgment this leads to thoughtlessness, if there is a failure to carry out an action this leads to inconstancy. Flaws at any stage of taking counsel, judging and action lead to analogous vices. Imperfections of prudence at the first stage of cognition come about through a failure to be still in order to perceive reality. At the root of all these vices lies unchastity; that is, the failure to be detached from the seduction of pleasures of sense.[76] Prudence as a virtue overcomes this vice in allowing reasoning to order the moral life. One mode of imprudence is thoughtlessness, acting too quickly without sufficient time for consideration. Aquinas named negligence as a distinctive vice, namely one of *not* choosing the good, a failure in the implementation of prudence or its 'command'.[77] Like the subsidiary virtues of prudence, such as well advisedness, negligence is a subsidiary outcome of imprudence. Those who fail to act at all by irresoluteness are also lacking perfected prudence, as are those who cannot act in unexpected circumstances, who lack what is known as *solertia* (acumen) or clear sighted objec-tivity in the face of the unexpected. Sham prudence is prudence directed to the wrong end, namely 'the flesh' set up as the final goal of the human life. If 'the flesh' becomes an object of 'inordinate attachment' without becoming the goal of human life, this can amount to a venial sin, as opposed to the mortal sin of replacing the ultimate goal of life as goodness under God with care of the human body.[78] Yet Aquinas is not denying the value of worldly prudence, rather it has to be put in its place so that 'the flesh is lawfully loved in subordination to its end, the good of the soul'.[79] Another form of sham prudence comes through using false or deceitful means, namely cunning, to attain either a good or evil end. For Aquinas the underlying sin in the case of sham prudence is covetousness, the desire to have what is not rightfully one's own.[80] While it is difficult, given the multifaceted nature of prudence, to do justice to it through a simple definition, Pieper has come close through his summary of many aspects of prudence in the following paragraph:

> It holds within itself the humility of the silent, that is to say, of unbiased perception, the trueness to being of memory, the art of receiving counsel, alert, composed readiness for the unexpected. Prudence means studied seriousness and, as it were, the filter of deliberation, and at the same time the brave boldness to make final decisions. It means purity, straightforwardness, candour and simplicity of character, it means standing superior to the utilitarian complexities of mere 'tactics'.[81]

Given this understanding of prudence, such a task would be almost impossible given the propensity to err (sin) in all its varied facets without Aquinas's belief that perfection in prudence is only possible through the grace of God. The form of prudence to which the Christian aspires is prudence in the light of the three theological virtues of faith, hope and charity.[82] Such a consideration leads to an understanding that the ultimate goal for a Christian is not goodness in an abstract sense, but friendship and participation in the life of the Trinitarian God. Prudence as learned and prudence perfected by grace both move from cognition through to decision, volition and action. This is where the virtue of prudence as *learned* links with the theological virtues of faith, hope and love. Indeed, Aquinas speaks of the gift of understanding, the gift of counsel, the gift of science and the gift of wisdom, but does not have a specific section on the gift of prudence.[83]

In his treatise on prudence, counsel is named as the gift *corresponding* to prudence, focusing as it does on the way the mind might be moved to act under another's influence, namely that of the Holy Spirit.[84] The beatitude associated with such a gift is that of mercy, as he suggests that it is through mercy that the gift is received and then given to others. Naming counsel as the appropriate gift for prudence strikes the reader as a little forced in some respects, especially as prudence necessarily involves command or action. However, the advantage of such a gift being placed at this stage in prudential activity is that the freedom of the individual is still preserved, the Holy Spirit may speak words of counsel in allowing the perfected prudence to flower, decision and action are individual results of choosing to follow the Spirit. Commentators on prudence in Aquinas seem to have ignored the possibility of prudence acting under the influence of God's grace; it has proved to be an embarrassment to modern readers preferring to align themselves with secular concepts of prudence. However, if Christian ethics is to move beyond a simple endorsement of secular models, as exemplified, for example, through a detachment of natural law from its theological context, then some sense of the possibility at least of prudence given by grace is not only necessary, but vital in thinking through difficult questions that impinge on religious understandings of reality. Such a rich understanding of prudence when combined with love of God in charity leads to a higher plane of prudence, one that is detached from the compulsions of worldly desires. This does not come from human judgement about the world; such disdain would stem from arrogance and pride. Rather, it is the overwhelming love of God that relativizes all human efforts, while at the same time holding a clear perspective on human obligation and responsibility. I prefer to call this form of prudence wisdom, since it can be more readily identified as a theological category. While prudence is in one sense a form of wisdom, known as practical wisdom, wisdom in itself moves beyond even the scope of prudence delineated above.[85]

What are the advantages of a recovery of prudence for reflection on the ethics of nature? I suggest that all aspects of the natural world that I will be considering in this book do well to be approached through the category of prudence. The particular facets of prudence that are most relevant will depend on the particular issue under consideration. Yet, overall, the holistic method implicit in the notion of prudence through contemplation/consideration, judgement and action is vitally important to hold together in situations where there is a temptation to split action from judgement. For example, accurate reflection on environmental ethics needs due attention to policy-making, to how far such a desirable end will be achievable in practice. Distortions of prudence may be more exaggerated in one area rather than another, and Aquinas allows such distortions to be distinguished by categorizing the different facets of prudence. In the first place, the ability of prudence to be still, to deliberate well, is a quality desperately needed in the frenzied search for new methods and techniques in biological science that are considered to have particular usefulness for humanity. I suggest that taking the time to deliberate and reflect and listen to others by taking counsel does not come easily to the popular mind, concerned with instant results and instant gratification of desires. Second, unlike deontological approaches within Christian ethics that refer to particular traditions that seem unrelated to practical contexts, prudence demands full en-counter with experience, including the experience of science, taking time to per-ceive what is true in the natural world. Such close attention to reality as perceived in the scientific world involves a kind of studied attention, a listening to the Other in nature, without trying to force the natural world to conform to human catego-ries.[86] While Aquinas restricted his idea of taking counsel to other human subjects, in the present environmental context it is essential to try as far as possible to perceive from the perspective of all creatures, all of whom are loved by God and under God's providence.[87] Third, prudence invokes not just contemplation of the world, but positive action as well, action that has in mind the goodness of God. Consequentialist approaches to the ethics of nature have sought to frame decisions in terms of costs and benefits, or risks. While prudence would include some perception of risks where they are known, the ability to have accurate foresight depends on how far such decisions promote the overall goal of prudence towards goodness. It is the character of the agents that is as important as the particular consequences of individual decisions made. Hence, the good of humanity is included along with the goods of other creatures. While those who are not Christian will be able to identify with the goal of goodness, a Christian virtue ethic springing from prudence will seek to move to a particular understanding of goodness, one that coheres with the overall goodness for creation, as well as goodness for humanity. In a later section I argue that a Christian virtue ethic set in such a context encourages a wider framework of reference to include the cosmic community, rather than simply the human community.

Justice, fortitude and temperance

A discussion of the significance of prudence would not be complete without mention of the three other cardinal virtues of justice, fortitude and temperance. Justice is often split off from a consideration of virtue ethics, as it is more commonly associated with rule-based ethics. Onora O'Neill considers the rival views of justice according to universal principles, as opposed to virtue ethics with its concern for the particular. She believes, instead, that justice needs to be inclusive of virtues.[88] I suggest, alternatively, from the side of virtue ethics, that when considered as a virtue to be developed justice gives consideration of rules and principles a proper place in an overall ethical framework. In addition, a Christian understanding of justice differs from that of secular philosophy, so that it needs some further elaboration. Justice is concerned broadly with the idea that each is given her or his due. Unlike many other virtues, justice specifically governs relationships with others, and also unlike other virtues it is possible to act justly without necessarily having a proper attitude towards that action.[89] Justice is therefore located in the will, rather than the emotions, keeping right relations between individuals others and between others in community. Aquinas suggests that 'justice is the habit whereby a person with a lasting and constant will renders to each his due'.[90] A particular rule or pattern for prudence prescribes what is a just deed according to reason, and if this is written down it becomes law. One important facet of justice, as Aquinas understood it, is that it acts in a general way, directing the action of all other virtues towards the common good.[91]

By calling justice a habit Aquinas locates justice within the parameters of virtue, even while recognizing the importance of law through his threefold distinction of natural law, positive law and Eternal Law. Natural right, if nature were immutable, would be fixed. However, Aquinas recognizes that human nature is not fixed, but varies, so that which is 'natural' will not always satisfy the demands of justice, such as giving back a loan when one knows it will be used for criminal activity.[92] The *jus gentium* is constituted by natural reason and shared by all people, equivalent to what we might today term international law. Human will establishes laws by positive right that are commensurate with natural justice. Divine right, on the other hand, is that which God commands, either for good consequences or simply because they are commanded. It is from this kind of justice that other forms of justice take their cue, for 'God's justice is everlasting on the part of his eternal will and purpose; in this justice chiefly consists'.[93] Legal justice between the individual and state can be compared with distributive justice between the state and the individual and commutative justice between individuals. The question arises, what is due and to whom? How do we work out what is due? Aquinas is realistic about the place of human laws in prescribing rules for living. It is bound to be imperfect, in that it does not restrain all vice or enjoin every act of virtue that is found even in natural law. It restrains only those vices which 'the average man can avoid' and fosters those virtues that lead to acts that 'serve the common good'.[94] Some of his specific recommendations strike the modern reader as odd, such as his strict stance against any form of usury. However, such a prohibition needs to be situated in the context of the time. The standard practices of liberal modernity and capitalist economy would be incompatible with the detailed reading of Aquinas's broad account of justice.[95] Even so, in emergency situations it may be necessary to grant a dispensation towards those who break the law, without even referring to the governing body. We also, according to Aquinas, have no obligation to obey unjust laws where they are opposed to the divine good.[96]

An initial reading of Aquinas suggests that, like Aristotle, he had a thoroughly anthropocentric view of justice, or what becomes due. While Aquinas did not have a theory of 'rights' as such, his theory of justice would suggest that rights are given to persons because as persons they are spiritual beings created by God. Pieper seems to adopt this view of Aquinas in rejecting any sense that animals have rights.[97] It is clear that there are strands in Aquinas's ethics that encourage a lack of respect for non-human creatures, relating animals to humans simply through their usefulness to humanity. However, the picture is not as simple as it might appear, since his ontology suggests a strong continuity between plants, animals and humans as *creatures* made by God and sharing in Divine Providence. Such a view on creation gives rise to an ambiguity in his thought, and one that, as I will argue in subsequent chapters, lends itself to a more favourable interpretation of justice along rather less narrowly anthropocentric lines.[98] Moreover, it is important to point out that for Aquinas justice cannot flourish unless it is rooted and informed by the supernatural virtue of charity, given by gift of the Holy Spirit.[99] As God is also given the name Justice, it is the Justice of God that is the ultimate arbiter of justice; hence justice is more accurately described in Aquinas's scheme as theocentric, rather than anthropocentric. This is important, for it opens up the possibility of alternative interpretations of justice that are more inclusive of the moral standing of non-human creatures.[100] MacIntyre argues that Aquinas's view of justice 'is only fully intelligible, let alone defensible, as it emerges from an extended and complex tradition of argument and conflict that included far more than Aristotle and Augustine'.[101] While MacIntyre is correct to note the historical situation in which Aquinas's thought is rooted, it seems to me that his understanding of justice can still inform the way justice is conceived in contemporary culture, even though due account needs to be taken of the cultural norms in which his thought is situated. Indeed,

MacIntyre is not wholly consistent in this claim, for he argues in *After Virtue* that the Aristotelian tradition is still a viable alternative to the barren waste of modernity, though he is anxious to interpret Aristotle with due sensitivity to his historical context, rather than subsequent interpretations.[102] It is somewhat doubtful, however, that such a recovery of original hermeneutic can be achieved to the extent that MacIntyre implies.[103] Yet his conclusion is worth noting, namely that the tradition that has withstood the encounters with other traditions most successfully, and is therefore closer to the truth with respect to practical rationality and justice, is the one emerging from the Thomistic tradition.[104]

Fortitude, for Aquinas, springs from prudence and justice, it is informed by prudence in so far as it presumes a correct evaluation of things. Fortitude is the ability to stand firm in the face of difficult circumstances, to be willing to suffer for the good, with a clear-sighted knowledge of what that good might be. Fortitude is necessary in order to preserve the good that is perceived by prudence and established by justice. While fortitude meant, in its ultimate sense, the willingness to be a martyr for the sake of Christ, once the goal of goodness in Christ is perceived, such willingness becomes the spur for acting out of fortitude. Such a radical willingness to act in courageous ways, even to the point of death, seems too extreme for modern ears. Fortitude does not glorify in the injury itself, rather it takes delight in the goal of the good that preserves serenity in the face of hardship. Once the goal of goodness becomes inclusive of all creatures, as I indicate below, the willingness to suffer for the sake of justice and in the light of prudence takes on a new significance. This is particularly the case when we consider, for example, steps that we need to take in order for justice to be restored to the whole community of creation.

Fortitude is linked with the fourth cardinal virtue, temperance. Popular understanding of this word might imply some sense of restriction, or just not acting in excess. While there is an element of this in any interpretation of temperance, the classical meaning pointed to a real awareness and sense of the ordered unity of the human person. Out of this inner unity a serenity of spirit arises that fills the inner recesses of the human being.[105] For such a turning in towards self to be temperance, it must be *selfless*, rather than *selfish* in the sense of being destructive towards self. Intemperance is the misdirection of the desires for self-preservation in actions that are selfish, and ultimately self-destructive.

The natural desires towards sensual enjoyment preserve the individual as creature, but as the most primal urge towards self-preservation they also have the potential to become the most self-destructive once they degenerate into selfishness. Hence intemperance, like imprudence, is associated with unchastity, understood as a disordered sense of sensual enjoyment. Yet temperance is also associated with humility, the ability to be assertive of the self in a way that is genuinely directed towards self-preservation, and is a truthful estimation of one's worth, as opposed to pride, which is a false estimation of one's own worth. Unchastity has relevance in consideration of the range of goods that are parodied as needs, rather than wants, in Western consumer society, ultimately leading to excessive waste with associated environmentally destructive consequences. Pride and covetousness creep in when estimates of the benefits of new technologies overreach their genuine possibility and value.

Yet temperance has a remit even beyond such considerations of chastity and humility, for it also leads to a gentleness and mildness in the face of danger, a self-restraint governed by reason. Those campaigning for animal rights with a destructive and vengeful attitude could learn a lesson from this aspect of temperance, as indeed could those who overreact in any way in demanding their particular rights against a perceived injustice. Such self-restraint can degenerate in a more sophisticated way in the search for knowledge itself, so that 'inquisitiveness' or more accurately *curiositas* itself becomes a negative force, associated with a compulsive greed. It is an obsessive addiction to seeing, a 'concupiscence of the eyes', leading to a 'roaming unrest of spirit'. Is the almost obsessive drive to clone human beings a form of this *curiositas*, demonstrating a lack of the real desire to know what is true according to *studiositas*?

Temperance is, then, a complex term embracing other virtues, and includes chastity, continence, humility, gentleness, mildness, *studiositas*, while forms of intemperance are unchastity, incontinence, pride, uninhibited wrath and *curiositas*. Ultimately temperance renders the human person beautiful, arising from an ordered state of being, and is associated with true virility, hence affirming biological nature, rather than denying it. The opposite, intemperance, 'not only destroys beauty, it also makes man cowardly; intemperance more than any other thing renders man unable and unwilling to "take heart" against the wounding power of evil in the world'.[106]

Wisdom in the World as Created

So far I have suggested that a case can be made for developing a Christian understanding of virtue ethics, in particular drawing on the four cardinal virtues of prudence, justice, fortitude and temperance. While there has been an increasing interest among Christian ethicists in the idea of virtue, the focus has been on how such virtue ethics can be relevant to the particular practices of the Christian community as such. Ethical issues that are of particular significance to the relationships between humans are discussed in the context of virtue theory, rather than wider issues connected with an ethics of nature. Stanley Hauerwas has been highly influential in this respect. *A Community of Character*, for example, dealt with the Church and social policies on the family, sex and abortion, while *Vision and Virtue* dealt with these and other issues, such as euthanasia, in a wider political context.[107] It might even seem that virtue ethics, in its focus on human being, is too anthropocentric to be helpful in developing an ethic of nature. However, I suggest that unless we look to ourselves and are critical of what we might become or have become, then ethics simply directed towards nature becomes a false dawn. It emerges, further, from a disjointed sense of who we are as persons, a projection of self into the cosmos as in deep ecology, without any sense of what that self might be like.

As an alternative, I suggest that a Christian virtue ethic does lend itself to an appropriate awareness of the created reality in which we are situated, especially if we consider the context in which Aquinas developed his own understanding of the significance of the virtues. Aquinas insisted that all knowledge begins from the sense perception of the world, as against Augustine, who urges a strong independence of spiritual from sense knowledge. Commenting on Chesterton's book on Aquinas, Pieper notes that: 'If conformable to Carmelite custom, a fitting epithet such as John "of the Cross" or Therese "of the Child Jesus" were sought for Thomas Aquinas, the one most appropriate would be "Thomas of the Creator", *Thomas a Creatore.*'[108] It was Aristotle who gave Thomas the clearest picture of what creation was like. Commenting on Aristotle, the philosopher John Caputo suggests: 'were he alive today, I dare say his interests would be in theoretical physics, astrophysics, DNA-molecule research, and the other natural and social sciences which collectively go together to make up what Heidegger calls "cybernetics"'.[109] Aquinas aligned his strong affirmation of creation with the Gospel of John; hence the Word made Flesh excludes any Manichaean understanding of the body or creation as evil.

Aquinas struggled to mediate between Augustine's sharp separation of the spiritual and physical worlds and Latin Averroism, which maintained the complete independence of philosophy from faith and theology. The latter became a precursor of the Renaissance and modern science. The task of an ethic of nature is to mediate similarly between those who claim complete autonomy of philosophical ethics and those who insist that to take cues from philosophical thought is not true to the purity and witness of the message of Jesus Christ.

For Aquinas the essence of all things is that they arise from the creative activity of God, and as created their inner structure is defined. His other doctrines are set within this presupposition of reality as *created.*[110] Contemporary philosophy rejects the idea that truth can be predicated from what exists; rather, it arises from human thought. Modern science sees the world of nature as autonomous, separate from any idea of creatures called into being by God.[111] However, once we believe nature to be manufactured by human minds because there is no God, the result is the nihilism of Sartre. Aquinas postulates an existential relationship between God and creation, but also a view of human knowledge that can include scientific understanding. Hence things exist 'between the absolutely creative knowledge of God and the non-creative, reality conformed knowledge of man'.[112] His view of human knowledge is 'scientific' in the sense that he also affirms that things are unfathomable, so always in some sense provisional and imperfect. However, the cause of such a lack of perfection is different. For the secular scientist the failure to know is a simple result of the failure of human reason. For Thomas, while we can know the relationship between things and our minds, we can never penetrate fully into the mind of God, for 'it is too rich to be assimilated completely, it eludes the effort to comprehend it'.[113] Hence the unknowability of creation stems from the fact that

God creates it. As such, creation only gives an imperfect picture of what God is like, and we cannot simply read off God from the world in the manner suggested by much contemporary science and religion writing.[114] In addition, our minds are too crude an instrument to fathom the true nature of things; hence it is also because human beings are created that they cannot know fully the divine mind in things.

Such a view does not lead to agnosticism, because it presupposes the idea of a Creator, but an awareness that we are always 'on the way'. Nor does it lead to a rejection of science, for even in their imperfect form creation shows the light of God as it were in a mirror. How can we best describe this search for knowledge that is also a search into the mind of God? I suggest that such as search can be described in terms of *wisdom*. For wisdom is also an expression of the eternal mind of God, while at the same time affirming what can be known in creaturely existence.[115] Aquinas describes wisdom as integral to God's being in the following way, for 'The divine essence itself is charity, even as it is wisdom and goodness. Now we are said to be good with the goodness which is God and wise with the wisdom which is God, because of the very qualities which make us formally so are participations in the divine goodness and wisdom . . . so too the charity by which we formally love our neighbour is a sharing in the divine charity.'[116] Wisdom is, then, the virtue that can express the mediation between scientific reasoning and faith, between the discoveries of the creaturely world and the telos of the created order as participation in God.

Wisdom as a virtue is also distinguished from prudence, even while being related to it, for while prudence is practical wisdom, wisdom is also one of the intellectual virtues of theoretical reason, along with understanding and science. While prudence is wisdom in human affairs, wisdom pure and simple surpasses this, as its aims directly at God, at knowledge of divine things. The priority that Aquinas gives to wisdom over prudence is particularly interesting, for 'prudence, or political art, therefore is, in this way, the servant of wisdom; for it leads to wisdom, preparing the way for her, as the door keeper for the king'.[117] It has the facility to act as 'judge' over all the sciences, both in the conclusions and premises, and it is for this reason that Aquinas names wisdom as more appropriately called a virtue compared with science.[118] While science is knowledge of a demonstrated conclusion, understanding is insight into principles, and wisdom knowledge of ultimate truth.[119] Aquinas also believes that understanding, wisdom and science can be gifts of the Holy Spirit. While the interpretation of wisdom as gift is relatively easy to envisage, this is more difficult in the case of understanding and science. Aquinas, in particular, believes that, like prudence, we can only get so far through our natural understanding. In order to penetrate to the fullest degree into reality, he suggests that we need the supernatural light of understanding as gift, added to our nature as an enhancement, given through the grace of God. He rejects the idea that understanding is just about insight into contemplative knowledge; rather, it includes practical matters as well. Hence, 'first that we should penetrate and grasp them with insight, this is the role of the gift of understanding. Secondly, that we should judge them aright, and appreciate how we should cling to them and shun their opposites. As for divine things such judgement is the role of the gift of wisdom, as for creaturely things of the gift of science, as for applying itself to individual actions of the gift of counsel.'[120] The gift of science can distinguish what is to be believed from what is not. Yet the gift has two roles, in discerning what is a matter of faith and ought to be believed, but also in how to bear witness to this belief. As a gift, that of science is nobler than its corresponding intellectual virtue, but falls under the theological virtues of faith, hope and charity. For Aquinas science is distinct from the gift of wisdom, in that science is about the certitude of judgement that arises out of secondary human or created things, while wisdom is judgement about the highest cause, namely God. The gift of science can be related to the judging activity in prudence, just as the deliberating activity is related to the gift of counsel. In as far as a person comes to know God through created things, this is the office of the gift of science, but the judgement of created things in the light of divine things is the gift of wisdom. This distinction is of great interest in the light of attempts by scientists to find God through their investigations of the natural world. Thomas would suggest that such intimations of divine reality are the result of the gift of science, but while science might give knowledge as to what one might believe, wisdom affords a deeper relationship with God in a way that science cannot. Hence, he is able to qualify both the provision and the limits of scientific knowledge.

Aquinas's admission of the partial nature of our knowledge is particularly significant in this context. For those seeking to find ways of understanding the world as created in a scientific context have summarily dismissed the classical view of God's relationship with the world.[121] The fear of ideas about an 'interventionist' God has pushed an understanding of God's action in creation towards unknowability in *God*, rather than in *human* understanding. While it is possible to see the benefits of the idea of kenosis for theodicy, such unknowability in Christ, understood in kenotic categories, once extended to the Creator, leads to the radical idea that even God does not know fully the outcome of God's creative activity. This seems to be the thrust of John Polkinghorne's analysis, even though he claims to affirm traditional Christian theology.[122] However, it seems to me, with Sarah Coakley, that Christ's kenosis has been rarefied to a principle far beyond that for which it was intended in Christian theology.[123]

It is worth asking if the evacuation of power from God in order to affirm human freedom is a misconception of that freedom, couched in terms that deny any admission of dependence. Such a view is inconsistent with other strands of theological reflection, which refer to God in maternal categories. Or, more specifically, is it symbolic of 'a normative masculine self who gains independence by setting himself apart from that which gave him life and continues to sustain him'?[124] For it is also possible to envisage an act as being the most free when *aligned* with God's providential will. This is the thrust of an ethics of virtue and an ethics of wisdom, namely to search after and seek to participate in the Eternal Wisdom of God. Wisdom, moreover, is rooted in charity, so that 'From his habit of charity the spiritual man has a bent to judge all things aright according to divine standards, and his judgment is pronounced through the gift of Wisdom, even as the just man pronounces according to juridical standards through the virtue of prudence.'[125] The alternative, libertarian freedom, seems to enjoin a freedom apart from God, since God's power is evacuated of content. The ethical outcome of such freedom negates the possibility of alignment with the Goodness and Beauty of God, since such concepts have no reality in and of themselves apart from the created world. The source of value in this context is humanity turned in on itself, freely open to the temptation of *curiositas*. It is for this reason that Stephen Clark's comments become most apt, namely 'if there were no forms of beauty, we could not do science. We could not even live.'[126]

Not only is wisdom fruitful in delineating the relationship between God and creation in the context of contemporary science, but also wisdom becomes most fruitful in the context of the Christian community when it is understood as a Trinitarian theological term.[127] Such Wisdom holds together the ideas of creation with redemption: Christ as Logos is *also* Sophia incarnate.[128] It gets round the difficulty identified by Gilbert Meilaender that attention to the virtues simply as the fulfilled life seems to clash with the Christian ideas of self-sacrifice and God's grace.[129] Wisdom is particularly useful as a starting point for ethical reflection on genetic engineering, both in the human sphere and in the context of environmental issues. How might such a wisdom ethic, identified as it is with prudence and thus the four cardinal virtues discussed above, be relevant to thinking about specific areas in an ethics of nature? Rather than begin with problems centred on the scientific understanding of human nature as such, I intend deliberately to begin with consideration of environmental ethics. For it is in this area above all that virtue ethics, at first sight, would not be expected to be able to make a contribution. I suggest not only that a virtue ethic understood through the Thomistic categories of prudence, justice, fortitude and temperance is particularly helpful, but also that wisdom as created, yet involving God in creation, does lend itself to such an extension into consideration of the natural world.

Notes

1   A. MacIntyre, *After Virtue: A Study in Moral Theory*, 2nd edn (London: Duckworth, 1985), p. 1.

2   See, for example, R. Crisp, ed.: *How Should One Live? Essays on the Virtues* (Oxford: Clarendon Press, 1996); D. Statman, ed.: *Virtue Ethics: A Critical Reader* (Edinburgh: Edinburgh University Press, 1997); R. Crisp and M. Slote, eds: *Virtue Ethics* (Oxford: Oxford University Press, 1997); R. Hursthouse: *On Virtue Ethics* (Oxford: Oxford University Press, 1999); S. Darwell, ed.: *Virtue Ethics* (Oxford, Blackwell, 2002).

3   An exception to this trend is Jamie Schaefer's doctoral thesis. See J. Schaefer: 'Ethical Implications of Applying Aquinas's Notions of the Unity and Diversity of Creation to Human Functioning in Ecosystems' (Marquetter University, PhD thesis, 1994).

4   Such a view is common. See, for example, A. Linsey: *Animal Theology* (London: SCM Press, 1994), esp. pp. 12–15.

5   Louke van Wensveen sees a contradiction between dynamic ecological virtue lan-
    guage and the systematic approach of Aquinas that she hints amounts to 'a closed
    intellectual system with strong claims to ultimacy'. I argue, instead, that while Aquinas's
    thought needs to be adjusted in some respects in the light of post-Darwinian science,
    the strength of his position is that is allows for a bridge into Aristotelian thinking that
    is far from being an 'oxymoron'; rather, it is one way of appropriating the Christian
    tradition as situated in a particular community. L.van Wensveen: *Dirty Virtues: The
    Emergence of Ecological Ethics* (New York: Humanity Books, 2000), p. 16.

6   For a range of Christian approaches to bioethics see N. Messer, ed.: *Theological Issues
    in Bioethics: An Introduction with Readings* (London: Darton, Longman and Todd,
    2002).

7   M. Banner: *Christian Ethics and Contemporary Moral Problems* (Cambridge: Cambridge
    University Press, 1999), pp. xi–xii.

8   Banner: *Christian Ethics*, pp. 5–6.

9   Banner: *Christian Ethics*, pp. 204–24.

10 M. Banner: 'Barth, Burke and the Sabbath: On Preferring the Sabbath to the Sub-
    lime: Some Preliminary Thoughts', in C. Deane-Drummond and B. Szerszynski, eds:
    Re-ordering Nature: Theology, Society and the New Genetics (Edinburgh: T & T Clark,
    2003), pp. 68–76.

11 Banner: *Christian Ethics*, pp. 163–203.

12 N. Biggar: 'Karl Barth and Germain Grisez on the Human Good: An Ecumenical
    Rapprochement', in N. Biggar and R. Black, eds.: *The Revival of Natural Law: Philo-
    sophical, Theological and Ethical Responses to the Finnis–Grisez School* (Aldershot: Ashgate,
    2000), pp. 164–83.

13 E. Reed: *The Genesis of Ethics: On the Authority of God as the Origin of Christian Ethics*
    (London: Darton, Longman and Todd, 2000).

14 J. Gustafson: 'The Sectarian Temptation: Reflections on Theology, Church, and the
    University', *Proceedings of the Catholic Theological Society*, 40 (1985), pp. 83–94, esp. p. 84.

15 J. Gustafson: 'A Response to Critics', *Journal of Religious Ethics*, 13 (1985), pp. 185–209,
    esp. p. 189.

16 J. Gustafson: *Ethics from a Theocentric Perspective. Volume 2: Ethics and Theology*
    (London: University of Chicago Press, 1984).

17 A similar observation has been highlighted by J. Porter: *The Recovery of Virtue*
    (London: SPCK, 1990), pp. 60–2.

18 I will be taking up a critical discussion with Gustafson's work in the final chapter.

19 For a recent response to this shift see Biggar and Black, eds: *The Revival of Natural
    Law*.

20 R. Black: 'Introduction: The New Natural Law Theory', in Biggar and Black, eds.:
    The Revival of Natural Law, pp. 1–25, esp. p. 5.

21 S. Hauerwas: *The Peaceable Kingdom* (Notre Dame, IN: University of Notre Dame
    Press, 1983), esp. p. 51.

22 R. Black: 'Is the New Natural Law Theory Christian?', in Biggar and Black, eds: *The
    Revival of Natural Law*, pp. 148–63, esp. p. 157.

23 J. Porter: *The Recovery of Virtue* (London: SPCK, 1994), p. 15. See also J. Porter:
    Moral Action and Christian Ethics (Cambridge: Cambridge University Press, 1995).

24 Porter: *Moral Action*, pp. 89–92; D. J. M. Bardley: *Aquinas on the Twofold Human
    Good: Reason and Human Happiness in Aquinas's Moral Science* (Washington, DC: The
    Catholic University of America Press, 1997).

25   S. Hauerwas: *A Community of Character: Towards a Constructive Christian Social Ethic* (Notre Dame, IN: University of Notre Dame Press, 1981), pp. 111–35.

26   Banner: *Christian Ethics*, p. 39.

27   See, for example, E. Lohse: *Theological Ethics of the New Testament*, trans. M. E. Boring (Philadelphia: Fortress Press, 1991).

28   L. White: *The Historic Roots of our Ecological Crisis, Science*, 145 (1967), pp. 1203–7; C. Deane-Drummond: *Theology and Biotechnology: Implications for a New Science* (London: Geoffrey Chapman, 1997), p. 28.

29   A. Thiselton: *The Two Horizons: New Testament Hermeneutics and Philosophical Description*, 2nd edn (Grand Rapids, MI: Eerdmans, 1993).

30   I will discuss particular examples of consequentialism as applied to biology in more detail in subsequent chapters. See also C. Deane-Drummond: *Biology and Theology Today: Exploring the Boundaries* (London: SCM Press, 2001), pp. 119–28.

31   Louke van Wensveen has conducted an extensive and careful survey of the ecological literature for virtue language. She recognizes that this is not self-conscious avocation of virtues, so to call this, as she does in the title of her book, an *emergence* of ecological virtue ethics is rather overstated. When speaking of the relative lack of a virtue ethic approach to the natural world I am referring to the primary and self-conscious development of virtue ethics. See L. van Wensveen: *Dirty Virtues: The Emergence of Ecological Virtue Ethics* (New York: Humanity Books, 2000), p. 5. She lists a handful of writers who have called for, developed or explored virtue-based approaches, (p. 19, fn. 7), though close examination of this literature shows that even in these examples the particular development of a virtue-based approach is somewhat limited. For example, James Nash in his *Loving Nature* devotes only five out of 251 pages specifically to nine ecological virtues, and these are defined in terms of pragmatic utility, namely sustainability, adaptability, relationality, frugality, equity, solidarity, biodiversity, sufficiency and humility. J. Nash: *Loving Nature: Ecological Integrity and Christian Responsibility*, The Churches' Center for Theology and Public Policy (Nashville, TN: Abingdon Press, 1991), pp. 63–7.

32   See, for example, Deane-Drummond and Szerszynski: *ReOrdering Nature*.

33   MacIntyre: *After Virtue*, esp. pp. 204–25.

34   Hursthouse: *On Virtue Ethics*, p. 13.

35   A. MacIntyre: *Dependent Rational Animals: Why Human Beings Need the Virtues* (London: Duckworth, 1999), p. x.

36   MacIntyre: *Dependent Rational Animals*, pp. xi, 5–6.

37   This takes us into the domain of evolutionary psychology, which I will return to in a later chapter. How far and to what extent our behaviour is related to that of the animals has become an area for current discussion among theologians interested in environmental concern. See, for example, J. Habgood: *The Concept of Nature* (London: Darton, Longman and Todd, 2002), pp. 80–111.

38   I will discuss the particular way such choices can be worked through in later chapters.

39   Hursthouse: *On Virtue Ethics*, pp. 71–4.

40   S. Clark: *Biology and Christian Ethics* (Cambridge: Cambridge University Press, 2000), p. 72.

41   Clark: *Biology and Christian Ethics*, p. 77.

42   Clark: *Biology and Christian Ethics*, p. 217.

43   Clark: *Biology and Christian Ethics*, p. 309.

44 John Haught argues for a revised understanding of God in the light of Darwinian theory, and thereby a revised ethical alternative. See J. F. Haught: *God After Darwin: A Theology of Evolution* (Boulder, CO: Westview Press, 2000). I will take up a critical discussion with Haught again in the final chapter.

45 Joseph Kotva discusses this possibility in J. Kotva: *The Christian Case for Virtue Ethics* (Washington, DC: Georgetown University Press, 1996), pp. 48ff. I will show later that there is a sense in which divine law is retained once wisdom is appropriated as a virtue, but the important point to note here is that the virtues take priority in ethical reflection on divine/natural law, rather than presuming a starting point in either a simple denial or avocation of divine law.

46 R. Taylor: *Ethics, Faith and Reason* (Englewood Cliffs, NJ: Prentice Hall, 1985), pp. 22–5, 77–87.

47 See S. Hauerwas: *Character and the Christian Life: A Study in Theological Ethics* (San Antonio, TX: Trinity University Press, 1975).

48 Kotva: *The Christian Case*, p. 59.

49 This highlights one of the difficulties of searching for virtue language. For example, respect or love can become rules that are then applied, and instead the particular context in which the virtue language is situated needs to be considered. For example, Wensveen points to the integral relationship between virtue language and social theory in Murray Bookchin's *The Ecology of Freedom*, though I suggest that it is the latter that is more dominant in his approach to environmental ethics. Wensveen: *Dirty Virtues*, pp. 43–61; M. Bookchin: *The Ecology of Freedom: The Emergence and Dissolution of Hierarchy* (New York: Black Rose Books, 1991).

50 Paul Ramsey is an influential Christian theologian whose avocation of a love ethic has become a classic text. See P. Ramsey: *Basic Christian Ethics* (Louisville, KY: Westminster John Knox Press, 1950). Kotva challenges the adequacy of such an ethic in Kotva: *The Christian Case*, pp. 113–14.

51 Kotva: *The Christian Case*, p. 104.

52 Kotva: *The Christian Case*, pp. 106–7.

53 G. Loughlin: *The Bible as Narrative* (Cambridge: Cambridge University Press, 1999).

54 Kotva: *The Christian Case*, p. 119.

55 Kotva: *The Christian Case*, p. 123.

56 Some biblical ethicists have rejected virtue ethics as too self-centred. For example, see W. Schrage: *The Ethics of the New Testament*, trans. D. Green (Philadelphia: Fortress Press, 1988), p. 79.

57 For a discussion of the four virtues see Josef Pieper: *The Four Cardinal Virtues* (Notre Dame, IN: University of Notre Dame Press, 1966); first published by Faber and Faber in three volumes, *Prudence*, trans. R. Winston and C. Winston (1959); *Justice*, trans. L. Lynch (1955); *Fortitude and Temperance*, trans. D. Coogan (1954). I am suggesting not that this is the only way to approach the virtues in this context, but that this focus brings to light issues that would not otherwise be considered in a fruitful and constructive way. Pieper did not apply the virtues to reflection on an ethics of nature.

58 See F. Kerr: *After Aquinas: Versions of Thomism* (Oxford: Blackwell, 2002), pp. 134–48.

59 Pieper: *Prudence*, p. 11.

60 I will come back to contemporary debates about the place of biological instincts as orientated towards altruism in subsequent chapters.

61 Pieper: *Prudence*, p. 16.

62 Pieper: *Prudence*, p. 17.

63 I will come back to the issue of natural law in subsequent chapters. See also, C. Deane-Drummond: 'Aquinas, Wisdom Ethics and the New Genetics', in Deane-Drummond and Szerszynski eds: *Re-ordering Nature*, pp. 293–311.

64 Aquinas: *Summa Theologiae, volume 36, Prudence*, trans. T. Gilby (Oxford: Blackfriars, 1974), 2a2ae, Qu. 47.2.

65 Aquinas: *Summa Theologiae, volume 36*, 2a2ae, Qu. 47.4, 47.5.

66 Both facets come through clearly in *Summa Theologiae*, 2a2ae, Qu. 47.6 and Qu. 47.7. Jean Porter has emphasized the second characteristic of the 'mean' of a virtue, but Aquinas includes both aspects in sequence, suggesting that both need to be considered together. See J. Porter: *The Recovery of Virtue* (Cambridge: Cambridge University Press, 1996), pp. 156–62.

67 Aquinas: *Summa Theologiae, volume 36*, 2a2ae, Qu. 47.7.

68 A. MacIntyre: *Whose Justice? Which Rationality?* (London: Duckworth, 1988), p. 196.

69 Such an approach can be compared usefully with Bernard Lonergan's philosophy of *Insight*, which focuses on the understanding, a virtue that Aquinas names as subsidiary to prudence as it refers to one's inner state, rather than being open to another through the gift of counsel. Yet Aquinas also lists insight as one of the aspects of prudence, so it is not entirely clear how far insight can be seen as integral to prudential activity. While I have included it under the list of prudential characteristics, it does not serve the same weight as that given in Lonergan's philosophical approach.

70 Aquinas: *Summa Theologiae, volume 36*, 2a2ae, Qu. 47.9.

71 Aquinas: *Summa Theologiae, volume 36*, 2a2ae, Qu. 51.2.

72 Aquinas: *Summa Theologiae, volume 36*, 2a2ae, Qu. 51.3.

73 Aquinas: *Summa Theologiae, volume 36*, 2a2ae, Qu. 51.4.

74 Aquinas: *Summa Theologiae, volume 36*, 2a2ae, Qu. 49.

75 Aquinas: *Summa Theologiae, volume 36*, 2a2ae, Qu. 47.11. For a more general discussion of the relationship between the common good and Christian ethics see D. Hollenbach: *The Common Good and Christian Ethics* (Cambridge: Cambridge University Press, 2002).

76 Aquinas: *Summa Theologiae, volume 36*, 2a2ae, Qu. 53.6.

77 Aquinas: *Summa Theologiae, volume 36*, 2a2ae, Qu. 54.1, Qu. 54.2.

78 Aquinas: *Summa Theologiae, volume 36*, 2a2ae, Qu. 55.2.

79 Aquinas: *Summa Theologiae, volume 36*, 2a2ae, Qu. 55.1.

80 Aquinas: *Summa Theologiae, volume 36*, 2a2ae, Qu. 55.8.

81 Pieper: *Prudence*, p. 36. Pieper, in using the term 'tactics', may be referring to Aquinas's rejection of cunning as an appropriate means to an end, even if such an end is a good one. Aquinas: *Summa Theologiae, volume 36*, 2a2ae, Qu. 55.3

82 One of the main differences between Christian understanding of prudence and its 'pagan' counterpart is the emphasis on charity, and the priority of prudence over justice. For discussion see, S. Hauerwas and C. Pinches: *Christians among the Virtues: Theological Conversations with Ancient and Modern Ethics* (Notre Dame, IN: University of Notre Dame Press, 1997), pp. 89–109.

83 In this Aquinas is following the list of the seven gifts of the Spirit taken from Isaiah.

84 Aquinas: *Summa Theologiae, volume 36*, 2a2ae, Qu. 52.2. He also suggests that the gift of understanding enlarges and helps prudence, but the gift most closely linked with

prudence is counsel, since it involves taking advice from another, namely the Holy Spirit.

85   See C. Deane-Drummond, *Creation through Wisdom: Theology and the New Biology* (Edinburgh: T & T Clark, 2000), pp. 99–103; Deane-Drummond: 'Aquinas, Wisdom Ethics and the New Genetics'.

86   For example, those who try to read into the natural world human values and desires are making what Holmes Rolston calls a category mistake. H. Rolston: *Genes, Genesis and God: Values and Their Origins in Natural and Human History* (Cambridge: Cambridge University Press, 1999), pp. 277–80.

87   This does not move against Aquinas's ontology, which insisted that all creatures are subject to the Divine Law, for 'even non-rational creatures are subject to it through being moved by divine Providence . . . so participate in the divine reason by way of obedience'. The difference between creatures with reason and those without is that non-rational creatures cannot perceive the meaning of the law, but are simply ruled by divine Providence. See Aquinas: *Summa Theologiae, volume 28, Law and Political Theory*, trans. T. Gilby (Oxford: Blackfriars, 1966), 1a2ae, Qu. 91.3.

88   O. O'Neill: *Towards Justice and Virtue: A Constructive Account of Practical Reasoning* (Cambridge: Cambridge University Press, 1996).

89   Aquinas: *Summa Theologiae, volume 37, Justice*, trans. T. Gilby (London: Blackfriars, 1974), 2a2ae, Qu. 57.1

90   Aquinas: *Summa Theologiae, volume 37*, 2a2ae, Qu. 58.1.

91   Aquinas: *Summa Theologiae, volume 37*, 2a2ae, Qu. 58.5.

92   Aquinas: *Summa Theologiae, volume 37*, 2a2ae, Qu. 57.2.

93   Aquinas: *Summa Theologiae, volume 37*, 2a2ae, Qu. 58.2.

94   Aquinas: *Summa Theologiae, volume 28, Law and Political Theory*, 1a2ae, Qu. 96.2, 96.3.

95   Alasdair MacIntyre comments on this in *Whose Justice?*, pp. 198–200. It is also worth noting that Aquinas's views were controversial even in his own time, such as the absolute prohibition against lying (p. 203). Yet while specific aspects of Aquinas's thought, such as his views on politics and women, were most understandable in the historical context of his time, his approach to ethics still has a significant bearing on how to approach ethical issues in a contemporary context.

96   Aquinas: *Summa Theologiae, volume 28, Law and Political Theory*, 1a2ae, Qu. 96.6.

97   Pieper: *The Four Cardinal Virtues*, p. 49.

98   I will come back to this discussion again in the chapters on environmental ethics and animal rights. For a reconsideration of Aquinas's view on animals see in particular J. Barad: *Aquinas on the Nature and the Treatment of Animals* (San Francisco: International Scholars Publications, 1995).

99   MacIntyre: *Whose Justice?*, p. 205.

100 That is, non-humans are significant others that need to be taken into account in human actions named as just, rather than attributing the possibility of just action to non-human mammals as moral agents. I will return to this issue in chapter 3.

101 MacIntyre: *Whose Justice?*, p. 205.

102 MacIntyre: *After Virtue*, pp. 260–3.

103 I would agree with MacIntyre that there is no wholly neutral, socially disembodied standpoint from which to elucidate rationality as such, but such standpoints do not mean that there is no such thing as a truth claim, as accordingly to relativism or perspectivism. MacIntyre: *Whose Justice?*, pp. 365–9.

104 MacIntyre: *Whose Justice?*, pp. 402–3.

105   Pieper: *The Four Cardinal Virtues*, pp. 146–7.

106   Pieper: *The Four Cardinal Virtues*, p. 203.

107   Hauerwas: *A Community of Character*; S. Hauerwas: *Vision and Virtue* (Notre Dame, IN: University of Notre Dame Press, 1981).

108   J. Pieper: *The Silence of St Thomas*, trans. D. O'Connor (London: Faber and Faber, 1957), p. 39.

109   J. D. Caputo: *Heidegger and Aquinas: An Essay on Overcoming Metaphysics* (New York: Fordham University Press, 1982), p. 251.

110   Pieper: *The Silence*, p. 55.

111   For a discussion of the emergence of the idea of autonomy, see Deane-Drummond: *Biology and Theology Today*, pp. 13–16.

112   Pieper: *The Silence*, p. 59.

113   Pieper: *The Silence*, p. 65.

114   This tendency is reflected in prominent science and religion authors. See, for example, A. Peacocke: *The Paths from Science to God* (Oxford: Oneworld, 2001).

115   For a detailed discussion of the theological basis for wisdom, see Deane-Drummond: *Creation through Wisdom*.

116   Aquinas: *Summa Theologiae, volume 34, Charity*, trans. R. J. Batten (Oxford: Blackfriars, 1975), 2a2ae, Qu. 23.2.

117   Aquinas: *Summa Theologiae, Volume 23, Virtue*, trans. W. D. Hughes, (Oxford: Blackfriars, 1969), 1a2ae, Qu. 66.5.

118   Aquinas: *Summa Theologiae, Volume 23, Virtue*, 1a2ae, Qu. 57.2.

119   According to Aquinas science was reserved for deductive knowledge. While such an understanding of science is much expanded today, his understanding of the relationship between science and wisdom offers a significant point of departure for contemporary reflection.

120   Aquinas: *Summa Theologiae, volume 32, Consequences of Faith*, trans. T. Gilby (Oxford: Blackfriars, 1975), 2a2ae, Qu. 8.6.

121   J. Polkinghorne, ed.: *The Work of Love: Creation as Kenosis* (London: SPCK, 2001).

122   J. Polkinghorne: 'Kenotic Creation and Divine Action', in Polkinghorne, ed.: *The Work of Love*, pp. 90–106.

123   S. Coakley: 'Kenosis: Theological Meanings and Gender Connotations', in Polkinghorne, ed.: *The Work of Love*, pp. 192–210.

124   Coakley, 'Kenosis', p. 205.

125   Aquinas: *Summa Theologiae, volume 37*, 2a2ae, Qu. 60.1.

126   Clark: *Biology and Christian Ethics*, p. 310.

127   See Deane-Drummond, *Biology and Theology Today*; *Creation through Wisdom*, pp. 124–31.

128   C. Deane-Drummond: 'Logos as Sophia: A Starting Point for a Sophianic Theology of Creation', in A. Peacocke and P. Clayton, eds: *In Whom We Live and Move and Have Our Being: Reflections on Panentheism in an Age of Science* (New York: Eerdmans, 2003).

129   G. Meilaender: *The Theory and Practice of Virtue* (Notre Dame, IN: University of Notre Dame Press, 1984). Wensveen suggests that this difficulty is caused by a somewhat incoherent combination of Lutheran emphasis on sin and Catholic reflection on natural law (p. 28). I suggest that willingness to suffer for the sake of the good is an integral aspect of fortitude, one of the four cardinal virtues, as I discussed above. This need not necessarily lead to the denial of the goodness of creation or its affective dimension in the way van Wensveen suggests.

Chapter 2

Environmental Ethics

Debates about how to treat the natural world need to be set in the context of present environmental problems. Current scientific thinking on the most likely environmental pressures in the twenty-first century include climate change, availability of water resources and water pollution, along with deforestation, desertification and environmental damage caused by poor national and international management.[1] These problems are not new, but are likely to get worse because of the lack of attention by policy-makers in many countries. However, in addition to these issues, the United Nations Environment Programme's *Global Environment Outlook 2000* suggests that new environmental problems will emerge. These come about first as a result of unforeseen events, or second because existing problems take a new unexpected turn, or third when areas that are currently neglected suddenly become significant.[2] Similar findings were reported in the *Global Environmental Outlook 3* report in preparation for the Summit on Sustainable Development in Johannesburg in 2002.[3] Such results suggest a measure of contingency and unpredictability in environmental problems, and are clear signals that any sense of complacency is premature. Moreover, the lack of complete scientific knowledge, as well as its enormous complexity, gives us reason to be careful of any trite solutions from philosophical or theological ivory towers.

While environmental scientists have become more aware of the mutual interdependence of the human and non-human, expressed as the relationship between socio-economic and environmental systems, the natural world remains an 'other' to be objectified and analysed according to the methods of science. How far and to what extent we ought to value the natural world depends on the relative value attached to humanity, expressed as the philosophical debate between a focus on humanity, or anthropocentrism, and a revised focus on the whole complex of living beings, or biocentrism. The premise of anthropocentrism is that value can only arise from human beings as free-thinking rational animals, while that of biocentrism is that such values have failed the environment, or even contributed to the environmental crisis. There arise, then, two opposing philosophies of nature, between mechanism and organicism, reductionism and holism, dualism and unity of mind and nature, reason and intuition/feeling, instrumentalism and intrinsic value, alienation and primordial harmony of being. The ideals of harmony, holism and unity seem to link together in a complex way to assure that nature is valued. While such a claim of harmonious interdependence purports to rest on ecological understanding, I shall argue that such a claim is false, as it is out of touch with ecological science. Moreover, using ecology as a foundation for ethics is itself fraught with difficulties. Indeed, the divorce of romanticized versions of philosophies of nature from practical ecological consideration undermines their credibility still further. What might be an alternative to the form of anthropocentrism that seems to have failed the environment? I suggest, instead, that a return to a virtue ethic, particularly that of prudence and wisdom, offers a way of affirming creation, while at the same time recognizing it as 'other' than human. Moreover, such a wisdom ethic is situated not so much in self-interest as in the context of knowing the world is created as 'other', leading to ecological justice for the earth.

The Biocentric Alternative

Given that we seem to have undervalued the natural world and are likely to continue to do so, as expressed in environmental problems cited above, philosophers have sought to find alternative ways of valuing nature that place greater emphasis on the importance of the natural world. As opposed to the instrumental view of natural systems, where nature is an object for the benefit of humanity, an alternative philosophy stresses intrinsic value of the natural world. Intrinsic value is a somewhat ambiguous term, as different philosophers have used it in different ways. It can mean value given to nature in and of itself, because of internal properties. Second, it can also mean that which is opposed to instrumental value. Third, it can mean that which is valued in independence of the valuing subject. All three varieties of intrinsic value have a tendency to coalesce.[4] Biocentric philosophers associate the anthropocentric alternative with the instrumental use of nature. It is clear, however, that those who still adhere to an anthropocentrism do so on the basis that it makes no sense to value the world in detachment from human valuing. However, it does not follow that those who reject biocentrism also adhere to an instrumental view of nature in the way that some biocentric philosophers would have us believe.

At one end of the scale we have those who argue that existing moral categories are all that are required for an environmental ethic. At the other end we have those who insist on a radical restructuring of value, so that it is no longer focused on human beings. In between are those who wish to extend moral categories of 'good', 'right', 'duty', 'care' and 'value' from human beings to the natural world.[5] I will return to a full discussion of the extension of moral categories to animals in the following chapter. I will also return to a discussion of the merits of various forms of holism in chapter 7, on Gaia. For the time being it is worth noting that to be credible an environmental philosophy needs to have four key components. These consist of: (a) a theory about what nature is; (b) a theory about human beings; (c) a theory of value and evaluation of human action; and (d) a theory of method, or standards against which claims are to be tested or confirmed. Current discussion has focused almost exclusively on ideas about value.[6] Perhaps counter-intuitively there is also little evidence that biocentric philosophy actually leads to more ecologically responsible behaviour.[7] I seek to address here both the lack of attention to an adequate theory about human being and the failure to address methodological issues.

Communitarianism or Cosmopolitanism?

It is possible to arrive at an environmental ethic primarily through consideration of historical socio-political factors that gave rise to the crisis. Michael Northcott, for example, considers the different facets of modernity that he suggests have contributed to environmental stress. These have very early roots in the changes in agricultural systems and land use that emerged following the early transition to a settled agricultural society. However, he argues that the problem is exacerbated by the development of a market economy from the time of the enclosures onwards, so that the idea of nature as sacred is replaced by the idea of nature as a commodity.[8] Northcott also considers that the development of modern science and technology, embedded in a Cartesian mechanistic attitude, fostered the abuse of nature.[9] Any purpose of nature is reduced to human willing; there is a 'hominization' of nature such that it is there simply to serve human interests. Science and technology become part of his critique of modernity as such, so that 'modernity substitutes material wealth and globalised Western technology and culture for human community, ecological richness and local knowledge'.[10] It amounts to a 'disembedding' of human consciousness and community from the 'sacred cosmos'. Not surprisingly, he associates the harmonious human relationships with nature with 'religious sensibilities and rituals by which these were traditionally sustained'.[11] However, because he has traced the early disruption of our relationship with nature to the first agricultural phase of human civilization, he needs to seek for models of human relationships with nature in early primitive culture, including the aboriginals. They become for him models of ethical conduct, in their 'deep primal respect and reverence for the natural order'.[12]

While I welcome the breadth of social and economic analysis that Northcott includes in his critique, I suggest that Northcott's attachment to primal cultures is far too idealistic. Anthropological studies have demonstrated that:

> It is unrealistic to lump together all indigenous and traditional peoples and claim that they understand their environments in ways that contrast sharply with Western models. Indigenous and traditional societies embrace a wide range of ecological practices, which generate a diversity of environmental perspectives, some of which are as ambiguous and contradictory as Western concepts of 'nature'.[13]

Northcott's critique of science and technology is also somewhat ambiguous. On the one hand he suggests that it is simply the *application* of modern science in industrialized technology that is partly responsible for the environmental crisis.[14] On the other hand he suggests that Kant and Newton laid a scientific and philosophical ground for an atheistic cosmology, so that 'The evacuation of purposiveness and moral order from nature independent of human willing and purposiveness is therefore inherent in the world-view of modern science'.[15] It is not entirely clear which aspect of science is the most important in fostering environmental stress. For him, modern scientists lack the ability to see any 'enduring significance, physical, spiritual or moral' in any aspect of the natural world. Above all, 'It is this mechanistic Cartesian approach to the natural world which is in part responsible for the abuses of nature which characterise modern civilisation.'[16] He contrasts this mechanistic approach with the more contemporary 'chaos' theory in modern physics and ecology/Gaia, which he suggests are more holistic and interactive. Yet, as John Brooke and Geoffrey Cantor have observed, to posit the history of science in terms of the Cartesian villains versus the heroic work of Einstein and others, including ecologists, is far too simplistic.[17] While Fritjof Capra looks to Eastern religious views, Northcott prefers the aboriginal. Both assume that there is an ideal towards which the new physics/ecology approaches. Both seem to attribute to early science the idea of mechanism, when in practice there were a number of competing philosophies, not least a romanticism that was present, but failed to win institutional support.[18] More importantly, perhaps, for historians of science, the suggestion that Cartesian metaphysics is in any sense causative of the ecological crisis puts far too much emphasis on the influence of metaphysical ideas. To be fair Northcott has, quite rightly in my view, considered other social, political, religious and technological forces, but he still seems to have portrayed science in the form of a 'master narrative', and attributed to holism a role that is unlikely to be justified. In addition, later in his account he seems to approve of modern scientific method, for:

> it is precisely the modern scientific method of empirical observation, applied with true ethological consistency to animal sociality and organic connections in the non-human world, which allows us to dare to believe that the non-human world, as well as human society, still contains within it marks of the moral order, as well as the physical design, of the creator God who first affirmed its goodness.[19]

Yet can this method of empirical observation be detached from the philosophical idea of the natural world as in some sense mechanistic? He believes that ethological science and ecology can be used, but this is only possible if they are detached from a modern scientific mechanistic narrative of the cosmos. Now if this means that some scientists are acceptable because they look at things more holistically, then this is inconsistent with his earlier claim that modern scientists lack the ability to see the spiritual in the natural world mentioned above.[20] His perception that ecology is operating out of a rather different philosophy compared with other 'harder' sciences, such as genetics, coheres with my own view, though I suggest that his implicit attachment of holism to ecology is not necessarily justified, as I will elaborate further below. Moreover, the boundaries between different sciences are more blurred than is implied in this account. A mechanistic science existed alongside more holistic views and vice versa. Just as the new physics still contains in it elements of Newtonian understanding, so too the classical physics also led to some extent to a sense of intimacy between the experimenter and the experiment.[21] This does not mean, of course, that we cannot be critical of tendencies in the philosophy of science, but to attribute to such tendencies responsibility for the ecological crisis seems to be overdrawn.

The alternative to mechanistic science is, for Northcott, the ideal of community, as expressed in the work of a pioneer in the field, Aldo Leopold. Leopold's land ethic fills the same epistemological space occupied by the new physics, though in this case it takes inspiration from ecology, rather than physics. Leopold localized his ethic in an ecological understanding that viewed ecology in terms of energy flows and nutritional cycles between different members of a holistic ecological community.[22] For him all parts of the ecological community are worthy of respect, they are all valued as citizens. In one sense Leopold might seem to be arguing for an extension of ideals of human community on to the wider ecological community. On the other hand, there are strands in his thinking that are more radical, and indicate that the human community has to be understood in terms of the ecological community. Overall his views seem to affirm the more holistic alternative, so that 'moral value is attached to the balanced functioning of the ecosystem, rather than to particular individual animals or plants within the ecosystem'.[23] Individuals become in this scenario less important compared with the biotic whole, including an acceptance of the pain inflicted by natural predators. Northcott distances himself from the ethical priority given to the land in Leopold's analysis; for him if moral value is to have biblical roots, then it must necessarily be linked with the human moral and social order.[24] In this respect Northcott locates his views between the extremes of biocentrism and anthropocentrism in a helpful way. None the less, Northcott seems to accept as given the idea of ecological stability, for 'ecological order is characterised by species diversity, by a stable biomass and by the preservation of nutrients in ecosystems by recycling processes. These processes are reliable and repetitive, they are mostly threatened not by natural competition or predation, but by humanly originated intervention.'[25] Moreover, while he is wary of any reading into the natural world of models for human behaviour, the link between religious community and ecological community of the land is a recurrent theme; the two intersect in a way that is bolstered still further by the idea of natural law.[26]

Other prominent writers on religion and environmental issues that are similarly positioned midway between anthropocentric and biocentric extremes make similar claims about the nature of ecology in terms of stable interconnected systems. Holmes Rolston, for example, rejects the idea that morality can be read off the natural world, or that sentient animals and plants and ecosystems are moral agents, but that does not mean that non-human nature is morally unimportant; it is, in other words, morally considerable.[27] He is novel in his insistence on the possibility of systemic value, arising out of consideration of the functioning of the whole ecological system. While he does recognize the dynamic nature of ecological systems, he seems to assume that there is 'beauty, integrity and persistence in the biotic community'.[28] Furthermore, he suggests that by looking for compassion, charity, rights or other values in nature we are making a 'category mistake'. On the other hand, for him, environmental ethics needs to be based upon but exceed biological and ecological science, so that the way the world is *informs* the way it ought to be. He claims, 'what humans value in nature is an ecology, a pregnant Earth, a projective and prolife system in which (considering biology alone, not culture) individuals can prosper but are also sacrificed indifferently to their pains and pleasures, individual well-being a lofty and passing role in a storied natural history'.[29] Eric Katz similarly insists that natural entities and natural ecological systems deserve moral consideration as part of an interdependent community of life. For him, 'there is a connection between ontology and ethics: what an entity is, free of the imposition of human desires and interests, determines its moral value and the moral obligations owed to it'.[30] None the less, he seems to go further towards biocentrism than Holmes Rolston in declaring that nature is 'an autonomous moral subject'. Other authors write in much the same vein, praising the value of ecological communities.[31]

The ideal of community has been criticized by Robin Attfield, who argues instead for cosmopolitanism, so that ethical obligations are not just within communities, but also to any agent or community, either individually or corporately.[32] He suggests that agents bereft of relationships still have responsibilities. A communitarian response would be to relocate such individuals back into a community, rooted in local traditions. Attfield suggests that a narrow, local focus fails to take into account the fact that cosmopolitanism is part of a tradition. In addition, he argues for a form of consequentialism that is not narrowly utilitarian or centred on human interest, but is both biocentric and consequentialist. How far his position is fully biocentric in the sense of transferring value to the non-human world is open to question. However, he does admit to the idea that non-human nature has moral standing, which means for him that it has a good of its own, even if it does not have moral significance. He redefines intrinsic value for biocentric consequentialism as the good or well being of the bearers of moral standing.[33] He rejects the idea that ecosystems have distinct intrinsic value or moral standing, since for him it seems a pointless exercise, as the individual moral standing of its members already covers its value. Hence, 'once biodiversity is recognised as a precondition of all terrestrial value, and valuable for this reason, no point remains in assigning it an additional value on a par with the individual creatures that it nourishes'.[34] Of course, he assumes here that the ecosystem as a whole has no properties beyond that of the individual members that are worth valuing. In this sense he is strongly opposed to any holism or ideals drawn from ecological narratives. For him consequentialism is better equipped to look at the global nature of problems. Furthermore, he argues for a strong sense of stewardship as a way of delineating the task of humanity towards the natural world. He finds in Jean Calvin the roots of the idea of stewardship, though the concept of cooperation with nature goes further back than this, to the early centuries of Christian thought.[35]

Attfield's emphasis on the global scale of environmental concern is realistic from a practical point of view. However, I suggest that his attachment to consequentialism is not inherent in cosmopolitanism.[36] A rather different version of cosmopolitanism is developed by Laura Westra, who argues for the principle of integrity as the basis for a global ethic.[37] Her position is interesting, in that while it takes inspiration from Leopold's land ethic, it is transferred not just to local ecological communities, but to a neo-Kantian principle of duty. Hence, 'the principle of integrity is essentially the injunction to respect the integrity of ecological and biological processes (save for the purposes of self-defence)'.[38] Her case rests on the assumption that ecological integrity is real and identifiable in the natural world. None the less, she seems to locate integrity in 'wild' nature, removed from human interference. The affirmation of the wild is based on her believe that 'unmanipulated natural systems would be closest to a state of real integrity and hence possess the utmost capacity (c) for sustaining and continuing the full range of potential evolutionary paths for a specific system at its specific time and location'.[39] She suggests that the radical uncertainty found in the unpredictability of ecological problems arising from apparently innocent human activity calls for a principle to be adopted, namely that of integrity. Yet how are we to identify the integrity of wild nature and does this lead to complete lack of human interference? She does, none the less, resist an egalitarian view of nature that is common among those who find a basis for value in ecosystems and for her amounts to a 'flattened view of all that exists'.[40] She affirms, instead, a virtue ethics approach, but one that is related to the principle of integrity.

Richard Fern similarly draws on Leopold and the ideal of wild nature for the development of his environmental ethic, but also on Holmes Rolston III in envisioning what he terms a sentiotic view of nature, which relates to the productivity and purposefulness of life on earth.[41] Like the previous authors he is keen to balance holism and anthropocentrism, so that while his sentiotic view is overtly holistic, his understanding of ethics is that it necessarily must take due cognizance of the special value of human beings, quite apart from specific characteristics such as sentience. Like Holmes Rolston he positions himself midway between holism and anthropocentrism, arguing for what he terms *humane holism*. He also offers an interesting critique of those who wish to ground their environmental ethics on science, be it evolutionary or ecological science.[42] While being more positive about modernity than Northcott, for example, he believes that science cannot be used to justify an ethics of nature, even though ethics needs to be *consistent* with scientific observations. He is making a bold attempt to set up a secular argument for purposefulness within the natural world prior to his theological discussion, which emphasizes traditional theism alongside a strong sense of God's immanence in the created world. The question arises as to whether his understanding of sentiotic nature comes too close to vitalism, and hence is inconsistent with a scientific understanding of reality.

The Nature of Ecological Understanding

Given that the idea of ecological stability and integrity is so widespread in the literature, and that theories of human obligation commonly take their inspiration from what is perceived to be a scientific ontology of nature, it is important to examine closely the concept of stability in ecosystems.[43] Ecology is characterized by hypotheses that are probable, rather than ones that can be rejected as true or false in the manner of Popperian science.[44] Furthermore, theories are sets of conceptual constructs that apply within a set of observable phenomena of a specified domain. Examples of concepts used in ecology are mutualism, parasitism, competition, symbiosis, commensalisms and so on.[45] Notions are the raw material from which theory is generated and are 'metaphors, analogies, personal intuitions'.[46] Certain facts are assumed to be the case by different branches of ecology. Evolutionary biology, for example, assumes that individuals are distinct and are distinguishable. Population ecology assumes that the density of a population functionally represents the intensity of interactions between individuals of a population. In ecosystems ecology the system itself is assumed to be bounded in terms of calculation of nutrient budgets etc. Concepts, such as adaptation, are testable and it is from these concepts that ecological theories develop; that is, they arise through an inductive process based on observation. The social dimension is true of ecological science as much as any other science. Hence particular 'lineages' of work emerge through training in one particular school or laboratory. The choice of method also affects the way ecology develops; for example, should it be comparative or experimental, focused on one factor or a number of factors, specific or broad in scope? Personality may also draw some researchers to particular topics and methods. Yet scientists insist that while these social biases are present, implicit in the method of science is the capacity to move beyond distortions imposed by social factors: 'The social biases are purged from science when people from various backgrounds identify some previously unstated or unsuspected background assumption that has become part of a paradigm, and therefore open the assumption to analysis'.[47] One paradigm that existed in ecology for nearly ninety years was the equilibrium paradigm.[48] This states that ecological systems:

- are essentially closed;
- are self-regulating;
- possess stable point or stable cycle equilibrium;
- have deterministic dynamics;
- are free of disturbance;
- are independent of human influences.

The ideal of 'wild' nature, fixed in a stable but dynamic equilibrium, is the view used as foundational for much environmental ethics, as I discussed above. As Sam Berry has pointed out, 'In the early years of professional ecology, most ecologists took it for granted that communities of animals and plants existed as natural, repeated, internally organised units with a considerable degree of integration.'[49] However, data have gradually accumulated that make this assumption highly questionable. Ecosystem boundaries were discovered to be much more fluid than had been previously anticipated. Longer-term dynamics started to challenge the idea of self-regulation in ecosystems, so that it was impossible to arrive at any realistic predictions. Rather than any fixed form of equilibrium, the most that we can anticipate is 'an equilibrium distribution of patch types or some other attribute, rather than a persistent point equilibrium'.[50] The new paradigm that has replaced the old one of stable ordering is *non-equilibrium*. In this case, 'ecological systems can be thought to be open, to be regulated by factors internal and external to them, to lack a stable point equilibrium, to be non-deterministic and to incorporate disturbance and to admit human influence'.[51]

The replacement of the equilibrium view with the non-equilibrium position has been gradual, and even non-equilibrium advocates recognize that systems can be in an equilibrium state at certain times. None the less, not all ecosystems are capable of being in an equilibrium state. Hence the cultural idea of the 'balance of nature' bolstered the equilibrium view, so that it took many years for it to be challenged. The persistence of this myth is evident in contemporary philosophical writing on environmental ethics, especially where it claims to gain support from ecological science. The hypotheses of science are tested in the context of the scientific community, so that the idea of balance has proved wanting and in its place is the idea of continual flux and change. According to this model ecological systems:

- are in a continual state of flux;
- may at times be in an equilibrium state;
- are characterized by openness to external influences;
- are subject to a multiplicity of controls in a complex way;
- are subject to disturbance from different internal and external factors;
- are open to human influences.

The balance of nature approach implies either that human interference is not justified, the position most commonly adopted by those concerned with environmental ethics, or that the system is so stable that any human intervention will have no real effect. The latter view is one associated with some forms of Gaia theory, which I will return to later in this book. Berry believes that some ecologists are still wedded to a notion of ecology in terms of structured communities, while others are 'more impressed with contingency and adventitious opportunism in nature'.[52] The scale by which ecological changes are measured can, if sufficiently large or short-term, give the appearance of stability. If we reject the idea that ecosystems have inherent stability and integrity, what happens to environmental ethics? Robert Kirkman is one of the few authors to have commented on this possible scenario. He suggests a dramatic change, so that 'the locus of environmental values might shift – or the project of environmental ethics might simply fall apart'.[53] Richard

Fern is wary of drawing out a naturalistic ethic based on ecological science. However, this leads him to conclude that ethics cannot be 'scientized', even though it needs to be 'naturalized'.[54] While, like Fern, I agree that contemporary understandings of ecology are not necessary suitable bearers of an environmental ethic, it seems to me that ethics needs to take such research into account in arriving at its recommendations. Baird Callicott faces up to this issue in asking if the land ethic is still tenable in the context of contemporary understandings of ecology in terms of dynamic flux.[55] He suggests that an adjustment in Leopold's theory is necessary, taking into account the normal special and temporal scales of disturbance that currently exist within a biotic community. How far such an approach can still envisage stability of land communities in the way that Leopold envisaged is open to question; in other words, once we allow for dynamism and flux in natural communities, the philosophical work done by notions of balance and stability integral to nature itself seems to be undermined. A similar problem exists in the issue of the 'naturalization' of natural law, discussed below.

The Recovery of Natural Law

Given the view of ecological systems discovered by more recent ecological research, what might be an appropriate Christian response to environmental ethics? The paradigm of small stable human communities, alongside or integrated with ecological communities, seems open to doubt. Is the new ecology still *consistent with* the concept of natural law, which might at first sight seem to imply coherence with concepts such as integrity and stability?[56] As one might expect, Michael Northcott has approached natural law from a perspective committed to including environmental issues and he strongly criticizes those prominent in the Grisez–Finnis school for being far too anthropocentric and effectively denying the possibility of an environmental ethic.[57] As he suggests, it is almost impossible to avoid taking into account factual statements about the way the world is in order to arrive at moral imperatives. He criticizes the philosophy of science for denying purpose in nature, while at the same time drawing on scientific observations of altruism among mammals in order to show that animals are not so different from humans.[58] The idea of purpose in the universe, or the concept of design, is rather more ambiguous in evolutionary science than he implies. Simon Conway Morris, for example, argues strongly against Stephen Jay Gould that the outcomes of biological evolution are random; rather, they seem to operate according to prescriptive limits, leading to convergent evolutionary forms in given environments despite genetically divergent histories.[59] For Northcott, the concept of ecological stability proves indispensable, so that 'the order and stability of the world, and the reciprocal relationship between this order and moral order of human society, is built into the very nature of reality'.[60] Natural law must be *naturalist*, an idea that he supports by the Gaia hypothesis, primatology and the moral standing of trees. Furthermore, he argues that 'right relations and balances between creatures are connected to incipient moral qualities'.[61] Yet while natural law may be useful as a guidepost for reflection on environmental ethics, the language of rights is more often than not less helpful.[62]

The final outcome of the integration of ecological community with human community is the extension of rights to 'beings and communities of life which also express richness in their nurturing and preservation of life'.[63] Now I could argue that the lack of order acknowledged by contemporary ecological science is simply a denial of ordering that is really present, in the same way as it is possible to reject the lack of purpose implicit in much modern science. However, while a lack of purpose in the universe cannot be supported by empirical evidence, for we simply cannot prove one way or another if there is an ultimate purpose or not, the question of ordering is rather different. It is here that I part company with Fern, for he seems to presume a naturalistic understanding of purpose, though outside the boundaries of current science, through the notion of sentiosis, prior to religious endorsement of it.[64] Such sentiosis leads to both purposefulness and ordering. Northcott hints at the same idea through his interpretation of natural law in ecological ways. While I agree with Northcott that natural law can be extended in order to take into account the common ground between human and non-human nature, I prefer to put more emphasis on the *theological* aspects of natural law, thus taking into account contemporary discussion in ecology.[65] The discovery of ecological instability and apparent flux betrays the fragile nature of any ordering that seems apparent to the casual observer. I suggest, rather, that the cultural belief in the *balance of nature* has coloured the science and that ecology has then been used to support this myth. While Fern does not make the mistake of claiming ecological warrant for his ideas, other philosophers, as I noted earlier, are less cautious.

Given this sense of the precariousness of natural ecosystems, should the idea of a 'naturalist' natural law be abandoned altogether? It is worth asking if all concepts about divine ordering and the chain of being actually reinforce the myth of the balance of nature that I have been arguing needs to be superseded. First of all, it seems to me that an escape into an exclusively anthropocentric focus of natural law is unhelpful, in that it denies the reality of God as creator that Aquinas also affirms through his concept of natural law. Second, we need to look at the idea of natural law in more detail, in order to see how far natural law can be said to be appropriately 'naturalist'. Philosophical renditions of natural law seem to have forgotten that natural law is above all a *theological concept*; it is 'participation in the eternal law' by rational creatures.

The first principle of natural law is that good needs to be sought and evil avoided, understood through reason characteristic of human nature. While the ability to reason could be extended to non-human creatures, the ability to stand back, take account of a multiplicity of circumstances and plan for the future is a uniquely human attribute.[66] Furthermore, this focus on reason needs to be set in the context of both Aquinas's understanding of reason as not rationalism in the post-Cartesian sense and his qualification of the importance of reason in relation to faith. Hence, for Aquinas, 'reason is subordinate to faith, to mysticism and in the end, the eschatological consummation of intelligence in the beatific vision'.[67]

Natural law is related, in the second instance, to natural inclinations. What are natural inclinations? For Aquinas this has three facets. The 'order in which commands of the law of nature are ranged corresponds to that of our natural tendencies'.[68] Such natural tendencies include that basic to all life forms, namely self-preservation. A *correspondence* exists between our natural inclinations and the commands of natural law, which are found in the twin injunction to love God and our neighbour.[69] Hence natural inclinations do not *produce* the natural law that Aquinas envisages; rather, ordering of divine law is in scripture, and this corresponds with ordering in nature as created. There are other correspondences 'which nature teaches all animals', including humans, such as copulation and the rearing of young. Finally, there is the 'appetite for the good of his nature as rational', unique to human beings.[70] Hence the natural law that Aquinas envisages relates to basic human activities such as self-preservation, rearing of young and reasoning.

This understanding of natural law suggests not as much a fixed balance or community of nature as a dynamic movement of all creation towards flourishing and the good. Most geneticists would argue that evolutionary processes through natural selection are opportunistic and pragmatic, rather than optimizing and perfecting.[71] Hence the teleology of ecology in the short term does not seem to have a particular goal or direction. Yet it is important to note that while processes are dynamic and seemingly wandering in their goals, overall patterns do come into view, and such patterns combined with dynamic processes can be thought of as being *consistent with* teleology of the good. While Aquinas believed in a hierarchical ordering of nature, his ontology suggests a commonality between human beings and creatures, in correspondence with the creative ordering of God. As Aquinas suggests, 'non-rational creatures do not share in the workings of human reason, nor do they obey them, yet they participate in the divine reason by way of obedience: the power of divine reason extends to more things than come under human reason. . . . Non-rational things are moved by God without thereby being rational.'[72] It is worth noting that non-rational did not mean for Aquinas a complete lack of any cognitive reasoning ability; rather, it was more specifically associated with willing and conscious choice. Once this is clear, his understanding of the gap between humans and animals is less stark than it appears at first sight.[73] Some flexibility in the concept of natural law is clear from Aquinas's admission that the more details are considered, the more exceptions to the general rule appear.[74] Some have even suggested that the flexibility in his account lays him open to the charge of relativism.[75] In addition, while the primary goal of natural law, to avoid evil and do good, does not change, its secondary precepts can change, in order to be useful for the human life. In other words, it is possible to adjust the concept of natural law so as to take into account contemporary understanding of ecological and evolutionary science. The final purpose, or telos, of natural law cannot be changed, but the means through which it is reached are adjustable.

The belief in the ordering power of God in the face of chaos is a very ancient one, harking back to the story of Genesis, where God's ordering held back the power of chaos, and expressed more fully in the apocalyptic literature such as 1 Enoch.[76] The covenant between God and all creation gives reason to hope in the face of insecurity and instability. It seems to me that this is a more realistic theological response. Rather than denying the possibility of disorder and unpredictability, to which ecological science and environmental science point, Christian ethics affirms its belief in a Creator.[77] Natural inclinations, I suggest, are useful in pointing to the common ground that we share with all other creatures. While in Aquinas natural law is not applied to non-rational creatures in terms of their behaviour, for they simply follow divine Providence in an unconscious way, natural law in humans *corresponds* with the common creaturely existence found in all life, including that of animals. A more helpful way of interpreting natural law is through revisiting our understanding of justice. I will return to this again below.

An Environmental Wisdom Ethic

I have suggested so far that principles in nature, such as the supposed principle of integrity or natural law, fail to serve an environmental ethic as they fail be consistent with current understanding of the natural world that views ecology more in terms of a dynamic and fluid complex of ever-changing relationships. Indeed, like Fern, I suggest that it would be precarious to base any ethical principle simply on scientific discoveries, subject to change, revision and modification. None the less, it seems to me that current knowledge about science needs to be taken into account in arriving at ethical mandates for human action. Just as Aquinas believed that scientific understanding could take us some way towards the truth, so modern science can, by analogy, serve to indicate something of the way God relates to the world.

Contemporary discussion of environmental problems has become more sensitive to the interaction between human society/community and 'raw' natural systems. It is therefore entirely appropriate to begin with a discussion of who we are as persons in such a community, rather than branding any such consideration as 'anthropocentric'.[78] I suggest that one way of developing an environmental ethic is through consideration of the virtues. It might seem surprising that environmental philosophers have paid relatively little attention specifically to virtue ethics, even though they may sprinkle their discussion with the environmental merits of various virtues.[79] Michael Northcott, for example, discusses the need for virtues to be developed as part of our environmental concern, but it is in the context of his strong sense of the requirement for an ecological community, rooted in local Christian community action and worship. The virtues he mentions are care and respect for life, justice and compassion/love, prudence, temperance and courage. He does not draw on the virtues specifically in order to develop his theological understanding of creation. Above all, for Northcott *relationality* to God, land and people remains primary for the moral quest, and he argues that pursuit of the virtues flows from this relationality.[80] One reason why the virtues have had relatively little attention may be that they are seen as part of the ancient systems of morality that have little chance of offering any new insights. Louke van Wensveen has carefully analysed the way virtues crop up in ecological literature, from social theorists such as Murray Bookchin though to the cosmic creation story of Thomas Berry.[81] However, while these and other authors include virtues in their reflections, they have not deliberately set out to develop a virtue ethic, but have situated such virtues in the context of their own particular framework for discussion. Although van Wensveen has accurately perceived the significance of virtues and vices for environmental ethics, other authors share the attitude of Robin Attfield, that virtues have little hope of giving real guidance in practical environmental decision-making. He dismisses the possibility of a virtue ethics of the environment in one short paragraph:

> Without principles of obligation, virtues are shortsighted if not blind. This is amply illustrated by environmental issues concerning choices of what habitats to preserve, what technology to use, or what limits to pollution to require, as by other ethical issues such as punishment or welfare policies. So theories about virtues or about caring cannot supersede or supplant theories of obligation or of justice; at the same time this fact does not make virtues and caring any less important in matters of practice.[82]

Yet his view seems to presuppose that virtues cannot be applied to practical action. Prudence is the basis for correct decision-making, requiring us to act in certain ways in correspondence with the good. Of course, a non-teleological theory of virtues may have more difficulty, but Attfield fails to recognize the different possible frameworks for virtue ethics. Moreover, I suggest that according to Aquinas's understanding of the virtues, justice is inclusive of a virtue ethic and is indeed one of the virtues. Without the virtues any principles of obligation fall on deaf ears. The criticism of the possibility of a virtue ethic also comes from those committed to more holistic interpretations of environmental value. Eric Katz, for example, equates instrumental rationality with prudence, so that 'environmental policy will be based on a secure foundation of philosophical and ethical reasoning, not the unstable and variable dictates of prudential self-interest'.[83]

Both sets of criticisms seem to reject virtue ethics without considering its original Aristotelian framework. John O'Neill has posited a modified version of Aristotelian philosophy as applied to environmental concern. He rejects the idea that moral concern about human well-being precludes consideration of the environment. While he notes Aristotle's own view that animals are made simply to serve human interests, this does not mean we have to follow Aristotle in this respect. However, he does suggest that the flourishing of all living things needs to be promoted, as it is constitutive of our own flourishing.[84] He rejects the cost–benefit analysis that has dominated economically driven interpretations of environmental problems. In addition, while a proper scepticism towards some of the claims of science is rational, once it degenerates into 'a quite general belief in any claim made by science, such scepticism becomes dangerous'.[85] He is particularly concerned about the hostility towards science of some green activists. None the less, there is a difference between technical knowledge and practical knowing from experience, which 'requires capacities of judgement and perception of particular cases that can be learned only by habituation and which cannot, like technical knowledge, be found in books'.[86] He recognizes, correctly, that it is possible to misuse science in policy-making by abstracting particular scientific principles and applying them inappropriately to other contexts. For example, a biochemist who claims that since all reactions are chemical it is legitimate to use inorganic fertilizers in agriculture is applying biochemical principles in an inappropriate way to deliver moral guidance.

O'Neill's conclusion that science is necessary, reliable but insufficient in making moral choices seems entirely apt. Moreover, I concur with his suggestion that in the environmental sphere science cannot be ignored: 'it is as reliable an epistemological friend as we could hope for'.[87] Mikael Stenmark's analysis of philosophical ethics is valuable in as much as he shows how environmental values influence environmental policy and the significance of taking scientific research into account in arriving at such policy decisions.[88] A commonly used strategy to support environmental decision-making is known as mini-max: the worst possible outcome of each policy is considered and the one that gives the least damage is chosen. However, consideration needs to be given to the plausibility of each claim in order to assess their merits.[89]

What kind of qualities do we need in order to come to appropriate decisions? I suggest that in complex cases the simple precautionary principle is not enough, for it is directed simply by the worst possible imagined scenario. Rather, we need to include different facets of prudence. One facet is the ability to deliberate. Moreover, deliberation relies not just on the expertise of a few, but on common deliberation of citizens drawing on their own experience. The capacities to make decisions in emergency situations, to take advice from others, to have foresight in a way that accurately anticipates the future as far as it is feasible to do so; all these qualities of prudence are, I suggest, vital in environmental decision-making. Moreover, Aquinas's rejection of over-attachment to material goods provides a corrective to policy-making that benefits the few at the expense of the greater good.

How far can we adhere to the suggestion that the flourishing of all creatures needs to be promoted, as it is constitutive of our own flourishing? I suggest that this might be one reason for promoting environmental concern. However, the worth of creatures as created is more than simply their relative worth for human beings, even if this leads indirectly to the promotion of their welfare. At the same time there is no need to extend our sense of self to the non-human world in the way that assumes a radically holistic ontology. Portraying non-humans as active participants in a moral community amounts to a subtle form of anthropocentrism that fails to take sufficient account of the difference between humans and non-human species. It is on account of the separate identities of other creatures that their true worth can be found.

One way of extending the notion of prudence so that it takes account of the individual worth of all creatures is through the concept of wisdom. I suggest that wisdom is particularly useful, in that it can act like a bridge between the philosophical concepts of prudence and theological ideas about who God is as Creator.

Yet wisdom in the theological sense does not describe God in a deist fashion. Rather, wisdom shows forth the creative action of God as Spirit in the beginning of the world, the affirmation of creation in the incarnation of Christ as Logos/Sophia and the qualification of all human knowing through the wisdom of the cross.[90] Wisdom includes ideas about practical prudential knowledge, but is more than this, in that it points to theological understanding: God is the author of all that exists. Creation is in love, but through wisdom.

How might this depart from an Aristotelian stance towards environmental ethics? While, as I have indicated above, there is common ground in the search for particular qualities such as prudence, wisdom affirms the worth of all creatures in and of themselves. It is after the pattern of Divine Wisdom that creaturely existence is called into being. Yet while traces of wisdom are found in all creatures of the earth, in humanity wisdom can take the form of the imitation of Christ, wisdom not just as an ontological state of being, but as an ethical directive. In this humanity has supreme responsibility to care for the earth, not out of a sense of duty towards other creatures in a narrow legalistic sense, but in expressing divine wisdom more fully in the world.

The ideal of stewardship is popular among Christian ethicists concerned about the environment, but it is somewhat ambiguous in its meaning. On the one hand it can be interpreted to mean human management of natural resources, a further step in the commodification of nature.[91] On the other hand, those who are more favourably disposed towards anthropocentric views suggest that it 'makes neither humanity nor God a despot, but teaches a salutary humility, especially to people intent on remoulding the planet solely for human benefit'.[92] For one who is hostile towards the development of a virtue ethic, Attfield puts surprising weight on the idea of humility. How might stewardship teach such humility? Berry comes close in his suggestion that stewardship is linked with prudence, but such an association might imply human 'management' that is somewhat counter to the form of prudence that I have been arguing for in this book.[93] I suggest that it is only in the context of wisdom – that is, according to Aquinas – that a real sense of humility can be gained. For 'wisdom, to which the knowledge of God belongs, is beyond man's reach, especially in this life, as though he could grasp; for this is for God alone, as is recognised by the Metaphysics. Yet the modicum which can be had through wisdom is preferable to all other knowledge.'[94] While prudence considers the means of acquiring happiness, wisdom considers the object of happiness, namely the supreme truth, or God. The sense that wisdom is always out of reach instils not so much despair, but an anticipation of the future happiness that we can expect in the next life. While prudence is the practical grounding for ethical decision-making, wisdom is its theological counterpart, encouraging the search through fellowship with God.

Aquinas's understanding of wisdom as in some sense surpassing natural capacities for human judgement points in the direction of divine grace. For example, Aquinas distinguishes the wisdom that comes from the world with the wisdom that issues from charity as a gift of the Holy Spirit. He suggests that, for Christians, life is directed towards the essential possession of God and its principle orientations are those deriving from our participation in the divine nature by way of grace, with the result that we do not look upon wisdom as merely yielding knowledge about God (as do the philosophers), but even as directing human life; and in fact, not according to human standards, but also in accord with divine norms, as St Augustine observes.[95]

Hence wisdom is not just knowledge about God in a speculative sense, but is both speculative and practical, located in the context of salvation history and carrying certain moral obligations. Hence, 'to regulate human life according to divine norms is in fact the work of wisdom, and the first indications of this ought to be reverence for God and subjection to him, with the consequence that in all things whatsoever a person will shape his life in reference to God'.[96] Hence wisdom is necessary in order to focus correctly on the ultimate goal of participation in God. According to this view, an ethic flows from wisdom and allows a person to reach towards those standards set by the commandments of God. This movement involves not just a passive acceptance of God in faith, but an active searching as well as an openness to receive grace.

The need for a wisdom ethic for the environment stems from not only a requirement for practical wisdom or prudence in complex environmental decision-making, but also the need to bring hope in an uncertain world. I suggest that this Christian virtue of hope is critical in framing environmental decisions, for without hope it would be easy to give up on our responsibilities out of a sense of despair. Such hope is not necessarily inspired by a simple resacralization of nature, an issue that I will return to in chapter 7. Contemporary ecology points less to stability than to flux and uncertainty. There is a sense in which God participates in this uncertainty through allowing creation to be itself. The pattern or orderliness that we can perceive in the natural world is despite its contingency, though it remains a dynamic, rather than static, orderliness. As such it represents the dynamic ordering in God, who is Trinity not in a static sense, but through perichoresis, a mutual indwelling of each divine person in the other. The wisdom of creation mirrors the Wisdom of God. Moreover, as well as being aligned to humility and hope, wisdom issues forth in the virtue of justice.

Ecological Justice

I suggested in the first chapter that justice was one of the cardinal virtues particularly relevant in consideration of an ethics of nature. Justice is normally associated with deontological approaches to environmental decision-making. Rule-based approaches to ethics are sharply separated from virtue ethics, natural law approaches from those taken by contemporary virtue ethicists. Onora O'Neill points to the tendency among philosophers following Aristotle to adopt a particularist approach, focusing on particular situations rather than appeals to universal norms.[97] The debate has some similarity with communitarianism and cosmopolitanism, discussed above. For particularists there is a deep suspicion of principles of obligation where the embeddedness of the human agent in social relationships seems to be overlooked, leading to oppressive policies that lack any sensitivity to the individual. Moreover, in a fragmented postmodern world how can justice be inscribed? On the other hand, those who appeal to justice traditions point out that there need to be some criteria to test whether local customs are evil or good, and complex legal and economic systems are overlooked in the process of simple focusing on virtues of the agent. O'Neill suggests combining virtue with justice from a neo-Kantian perspective. For her, practical reason is informed by principles that all can follow within a given ethical domain. By insisting that all can follow such principles she seeks to avoid an oppressive imposition of rules through external authority.[98] Yet how do we decide what might be 'followable by all'? Rather than attempting to combine virtue with justice, an alternative might be to consider the classical view that justice is simply *one* of the virtues.

If justice is one of the virtues, does this mean that it is simply an individual good to be pursued? Certainly, the idea of creating local communities that have values sensitive to ecological health is a common theme in environmental literature.[99] More unusual is the idea of a virtuous cooperator, modelled from Aquinas's understanding of prudence, temperance, justice and fortitude.[100] The idea of justice emerging from bounded social realities can be counterposed to discourse about justice from unbounded global relationships. Yet, as Nicholas Low and Brenda Gleeson point out:

> What has to be discovered is a conception of justice not for a homogenous world of cultural uniformity, nor for a world of sealed off bounded communities, but for a web of interacting, overlapping cultural diversity in which both the reality of belonging to a local community and to an unbounded – ultimately global – community are given due recognition.[101]

Aquinas found a way of linking individual, community and global justice, so I suggest that it is helpful to consider his views and ask how far these might be appropriated in the contemporary ecological context. He defines justice as a virtue of the will, 'the habit whereby a person with a lasting and constant will renders to each person his due'.[102] That is, each is given what he or she deserves. Furthermore, for Aquinas it implies 'a certain balance of equality' whereby 'that which is correct is constituted by a relation to another'.[103] Hence a second principle is that each is given according to their needs. Third, Aquinas introduces the idea of positive rights – that is, rights according to human law – as long as they do not conflict with natural law:

> By mutual agreement the human will can establish that which is just in matters which of themselves do not conflict with natural justice. It is here that positive right has its place. However, if anything conflict with natural right, human will cannot make it just, for instance by decreeing that one may rightfully steal or commit adultery.[104]

Note that positive rights do not emerge from natural law or justice, but they are not in conflict with it. Finally, he has a global conception of rights between all peoples, the *jus gentium*: 'that which natural reason constitutes between all men and is observed by all people is called the *jus gentium*'.[105] For Aquinas, justice is our Christian vocation, so that 'it is written that God's wisdom teaches temperance and prudence and justice and fortitude'.[106]

The first principle of natural law (good sought and evil avoided) cannot be changed, but secondary precepts of natural law are alterable where they are beneficial to social existence.[107] Furthermore, human law always falls short of natural law, which is a sharing in the Eternal law of God. The relationship between human law and the virtues are as follows:

> human law does not enjoin every act of every virtue, but those acts only which serve the common good, either immediately as when the social order is directly involved, from the nature of things, or mediately, as when measures of good discipline are passed by the legislator to train citizens to maintain justice and peace in the community.[108]

The idea that natural law in its secondary sense can be altered gives a measure of flexibility in Aquinas's understanding of justice. How might we adapt his idea of giving each person his or her due? His affirmation of all of life in self-preservation in natural inclinations that correspond with natural law suggests the principle that every natural entity is entitled to enjoy the fullness of its own life. His second principle of equality among humans through relationships does not make sense in an ecological context, so it needs to be changed in order to take into account the fact that all life forms are mutually interdependent on each other and on non-life forms. His concept of natural law as applied to humans as uniquely rational animals only makes sense on the basis that humanity does have precedence over other life forms. However, while the concept of human rights is a modern one, Aquinas's conception of the unity of life and the rootedness of human life in the created world need not deny that some justice for non-human life exists, though such *forms* of justice will be necessarily different from that given to humans. I suggest it is justice *for* non-human life from the perspective of a human community in *kinship with* the non-human community, rather than justice between non-humans by analogy with the human condition.[109]

Conclusions

Jean Porter suggests that the demands of justice that Aquinas presents need to be tempered by consideration of mercy.[110] Decisions may be particularly difficult when justice suggests one action, but compassion another.[111] None the less, the priority that Aquinas gives prudence in his scheme seems to allow for such an adjustment. Justice includes conscientiousness and fairness, but this needs to be balanced with caring: 'The person who is able consistently to achieve a felicitous balance between the demands of caring and the demands of conscientiousness will necessarily be a prudent person, whose wisdom is grounded in a sound and reflective conception of the human good.'[112] For Porter, the human good, which forms the basis for justice, includes notions of human dignity, grounded in the idea of restraint and forthrightness, kindliness, decency, caring, fairness and responsibility.[113]

I have tried to show here that an environmental ethic needs to take cognizance of ecological science if it is to make sense at a practical level. Furthermore, communitarian views that rely on the concept of the balance of nature in order to support their ideas are dependent on a false paradigm in ecology that has now been replaced. None the less, the idea of natural law needs to be modified to take into account this shift to a new ecology. I have suggested that the theological concept of wisdom can be joined with more philosophical understandings of prudence and justice in order to inform appropriate environmental decision-making. Such a focus on the virtues reaches beyond self to the natural world, beyond local communities to a cosmopolitan framework for action. It is not as much a choice either between natural law and virtue ethics or between communitarianism and cosmopolitanism as the subtle interplay of all facets weaving into deliberative moral action.

How should we consider the particular claims of those creatures closest to us, namely the animals? The question of how we should treat animals is the subject of the following chapter. There is also another question to be asked, namely how do we arrive at a just distribution of environments between peoples? I include a discussion of environmental justice in chapter 4, on biotechnology. What other virtues need to inform an environmental ethic? I suggest that fortitude or courage and temperance are significant attitudes to adopt in relationship with nature. Moreover, the ability to wonder, to have awe in the face of the complexity of the natural world, is a virtue that could in one sense be fostered by our knowledge of ecology. As these virtues (fortitude, temperance and wonder) apply to our scientific treatment of nature generally, I will be coming back to them in later chapters.

Notes

1 Scientific Committee on Problems of the Environment (SCOPE) survey of two hundred scientists in fifty countries, carried out in 1999, published in C. Park: *Environment: Principles and Applications*, 2nd edn (London: Routledge, 2001), pp. 632–3.

2 An example of an unforeseen problem is the depletion of ozone in the stratosphere, discovered in 1974, but only addressed as a serious issue in 1985. See Park: *Environment*, pp. 632–3.

3 United Nations Environment Programme: *Global Environment Outlook 3: Past, Present and Future Perspectives* (London: Earthscan, 2002).

4 John O'Neill is critical of this lack of precision. See J. O'Neill: *Ecology, Policy and Politics: Human Well Being and the Natural World* (London: Routledge, 1993), pp. 6–10.

5 For a useful summary of the debates see R. Elliot: 'Introduction', in R. Elliot, ed.: *Environmental Ethics* (Oxford: Oxford University Press, 1995), pp. 1–20.

6 See A. Brennan: 'Introduction', in A. Brennan, ed.: *The Ethics of the Environment* (Brookfield: Dartmouth Publishing, 1995), pp. xv–xvii.

7   For a discussion see R. J. Berry: *God's Book of Works: The Nature and Theology of Nature* (London: T. & T. Clark/Continuum, 2003), pp. 88–9.

8   M. Northcott: *The Environment and Christian Ethics* (Cambridge: Cambridge University Press, 1996), pp. 38–55.

9   Northcott: *Environment*, p. 60.

10 Northcott: *Environment*, p. 83.

11 Northcott: *Environment*, p. 84.

12 Northcott: *Environment*, p. 85.

13 K. Milton: 'Nature and the Environment in Indigenous and Traditional Cultures', in D. E. Cooper and J. A. Palmer, eds: *Spirit of the Environment: Religion, Value and Environmental Concern* (London: Routledge, 1998), pp. 86–99.

14 Northcott: *Environment*, p. 57.

15 Northcott: *Environment*, p. 59.

16 Northcott: *Environment*, p. 60.

17 J. Brooke and G. Cantor: *Reconstructing Nature: The Engagement of Science and Religion* (Edinburgh: T & T Clark, 1997), pp. 80–1.

18 Booke and Cantor: *Reconstructing Nature*, p. 100.

19 Northcott: *Environment*, pp. 132–3.

20 Northcott does seem to mean this, namely that there are some sciences which are inherently more favourable towards environmental thinking than others.

21 Brooke and Cantor: *Reconstructing Nature*, p. 100.

22 A. Leopold: *A Sand County Almanac and Sketches Here and There* (New York: Oxford University Press, 1968, first published 1949).

23 Northcott: *Environment*, p. 107.

24 Northcott: *Environment*, p. 109. In later work he suggests that animals could be considered as part of the human moral community; see chapter 3.

25 Northcott: *Environment*, p. 176.

26 Northcott: *Environment*, pp. 257–327. I return to a discussion of natural law below.

27 H. Rolston III: *Environmental Ethics: Duties to and Values in the Natural World* (Philadelphia: Temple University Press, 1988), 39–40.

28 Rolston III: *Environmental Ethics*, p. 188.

29 Rolston III: *Environmental Ethics*, p. 225.

30 E. Katz: *Nature as Subject: Human Obligation and Natural Community* (Lanham, MD: Rowman and Littlefield, 1997), p. xxiv.

31 For a collection of readings see R. Gottlieb: *The Ecological Community* (London: Routledge, 1997).

32 R. Attfield: *The Ethics of the Global Environment* (Edinburgh: Edinburgh University Press,1999).

33 Attfield: *Ethics of the Global Environment*, p. 39.

34 Attfield: *Ethics of the Global Environment*, p. 40.

35 Attfield: *Ethics of the Global Environment*, pp. 47–50.

36 Attfield does admit that cosmopolitans can take their theoretical position from Kantian or rights or contract theory. Attfield: *Ethics of the Global Environment*, p. 34.

37 L. Westra: *Living in Integrity: A Global Ethic to Restore a Fragmented Earth* (Lanham, MD: Rowman and Littlefield, 1998).

38 A. Holland: 'Foreword', in Westra: *Living in Integrity*, p. xi.

39 Westra: *Living in Integrity*, p. 43.

40 Westra: *Living in Integrity*, p. 148.

41   R. Fern: *Nature, God and Humanity: Envisioning an Ethics of Nature* (Cambridge: Cambridge University Press, 2002).

42   Fern: *Nature, God and* Humanity, pp. 69–102.

43   C. Deane-Drummond: *Biology and Theology Today: Exploring the Boundaries* (London: SCM Press, 2001), pp. 39–42.

44   S. T. A. Pickett, J. Kolasa and C. G. Jones: *Ecological Understanding: The Nature of Theory and the Theory of Nature* (London: Academic Press, 1994), pp. 12–16.

45   Berry, *God's Book of Works*, p. 117.

46   Pickett et al.: *Ecological Understanding*, p. 57

47   Pickett et al.: *Ecological Understanding*, p. 157.

48   Pickett et al.: *Ecological Understanding*, p. 159.

49   Berry: *God's Book of Works*, p. 111.

50   Pickett et al.: *Ecological Understanding*, p. 160.

51   Pickett et al.: *Ecological Understanding*, p. 161; Deane-Drummond: *Biology and Theology Today*, pp. 40–1.

52   Berry: *God's Book of Works*, p. 112. While Berry has described this debate as 'continued and unresolved', the credibility of the contingent approach is gaining ground. Even Elton, the founder of modern ecology, rejected the 'balance of nature approach' in work published in 1930 (cited in Berry, p. 113).

53   R. Kirkman: 'The Problem of Knowledge in Environmental Thought: A Counter Challenge', in Gottlieb, ed.: *The Ecological Community*, pp. 193–207, esp. p.199.

54   Fern: *Nature, God and Humanity*, pp. 69–102.

55   See B. Callicott: 'From the Balance of Nature to the Flux of Nature: The Land Ethic in a Time of Change', in R. L. Knight and S. Reidel, eds: *Aldo Leopold and the Ecological Conscience* (Oxford: Oxford University Press, 2002), pp. 90–105.

56   See N. Biggar and R. Black, eds: *The Revival of Natural Law: Philosophical, Theological and Ethical Responses to the Finnis–Grisez School* (Aldershot: Ashgate, 2000).

57   Northcott: *Environment*, pp. 245ff. Northcott develops this argument further in M. Northcott: 'The Moral Standing of Nature and the New Natural Law', in Biggar and Black, eds: *The Revival of Natural Law*, pp. 262–81.

58   Northcott: *Environment*, pp. 250–1. I will return to a discussion of purpose in nature in the final chapter.

59   A full discussion of this topic is outside the scope of this chapter. However, it is worth noting that the probability of complex forms emerging in evolution purely by chance is an area of scientific dispute. Overall, the eschatology projected by scientific analysis is, as Northcott indicates, pessimistic, especially when due account is taken of physical constraints operating towards the eventual destruction of planet earth. See S. Conway Morris: *The Crucible of Creation* (Oxford: Oxford University Press, 1998).

60   Northcott: *Environment*, pp. 253–4.

61   Northcott: 'The Moral Standing of Nature', p. 275.

62   I agree with Sam Berry in this respect. See Berry: *God's Book of Works*, p. 171.

63   Northcott: 'The Moral Standing of Nature', p. 279.

64   I will come back to the discussion of whether there is identifiable purpose and order in the world in the final chapter.

65   The difference between Northcott's position and mine may be related to the extent to which we believe science is a social construct. While I admit that such social construction needs to be taken into account, I resist the idea that science is purely a construct, and therefore take more seriously contemporary movements in science

compared with theories that have become more obsolete. I take up a discussion of how to apply the concept of natural law later in this chapter.

66 I will take up a discussion of this topic again in chapter 3.

67 J. D. Caputo: *Heidegger and Aquinas: An Essay on Overcoming Metaphysics* (New York: Fordham University Press, 1982), p. 250.

68 Aquinas: *Summa Theologiae, volume 28, Law and Political Theory*, trans. T. Gilby (London: Blackfriars, 1966), 1a2ae, Qu. 94.2.

69 J. Porter: *Moral Action and Christian Ethics* (Cambridge: Cambridge University Press, 1995), p. 108.

70 Aquinas: *Summa Theologiae, volume 28*, Qu. 94.2.

71 See, for example, Berry: *God's Book of Works*, p. 116.

72 Aquinas, *Summa Theologiae, volume 28*, 1a2ae, Qu. 93.5.

73 This comes through clearly in, for example, his comment that 'It should be said that although these powers [the irascible and concupiscible appetites] are found in brutes, in them they do not participate in reason and thus they cannot have moral virtues.' Aquinas, 'Disputed Questions on the Virtues in General', art. 4, ad. 12 in R. McInerny, trans.: *Disputed Questions on Virtue* (South Bend, IN: St Augustine's Press, 1999), p. 29. The closest he comes to ascribing reasoning powers to non-humans is his notion of an estimative sense, able to act according to a particular universal, rather than an abstract universal.

74 Aquinas: *Summa Theologiae, volume 28*, 1a2ae, Qu. 94.4.

75 For discussion, see F. Kerr: *After Aquinas: Versions of Thomism* (Oxford: Blackwell, 2002), p. 98.

76 C. Deane-Drummond: *Creation through Wisdom: Theology and the New Biology* (Edinburgh: T & T Clark, 2000), p. 159. Other authors have pointed to the ordering power of God in chaos, as in physicist Sjoerd Bonting's *Chaos Theology: A Revised Creation Theology* (Toronto: Novalis/Saint Paul University, 2002). One of the author's main purposes in this book is to reject the idea of *creatio ex nihilo* and reinstate the biblical idea of creation out of chaos. It seems to me that the tradition of *ex nihilo* is important to preserve, even as a prelude for chaos, for without it there is something other than God at the beginning. While Bonting prefers to relegate this issue to 'mystery', I am content to affirm both creation out of chaos *and* creation out of nothing.

77 As indicated in the above reference, there is also considerable interest in chaos theory in physics. Yet chaos in ecology, as in physics, is not a destructive chaos, but the ground from which ordering can emerge. See Bonting: *Chaos Theology*, pp. 32–7. While I might be more wary than Bonting appears to be of tying God's work into particular chaos events, since it seems to marry scientific theory with the work of God as creator in a reductionist way, there is no reason not to affirm chaos events as an inherent aspect of the creation, created by God as good. It is in this *context* that God works out God's purposes.

78 Sam Berry believes that 'enlightened anthropocentrism may be the best approach for forming proper environmental attitudes'. Berry: *God's Book of Works*, p. 89.

79 See, for example, P. S. Wenz: *Environmental Ethics Today* (Oxford: Oxford University Press, 2001). One exception is John Benson, who includes a chapter on environmental virtues. However, the readings he cites are not specifically writing on environmental issues; rather, they are virtue ethicists who, Benson believes, are suggestive for an environmental ethic. J. Benson: *Environmental Ethics: An Introduction with Readings* (London: Routledge, 2000), pp. 67–84.

80   See Northcott: *Environment*, pp. 121–2, 226ff, 314–16.

81   L. van Wensveen: *Dirty Virtues: The Emergence of Ecological Virtue Ethics* (New York: Humanity Books, 2000).

82   Attfield: *Ethics of the Global Environment*, p. 156.

83   Katz: *Nature as Subject*, p. xvii.

84   J. O'Neill: *Ecology, Policy and Politics: Human Well-being and the Natural World* (London: Routledge, 1993), p. 24.

85   O'Neill: *Ecology, Policy and Politics*, p. 123.

86   O'Neill: *Ecology, Policy and Politics*, p. 125.

87   O'Neill: *Ecology, Policy and Politics*, p. 147.

88   M. Stenmark: *Environmental Ethics and Policy Making* (Ashgate: Aldershot, 2002).

89   A useful discussion of concrete examples of environmental problems and strategies used for their solution can be found in Berry: *God's Book of Works*, pp. 138–60.

90   Deane-Drummond: *Creation through Wisdom*, chapter 2.

91   C. Palmer: 'Stewardship: A Case Study in Environmental Ethics', in I. Ball, M. Goodall, C. Palmer and J. Reader, eds: *The Earth Beneath: A Critical Guide to Green Theology* (London: SPCK, 1992), pp. 67–86.

92   Attfield: *Ethics of the Global Environment*, p. 49.

93   Berry: *God's Book of Works*, p. 183. I would agree with Berry's criticism that notions such as that the planet will take care of itself are naive, but this view is also associated with the Gaia hypothesis that he later endorses. He spells out in a useful way the implications of stewardship as he understands it might be in environmental terms, though his filling out of the notion of stewardship seems to go beyond what the term suggests, and take its cue from reflection on the biblical parable of the rich landowner; for example, the idea that humankind needs to invest positively in change, while recognizing limits. Yet such limits are also set in the context of God as one who is a 'risk-taker', so, by implication, human kind is also called to a similar risk-taking task. While understanding what freedom means is an important aspect of our relationship with nature, I am less convinced that freedom envisaged as *choice* endorsed through the ideal of *stewardship* will be entirely helpful in the manner that Berry intends here. Instead, freedom *for excellence* or the good implies direction in decision-making that is best thought of in terms of the virtues.

94   Aquinas: *Summa Theologiae, volume 23, Virtue*, trans. W. D. Hughes (London: Blackfriars, 1969), 1a2ae, Qu. 66.5.

95   Aquinas: *Summa Theologiae, volume 33, Hope*, trans. W. J. Hill (London: Blackfriars, 1966), 2a2ae, Qu. 19.7.

96   Aquinas: *Summa Theologiae, volume 33*, Qu. 19.7.

97   O. O'Neill, *Towards Justice and Virtue: A Constructive Account of Practical Reasoning* (Cambridge: Cambridge University Press,1996), pp. 14–16.

98   O'Neill, *Towards Justice and Virtue*, p. 57.

99   This seems to be the thrust of Northcott's argument, as I pointed out earlier.

100   As this book goes to press, my attention has been drawn to J. Schaefer, 'The Virtuous Cooperator: Modelling the Human in an Ecologically Endangered Age', *Worldviews: Environment, Culture, Religion*, 7:1 (2003), pp. 171–95.

101   N. Low and B. Gleeson: *Justice, Society and Nature: An Exploration of Political Ecology* (London: Routledge, 1998), p. 42.

102   Aquinas, *Summa Theologiae, volume 37, Justice*, trans. T. Gilby (London: Blackfriars, 1974), 2a2ae, Qu. 58.1.

103   Aquinas: *Summa Theologiae, volume 37*, Qu. 57.1.

104   Aquinas: *Summa Theologiae, volume 37*, Qu. 57.2.

105   Aquinas: *Summa Theologiae, volume 37*, Qu. 57.3.

106   Aquinas: *Summa Theologiae, volume 37*, Qu. 58.3.

107   Aquinas: *Summa Theologiae, Law and Political Theory, volume 28*, trans. T. Gilby (London: Blackfriars, 1966), 1a2ae, Qu. 94.5.

108   Aquinas: *Summa Theologiae, volume 28*, Qu. 96.3.

109   I will take up a discussion of the possibility of non-humans as moral agents in the following chapter.

110   Porter: *Moral Action*, pp. 182–8.

111   Benson: *Environmental Ethics*, p. 69.

112   Porter: *Moral Action*, p. 196.

113   Porter: *Moral Action*, p. 198.

Chapter 3

Animal Ethics

Given that moral concern has progressively widened to include the environment, in what ways are animals morally considerable? The use of animals in all manner of 'factory farming' was highlighted in Britain in 2001 by the 'foot and mouth' crisis, supposedly originating from contaminated feed. In this instance the main worry seemed to be about the loss of income to farmers and the indirect effects on related industries, including the effects as a result of footpath closures that impacted on tourism, or the offence of witnessing burning pyres of animal carcases. Media discussion of the plight of the animals themselves took on a comparatively strange silence, considering the extent to which our treatment of animals has become a political issue. The desperate attempts to prevent the spread of disease through the drastic cull of healthy animals demonstrate their low esteem in the political sphere. Of course, the view that animals are simply 'walking larders', providers for human needs and outside the realm of human moral concern, is an ancient one and goes back to early Greek philosophy.[1] This view amounts to no concern for animals at all, they are simply there to serve human interests and any harm to animals is not morally considerable. Less extreme is *indirect* moral concern, followed by philosophers such as Immanuel Kant, namely that harm to an animal indirectly harms its human owner and so is, for this reason, morally irresponsible. A third view is that which focuses on the animals themselves and their ability to feel pain, or sentience, and this can take the form of moral consideration because of the consequences, or moral concern because animals have rights. This chapter focuses on the different versions of the third view and offers a critique in comparison with an alternative position drawing on virtue ethics of Aquinas.

From a Christian perspective it is possible to argue that God gives animals rights, since God created the animals. An alternative might be to consider our own attitudes to animals and how these need to be challenged by considering how far our human nature reflects Christian ideals. Aquinas has been branded by animal rights campaigners as irredeemably anthropocentric, or worse, only resisting animal cruelty on the basis that this fosters vice towards other humans. I argue in this chapter that while it is necessary to reject Aquinas's ethic towards animals, his theology points in another direction altogether, namely one that is affirmative towards other species. Furthermore, his focus on the virtues, particularly prudence, wisdom, charity and temperance, is instructive in outlining an alternative approach to the treatment of animals.

Regardless of the theoretical reasons for rejecting animals' moral status, the harsh treatment of animals by humans has become the subject of increasing concern to a growing number of people. The revulsion against animal cruelty goes back at least two hundred years in Britain.[2] Popular organizations such as the Battersea Dog's Home, the Cattle Trough Association, the Blue Cross, the Metropolitan Drinking Fountain and the National Canine Defence League all exerted a significant influence on British society, so that it became more empathetic towards the idea of the worth of animals in and of themselves.[3] John Wesley (1704–91), founder of the Methodist movement, and Humphrey Primatt (1725–80) were both clerics who consistently argued for the more humane treatment of animals.[4] While the influence of philosophical arguments in favour of the treatment of animals is important, it needs to be set in the context of this more general societal drift towards giving animals enhanced moral considerability.

Peter Singer's Utilitarian Case for Animals

Often regarded as the founder of the animal liberation movement, the American philosopher Peter Singer set out a case for animal worth against what he saw as anthropocentric alternatives.[5] It is worth considering his arguments in detail, as he set the stage for the development of animal rights and argued strongly that animals should be considered morally directly, rather than indirectly. After outlining his position, I will consider the difficulties inherent in his view. While I will argue that he is correct to consider animal ethics in a direct sense, rather than simply indirectly because of harm to human owners, his position is faulty for other reasons that I discuss below.

Singer argued that animals are morally equal with humans, and that not to give animals equal status amounts to unwarranted 'speciesism'. Furthermore, given the equal moral status of animals, not to treat them fairly contravenes the requirements of justice. Singer compares his avocation of moral equality of animals with other protest movements, such as those against sexism and racism. He acknowledges that humans anticipate suffering, which contributes to their anguish, in a way that animals do not, but this gives us reasons to believe that if we are to have experiments at all, then animals are to be preferred, or rather, those creatures that share the same capacity for pain, such as severely retarded human beings, 'since infants and retarded humans would also have no idea of what was going to happen to them'.[6] He admits that we cannot know precisely how an animal might suffer in given circumstances, but he suggests that 'precision is not essential'.[7] How might we adjudicate between different claims? Singer argues on the basis that if all creatures should be treated with respect then this means that their interests based on sentience count equally as well. Overall, whatever leads to maximization of interests of all parties, or aggregation of interests, constitutes moral action. In practice, whatever leads to the maximization of happiness, pleasure and so on and the minimization of pain and suffering shapes the correct moral choice. The definition of justice is grounded first on equal considerability, and then this leads to a utilitarian account of moral action.

In consideration of whether it is permissible to eat animals, Singer argues that human preference for meat eating is trivial compared with the loss of life of animals concerned. Furthermore, where the animals are reared in conditions where they suffer considerable hardship, this tilts the balance even further in their favour. Hence:

> Becoming a vegetarian is not merely a symbolic gesture. Nor is it an attempt to isolate oneself from the ugly realities of the world, to keep oneself pure and so without responsibility for the carnage all around. Becoming a vegetarian is a highly practical and effective step one can take toward ending both the killing of nonhuman animals and the infliction of suffering upon them.[8]

He argues that as 'an absolute minimum' we should give up eating animals or products of animals produced by 'factory' farming. Yet becoming a total vegetarian is the ideal we should look towards, not only because goods labelled 'organic' often just means simply that the animals were not injected with antibiotics, but also because of 'the belief that it is wrong to kill these creatures for the trivial purpose of pleasing our palates'.[9]

How far should we go down the evolutionary scale in restriction of killing? For Singer it is related to whether a creature has interests or not, in particular whether it is capable of suffering or not. He uses *biological* criteria to measure the latter, namely how far the behaviour of a creature indicates it is in pain, and whether or not it has a well developed nervous system.[10] Accordingly, fish can be included in this calculus as they show signs of distress when injured in any way. Does this mean that as long as killing is painless then it is morally acceptable? Singer responds to this by arguing that some animals can be classified as having preferences, which gives them added value over others that only have interests based on sentience.[11] This would introduce another criterion into evaluation of whether killing is lawful or not. Taking a life of a human being is worse than taking that of other beings as they are more future-orientated, so their future preferences need to be taken into account. This also applies to other creatures that have preferences to a lesser degree. For example, it would be more morally reprehensible to kill monkeys, which have clear preferences according to Singer's scheme, than chickens, which have interests, but no preferences.[12]

One problem with the utilitarian calculus is that it does not necessarily follow that equality of moral consideration leads to unambiguous moral action through consideration of interests and/or preferences. What happens, if, for example, other people reject the claim for justice for certain races? In this scenario the overall preference of the dominant group is the one that might well win out in the utilitarian calculus.[13] By the same token, it might be that if there were sufficient numbers of people strongly opposed to animal rights, then this would be the view adopted, as it would lead to the greatest amount of happiness overall. Stephen Clark rejects utilitarian portrayals of animal welfare for other reasons that are pertinent. He suggests, correctly in my view, that it attempts to calculate what is strictly beyond calculation. Moreover, once self-styled experts have taken over what could be counted as an 'objective' method of calculation, 'the road to tyranny is open'.[14] For it could be used in order to calculate that the overall sum of happiness is increased by, for example, using animals for experimentation on human diseases.[15] From a theological perspective there are also significant problems associated with Singer's position, for it seems to devalue human life on the basis of sentience and open the door to problematic ethical practices such as infanticide and euthanasia where brain function is impaired. It is, perhaps, for reasons such as these that his views have had a hostile reception among disability rights campaigners.

Might there be an alternative to Singer's utilitarian argument? Mark Rowlands suggests that instead of utilitarianism, a modified version of social contract theory can be wedded to Singer's critique of speciesism.[16] While this gets round the problems associated with utilitarianism mentioned above, it includes a strong rejection of speciesism. Rowlands suggests that since animals are worth equal moral consideration to humans, they can be included as recipients of a contract, even if they are not the originators of it.[17] His theory is novel, in that traditional interpretations of contract theory regard animals as outside the scope of justice, as they are held to be irrational beings, incapable of entering into and participating in contractual arrangements with human persons. I will also be taking a similar position to Rowlands regarding the *scope* of justice; however, he comes to different conclusions about the scale of comparability with humans, as he is tied to a Rawlsian view of equality according to social contract theory. Following John Rawls, Rowlands suggests that we use a 'veil of ignorance' about our 'original position', where no one knows his or her place in society. For Rowlands this original position includes whether we are members of the human species or not. Such an original position acts like a heuristic tool in order to help us decide which moral course to take. Sentience, too, becomes the boundary for moral considerability. Accordingly, he supports vegetarianism, as it would be against the claims of our original position if we were to do otherwise.

Rowlands suggests that while we may not be able to imagine what it is like to be an animal, we could equally not imagine what it is like to be another human individual. However, it seems to me that such a comparison is somewhat vacuous. The fact is that we are people and not sheep or goats or fish, and that it is easier, relatively, to imagine I am a member of another race or sex compared with imagining I am a member of another species. The problem, additionally, with Singer's anti-speciesist view is that while he may show some analogous relationships between the way we treat animals and the way we treat humans, or have treated them in the past, this does not mean that the two are identical. Those who argue that our treatment of animals is exactly like the slave trade fall into the same trap.[18] There are clear differences between different forms of oppression that we need to consider.

Mary Midgley has considered these differences in her book *Animals and Why They Matter*.[19] She provides what seems to me to be a convincing philosophical argument against the rejection of speciesism advocated by Singer and Rowlands and discussed above. She considers the special case for treating our own species differently on the basis of preference for bonding. For example, parents give special attention to children and are not condemned for so doing; in fact they are expected to show such preference. It is, furthermore, a natural preference, rather than one, like racism, produced by cultural norms. Yet she does not argue for 'familyism' on the basis of natural inclinations; rather, for her it contributes to human happiness. She suggests that charity may be limited by too much focus on the family. However, such family ties are:

> an absolutely central element of human happiness, and it seems unlikely that we could live at all without them. They are the root from which charity grows. Morality shows a constant tension between measures to secure justice and widen sympathy for outsiders. To handle this tension by working out particular priorities is our normal moral business. In handling species conflicts, the notion of simply rejecting all discrimination as speciesist looks like a seductively simple guide, an all-purpose formula.[20]

Moreover, Midgley goes on to suggest that our ability to form bonds within our own species can serve to enhance the bonds we have with other animals, drawn into our circle.[21] It is somewhat analogous to the ethic of care towards animals that some feminist authors have developed and that I will discuss further in chapter 8. The difficulties with this view relate to the problems associated with its particularity, so that it is hard to argue for moral responsibility towards those who are distant from the immediate circle of interests.

Stephen Clark adds another important dimension to the debate by pointing to the lack of real biological identity attached to the term 'species'. Hence, for him, 'There is no need to think that all and only species members have any shared character, save only that they have common ancestors and are still members of a population whose members may yet have common descendents.'[22] The objective form of humanism seems to break down in face of biological diversity of form and a lack of definition of species boundaries. He asks, further, 'What is there to mind about that all and only human beings share?'[23] Rationality alone does not get us very far, since other animals share to some extent in this capacity. Clark suggests, further, that if we choose the alternative – that is, to reject the implications of evolutionary theory that there is no such thing as a 'human nature' as such – then the form of humanity to which we aspire is likely to be the saint or sage, in which case we need to behave in a way that is humane towards other creatures.[24] Hence,

'Either we evolved along with them, by merely natural processes, or else we evolved, in part, to imitate a Divine Humanity. Neither theory licenses a radical disjunction between ourselves and other apes. Either may give us reason to esteem and serve the greater humankind.'[25] I suggest that while biological theory certainly rejects any 'radical disjunction' between ourselves and other species, especially primates, this does not mean that there are *no* differences whatsoever between species, especially between ourselves and other non-human animals. To reduce the human condition to biological common ancestors and descendents in the way Clark suggests above seems to me to be similar to the assumption that the scope and content of morality is restricted to genes, the interaction of genes and the survival of genes. There is likely to be a genetic component to morality, but to assume that there is nothing more than this is likely to impose falsely the content of biology on complex cultural constructs.[26]

In fact Clark has also provocatively imagined a scenario where there are no specific forms, where animals are genetically engineered to be self-perpetuating tumours of pure meat: 'chicken little' or 'pure pork'.[27] According to this position there could be no objection by reference to Singer's original theory, as such artefacts could not feel pain, so are objections in this case any more than a simple 'yuk' factor? What if other species boundaries were crossed so that hybrids were produced between say, apes and humans?[28] Clark rejects this idea on the basis that, following Plato's philosophy, all living things to be something must have a 'form'. Hence, 'To be is to be something. To be something is to embody, though perhaps ineptly, some one form of the many forms which shape, or are shaped in, the mosaic of the divine intellect. Every individual thing, that is, is a more or less distorted embodiment or reflection of that intellect.'[29] However, if we adhere to this view of the 'forms' of species, then this is inconsistent with Clark's argument from biology that I discussed earlier that there is, strictly speaking, no such thing as distinct biological species. I suggest that while Clark seems to imply that biology needs to be taken into account, but ultimately leads us down the blind alley of formless artefacts, biological distinctions are subtler than simply taking note of genetic similarities. To go, as he suggests, to the opposite extreme of Platonic fixed forms is not necessarily all that helpful, for it is inconsistent with current biological knowledge. Clark is correct to reject ethical reflection that just emerges from biological nature, but such biological nature needs to be taken into account in a way that includes other aspects of species diversity. Biologically speaking the lack of cross breeding between species implies a distinction, even if according to genetics such distinctions are blurred. Very small genetic differences can lead to very different species, as is obvious from the genetic similarity between the mouse and the human, and the human and the ape.

The difficulty with Clark's argument is also a philosophical one, namely that the focus on *species* means that the value of *individuals* in a species is lost. This contrasts strongly with the animal rights view that focuses much more on the worth of individual animals. While it is possible, then, to reject 'speciesism' if this means we think of the human species as necessarily superior in every respect to other creatures, a sense of distinctiveness of what it means to be human is necessary if we are to retain a sense of identity of ourselves and of other animals as 'Other' than us.[30] I suggest that such human identity can be fostered by considering human life as with animals, rather than as manipulators of animals. While a biological sense of the weakening of boundaries between species should give us cause to feel humble in the face of the myriad of other creatures so biologically alike to ourselves, a return to a belief in Plato's fixed forms is not necessarily a very helpful alternative, as it is *inconsistent* with biological science, even if the latter acknowledges some differences as well as similarities between species. A balance between concern for communities and concern for individuals is imperative, and thus far the focus on species has tended to ignore individual concern.

Rights Theory of Tom Regan and Andrew Linzey

While Peter Singer has commonly been accredited as the initiator of the animal rights movement, strictly speaking it was Tom Regan who developed a contemporary theory of the value of animals based on natural rights.[31] He believed that basing moral action on consequences was insufficient, though strictly speaking this misrepresents Singer, who argued on the basis of equality between animals and humans first, then went on to consider how this might be expressed in terms of equality of interests. Regan represents the turn to moral concern for the individual creature, both animals and humans. In as much as he represents acknowledgement of the value of individuals his views are welcome. However, his views do not take adequate account of animals and humans as integral to the biotic community as a whole. Andrew Linzey has developed a Christian version of Regan's theory, so I will discuss the theological implications of their views through a critique of Linzey's work in a latter section. For Regan all animals, humans and some non-human, *by their nature*, are 'subjects of a life' and therefore possess moral rights. Individuals are 'subjects of a life'

> If they have beliefs and desires, perception, memory, and a sense of the future, including their own future; an emotional life together with feelings of pleasure and pain; preference and welfare interests; the ability to initiate action in pursuit of their desires and goals; a psychological identify over time; and an individual welfare in the sense that their experiential life fares well or ill for them, logically independent of their utility for others and logically independent of their being the object of anyone else's interests.[32]

The above is satisfied by all humans, apart, perhaps, from those in a vegetative state or irreversible coma, as well as all mammalian species, many birds, some fish and possibly reptiles. However, Regan restricts his case to mammalian species only, since it might be doubted on empirical grounds that birds and reptiles fulfilled his criteria for 'subjects of a life'. How far an individual must satisfy all of the criteria that Regan lists, or only the majority of these criteria, is somewhat ambiguous.[33] Of course, one of the main difficulties with such a view is that it groups together members of different species depending on whether they possess a key characteristic, and thus differences tend to be ignored in ethical consideration.[34]

Regan also argues that individuals that are 'subjects of a life' have inherent value, which he understands to mean objective moral worth quite apart from whether they are valued by humans or not. It is more similar to the idea of intrinsic value that I discussed in the previous chapter, defined as value of something in and of itself. For him it does not matter whether human beings recognize the inherent value or rights of such non-human animals, they are simply there in an objective sense that they are a given part of the nature of the creatures themselves. As these rights derive from the being of animals, they are prior to any agreements that humans enter into with non-human animals. This is the crucial difference between his view and Singer's utilitarianism. For a utilitarian such as Singer, the worth of animals is dependent on their interests and preferences or feelings, so the individual as such does not have inherent worth. Hence as long as the sum total of happiness is enhanced, the means of attaining this goal is less significant. Both Regan and Singer adhere to the principle of equality between humans and animals, though Regan is more focused on mammals, and hence both are anti-speciesist. However, while for Singer moral difficulties can be overcome by considering the overall sum of interests on the basis of sentience, for Regan the inherent value of the individual confers particular rights that are equivalent to those held by human subjects.

Regan suggests that the conferral of naturalistic rights on animals has strong practical consequences, namely the total abolition of the use of animals in science, the total dissolution of commercial animal agriculture and the total elimination of commercial sport hunting and trapping.[35] His case relies on the assumption that it is possible to give animals rights in a legal sense, as he argues that they have ontological rights. But is this extension justified? The concept of rights is tied up with the legal context in which it is set. As Rosalind Hursthouse points out,

> laws, institutions and conventions are all unique features of human society. Only creatures who can devise, and agree to abide by, laws, conventions and the rules and regulations involved in setting up of institutions can have such things, and we are the only creatures who can. The concept of rights applies against a background of such laws, conventions and institutions; without such a background, it has no application, makes no sense.[36]

Of course, Regan could assert that according to this view the mentally handicapped, infants, the senile or the insane would also be excluded, and in one sense we could say that the law does do this, that parents dictate property of the child and so on. Prevention of abuse of animals *or* people does not necessarily mean that they share the same rights.

Even if we disagree with Regan that it is possible to extend legal rights to animals on the basis of 'natural' rights, we might ask ourselves if the current legislation framed around human rights is really adequate for the protection of animals. The difficulty with much of the legal framework in which we find ourselves is that animals are treated simply as human property.[37] In legal terms, any use of animals may be considered 'humane' and any level of pain inflicted on an animal 'necessary' as long as there is evidence of benefits to humans. The regulations, such as they exist in the USA, are there to control 'waste' of animal 'resources'. Hence, 'the law excludes animals from the scope of legal concern and enforces this exclusion through the doctrine of juridical standing, according to which most animal interests are disqualified from the outset from even being considered in courts of law'.[38]

If animals are treated as property, then it is inevitable that judgements will be made in favour of the interests of humans, who have rights, even if animal interests are considered as well. The dilemma is clear, so should we introduce some sort of language about rights as applied to animals, in order to afford a greater measure of protection than their consideration as property? The lawyer Gary Francione suggests the following:

> though it may not be meaningful to talk about animal rights within our present legal systems if what we mean by rights is what Regan means by rights, we may nevertheless be able to achieve some rights-like protection for animals, protection based on the recognition of animal interests that are not susceptible to sacrifice merely on account of consequential considerations.[39]

This is a point worth taking on board in thinking through animal ethics. In addition, I will be arguing that a shift in legislation towards animals can also be considered by ethical reflection that does not necessarily rely on the language of rights. Although Francione hints at such a possibility, he does not give any indication as to how we might arrive at 'rights-like' protection without recourse to animal rights language as such.

Andrew Linzey, like Regan, is an advocate of animal rights, though he writes as a theologian, rather than as a philosopher.[40] Andrew Linzey is certainly not alone in bracketing the thought of Thomas Aquinas with Descartes, who viewed animals as 'automata', devoid of reason, and had a thoroughly dualistic concept of matter and spirit.[41] Animals lack what humans have, namely reason, a soul and correspondingly human rights. For Linzey, the classical Thomistic–Aristotelian view that denies any moral status to animals remained virtually unchallenged from the eighteenth century. The equation of Aquinas's views with those of Descartes misinterprets Aquinas's reasons for rejecting the moral worth of animals.[42] Instead, it seems far more likely that Aquinas's attitude to animals was in response to Manicheanism, namely the view that the world was evil. The supposition that we were like animals was, incorrectly, equated with being selfish and materialistic. Furthermore, 'it was thought to be dangerous to advocate abstention from flesh foods and the like because this was taken to imply that the world of nature was evil, not such as to be decreed by a benevolent creator'.[43] Viewed in this light it becomes more understandable that Aquinas would have cause to reject the moral status of animals.

Linzey sought to base his concept of rights on the more theological idea of *theos-rights*.[44] This view envisages rights given to animals by God, rather than by humans, since God establishes the specific value of some living things. Hence rights are not so much given, as recognised. The argument takes three steps:

1   He suggests that God has 'rights' in creation, by which he seems to mean that God has authority over creation.
2   Spirit-filled breathing creatures of flesh and blood are subjects of inherent value to God.
3   Animals can make an objective moral claim, nothing less than the claim of God upon human beings.[45]

Linzey takes the idea of theos-rights from Dietrich Bonhoeffer. For him duties to other creatures derive from the rights given by God, they are like the reflected splendour of the glory of God's creation.[46] While Bonhoeffer almost certainly did not intend his idea of theos-rights to be applied to animals, Linzey believes it is entirely justified. He suggests that in the past the idea of giving rights to animals has been queried because animals cannot have duties, but the concept of theos-rights makes the discussion of duties irrelevant. In addition, whether the language of 'rights' is an appropriate way of speaking of God's involvement in creation is somewhat debatable, as it imposes a concept from human ethics on to the way God relates to God's creation. Of course, the claim could equally now be made that even if theos-rights are accepted, why not extend rights to all parts of creation, as God affirms all creation as good? Linzey gets round this difficulty by referring to some biblical texts that point to the association of beasts and humans in Joel. Furthermore, he suggests that human beings and animals share in the same 'flesh and blood'; this is of particular significance for the doctrine of the incarnation, where the Logos 'became flesh' and dwelt among us.[47] It is particularly significant for Linzey that Christ became a human *mammal*, for 'the flesh assumed in the incarnation is not some hermeneutically sealed, highly differentiated human flesh, it is the same organic flesh and blood which we share with other mammalian creatures. There is no human embodiment totally unsimilar to the flesh of other sentient creatures.'[48]

In earlier work he had suggested that sentience is the criterion for animal rights, now he suggests that the capacity to feel pain is implicated in the idea of creatures who share spirit/flesh/blood. He finds any suggestion that denies animals have souls highly objectionable.[49] For him rights are given to 'spirit-filled, breathing beings composed of flesh and blood', in other words mammals.[50]

But why should we just include mammals? Linzey's reply is perhaps a little surprising, namely that 'mammals so clearly live Spirit-filled lives which are analogous to human beings'.[51] While he suggests that mammals share something of the spiritual life of humans, for him we simply do not know if other species have any kind of spiritual life or not; hence while they do not have rights as such, they are still valuable as part of the community of created beings.[52] Yet Linzey is not content simply to state that mammals share something of the spiritual life of humans; instead, for him, they are 'individuals filled with the gift of the Spirit'.[53] This allows him to accord equal status to the rights of humans and mammals, and though he recognizes that conflict may occur, at least it gives the opportunity for the case of animals to be heard. Moreover, he suggests that while there may be circumstances in which rights can be overridden, where there is no justification, then this amounts to a sin against God.[54] Of course, Linzey's view assumes that God affords equal status to mammals and humans and that the conferral of rights on mammals is part of the will of God for creation.[55] The advantages of the idea of theos-rights for Linzey, as against what he perceives as 'the scholastic tradition' where animals are treated as property, is that it affirms the givenness of creation, it puts all creatures in the context of a covenant relationship with God and places humans in a unique position of responsibility for creation, to 'actualize' the divine will for all creatures.[56] The practical consequences of the conferral of animal rights are dramatic. For 'The attainment of animal rights goals would require a transformation of human society as we know it. Such a society would be characterised by a minimum disturbance to animal life and an end to all institutional abuse of animals in agriculture, science and sport.'[57]

Of course the case for theos-rights rests on Linzey's assumption that God does give special preference to animals as well as humans. Is he justified in claiming that the significance of the incarnation lies in the Word made *flesh*, with an emphasis on the latter? If we follow Linzey's argument to its logical conclusion, then only creatures with flesh and blood can be considered the subjects of covenant and redemption, but the Noahic covenant claims otherwise. All creatures of the earth, not just mammals, are included in God's providential intention. In addition, as I discussed earlier, the biological origin of species bespeaks of a much looser boundary between other living things and humans. Hence the incarnation is an not just affirmation of human beings, but set in the context of the creation as a whole affirmed as good.

Linzey also tries to defend the boundary between mammals and other creatures on the basis that mammals are 'filled with the spirit'. However, in biblical terms the cut-off point for special receipt of the particular gift of the Holy Spirit is humanity, made in the image of God. Of course, this need not imply that other creatures are outside divine providence, or do not in some sense share in the immanence of God's Spirit in creation.[58] However, Linzey appears to go beyond this in suggesting the spirit comes as *gift*, a term normally associated with the special outpouring of the Holy Spirit on humanity. Unlike Regan, Linzey is careful to distinguish the role of humans from that of mammals, though he does so in a surprisingly anthropocentric manner by claiming, in common with some of the earlier saints, that we are like priests for creation. He suggests that in the Eucharist 'There is something especially fitting about the idea that humanity should represent other creatures and in so doing exercise a priestly role in creation.'[59] In addition, 'Humanity is the one species chosen to look after the cosmic garden.'[60] Such a move is both hierarchical and thoroughly anthropocentric, the opposite of what Linzey seems to suggest in his notion of animals rights. As Richard Bauckham aptly suggests:

> If we are to recover the true value of joining in creation's praise, we must avoid a move that assimilates this theme to the hierarchical model of humanity mediating between God and the rest of creation. Such a move has proved irresistible in some parts of the Christian tradition, especially where the hierarchical model has been understood in a benevolent rather than dominating or exploitative way.[61]

Hence Linzey's own interpretation of the role of humanity in the Eucharist seems to undermine his own stated view of affording mammalian species equal rights with humans. This view is also reinforced by consideration of the development of his idea of generosity. According to this view, humans are called to imitate the divine generosity by caring for the weak and defenceless. As we focus on Christ crucified, we come to see that God identifies particularly with the vulnerable, both humans and animals.[62] But he goes beyond just saying that animals now share in the crucifixion of Christ: rather, they become the *particular* priority for our moral concern. He compares animals with children as subjects of special moral concern for humanity, though somewhat bizarrely he suggests that animals have an *even greater* claim on us than do children.[63] He believes that his own 'generosity theory', like welfare theory and rights theory, 'represents a real intellectual advance in terms of understanding the moral status of animals'.[64] The once monolithic tradition which denied animals moral status is breaking down, so that 'the animal rights and generosity theories anticipate an even greater weakening of this tradition and return us to some fundamental insights which have always been present within Western culture (to some degree) but which have been insufficiently recognised and articulated'.[65]

The theory of generosity for him complements the language of rights, so that 'talk of respect, care, generosity, love and gentleness to animals is not only appropriate, but also essential'.[66] The means to achieve this end emphatically is not, for him, through violence. We can ask ourselves here how far the idea of generosity carries with it something of a *condescending* attitude towards animals; we still seem to be relating to them on our own terms as 'caretakers' or 'managers' of the garden. Hence Linzey has not really freed himself from the anthropocentrism that he decries in the Christian tradition. However, his move towards thinking about human *attitudes* to animals is of interest, since it hints at an alternative approach that has been rarely aired, namely that of virtue ethics.[67] His theme of generosity is significant in that like the covenant ideal it stresses the relationship between God, humanity and animals.[68] However, given the stress on rights language the relationship is still domineering in tone, so the introduction of the idea of generosity reinforces an anthropocentric attitude, rather than challenges it.[69]

Aquinas, Animals and the Virtues

Stephen Clark is, understandably, reluctant to identify himself with either Singer's utilitarian case for animals or the case for animal rights in the narrow sense defined by Regan.[70] While he does not specifically claim to present a case for virtue ethics, he spells out the importance of considering who we are, our character traits, and how this is expressed in relation to animals. In his earlier work, for example, he describes those who are not vegetarian as committing the vice of gluttony: 'Flesh eating in our present circumstance is as empty a gluttony as any of these things. Those who still eat flesh when they could do otherwise have no claim to be serious moralists.'[71] This position seems somewhat extreme, though he has written in more moderate tones subsequently. The main point to note here is that he has, correctly in my view, paid close attention to attitudes and virtues. In addition, following Aristotle, he suggests that the good person acts well, so that actions arise

> from a stable state of character which brings to an integrated whole such emotional and intellectual capacities as are open to creatures of humankind. He relates realistically to things in the world, living and unliving, and finds the meaning of his life in natural friendships and the shared worship of natural beauty.[72]

While Clark may well have revised his views on the moral status of non-vegetarians, his intuition that our actions are related to who we are as personal moral agents is an important one. He takes up further themes from Aristotle's work in more recent volumes.[73] For him, our morality begins in the context of the family, but reaches out to include non-human companions. Hence, it is through 'domestic virtues' that the moral life is born, so our first charge is 'to be loyal to those with whom we have bonds of affection and familiarity'.[74] In other words, while he agrees with Midgley that our first loyalty is towards family members, he argues that this family cannot be separated from those animals that share the same society as ourselves. This is set in a wider, global context, so that 'The final context of our worldly activity is not our immediate household or nation state, nor yet the socio-political nexus of suffering humanity, but the whole earth.'[75] His accommodation of virtue ethics into animal ethics is particularly welcome, as is his distinction between domestic animals and other animals. The utilitarian calculus of Singer and rights language of Regan, bent as they are on a rejection of speciesism, fail to make such distinctions apparent.

In addition, Clark argues that attempts to draw from a single moral theory, such as utilitarianism or humanism, all that might be required in deliberation about our treatment of animals is to expect too much, for 'Morality is the record of "our" past conclusions, the testimony of those who seriously sought to be virtuous, and to see things clearly.'[76] Yet while the tradition of the past has claimed that animals deserve little respect, there is nothing in tradition that suggests this aspect cannot be changed. Of particular significance is his injunction that:

> Those who would live virtuously, tradition tells us, must seek to allow each creature its own place, and to appreciate the beauty of the whole. It is because human beings can sometimes come to see that whole, and know their own place in it, that – in a sense – they are superior to other forms. Our 'superiority', insofar as that is real, rests not upon our self-claimed right always to have more than other creatures do (which is what our modern humanism amounts to), but on the possibility that we may (and the corresponding duty that we should) allow our fellow creatures their part of the action.[77]

In other words, Clark has found a way of expressing the *difference* between humanity and other creatures, while denying any hierarchical superiority or condescension. This is a preferable strand in his thought compared with his discussion of 'forms' that I mentioned above. This emphasis on distinction and difference is an important aspect that has already been noted by feminist critiques of animal rights advocates. Palmer, for example, suggests that a focus on relationships is critical, so that it would be 'flexible enough to take into account matters such as species difference, contextual differences and differences of origin between animals'.[78] This coheres well with the concept of virtue ethics that I will elaborate further below. However, Clark's view is more sophisticated than simply an avocation of the virtues, for he relies on an ideal concept of beauty that is also tied into a theistic framework.[79] Hence:

> Our duty is to admire and to sustain the world in beauty, and not to impose on others pains and penalties that we could not bear ourselves. . . . We ought to live by those laws that an ideal observer or Creator-God would make (maybe has made) for the world: to respect the integrity of every creature, and not to seize more for ourselves and our immediate kin than would be granted under such a dispensation.[80]

But where might we find such a discussion of the moral life in terms of virtues, with its goal towards beauty and respect of the value of all creation? I suggest that, contrary perhaps to expectation from critics such as Andrew Linzey, it is the tradition of Thomas Aquinas that lends itself to thinking through the moral status of animals in this way.

Aquinas on animals

Aquinas's negative view on the ethics of our treatment of animals is well known and thoroughly castigated by those committed to animal rights. Not only is he portrayed as one who simply advocates a benign anthropocentrism; rather, his views actually seem to support more serious human *abuse* of animals. The following extract, taken from a book of readings on animals and Christianity, highlights why it is that he has come to be regarded as the 'bête noir' of animal rights:

> Dumb animals and plants are devoid of the life of reason whereby to set themselves in motion; they are moved, as it were, by a kind of natural impulse, a sign of which is that they are naturally enslaved and accommodated to the uses of others. He that kills another's ox, sins, not through killing the ox, but through injuring another man in his property. Wherefore this is not a species of the sin of murder, but of the sin of theft or robbery.[81]

Aquinas also considers the possibility of whether animals should be loved out of charity, since God created all creatures. However, he suggests that the idea of extending neighbourly relations with animals is false, for irrational creatures cannot possess the good, nor, for this reason, could we join with them in friendship; in other words, they cannot be on equal terms with humans. Irrational creatures cannot, therefore, have fellowship with human beings, nor are they destined for 'everlasting happiness'. The only possible reason we might have for showing charity towards an animal is if it gives pleasure to its human owner.[82] In addition, he suggests that if we are kind to animals, we are more likely to show kindness to other human beings, and vice versa, cruelty to animals may lead to further human abuse.[83]

While it is possible to agree with Aquinas in this latter point only, namely that animals abuse fosters other immoral behaviour, it is clear that as far as he is concerned animals can be treated as instruments for human use and have little value in and of themselves. Aquinas's seeming rejection of full reasoning ability in animals also means that for him they are not morally culpable. Children are also not culpable, in that they have not yet developed the kind of reasoning that allows them to make moral choices. But he rejects the idea that children (like animals) should be treated as instruments. The difference seems to rest simply on the idea that children are capable of entering everlasting happiness, whereas animals are not. While lack of moral culpability in animals is reasonable, to treat animals simply as instruments is unacceptable. However, this does not mean that all strands of Aquinas's thought are irrelevant to animal ethics. I will argue below that contrary to expectation, his ontology and focus on virtues encourage appropriate ethical action towards animals. Those concerned with animal ethics have largely castigated his views for the reasons suggested above, but I suggest that they have been too hasty in rejecting the scholastic tradition as a whole, without giving due attention to its possible significance.

Aquinas believed that plants, animals and humans are closely connected through a great Chain of Being. Humanity is humanity situated in creation as a whole. Yet the divisions are not as sharp as this image might suggest, for, following Aristotle, 'the lowest in the higher genus touches [*contingere*] the highest of the lower species', such touching causing a similarity between the two, leading to a very gradual but orderly succession.[84] The perfection of a being increases the nearer it is to the divine likeness. The concept of gradual succession means that certain plants are very close to inanimate things, certain animals are very close to plants and, by implication, certain animals are very close to humans.[85] The latter point is reinforced by Aquinas's suggestion that in sin human beings can move away from their human dignity, and become ranked 'lower' than the beasts.[86] Within each general category of being there is a higher and lower type, so that there is a movement from plant life to animal life lacking locomotive power, through to animals with locomotive power and finally the human animal, possessing full reasoning ability.[87] Judith Barad suggests that in this respect Aquinas is surprisingly close to current evolutionary theory compared with Descartes, including, for example, his distinctions between lower animals, such as mussels and other shellfish, and higher animals.[88] While Aquinas had no knowledge of the biological or evolutionary origin of species, his interpretation of the 'chain' of being is not as fixed as one might expect. However, it seems to me that while Aquinas has tried to blur the boundaries between species, as is also the case with evolutionary theory, ultimately his scientific understanding of the world stressed hierarchical distinction rather than continuity. Judith Barad's thesis that Aquinas's ideas are essentially 'evolutionary' is somewhat strained, even if she is right to point out that his views are not as hostile to evolutionary ideas as has been supposed in the past. For example, his insistence on a linear progression between species is not characteristic of current ideas about evolution, which perceive a branch-like development through time, rather than a linear hierarchy.[89] A further important difference between Aquinas and evolutionary ideas is that while Aquinas believed in forms as given by God in hierarchical ordered relationships *over space*, taking account of both scientific knowledge of the time and the Genesis account as the basis for his reflection, contemporary evolutionary ideas envisage a slow progression and emergence of living forms *over time*, even though it is not linear and directed simply towards human beings in the way that Aquinas envisaged.[90] The chain of being might also reinforce the idea of a 'balance of nature' that has proved to be incommensurate with ecological thinking, as discussed in chapter 2. However, the dynamic interplay in patterns of populations of species that is characteristic of current ecological thought is still commensurate with the basic knowledge of speciation as divergence between non-breeding populations. The chain of being stressed this divergence and increased capacity for consciousness, but also was set in an understanding of the natural world as a whole expressing God's goodness.[91]

Another significant aspect of Aquinas's ontology is that he believed we could learn more about ourselves by close study of the natural world and non-human animals in particular.[92] For him 'sensible beings resemble in their own way, intellectual beings. Thus from the resemblance of sense to intellect we can mount to some knowledge of intellectual beings.'[93] There is some continuity with plant life as well, since plants have a vegetative soul, animals a sensitive soul and humans a rational soul. Against the Manicheans, Aquinas envisages a soul as having bodily form; hence it is by definition corporeal.[94] Judith Barad rejects Aquinas's suggestion that plants have souls on the basis that, unlike animals, they cannot transcend their own nature and limitations. In other words, plant activity can be explained through material explanations, without recourse to the idea of a 'soul' within it.[95] It is worth noting that even if Aquinas believed that animals have souls, he rejected the idea that they share in eternal salvation. His affirmation of the variety and goodness of creation jars with his anthropological eschatology.[96]

Aquinas also arranges the appetites found in creatures in a hierarchical way, into the natural, the sensitive and the rational. Plants and inanimate things carry out activities without any knowledge according to natural appetite.[97] The sensitive appetite, on the other hand, shared by all animals, is a response to a perceived good, and it shows the ability to distinguish between what is desired and what is not. For Aquinas, all animals have desire based on the ability to touch: 'For everything touched is either congenial to the one touching, and then it gives pleasure, or uncongenial, and then it gives pain. But whatever can feel pain and pleasure can desire the pleasant. Since then, all animals without exception, have a sense of touch, all can desire.'[98]

He also suggested that animals could have inner emotions.[99] Such emotions are analogous to those found in humans, and hence, with respect to anger, 'the brute animals are divinely endowed with a natural instinct for internal and external reactions analogous to the operations of reason'.[100] He distinguishes concupiscible appetite from irascible appetite. The former leads animals to desire those things associated with the pleasures of sense, and includes primarily love and hate, but also desire, disgust, joy and sorrow. However, the irascible appetite commonly leads to aggression and follows from the frustrations of the concupiscible appetite, including emotions such as hope, despair, fear, daring and anger. All animals are capable of feeling all such emotions, but whereas in the human animal such emotions are tempered by reason, in non-humans no such restraint is present.[101]

In addition to these complex emotional states that he attributed to all animals, he suggests that animals have a sensitive soul, one that attains 'nobility' as it relates to the movement of the heart, analogous to movement in the heavens.[102] Furthermore, importantly, Aquinas attributes some cognitive powers to all animals, the difference between humans and animals being one of *degree* or excellence, rather than an absolute difference.[103] Judith Barad suggests:

> Just as Aquinas acknowledges that there is continuity between the highest form of animal life and the lowest form of human nature, he notes parallel continuity in the cognitive sphere. Like biological characteristics, cognitive experiences constitute evolutionary continuity. There are degrees of cognition found throughout the various animal species. It is not an all-or-nothing affair, either fully present, exhibited only in highly abstract thought, or totally lacking.[104]

While the degrees of cognition are worth taking into account, Barad's claim that such development is 'evolutionary' is a misnomer for reasons I have suggested above. Evolution implies development over time in a way that Aquinas could not take into account given the cosmological assumptions of his time. However, the ontological continuity between species is something that is still acceptable in a contemporary context, even if the means by which such difference has taken place requires adjustment.[105] In addition, higher animals have faculties of imagination and memory, and it is the memory that constitutes the sum of experience. Even more complex still is what Aquinas calls the 'estimative sense'. This sense is particularly significant, as it is able to share in reason, and it is through this sense that Aristotle claimed that some 'animals are said to have a sort of prudence'.[106] It is worth noting that when Aquinas rejects the idea that animals have reason, as noted earlier in the discussion, he seems to mean lacking in full reasoning powers of humans. However, Barad's belief in the possibility of a kind of prudence in animals seems to misinterpret Aquinas in attributing moral activities to animals that are analogous to that found in humans.[107] On the other hand, with Barad, it is likely to be incorrect to call the estimative sense found in Aquinas simply 'instinct', as the term today has connotations associated with unthinking or unconscious behaviour.[108]

Given the knowledge available at the time, it is very unlikely that Aquinas perceived the closeness between animals and humans that has since become available through study of primate behaviour, especially that of the great apes. It is also important not to read into animal behaviour human awareness that we take for granted. For example, great apes, in comparison with monkeys, are able to undertake simple planning tasks, use others' behaviour as a source of new ideas and sometimes understand the intentions of another's actions.[109] Barad has also suggested that Aquinas claimed that animals have the ability to communicate with each other through a kind of primitive language, but human beings are more advanced in this ability to communicate.[110] If this interpretation is correct, then the 'language test' often used to distinguish humans from other animals simply does not apply.[111] Only the very lowest forms of animals are restricted to 'instinct' in the modern sense that their actions are totally determinate, lacking in any learned behaviour.

Barad also considers that Aquinas attributes some spiritual activity to all higher animals. She suggests that spiritual activity usually involves their bodily organs, but the process of intelligent knowing can sometimes have immaterial characteristics. She has pointed to Aquinas's texts that distinguish higher animals from humans by suggesting that while all animals can achieve a *particular* universal based on prior experience, humans are able to abstract further than this to an *abstract* universal.[112] Hence Barad suggests that 'In the ability to receive a form without matter, in the construction of a particular universal, and in being able to know potentially all physical things in their individuality, an animal manifests immaterial activity.'[113] From this it follows that souls of animals are to some extent immaterial, even if they do not have the same degree of immateriality compared with human beings. Yet given Aquinas's rejection of eternal life for animals, it is doubtful if any kind of immateriality can be read into Aquinas's texts without some distortion and it is not clear what such partial immateriality would mean in practice.[114] Hence it seems to me more accurate to allow for the fact that while immateriality is not definitively ruled out by Aquinas, he does not specifically suggest that this is the case in the way Barad suggests. In the light of contemporary understanding of animal intelligence, we might want to shift towards this direction from a theistic perspective, though the possibility of spiritual activity in animals is a matter of open debate.[115]

It is also worth pointing out that evolutionary biology indicates that the common ancestor to apes and humans that had more sophisticated cognitive ability, such as being able to detect another's intentions, emerged only about twelve million years ago.[116] This research is significant in that it serves as a salutary warning against reading into animal behaviour particular human intentions and feelings. A certain type of grin on a chimpanzee, for example, does not have the meaning of a human smile. The primatologist Richard Bryne comments:

It is tempting, when we see an animal use a smart trick to get what it wants, to assume that they understand the situation as we do: to think that the female gorilla mates silently because she *knows* that if her leader male hears her call he will *realize* he is being cuckolded; the young baboon screams because he *wants* his mother to *think* he has been hurt. We may be quite wrong. We have noted that the acquisition of deception by rapid learning is sometimes not at all implausible; a deep comprehension of the situation may not be necessary: In fact, experimental evidence indicates that monkeys do not understand the mental states of other individuals (what they want, what they intend to do, what they know).[117]

When monkeys were exposed to a predator that put their infants at risk, they were just as likely to give an alarm call if their infants could see the predator or if they could not, which implies an inability to understand another's mental state, and 'helps explain the puzzle that animals manipulated by deception often do not seem to understand what is happening'.[118] By contrast, chimpanzees and other great apes did show some evidence of knowing what another individual thought or intended. The increase in cognitive ability among primates is likely to be related to increase in size of the neocortex.[119] However, it is also worth noting that the evolution of the first human species, from *Australopithecus habilis* to *Homo erectus*, which occurred around 1.8 million years ago, involved a much greater increase in brain size than previously during ape evolution, almost *doubling* brain size to over one thousand cubic centimetres.[120] *Homo sapiens*, our current species, is generally regarded as having evolved between 150,000 and 200,000 years ago. A more recent theory is that the species prior to *Homo sapiens* was *Homo heidelbergensis*, living in a restricted area of Africa.[121] While it is possible, therefore, to find some evidence of cultural evolution in primates, especially apes, even of patterns of social communication that express forms of 'altruism', and even find complex emotional states in animals that suggest some awareness of their own behaviour and how it affects others, the difference in brain size and cognitive ability is a reminder of the difference between apes and humans. Michael Northcott notes the range of behaviours in many animals, including non-primates such as dolphins and elephants, that seem to correspond with showing grief, empathy, care, even social restraint on aggression, and suggests that 'there is a great deal of common ground between humans and their mammalian relatives in moral behaviour'. For this reason he suggests that mammals should be considered part of the human *moral* community.[122] Yet, for reasons given above, I argue that reading into animal behaviour moral agency in a strong sense as *morally culpable* is a mistake, that there remain crucial differences between animals and humans that should not be underestimated so as to interpret in animal behaviour capabilities for being included as *moral agents* as part of human moral communities.[123] In addition, it partly depends on one's preconceived ideas as to what characteristics will be found in non-human species, since it will serve to shape which particular scientific research questions are asked and the way they are asked. For example, a range of behaviours have been found in apes, from violence to sexual promiscuity to peace making, interpreted by sociobiologists as in some sense normative for human behaviour, and animal rights campaigners as indicative of the closeness between animals and humans, namely that they are really 'like us'.[124] I suggest that the inclusion of animals in the moral community of humans is not so much with reference to the specific behaviour of animals as being 'moral', like humans, even though they may act in ways that are in some sense *precursors* of human morality, but rather it is the choice of humans to welcome those unlike as well as like ourselves as those *to whom* we have specific responsibilities and *with whom* we share a common life.

Aquinas and animal rights

While Aquinas clearly gives high ontological status to non-human animals, his recommendations for their treatment, as Barad points out, confront us with a 'glaring inconsistency'.[125] He does not recommend that we treat them in the way his ontology suggests; though the gap may not be quite as wide as she has implied, it is certainly there and worth consideration. If animals are simply instruments in the way his specific ethical recommendations suggest, then this requires a much greater adjustment to his ontology than rejecting this notion altogether. As well as the relatively high ontological status given to higher animals, Aquinas also suggests that the *telos* or end of any creature is valuable, so this would imply something is due to animals in this respect.[126] Is Barad correct to claim that 'the admission that an animal can have his due violated constitutes a tacit ascription of rights to an animal'?[127] This seems to be based on her belief that Aquinas suggests that all animals share in 'natural law'.[128] 'Natural law' is more commonly interpreted as human participation in the eternal law through use of reason.[129] Barad suggests that Aquinas implies animals have natural 'rights', but this is an interpretation of Aquinas that is not immediately obvious from the text, even if we assume, as Barad does, that animals are also, like humans, sharing in natural law.[130] Rights, according to the principles of justice, are set up by relationships with others. Barad believes that these others include individuals capable of action and, according to Aquinas's ontology, are inclusive of animals. Yet while I would agree that for Aquinas all beings are directed towards the eternal reason, and participate in it, the action of animals does not have the same *deliberative* quality that takes into account past, present and future in a sophisticated way that is based on the higher activity of the intellect and will as it exists in humans, and hence animals cannot share in moral responsibility in the same way.[131] As I discussed in chapter 2, there is nothing in Aquinas to suggest that natural law is fixed for all time in its secondary principles, only the first principle, to desire good and avoid evil, cannot be changed. The question to be asked is: can the understanding of natural law be extended in order to be rather more inclusive of animals? I suggest that while the idea of giving animals 'rights' would not necessarily be an appropriate extension of Aquinas's thought, the application of natural law theory so that it includes responsible *human* behaviour towards animals is entirely justified. This does not mean that we automatically have to accept that animals somehow *consciously share* in the natural law, though some scholars have put this forward, as I suggested above. Rather, given the close relationship between human natural inclinations and those of other species, this implies a relationship and human responsibility towards animals that goes beyond a simple instrumental view towards them. In other words, Aquinas's ontology implies inherent value for animals and plants on a hierarchical scale that takes into account the complexity of a species relative to human beings. Prudential decision-making directed towards the good is that defined by natural law in a way that takes into account natural inclinations as the *common ground* of both human and animal life. Moreover, the good is not simply that for an individual or human species alone, it must be directed towards the universal good, though the good of individuals is respected in so far as it does not damage the common good. It is worth reinforcing once again the goodness that Aquinas perceived in the variety of creation:

> And because one single creature was not enough, he produced many diverse creatures, so that what was wanting in one expression of divine goodness might be supplied by another; for goodness, which in God is single and all together, in creatures is multiple and scattered. Hence the whole universe less incompletely than one alone shares and represents his goodness.[132]

Aquinas's account of justice does not depend on the assumption that all parties are moral agents in the same sense. Rather, as agents of natural law, humans have duties towards others who participate in the eternal law. Hence I suggest that it is more accurate to suggest that Aquinas points more in the direction of *duties* towards all creatures, rather than 'rights' as understood in the legal sense through an implicit contract theory. In other words, his philosophical theology hints at forms of protection that give some sense of responsibility owed to other creatures through natural law, without making human beings and animals equivalent right holders. It is therefore subtler than simply ascribing rights to animals in a mechanical way according to certain attributes deemed similar to humans, which tends to be the case for the animal rights campaigners discussed above. While human beings obey eternal law through an understanding of the divine commandment, for Thomas 'all actions and movements of the whole of nature are subject to the eternal law, through being moved by Divine providence'.[133] Hence animals, as *fellow creatures sharing in the eternal law and the goodness of God* deserve our respect.[134] This concurs with Thomas that 'in all creatures there is to be found the trace of the Trinity, inasmuch as in every creature are found some things which are necessarily reduced to the divine Persons as to their cause'.[135] Moreover, animals are part of the community of creation in which humans share with all others, so their particular goals need to be acknowledged.

Aquinas and the virtues

Aquinas's theology is not only capable of giving a more subtle interpretation of animal ethics under the auspices of natural law, in addition it requires us to focus much more on the virtues of the agent. Given that I have argued for an adjustment of natural law theory so that it takes into account Aquinas's affirmation of the goodness of all creatures and their subjection to the eternal law, how might this influence the way particular virtues are interpreted in the present context? I have argued above (*contra* Barad) that prudence, properly understood, is a unique characteristic of humans. However, such additional skills require a greater sense of responsibility. Prudential activity needs to come prior to considerations of justice, as I discussed in the first chapter. Hence, the particular ability of prudence to have an accurate perception of reality is desperately needed when it comes to discerning moral action in relation to animals. Prudence includes a memory of the past, as well as foresight about the future.[136] In concrete terms such memory may lead to shame, especially where human activities have led to cruel treatment of animals. Yet the memory of those who have called animals 'brothers and sisters', who have been able to welcome animals as in some sense part of the human community, bespeaks of a more cosmic vision in which all creatures are honoured for their own sake.

Does this mean that anyone other than a vegetarian is guilty of the vice of gluttony? I suggest that such a move is inappropriate, since it focuses on just one aspect of the complex interdependent lives of humans and animals. Of course, animals deserve our respect and deserve to be treated with compassion and consideration. A prudential approach would reject, in principle, all forms of factory farming and cruel practices that restrict the well-being of animals. It would also be highly critical of those who use animals for pleasure through sport hunting. However, while the ideal state may be one that is totally vegetarian, I suggest that it is imprudent to expect this to be adopted as a *universal* practice, for the good of the whole community needs to be taken into account. I suggest this because farm animals are not and can never simply become household pets; their role and place in the human community is different compared with those animals in our immediate household. Moreover, for health reasons it may not always be possible to adopt a strictly vegetarian diet. This might include, for example, gestating or lactating women.[137] To be thoroughly consistent in claiming 'the rights' of animals in industrialized societies it would be necessary for everyone to become vegan and not use leather shoes, but many draw the line before this point is reached. It is more reasonable, and I suggest more prudent, to expect everyone to reduce their meat consumption and as far as possible restrict this to those animals that are reared in 'free range' conditions. While we might be suspicious of 'free range' labels where this is a distortion of the truth (sham prudence), the extra cost of such freedoms is ultimately born by the consumer. It therefore requires a measure of temperance in practice. It is important to qualify that which operates according to individual prudence in the light of household and political prudence. Such political prudence sets the needs of individuals in a relational and ecological context.[138] There are, then, special obligations to those animals that are near extinction; the use of such animals for food is not likely to be justified.

However, in addition to prudence, Aquinas invites Christians to develop their capacity for wisdom, wisdom understood as being both learned and a gift of the

Holy Spirit. Traces of the Spirit of wisdom are found throughout the community of creation, though as gift it is confined to the human community.[139] Given that all creatures share in this wisdom, all are owed respect. Moreover, wisdom and charity coexist with each other, so that wisdom is only possible if it coheres with charity. Such charity allows other creatures to be different and recognized as valuable not just through shared characteristics, but through acknowledgement and acceptance of difference. Wisdom, then, is the ability to perceive both similarities where they are present and differences. *Moral* responsibility is to exercise such wisdom with charity. This view resonates with the ethic of care that is currently being developed by feminist thinkers, though it seems to me that caring needs to be complemented by other virtues, such as wisdom and justice.[140] This conjoining of wisdom and charity suggests that simply rational prudential consideration of animals is not sufficient; instead, we need to develop compassion for animals, but also compassion for those who are not able for whatever reason to fulfil this role. Those poorer communities struggling for survival cannot be expected to reduce their meat intake where this would lead to starvation, though we might expect them not to treat animals with cruelty. Prudential thinking can set normative guidelines, but also includes *gnome*, the ability to realize when exceptions to certain rules apply. Frans de Waal, an ethologist who specializes in primatology, suggests that our circle of morality reaches out like an inverted pyramid from self, family, group, tribe, humanity and all life forms. It is only when our own basic needs are met in the inner circle that compassion can realistically extend to others unlike ourselves. Hence 'people on the brink of starvation can afford only a tiny tip of the moral pyramid, it will be every man for himself'.[141] Like Aquinas, de Waal finds many examples of primate behaviour that mirrors that of humans, including sympathy, social rules, reciprocity and the ability to make peace. Yet de Waal suggests that it is condescending to see animals simply as 'retarded humans', in the way that those who campaign for animal rights suggest; instead, we need to respect them in their 'otherness'.[142] Wisdom includes the ability to see reality, which is the significance of other creatures in their commonality with humans as well as their uniqueness.

I suggest that wisdom takes account of both the similarities and the differences between human beings and animals, and, more importantly, is able to acknowledge the demands of social justice in the human community alongside the claims of those who share our planetary home. For the virtue of wisdom not only leads to just action in the community, but also encourages the virtue of temperance. As I suggested in the first chapter, temperance is associated with the misdirection of desires for self-preservation, leading to distorted desire for sensual enjoyment. As applied to human relationships with animals, those practices that encourage the treatment of animals as human property, to be manipulated at will for human enjoyment or entertainment, suffer from the vice of intemperance. Temperance also includes an accurate estimation of one's own self-worth. The idea that human beings are in any sense superior to other life forms is out of fashion in philosophy, even for those who confine moral agency to human beings. Human moral rights can be grounded in the particular ability of humans to show empathy and in this way 'we no longer need to appeal to the myth that humans are superior to all other living things in order to make sense of our special moral obligations to sentient human beings'.[143]

Yet humans do have greater skills in some areas, such as in their use of language or invention of technologies. This means that 'We are collectively more powerful – and more destructive – than other terrestrial animals; but however much we may value that power, it does not make us more valuable in the universe.'[144] In Christian terms we could say that temperance involves an accurate appraisal of ourselves as those with special powers, but not necessarily superiority in the sense of having licence to do what we will with the universe. Warren suggests that the medieval understanding of the Chain of Being automatically makes human beings superior to other animals.[145] I suggest that once understood in the context of evolutionary categories, the Chain of Being instead affirms the continuity of human life with all life forms: we are an integral part of the whole complex chain of creation. In so far as the Chain of Being infers superiority, this needs to be rejected on the basis of temperance. For temperance also includes the idea of self-restraint governed by reason. Unlike other animals, we do have the ability to choose how we are to live, we have the power to deliberate at *an abstract level* in a way that is not possible for other animals. This power need not lead us to a sense of pride or superiority; instead, we should have a humble estimation of our place in the wider community of the earth.

In conclusion, I suggest that, contrary to expectations, Aquinas's thought can lead to a positive appraisal of the place and worth of animals. Such justice only makes sense in its context as one of the cardinal virtues, the first of which is prudence, but also includes the idea of temperance. Wisdom, as related to prudence, is the theological goal to which humanity aspires, since it is through wisdom that the Eternal law becomes visible. Wisdom reaches out to those forms of beauty that are there in the mind of the Creator. As applied to our treatment of animals, consideration of the virtues forces us to stop and reflect, not just on how to treat animals, but on how we balance the demands of justice for animals with those for the human community and members of our own family and household. None the less, such a discussion needs to be set in another context again, namely that of the increasing drive towards biotechnology. What particular issues does biotechnology raise for an ethics of nature? I attempt to address this question in the chapter that follows.

Notes

1   S. Clark: *The Political Animal* (London: Routledge, 1999), p. 155.
2   See H. Kean: *Animal Rights: Political and Social Change in Britain since 1800* (London: Reaction Books, 1998).
3   Kean: *Animal Rights*, p.10.
4   See entries in M. Berkoff, ed.: *Encyclopedia of Animal Rights and Animal Welfare* (London: Fitzroy Dearborn, 1998), pp. 280, 361–2.

5 His book, first published in 1976, has become something of a classic text for those campaigning on behalf of animals. P. Singer: *Animal Liberation* (London: Pimlico, 1990).

6 Singer: *Animal Liberation*, p. 16.

7 Singer: *Animal Liberation*, p. 16.

   8 Singer: Animal Liberation, p. 161.

   9 Singer: *Animal Liberation*, p. 171.

   10 Singer: *Animal Liberation*, p. 171.

11 This is detailed in work that was published after *Animal Liberation*. See, for example, *Practical Ethics*, 2nd edn (Cambridge: Cambridge University Press, 1993).

12 Singer lists the following animals that should be excluded from killing: whales, dolphins, monkeys, dogs, cats, pigs, seals, bears, cattle, sheep. He also suggests that animals without rationality and self-consciousness can be killed, and as long as they are kept in 'free range' conditions, they are replaceable. His argument for replaceability does not apply to more advanced creatures, since their future happiness needs to be taken into account. See Singer: *Practical Ethics*, pp. 132–4.

13 See M. Rowlands, *Animal Rights: A Philosophical Defence* (Basingstoke: Macmillan Press, 1998), pp. 74–5.

14 Clark: *The Political Animal*, p. 6. See also S. Clark: *Animals and Their Moral Standing* (London: Routledge, 1997), pp. 161–4.

15 Clark: *Animals*, p. 162.

16 Mark Rowlands is not the only author to advocate a social contract version of Singer's theory. His approach is probably one of the most thoroughly developed positions in this vein. For other examples of modified versions of Rawls's position as applied to animals see R. Elliot: 'Rawlsian Justice and Non-human Animals', *Journal of Applied Philosophy*, 1 (1984), pp. 95–106; A. Fuchs: 'Duties to Animals: Rawls' Alleged Dilemma', *Ethics and Animals*, 2 (1981), pp. 83–7.

17 Rowlands: *Animal Rights*, pp. 120–58.

18 A view that is common among those who support animal rights. See, for example, M. Spiegel: *The Dreaded Comparison: Human and Animal Slavery*, 2nd edn (New York: Mirror Books, 1996).

19 M. Midgley: *Animals and Why They Matter* (London: Penguin, 1983). See also her earlier book, *Beasts and Man* (London: Methuen, 1980) and her subsequent book, *Utopias, Dolphins and Computers: Problems of Philosophical Plumbing* (London: Routledge, 1996).

20 Midgley: *Animals and Why They Matter*, p. 103.

21 Midgley: *Animals and Why They Matter*, p. 111.

22 Clark: *Animals*, p. 160.

23 Clark: *Animals*, p. 161.

24 Clark: *The Political Animal*, p. 132.

25 Clark: *The Political Animal*, p. 133.

26 See Holmes Rolston III: *Genes, Genesis and God: Values and Their Origins in Natural and Human History* (Cambridge: Cambridge University Press, 1999). For discussion of genetic components to religious traits see L. B. Eaves: 'Ought in World that Just Is', in W. Drees, ed.: *Is Nature Ever Evil? Religion, Science and Value* (London: Routledge, 2003), pp. 284–309.

27 S. L. Clark: 'Making up Animals: The View from Science Fiction', in A. Holland and A. Johnson eds: *Animal Biotechnology and Ethics* (London: Chapman and Hall, 1997), pp. 209–24.

28   This has, in fact, been achieved between a goat and a sheep at the University of California in 1999. Ted Peters: personal communication.

29   Clark: 'Making up Animals', p. 222.

30   I will be taking up a discussion of 'other animal ethics' in the final chapter.

31   T. Regan: *The Case for Animal Rights* (Berkeley: University of California, 1984; reprinted London: Routledge, 1988). One of the first authors to initiate the term 'rights' for animals was Henry Salt, writing in the late nineteenth century. See H. Salt: *Animal Rights Considered in Relation to Social Progress* (Fontwell: Centaur Press, 1985; 1st edn 1892).

32   Regan: *The Case for Animal Rights*, p. 243.

33   For further comment, see Rowlands: *Animal Rights*, pp. 88–9.

34   For discussion of the problems with the emphasis on 'sameness' see C. Pinches and J. McDaniel, eds: *Good News for Animals? Christian Approaches to Animal Wellbeing* (Maryknoll, NY: Orbis Books, 1993).

35   T. Regan: 'The Case for Animal Rights', in D. van de Veer and C. Pierce, eds: *People, Penguins and Plastic Trees; Basic Issues in Environmental Ethics* (Belmont, CA: Wadsworth, 1986), p. 39. For a brief discussion, see C. Deane-Drummond: *Theology and Biotechnology: Implications for a New Science* (London: Geoffrey Chapman, 1997), pp. 61–2.

36   R. Hursthouse: *Ethics, Humans and Other Animals: An Introduction with Readings* (London: Routledge, 2000), p. 103.

37   G. L. Francione: *Animals, Property and the Law* (Philadelphia: Temple University Press, 1995).

38   Francione: *Animals, Property and the Law*, p. 115.

39   Francione: *Animals, Property and the Law*, p. 260.

40   He claims that his first book, *Animal Rights: A Christian Assessment*, was the first one that promoted the idea of conferring rights to animals, though, as I indicated earlier, the idea that animals could have rights was aired much earlier than this in the nineteenth century. See A. Linzey: *Animal Rights: A Christian Assessment* (London: SCM Press, 1976).

41   A. Linzey: 'Animal Rights', in P. Clarke and A. Linzey, eds: *Dictionary of Ethics, Theology and Society* (London: Routledge, 1996), pp. 29–33.

42   It is also worth noting that Descartes's views on animals may not be as extreme as Linzey and others have implied. While Descartes thought that animals were machines, automata that did not think, he did not say that they were totally without feeling, but such a 'monstrous' view has been read into his work in an illegitimate way. Instead, a close reading of Descartes shows that he did believe animals had feelings, including fear, hope and joy in horses, dogs and monkey. However, he believed that these feelings were without thought, by which he meant without conscious self-reflection. His dualistic Cartesian philosophy might point in another direction, but such evidence shows that with respect to animals he was inconsistent in strict application of a Cartesian framework. For discussion see J. Cottingham: 'A Brute to the Brutes? Descartes' Treatment of Animals', *Philosophy*, 53 (1978), pp. 551–9. My main concern here is that Linzey is misrepresenting Aquinas's views, though due account needs to be taken of distortions of Descartes's position as well.

43   S. Clark: *Animals*, p. 105.

44   A. Linzey: *Christianity and the Rights of Animals* (London: SPCK, 1987).

45   Linzey: *Christianity and the Rights of Animals*, p. 69.

46   Linzey: *Christianity and the Rights of Animals*, p. 70.

47   Linzey: *Christianity and the Rights of Animals*, pp. 78–81.

48   A. Linzey: *Animal Rites: Liturgies of Animal Care* (London: SPCK, 1999), p. 5.

49   He notes that Aquinas gives plants, animals and humans different kinds of soul – vegetative, sensitive and rational – but queries the biblical basis for this distinction. I discuss this point again below. Linzey: *Christianity and the Rights of Animals*, p. 36.

50   Linzey: *Christianity and the Rights of Animals*, p. 84.

51   Linzey: *Christianity and the Rights of Animals*, p. 84.

52   Linzey sets his discussion of animal rights in the context of the idea of a covenant community between God and all creatures. Linzey: *Christianity and the Rights of Animals*, pp. 29–39, 85.

53   Linzey: *Christianity and the Rights of Animals*, p. 86. This seems to be a Christian version of Regan's idea of 'subjects of a life'. Clare Palmer suggests that Linzey gives animals inherent value by their capacity to respond to God. However, this is as problematic as other attempts by Singer and Regan to found ethics based on specific capacities possessed by individuals. See C. Palmer: 'Animals in Christian Ethics: Developing a Relational Approach', *Ecotheology*, 7:2 (2003), p. 168.

54   Linzey: *Christianity and the Rights of Animals*, pp. 90–1.

55   He qualifies this suggestion by allowing for the fact that while it is the best way of defining the divine imperative for now, it may be superseded in the future by other theological alternatives. Moreover, it may not be fully comprehensive. Linzey: *Christianity and the Rights of Animals*, pp. 94–5.

56   Linzey: *Christianity and the Rights of Animals*, pp. 97–8.

57   Linzey, 'Animal Rights', p. 31.

58   C. Deane-Drummond: *Creation through Wisdom: Theology and the New Biology* (Edinburgh: T & T Clark, 2000).

59   Linzey: *Animal Rites*, p. 45.

60   A. Linzey: 'The Theological Basis for Animal Rights', *The Christian Century*, 9 October (1991), pp. 906–9, see p. 908

61   R. Bauckham: 'Joining Creation's Praise', *Ecotheology*, 7:1 (2002), pp. 45–59, citation p. 49.

62   A. Linzey: *Animal Theology* (London: SCM Press, 1994), pp. 50–2.

63   Linzey: 'Animal Rights', p. 32.

64   Linzey: 'Animal Rights', p. 32.

65   Linzey: 'Animal Rights', p. 32.

66   Linzey: 'Animal Rights', p. 32.

67   Rosalind Hursthouse comments after a chapter on virtue ethics in her latest book: 'Given the relatively recent appearance of virtue ethics on the scene, what you have just read is so far (as I write in 1999) the only available application of virtue ethics to our treatment of animals.' Hursthouse: *Ethics, Humans and Other Animals*, p. 164.

68   Clare Palmer criticizes Linzey for his focus on rights, rather than on relationships. However, while I agree with her observation that a rights approach shifts attention away from relationships, his theme of generosity attempts to counter it, though it remains unsuccessful, as it is still wedded to a hierarchical view of the relationship between humanity and nature, expressed in terms of humanity as priests of creation. See C. Palmer: 'Animals in Christian Ethics', pp. 164–86.

69   Linzey's rendering of God in hierarchical terms is also criticized strongly by Clare Palmer. However, I doubt that he can really be characterized as portraying God as

'absolute power', since he also stresses the idea of the suffering and compassion of God. While Palmer notes that this is inconsistent, it seems to me that his view is hierarchical and anthropocentric, but not as absolutist as she implies. See Palmer: 'Animals in Christian Ethics', p. 171.

70 Clark: *Animals and Their Moral Standing*, p. 2. Clark does suggest that animals do have rights, but he does not usually choose to argue for their worth on this basis: see pp. 9ff. See, however, 'The Rights of Wild Things', pp. 16–30. He also, significantly, suggests that rights only make sense in the context of *cosmic* democracy. *Animals and Their Moral Standing*, pp. 70–86.

71 S. Clark: *The Moral Status of Animals* (Oxford: Clarendon, 1977), p. 183.

72 Clark: *The Moral Status of Animals*, p. 183.

73 See especially Clark: *The Political Animal*. Here he argues the case for considering the significance of particular bonds with family and our non-human companions.

74 Clark: *The Moral Status of Animals*, p. 106.

75 Clark: *The Moral Status of Animals*, p. 108. I am less nervous than Clare Palmer seems to be in extending ethical concern about animals to wider ecological considerations of the relationship between humanity and the environment, while recognizing, like she does, that domestication is significant and introduces different obligations compared with human relationships with wild animals. See Palmer: 'Animals in Christian Ethics', pp. 176–7.

76 Clark: *The Moral Status of Animals*, p. 167.

77 Clark: *The Moral Status of Animals*, p. 168.

78 Palmer: 'Animals in Christian Ethics', p. 170.

79 I will be coming back to a critical discussion of the aesthetic basis for value in the final chapter.

80 Clark: *The Moral Status of Animals*, p. 168.

81 Aquinas, *Summa Theologiae*, Part 2, Qu. 64.1, cited in A. Linzey and T. Regan, eds: *Animals and Christianity* (London: SPCK, 1989), p. 125.

82 Aquinas, *Summa Theologiae*, Part 2, Qu. 65.3; cited in Linzey and Regan: *Animals and Christianity*, pp. 125–7.

83 For comment on this aspect of Aquinas's thinking on animals, see R. Rudd: *Biology, Ethics and Animals* (New York: Oxford University Press, 1990), pp. 224–7.

84 Aquinas: *Summa Contra Gentiles*, 11, 68, cited in J. Barad: *Aquinas, On the Nature and Treatment of Animals* (London and San Francisco: International Scholars Publications, 1995), p. 39.

85 Barad: *Aquinas*, pp. 41–2.

86 This reinforces the point I made above, that one of the reasons why Aquinas is so harsh in his disposition towards animals is that he assumed they were incapable of anything other than 'selfish' behaviour. Of course, he was likely to be wrong in this assumption, as higher animals show tendencies towards altruism that are implicit forms of that found in humans, though the capacity for true altruism is also particularly noticeable when altruism is defined according to the Christian tradition. How far 'selfish' genes can explain animal altruism is also a matter for scientific debate. See C. Grant: *Altruism and Christian Ethics* (Cambridge: Cambridge University Press, 2001).

87 Barad: *Aquinas*, pp. 46–7.

88 Barad: *Aquinas*, p. 49.

89 Barad has not taken branch theory into account in her affirmation of Aquinas's ontology in terms of evolutionary ideas.

90   See note 104 below.

91   Gustafson strongly objects to Aquinas's chain of being on the basis that it implies
     dependence, rather than interdependence, and ignores the possibility of altering the
     natural order. Janet Porter believes that James Gustafson has seriously misunderstood
     Aquinas in this respect, believing that local ecological variations are perfectly com-
     mensurate with Aquinas's understanding of a chain of being. In other words, ecologi-
     cal interdependence is still feasible in Aquinas's account. Yet in as much as Gustafson
     may be referring to the ability to *change* the natural order by genetic mixing between
     species, he is correct to assert that this goes against the concept of a 'fixed' chain of
     being. None the less, even in this respect Aquinas does not regard 'fixity' as 'immut-
     ability'. See J. Gustafson: *Ethics from a Theocentric Perspective. Volume 2: Ethics and
     Theology* (London: University of Chicago Press, 1984), pp. 57–8; J. Porter: *The
     Recovery of Virtue* (London: SPCK, 1990), pp. 52, 60–2.

92   This view is implicit in many contemporary studies of animal behaviour, especially in
     the primates.

93   Aquinas: *Compendium Theologica*, trans. C. Vollert (London: B. Herder, 1947), p. 80
     (also cited in Barad: *Aquinas*, p. 50).

94   Aquinas: *Summa Theologiae, volume 11, Man*, trans. T. Suttor (London: Blackfriars,
     1970), 1a, Qu. 75.1.

95   Barad: *Aquinas*, pp. 55–76. The idea that there might be a 'life principle' or 'vitalism'
     within nature was rejected early on in the history of biology. See C. Deane-Drummond:
     Biology and Theology Today: Exploring the Boundaries (London: SCM Press), pp. 3, 45.
     Does Aquinas support vitalism? Barad seems to think that he does, in that vegetative
     souls are generated from the potency of matter, and sensitive souls, somewhat bizarrely,
     come from the power of life in the semen. He also believed that in human develop-
     ment human embryos acquire a vegetative, then sensitive, then rational soul. This
     reflects the archaic biology and epigenetic teaching that he inherited from Aristotle,
     though he seemed to differ from Aristotle in allowing for some change in nature due
     to 'accidental failures', by 'unanticipated sets of circumstances'. (Aquinas: *On Truth*,
     23.2). Rational souls, on the other hand, are infused directly by God. Barad describes
     Aquinas as supporting the idea of a soul as 'the principle of life'; see Barad: *Aquinas*,
     p. 32. Unlike the Manicheans, he rejected a dualistic separation of the spiritual from
     the material. While this is a welcome aspect of his theology, his understanding of
     ensoulment in as much as it leans towards a principle of vitalism is problematic
     and needs to be adjusted in the light of modern biological theory. Barad does not
     consider this difficulty in relation to the ensoulment of non-human creatures. The
     possibility suggested by Barad that Aquinas believed that humans had animal souls
     prior to having rational souls is interesting, but pure speculation; see Barad: *Animals*,
     p. 34.

96   For further discussion of this point, see M. Atkins: 'Could There Be Squirrels in
     Heaven?', *Theology in Green*, October (1992), pp. 17–28.

97   Aquinas: *Disputed Questions Concerning Evil*, trans. R. Ingardia, 1, Qu. 80.1.

98   Aquinas: *Commentary on de Anima*, Lectio 5, cited in Barad: *Aquinas*, p. 108.

99   Aquinas: *Summa Theologiae, volume 21, Fear and Anger*, trans. J. P. Reid, (London:
     Blackfriars, 1965), 1a2ae, Qu. 40.3.

100 Aquinas, *Summa Theologiae, volume 21*, 1a2ae, Qu. 46.4.

101 Barad: *Aquinas*, pp. 110–11.

102 Barad: *Aquinas*, pp. 81–3.

103 Aquinas: *Summa Theologiae, volume 11,* 1a, Qu. 79.1. He suggests here that 'appetite shares something with intellect and something with sense so far as acting with or without a bodily organ is concerned, for appetite depends on knowledge'.

104 Barad: *Aquinas,* p. 84.

105 A full discussion of the relationship between evolutionary science and Christian theology is outside the scope of this chapter. It is sufficient to note that evolutionary ideas are not necessarily incompatible with a theist interpretation of creation; in other words, evolution becomes the means through which God has created the world. The materialistic assumptions implicit in scientific evolutionary ideas need to be rejected in the light of Christian theology; that is, the goal of evolution is one that can be affirmed as good, just as Aquinas believed that the goal of life is one directed towards the good in the moral sphere and truth in the ontological sphere.

106 Aquinas seems to link any intellectual activity in animals with bodily organs (Aquinas: *Summa Contra Gentiles, book 2: Creation,* trans. James Anderson (Notre Dame, IN: University of Notre Dame Press, 1975), chapter 68, para. 11. Judith Barad is likely to be mistaken in arguing specifically for 'prudence' in animals according to Aquinas. While, in the *Summa,* he does cite Aristotle initially in the claim that 'animals have a kind of prudence', later in the article he draws back from this suggestion and qualifies prudence by suggesting that 'we conclude it is not in us by nature', since it is about indeterminate means to particular ends, while admitting that 'by natural temperament one may be more discerning than another, as also is the case regarding the conclusions of the theoretic sciences'. But 'with animals the ways of reaching an end are determinate, and so we observe that all of the same species act in like manner. This is not the case with men, because their reason, by knowing universals, can reach over to numberless universals'. As such, since Aquinas believed that, in general, animals act through determinate means to an end, it is difficult to envisage in them any quality approaching prudence. He recognized that animals had an estimative sense, which qualifies this, though not sufficiently to imply prudence. His views on animals acting simply through 'determinate' means were in ignorance of contemporary primatology studies that I discuss further below. Aquinas: *Summa Theologiae, volume 36, Prudence,* trans. T. Gilby (London: Blackfriars, 1973), 2a2ae, Qu. 47.15. The suggestion that animals may have a 'natural prudence' in other texts still assumes that the process of deliberation is missing entirely, that judgement arises from a 'natural estimate' and is focused on limited 'objects', so it seems to me that 'prudence' is a confusing term to use in this context. Aquinas: *On Truth,* 24.2, cited in Barad: *Aquinas,* p. 113.

107 Barad: *Aquinas,* p. 90.

108 Barad: *Aquinas,* pp. 97–9. The Blackfriars translation does render this term 'instinct', but it is clear that the term is associated with perception, for 'instinct grasps intentions which are not objects of simple sensation . . . the reason for remembering in animals is an intention of this kind'. Aquinas: *Summa Theologiae, volume 11, Man,* 1a, Qu. 77.3.

109 See, for example, R. W. Bryne, 'Social and Technical Forms of Primate Intelligence', in F. de Waal, ed.: *Tree of Origin: What Primate Behaviour Can Tell Us about Social Evolution* (Cambridge, MA: Harvard University Press, 2001), pp. 147–72. The author suggests that the reason for this ability emerging is most likely to be connected with the need to cope with more complex social interactions. This counters, somewhat, statements by philosophers who have implied that there is no real evolutionary advantage of increased intelligence.

110   Aquinas: *On Kingship to the Kind of Cyprus*, trans. G. Phelan (Toronto: The Pontifical Institute of Medieval Studies, 1949), book 1, chapter 1, cited in Barad: *Aquinas*, p. 103.

111   For further discussion of the development of communication skills in animals, see S. T. Parker and K. R. Gibson, eds: *Language and Intelligence in Monkeys and Apes* (Cambridge: Cambridge University Press, 1990).

112   Barad: *Aquinas*, pp. 123–5.

113   Barad: *Aquinas*, p. 127.

114   See discussion above about animal and plant souls.

115   For a fuller discussion of emotions in animals see M. Nussbaum: *Upheavals of Thought* (Cambridge: Cambridge University Press, 2001), pp. 89–139.

116   Bryne: 'Social and Technical Forms of Primate Intelligence', p. 170.

117   Bryne: 'Social and Technical Forms of Primate Intelligence', p. 158.

118   Bryne: 'Social and Technical Forms of Primate Intelligence', p. 159.

119   R. I. M. Dunbar: 'Brains on Two Legs: Group Size and the Evolution of Intelligence', in de Waal, ed.: *Tree of Origin*, pp. 173–91.

120   Living humans have an average brain size of 1355 cubic centimetres, remarkably close to these human ancestors. Other changes included a 60 per cent increase in the size of females, smaller teeth, smaller guts, arms that were no longer adapted to hanging in trees and longer legs. Males were now only 15 per cent bigger than females. For discussion see R. W. Wrangham: 'Out of the Pan, into the Fire', in de Waal, ed.: *Tree of Origin*, pp. 122–6.

121   The details need not concern us here; the main point is that *Homo sapiens* evolved about 200,000 years ago from earlier human ancestors. See N. M. van Straalen and J. Stein: 'Evolutionary Views on the Biological Basis of Religion', in W. Drees, ed.: *Is Nature Ever Evil? Religion, Science and Value* (London: Routledge, 2003), pp. 321–2.

122   M. Northcott: 'The Moral Standing of Nature and the New Natural Law', in N. Biggar and R. Black, eds: *The Revival of Natural Law: Philosophical, Theological and Ethical Responses* (Aldershot: Ashgate, 2000), pp. 276–7. The implication of this view is that animals could be judged as 'guilty' or 'innocent' of crimes, in relation to either humans or each other, and while such judging by humans of animals did occur in medieval times, Northcott does not follow through the practical implications of this suggestion here.

123   Michael Northcott also believes that the similarities between humans and non-humans are such that non-humans can be considered as having moral agency (personal communication, February 2003). Given the differences in brain size and cognitive abilities of humans and animals, I am more inclined to reject this suggestion, if it means the strong sense of being morally culpable, while recognizing that the differences between humans and other closely related species are not as extreme as was once thought. In other words, some animal behaviours are precursors to what later becomes more sophisticated moral action in humans. Apes show a greater degree of awareness of self and of others' intentions, but this does not amount to moral culpability. As Holmes Rolston suggests, 'We humans do not take our moral standards from nature, nor should we fault nature as though it were moral. That is a category mistake': 'Naturalising and Systematizing Evil', in Drees, ed.: *Is Nature Ever Evil?*, p. 67.

124   For discussion see T. Visak: 'The Normative Relevance of Disputes in Primatology', in Drees, ed.: *Is Nature Ever Evil?*, pp. 313–20.

125   Barad: *Aquinas*, p. 145.

126 Is such a view of the value of creatures' *telos* tenable in the light of knowledge of extinctions during evolutionary processes? I suggest that this is only acceptable in the context of eschatology, which claims that in God all creaturely existence will find a place and value, even the lives of creatures that have had limited histories on planet earth. A full discussion of ecological eschatology is outside the scope of this chapter.

127 Barad: *Aquinas*, pp. 148–9.

128 For Aquinas even non-rational creatures share in Eternal Reason in their own way and 'natural law is nothing other than the sharing in the Eternal Law by intelligent creatures'. This would imply that only intelligent creatures share in natural law in the sense of being subject to it, even though ontologically natural law itself has some correspondence with natural inclinations common to both plants and animals, as discussed in the previous chapter. Aquinas: *Summa Theologiae, volume 28, Law and Political Theory*, trans. T. Gilby (London: Blackfriars, 1966), 1a2ae, Qu. 91.2; Barad: *Aquinas*, pp. 148–9.

129 Crowe suggests that Aquinas defends the 'Ulpian' version of natural law as that which nature has taught all animals, against the definition of his contemporaries, such as Albert the Great, who held that natural law existed for human beings alone. How far this interpretation is correct is a matter of scholarly debate that is outside the scope of this discussion. I will be assuming, for the purposes of the argument here, that the more conservative interpretation is correct. Barad follows Crowe's interpretation as it reinforces her desire to give animals rights. M. Crowe: 'St Thomas and Ulpian's Natural Law', in *St Thomas Aquinas: Commemorative Studies* (Toronto: Pontifical Institute of Medieval Studies, 1974), p. 261. Cited in Barad: *Aquinas*, p. 162.

130 Rights language is a relatively recent historical development in the liberal tradition. See A. MacIntyre: *Whose Justice? Whose Rationality?* (London: Duckworth, 1988), pp. 342–4: 'the lawyers, not the philosophers, are the clergy of liberalism', p. 344.

131 See earlier section for a discussion of the difference in cognitive ability of humans and animals.

132 Aquinas: *Summa Theologiae, Man*, 1a, Qu. 47.1.

133 Aquinas: *Summa Theologiae, Law and Political Theory*, 1a2ae, Qu. 93.5.

134 A sharing in eternal law is not meant to imply deliberate choice, but a further way of affirming the goodness of all created life.

135 Aquinas: *Summa Theologiae, Man*, 1a, Qu. 45.7.

136 For a full discussion of the various facets of prudence see the introductory chapter.

137 See K. George: 'Should Feminists Be Vegetarians?', *Signs: Journal of Women in Culture and Society*, 19:1 (1994), pp. 405–34.

138 A full discussion of the political implications is outside the scope of this chapter; for a creative integration of theology, politics and ecology see P. Scott: *A Political Theology of Nature* (Cambridge: Cambridge University Press, 2003).

139 Deane-Drummond: *Creation through Wisdom*, pp. 142–3.

140 See, for example, Palmer: 'Animals in Christian Ethics'. I will return to the feminist discussion of care as a basis for ethics again in chapter 8.

141 F. de Waal: *Good Natured: The Origins of Right and Wrong in Humans and Other Animals* (Cambridge, MA: Harvard University Press, 1996), p. 212.

142 De Waal: *Good Natured*, p. 215.

143 M. Warren: *Moral Status: Obligations to Persons and Other Living Things* (Oxford: Oxford University Press, 1997), p. 229.

144 Warren: *Moral Status*, p. 239.

145 Warren: *Moral Status*, p. 238.

Chapter 4

The Ethics of Biotechnology

The boom in biotechnology at the close of the twentieth century and the dawn of the new millennium is likely to continue to challenge the way we think of ourselves in relation to the natural world. The particular focus of this chapter is on biotechnology as applied to agricultural technology, rather than as applied specifically to genetic manipulation of humans. One of the current debates is how far issues in biotechnology, or more specifically genetic engineering, raise new issues for ethical debate, or whether this technology is simply an extension of traditional methods of cultivation and agriculture that have been practised since the dawn of civilization.[1] However, even if we accept the latter more conservative view, it is possible that a certain threshold will be reached whereby change is no longer considered to be acceptable. Furthermore, slow, more cumulative, changes allow, with hindsight, a reassessment of previous practice that was formerly unchallenged and uncontested.[2] Biotechnology, in common with environmental concern and animal ethics, discussed in the previous two chapters, has strong social and political connotations. It is therefore open to social critique as well as philosophical analysis. Indeed, the politicization of issues in debates such as that around the genetic modification of food is such that it could even be suggested that ethics is irrelevant, and instead the technical and political framings of biotechnology are the only ones really worth considering from a Christian perspective.[3] However, even though I agree that the social and political issues surrounding biotechnology are of crucial importance, this does not mean that there is no need to examine and consider possible ways in which biotechnology exerts a particular *ethical* demand on the relationship between humanity and nature. Indeed, I suggest, further, that it is through considering new ways of approaching such relationships in ethical terms that the ground for political and social reconstruction can gain greater validity. I begin this chapter with a discussion of the ethos of technology, setting out alternative possible philosophical stances towards technology in the light of social and political critique. Such preliminary remarks are important for two reasons. The first is that the discussion of agricultural biotechnology needs to be situated within a wider debate about the ethos of technology and its social ramifications in order to expose more clearly its promise and dangers. Second, it is important to critique alternative approaches to technology in order to show more clearly how my own particular approach, which focuses on the virtues, contrasts with these other alternatives. I build on a discussion of the virtues as set out in previous chapters. I also compare ethical approaches to agricultural biotechnology with different stances in environmental ethics as a way of highlighting points of convergence and divergence. Drawing on earlier discussion, the virtues that I argue are particularly relevant for considerations about biotechnology are wisdom, prudence, justice and wonder.

Jackie Stewart believes that the 'majority of theological comments on the GM [genetically modified] debate so far have concentrated on ethical questions, and there is a tendency to preach to science'.[4] She considers that 'it is clearly absurd to suppose that ethical guidelines for scientists can make any difference whatever to the promotion of GM technology, since they are employees in an industry and their work is within the law'.[5] However, even if it is true that dictates to the scientists themselves will be resisted by those secure in such employment, this does not mean that all ethical considerations about biotechnology are thereby invalidated in the way she seems to imply. In addition, if we believe that natural law is related to positive laws, then ethical and legal considerations need to be considered in dialectic relationship, rather than separately. Donald Bruce's work with the Church of Scotland's Society, Religion and Technology Project shows that biotechnology companies are at least open to ethical discussion and the concerns of Christian churches.[6] Biotechnology, like other commercial enterprises, still falls under the scrutiny of business ethics. Some business practices may not be illegal, but they may well be outside what is acceptable in moral terms. Companies do not like to be judged as immoral, if only because it influences sales. Moreover, the use of animals for biotechnological purposes has a clear ethical component and even if this is a voluntary mandate, it draws on current legislation, as is clear from the Banner Report.[7] In addition, ethical and moral constraints can serve to influence legislation, as parliamentary debates about hunting with dogs have demonstrated in the UK.

From the perspective of Christian ethics it is also useful to consider how far and in what sense there can be an ethics of biotechnology. In thinking through how we value nature and in what sense this might be possible through biotechnology, questions are bound to arise that challenge accepted policy. A radical environmentalism or radical animal rights perspective lends itself to hostility and suspicion of most if not all currently legal practices in agricultural biotechnology.[8] Much of this hostility is couched in terms of the risks to humanity, animals and ecological systems by the new biotechnological innovations. However, underlying this political activism there are more deontological commitments to the principle of affinity with and affirmation of the natural world.[9] The obvious and entirely understandable response of scientists is to challenge some of the details of the risks and emphasize instead the benefits of the new technology.[10] Simple assessment of the risks and benefits of genetic engineering does not take us very far.[11]

There are a number of alternative approaches that are worth considering. The first is to consider what kind of *ethos* is engendered by biotechnology. The relevant domain for discussion in this sphere necessarily includes the social and philosophical framing of biotechnology. Another approach is to review the way this ethos relates to alternative values found in ecology, discussed in chapter 2. Can the *clash in values* between commitment to biotechnology or ecology help us to discern some of the reasons for the hostility generated in the public debates to date? A third approach is to consider particular *virtues* that we need to recover in order to evaluate biotechnology. The virtues that I suggest are particularly relevant are wisdom/ prudence, justice and wonder. It is through consideration of such virtues that particular examples of biotechnological practice can be scrutinized. Of course, policy change requires more than just an urge to recover particular virtues.[12] However, I suggest that without the appropriate ethical grounding for such change there is little impetus for reform. In addition, it is vital that a sense of the public and political dimensions of biotechnology forms the backcloth to the discussions about virtue if the latter are to make practical differences in policy-making.

The Ethos of Biotechnology

Biotechnology, as its name implies, shares some common ground with the field of technology as such. Analysis of the philosophy of technology is therefore pertinent to understanding the particular ethos of biotechnology. Martin Heidegger offered an existentialist critique of technology based on what he saw as the inevitable growth of technological mastery of the world. He suggested that in contrast to art and craft, which allow for *techne*, or letting nature be itself, technology imposes an ordering on the world without reference to intrinsic meaning.[13] He distinguished between technique, which is the mindset embedded in technology, and technological activity as such. Technology is embedded within a wider horizon of technique.[14] Accordingly, science follows the mindset of technique that *also* shapes technology. The task of humanity for Heidegger seems to be to shift from seeing the world as a 'standing reserve' to be manipulated at will, integral to technique, to viewing the world in terms of *poiesis*, a coming forth that might appear to have some analogy to a theological interpretation of the world as gift from God.[15] The difficulty with this view is that there appear to be two stark alternatives, contemplation and technique, with no room for a realistic appraisal of the social context of technology.[16]

Jacques Ellul also heavily criticized the rise of technology in the West.[17] He suggested that the lack of conformity of nature to the ordered reductionistic ration- ality engendered by 'Technique' inevitably opens up the possibility for catastro- phe.[18] Technology is characterized by artificiality, which amounts to a subordination of nature, similar to Heidegger's analysis. Ellul refers to more social dimensions of technology, such as automatism; that is, it is directed by considerations of efficiency.

He also suggests that it is characterized by self-augmentation – that is, by collective and autonomous decisions – rather than being based on individual creativity, leading to a series of technological 'fixes' to circumvent new problems as they arise. The other features of technology that he highlights relate to shared values in technology that he calls 'monism', leading to technological integration and ultimately technological universalism. For Ellul the developing 'rationality' is a form of 'unreason' in features such as the pressure for change for its own sake, growth and speed. Jackie Stewart has highlighted the significance of Ellul for challenging the claim made by GM proponents that they are able to feed the world through the new biotechnology. Even though Stewart seems to distance herself from specific ethical considerations of biotechnology, I suggest that if it is true that the *values* engendered by biotechnology are the ones described by Ellul, then this inevitably has serious ethical implications.

Albert Borgmann believes that a way out of the negative tendencies in technology is to recover 'focal things and practices' that centre our lives in such a way that we are offered an alternative to the dominant mode of technology.[19] He suggests that the 'substantive' view of Ellul amounts to a 'demonizing' of technology.[20] Borgmann's view that technology is embedded in ordinary existence is worth taking seriously. However, like Heidegger and Ellul, he still seems to have a strong view of the power of technology. He suggests, for example, that the Aristotelian distinction between technology as human making or artefact and human doing such as political, religious and moral action no longer applies, for 'Human making has overgrown and suffocated human doing, truly political action in particular.'[21] Moreover, he likens technology to that which 'invades' the whole of our culture; for him the view that it is simply the way humans intervene in nature is too limited a view of the power of technology. The natural world, in particular the wilderness, becomes like 'islands in an ocean of technology'.[22] But the irony is that even through a wilderness experience, 'what really keeps us warm and nourished in the wilderness of nature are the blessings of technology, hiking boots, back packs, tents, stoves, freeze-dried foods, and all other compact light weight and efficient devices that we carry into the wilderness'.[23] In a manner rather akin to Heidegger, he offers a romantic alternative, but while technology may overcome nature it cannot overcome its beauty. Like other environmental ethicists such as Holmes Rolston, he seems to venerate the raw beauty of the 'wilderness' experience as a way of providing energy against the more negative elements in technology.[24] However, the wilderness is not the only 'focal' thing, and others might include music, gardening or running, even what he calls the 'culture of the table', rather than fast food.[25] He is hopeful that the excesses of technology will thereby become pruned and limited to its proper role in society. Peter Scott argues that the cogency of Borgmann's analysis depends in part on the relationship between the sacred and the profane, where focal things are similar in character to Paul Tillich's notion of ultimate concern.[26]

How accurate are these pictures of technology and do they apply specifically to biotechnology as well? One of the important questions to ask is how far such critiques of technology depend on particular essentialist readings. Andrew Feenberg finds such essentialism in Heidegger, Ellul and Borgmann.[27] In the first place, he argues that the essence of technology is not necessarily the obsession with rationality and efficiency in the way that essentialism implies. The substantive view of Heidegger is that nothing escapes from the culture of control engendered by technology, echoing Max Weber's concept of the 'iron cage' of rationalism.[28] When technological advance is described as automatic and unilinear in character, with a bias towards domination, then this amounts to essentialism. Feenberg challenges the idea that we are necessarily more 'rational' and orientated towards control than are earlier societies.[29] If Feenberg is wrong and contemporary society is dominated by the desire to control, then the alternative would be to develop virtues that are more in tune with the natural world, but without caving in to romantic perceptions of it. If he is right then the opposite of the kind of essentialism that is implied by Ellul and others is modernity's assumption of instrumentalism, which treats technology as neutral and value-free.[30] The belief that technology is value-free is congenial to liberal democratic traditions, where the state provides the means for a good life, but the pursuit of values is a private matter.[31] In this case the ends of technology are brushed aside and the ability of technology to change political policies is not taken into account. The popular understanding of technology, namely that it is simply applied science, is likely to be far too simplistic. In particular, Borgmann suggests that, 'if we accept the realistic view of science and admit that what our current scientific theories and explanations say of the world is true, then we must also admit that technology, if it is the necessary consequence or companion of science, is equally true'.[32]

Borgmann argues that in view of the fact that technology harbours forces that cannot be delineated by modern science, 'scientific knowledge is a necessary condition of modern technology, it is not, however, sufficient'.[33] However, the relationship between science and technology he envisages still implies a movement from science to technology, rather than the other way round. One of the unique features of *bio*technology is that the discoveries made in the service of application also contribute to scientific knowledge in unexpected ways. The cloning of Dolly the sheep, which I will discuss in the next chapter, is one example of this tendency. Hence those engaged in biotechnology can properly be referred to as scientists, even though their aims may be practical rather than theoretical. The view that science is value-free has come under considerable scrutiny and is less likely to be accepted by most contemporary scientists.[34] If science is inseparable from values, should science be re-evaluated according to the goals of wisdom? Much the same could be said of technology, though Mary Midgley has pointed to the tendency for scientists to abrogate responsibility for the way their discoveries are used.[35]

Of course, the application of science involves a far more complex social process than simply scientific decision-making. An alternative, more realistic, view of technology according to constructivists is that technology is neither autonomous nor neutral, but dependent on particular social origins. While at the design stage a whole range of personnel are involved in the creation of new technology, including business personnel, technicians, customers, politicians and bureaucrats, eventually a product adapts to a socially recognized demand and there is a 'closure', the social origins are forgotten and it becomes an accepted part of culture. What is of interest in this respect is the way particular products may in fact be rejected if there is sufficient public pressure against the adoption of the new technology. The sale of GM paste in Sainsbury's and other supermarkets from 1996 to 1999 and the withdrawal of all GM products from other food chains such as Iceland is a good example of the way public pressure has resisted technological change. In this it could be argued that consumers are exercising their own form of discernment, in this case a rejection of the validity of GM crops.

This leads to a different understanding of technology, namely that it is possible to arrive at a form of democratized technology.[36] The advantage of this view of technology is that it allows for appraisal and critique of technology as part of the social process of change. One could argue that where there is insufficient democratization of technology then as a last resort the public, as the above example suggests, will reject it. Where citizens are involved in action related to technical design then particular advances that favour opportunities for participation are likely to be encouraged, rather than alternatives that favour the autonomy of technical personnel. The importance of public engagement with new technologies may be dismissed, but Feenberg suggests that this is a very thin view of what democracy means: 'All too often public interventions into technology are dismissed as non-political or, worse yet, undemocratic because they mobilise only small minorities. Such movements never really satisfy thin democracy which emphasises rights and representation to the exclusion of the central role of citizen action.'[37]

This seems to me to offer a much more positive way of approaching technology compared with the essentialist critique, in that according to the former view it is possible to reformulate technology in the light of the common good. Of course, Ellul warns of potential dangers that may exist in technological thinking and the tendency, in particular, for limited means to become ends in themselves. However, I suggest that it is not simply a faulty collusion of ends and means, but the ends claimed need to be subject to critical appraisal. For example, where the claim to feed the world is offered as an incentive for yet more GM foods, the claim itself must be subject to ethical scrutiny. The real *motivation* behind the claim is the maximization of profit.[38] A similar situation exists in biotechnological innovations used in medical science. While few would deny the positive beneficial effects for medical science, the claim that the purpose behind such developments is just altruistic is oversimplified. In these cases any claim that the purpose is to alleviate suffering has to be evaluated in the light of the practical reality of the workings of business in the market economy.[39]

There are examples of disingenuous claims for environmental benefits of genetic modification of crops that are parroted in order to lend support for the genetic modification of plants.[40] Hence the ethical critique of biotechnology necessarily must include a critique of the *motivation* and *attitudes* of those involved. In some cases there may be genuine delusion about the likely benefits, in others there may be deliberate economizing with the truth in order to win public or political support. While such claims may not be illegal, they are certainly misleading. Such tendencies suggest the need to encourage a virtue ethic approach to biotechnology; it is an example of what Aquinas would term sham prudence. In addition, testing the merits of genetic engineering in narrow terms as that which simply overcomes human suffering is in itself mistaken. Peter Scott makes this point forcefully, wanting 'to argue the radical case that developments in genetic engineering must be tested not narrowly against the laudable desire to overcome human suffering but more widely by the "social" and "natural" goods secured by technologies of genetic engineering and by technologies in general'.[41] The question of how such tests might be carried out takes us into the province of the virtues, in particular the virtues of wisdom, prudence and justice. Such virtues, when embedded in social and political discourse, become ways of evaluating biotechnology that avoid the impasse expressed in the alternatives of romanticism opposed to essentialist technology or technology as neutral and value-free. Virtue ethicists have been criticized for not taking due account of the social and political order in which decisions are made, but once it is allowed that prudence is also relevant in the political sphere and justice is a virtue then it becomes possible to expand the concept of a democratized technology.

A Recovery of Wisdom

While there are a variety of ways of thinking about wisdom, I suggest that a wisdom ethic drawing on the works of Thomas Aquinas gives significant insights about the way to think about biotechnology.[42] Wisdom is one of the three intellectual virtues of speculative reason, the others being understanding, or grasping first principles, and *scientia*, or science, which denotes the comprehension of the causes of things and the relationship between them. Wisdom is the understanding of the fundamental causes of everything and their relationship to everything else. In alignment with practical wisdom or prudence, wisdom gives a means through which relationships, attitudes and motivations can be assessed. Psychologists have identified a subtlety to the thought processes in wise individuals, as well as a heightened awareness of motivations and the ability to integrate different forms of knowledge.[43] In Aquinas wisdom is expressed theologically, for God is the ultimate cause of all that exists in view of the fact that God is creator. Human wisdom is a virtue directed towards the Wisdom of God, for while wisdom can be learned it cannot be grasped or used for human aggrandisement. In the fullest sense human wisdom is only possible through the gift of the Holy Spirit by the grace of God.

Wisdom is closely related to one of the intellectual virtues of practical reason, namely prudence or practical wisdom. I have discussed the core elements of prudence in the introductory chapter and shown how distortions at any stage could lead to unethical decisions and actions. Prudence is particularly significant for ethics, since it sets the way individual virtues need to be expressed in particular circumstances. For example, prudence comes into play in discerning what is the most appropriate way of acting in given circumstances, moving through deliberation, judgement and action. The dialectic of prudence, which includes contemplative activity through to reasoned action, is particularly important in dealing with the ethics of technology, for the critical lens of ethical reflection is not confined to one or other stage in the process, but includes the full sweep of activity in a holistic way. Prudence as both individual and cooperative (political) refuses just to lay responsibility on individuals and individual ethical choices, but sets such ethical decision-making and acting in the context of the common good. Virtuous behaviour or its opposite may, in some circumstances, be related to the means of attaining a particular goal. For example, a company that genetically engineers seed so that it is sterile in order to force farmers to buy new seed every year from the same company could be seen as an inappropriate means in order to attain the goal of maximum profits.[44] The goal itself may also be challenged as an expression of imprudence where it eclipses other good goals, such as respect for the needs of the local community. In this case prudence may have decided that sterile seed is the best way of attaining the goal, but because the goal is not for the overall good of the community as a whole, this leads to what Aquinas describes as 'sham prudence'.[45] Perhaps more accurately we could say that the goal is a *partial* good, for it benefits relatively few people. It may also be a result of thoughtlessness or undue haste or failure of resolve, in which case this would be imprudence or 'incomplete prudence'. These distorted forms of prudence are worth bearing in mind, since from the perspective of a biotechnology company an action could look like it is entirely prudent. However, once the wider needs of the community are taken into account, prudence is shown to be incomplete.[46] In this scenario prudence relates strongly to justice, which I will discuss further below. Prudence may also be marred by exaggerated passions, which then further distort the use of reason and block the expression of prudence. A particular passion for expanding the area of knowledge of genetics, for example, may lead to a lack of sensitivity towards the social effects of its development.[47]

Virtues are subtler than exploring the consequences of actions according to crude cost–benefit analysis approaches, in that expressing a particular virtue cannot necessarily always be described through means and ends type of analysis. What would count as behaving virtuously in the context of the practice of science and technology? While the goals of genetic engineering and the means of attaining such goals may come under scrutiny through prudence, the humility to accept that the public may have important insights into social issues, the courage to challenge developments in those cases where the opinion of local farming communities have not been taken into account, actions such as these are not readily analysed simply in terms of means and ends. Prudence is also significant in that it necessarily leads to action, in contrast with art, which is simply the skill in making judgements.

Prudence includes a number of characteristics that are worth pondering in the context of biotechnology. Aquinas draws on five areas related to knowing, namely memory, reason, understanding, aptness to being taught and ingenuity. Clearly reason, understanding and ingenuity all come into play in developing new bio-technological methods for use in the plant and animal worlds. Yet these charac-teristics alone are not sufficient for prudence, since it includes memory as well. The ability to remember is associated with appreciation of history and tradition. The memory is used in a selective way in devising new technologies. From a historical perspective biotechnology has emerged as one more example of the way human-kind engages with the natural world. However, as Michael Northcott points out, it cannot be isolated from the social context of the culture of modern industrial farming.[48] While it may not be possible to return to earlier idealized communities, a deeper sense of relatedness to the land would shift what is envisaged in terms of prudence. I return to a discussion of this aspect in the section below on biotechnology and ecology.

The three areas of prudence that are related to doing include foresight, circum-spection and caution, or avoiding obstacles. Foresight ideally is free from particular biases and is able to discern how far the intended aim matches the overall goal of human life of ultimate goodness. Where these goals are narrowly portrayed in terms of the particular products of technology, then foresight is distorted. For example, does the introduction of vital vitamins to rice and other staple crops grown in the poorer nations of the world really solve the problem of nutrition in these nations? A technological fix can only be a temporary and even partial solu-tion, for it ignores the fact that world hunger is more often than not the result of economic and social problems. Even expecting multinational companies to solve the world food crisis is a failure of foresight, for it assumes that they will behave altruistically rather than be driven by market forces.[49] Circumspection is the ability to attend to circumstances, and will reflect a clear perception of the reality that is involved. For example, the decision of British governments to close down state-funded research into the development of GM technologies and rely instead on private investment exacerbates the problem of lack of adequate controls into re-search on the safety of GM crop trials.[50] Finally, prudence also expresses caution, or avoiding obstacles. There are numerous examples in genetic technology where there are clear risks involved. Where these risks are exaggerated, this amounts to a distortion of prudence. For example, many scientists consider that the research published by Dr Arpad Pusztai claiming that a modified lectin gene causes adverse effects in rats was not sufficiently subject to normal peer review and scrutiny prior to publication.[51] Moreover, campaigners and the media have used his later work to make irresponsible claims that genetic modification causes serious intestinal infec-tion in rats, when in fact his research simply describes the structure of the small intestine.[52] The precautionary principle is one frequently adopted by committees adjudicating on whether or not to approve particular developments in GM re-search. It is commonly defined as 'a strategy for dealing with environmental risk and uncertainty, which guides us to act cautiously and embark on a systematic programme of research to improve our understanding of the costs and benefits of particular actions'.[53] Of course, in this particular case the goal is defined simply in terms of costs and benefits, but the key element here is the idea of caution when it comes to assessing the merits or otherwise of genetic modification. Unfortunately, when risk is simply assessed in terms of costs, risks that cannot be easily quantified either because they are long term or because they act in synergy with other environmental or genetic influences are likely to be overlooked.[54]

The Significance of Justice as Virtue

I have argued throughout this book that justice is an appropriate companion to prudence and wisdom in framing appropriate ethical action. I traced the contours of justice as virtue in chapter 1, the nature of ecological justice in chapter 2 and the shift towards moral considerability of animals in chapter 3. I also suggested that since consideration of human treatment of animals falls under the remit of the natural law, since all creatures are subject to eternal law, humanity has particular duties towards others, including animals. But how might justice be particularly related to issues in biotechnology? Given that I have argued that the technological context in which biotechnology needs to be discussed is that of a democratic political society, in a just order, each is given his or her due. I therefore part company with Aquinas's view of monarchic social order as a social good, though I suggest that his theory of justice as virtue can be translated into a different political context. The logic of Aquinas's ontology allows us to extend the bounds of justice *towards* animals, by adjusting the secondary precepts of the natural law tradition.[55] This does not mean that animals will be able to express the virtue of justice and I argue against the possibility that animals express traces of prudence. Rather, the human virtue of justice can take into account the importance of the non-human species as part of the overall ecological community in which a democratic community is situated. Prudence is necessarily prior to considerations of justice, for without prudence there can be no sense of the right means towards justice becoming established, and the mean of justice, in other words what is a just action in particular circumstances. On the other hand, an act may be an act of fortitude, but where a risk is taken as part of the obligation owed to a community, then the act is also necessarily an act of justice.

How does justice relate not just to practical wisdom (prudence), but also to the virtue of speculative reason? The ancient sages were well aware of the link between justice and wisdom, indeed Proverbs personifies Lady wisdom as one who 'By me monarchs rule and princes issue just laws; by me rulers govern and the great impose justice on the world.'[56] In the monarchical society of the time, kingship, wisdom and justice were intertwined. I suggest that a more appropriate framework for thinking about the relationship between humanity and the natural world today is *kinship*, rather than *kingship*, but this shift need not deny the basic principle of linking justice and wisdom. Virtue ethicists have tended to associate justice with Kantian ethics, but for Aquinas justice is *also* a virtue to be acquired, alongside prudence or practical wisdom.[57] Indeed, when justice is defined in association with natural law, it no longer makes logical sense to speak of justice simply as that directed towards future generations, which is the premise of much environmental concern.[58] Wilfred Beckerman and Joanna Pasek are then forced to concede that additional ethical resources are required in order to elucidate obligations, and while they hint at the possibility of virtue theory making a contribution in this respect, it is not filled out in any detail and they also seem to assume that justice is not a virtue.[59] Of course, unlike the other virtues, justice also has an objective basis through particular acts that could be characterized as just or not.[60] In this sense justice moves away from virtue ethics *sensu stricto* in terms of agents and attitudes towards a more deontological position.[61] In a similar way I indicated earlier that consequences are also taken into account in making prudential choices. Yet in the same way that those following Kantian views can take into account some of the advantages gained through virtue ethics, so I suggest that it is possible to incorporate ideas about what counts as justice without losing the emphasis on the importance of the virtues. In a just order, each is given his or her due. This once again raises the priority of consideration of the needs of the poor when reflecting on biotechnological intervention, as well as consideration of non-human creatures and the wider environment. Once justice is considered to be a virtue it no longer has to be associated so closely with the language of rights.[62] The human virtue of justice, understood in terms of human obligations, can take into account the importance of the non-human species as part of the overall ecological community.

What are the duties of justice as virtue in relation to the 'others' in the community of life? Certainly, there may be *legally* binding actions that have to be undertaken, that are more based on particular objective rules, but there are *morally* binding ones as well that are more closely aligned with attitudes of the agents. Even within the moral sphere it is possible to distinguish that which is *dishonourable* as opposed to that which is *unseemly*. The distinction between these various forms of justice as virtue can be illustrated as follows. Ten thousand hectares of genetically engineered cotton was found growing in India in the western state of Gujarat.[63] The cotton had been genetically engineered to resist the bollworm using a gene from *Bacillus thuringiensis*. This gene (Bt) acts like an insecticide in the plants, so that they are no longer infected. The farmers purchased their seed from Navbharat, a company that originally purchased seed from the larger Maharashtra Hybrid Seeds Company, Mahyco. Monsato has a 26 per cent stake in the latter company and the seed is also freely available for purchase in the USA. The row exploded because Monsanto discovered Bt cotton on farms in Gujarat and they had not been paid for the patents. Navbharat could argue that it lacks the technology to detect transgenic strains. From a legal perspective the action of Navbharat is against the law, it is breaking the legal requirement to pay dividends for patents on particular 'inventions', in this case GM cotton. It is not clear if Monsato had been granted an Indian patent on Bt cotton as the work with Mahyco was still at the field trial stage. Mahyco had spent US$8 million on preparing to commercialize Bt cotton for the Indian market. In terms of business ethics Mahyco/Monsato did have their particular 'rights' violated according to patent law. It is also worth asking how far the

Indian regulatory system is able to ensure that the patent can be carried out in terms of monitoring the seed. The report suggests that the capacity for India to monitor breaches of patent law is insufficient, in which case Indian authorities were imprudent in granting a patent in the first place. The call in the report to spend more money (US$2 million) on tightening up the regulation system again begs a number of questions. Indeed, from the perspective of justice in the widest sense it is possible to ask whether the multinational giant Monsanto is *morally* justified in making such demands for patent payments when it is doubtful if India would *ever* have the resources for adequate monitoring.

In addition, actions such as the practice of Western companies indulging in 'gene piracy', or the lifting of genetic resources from poorer nations and then imposing a patent of them, as well as the introduction of particular genetic traits such as 'terminator genes', serve to break down the trust between larger companies and our neighbours in the Southern nations of the world.[64] Both Monsanto's attitude and their action could be said to be *dishonourable* in making demands for payments for patents from nations that can ill afford to pay. In addition, behind the imposition of patent law is the assumption that frameworks adequate for an industrialized Western nation can be applied in a crude way to a poorer 'developing' community. In other words, it raises wider questions about the whole system of patenting as applied on an international level. In addition, it is worth asking what might be the *social* consequences for subsistent farmers growing traditional crops if agricultural practice shifted significantly towards commercial GM crops. The motivation of Monsanto in developing GM cotton for the Indian market was clearly commercial. If the officials on either side behaved in such a way as to express hostility or anger, then such an attitude could be said to be *unseemly*. Justice is violated in this case because it serves to break down relationships in a community. All acts of virtue relate in one sense or another to justice; hence Aquinas refers to justice as the 'most perfect virtue'.[65] In the example just given environmental risks are also evident in this case, so developing cash crops specifically for use in the Indian subcontinent could be said to be an example of ecological injustice. The chairman of an Indian department of biotechnology committee is worried by these developments; accordingly he asks if 'this is a foretaste of a frightening situation where transgenics will be out of control and all over the place'.[66] Yet the 'solution' to this biotechnological problem is to press for Rs100 million to be spent on national laboratories to monitor GM organisms (GMOs). Given the reality of the shortage of funds for other work, is this a just use of resources?

The above example shows that an act of justice can be judged, as it were, from the outside in an objective way. This makes justice different from the other virtues such as temperance or fortitude. Acts of justice are not necessarily affected by particular dispositions towards another; hence it is possible to act justly while not having an inner disposition towards justice. In the above example, it may be that the Indian company mistakenly mixed up the seed used, in which case, while it was a legal injustice according to patent law, it would not render the company unjust. However, the ideal of justice as virtue requires *both* an inner assent to justice and an external just action. Justice also reflects obligations to the community; hence in Aquinas's scheme it is ranked higher than other virtues, such as temperance or fortitude, that relate simply to inner dispositions.

While justice as virtue is the starting point for effective environmental decision-making, consideration of wider concerns of justice locates the virtue in the context of a particular way of thinking in an objective sense about just relationships. Aquinas divided the just ordering in community life first to that between individuals, or commutative justice, second to that between the whole and the individual or distributive justice and third to that between the individual and social whole, or legal justice.[67] This division follows from the fact that the kind of legal protection afforded by the state is different in kind compared with that which is due between individuals. The philosopher Josef Pieper criticizes individualism in not taking sufficient account of the reality of the social whole in making just decisions.[68] On the other hand, there is an equal but opposite danger in collectivism, where no one individual enters a relationship in their own right. In this case no individual is given any right, and therefore none is given any due. The idea of justice collapses in this case. Some forms of deep ecology and Gaian thinking seem to me to lean far too heavily in this direction. Of course, Aquinas's scheme fails to take into account the corporate nature of contemporary existence in so far as today, legally speaking, multinational companies have rights. Hence particular companies have particular responsibilities to act according to the law.

Commutative justice is what is owed to a stranger and follows what is due according to particular contracts. For all intents and purposes commutative justice could be said to apply to biotechnological companies in relation to individuals and their claims for particular demands for what is due in their case. The relationship between parties needs to be one of mutual respect, rather than hostility, so that the task of commutative justice is 'to bring solace and order into the conflict of contending interests which by their nature are legitimate opposites and not easily reconcilable, to impose on them, as it were, a posterior order, is the office and task of commutative justice'.[69]

In the case of GMOs the task of commutative justice would be to ensure that no damage exists to someone or their property as a result of the release of GMOs. However, where accidents happen, such as in the case of accidental contamination of organic farms during field trials of GMOs, then compensation would be required, since some recompense needs to be made. Of course, this presupposes that it is *possible* for GMO field trials to take place without any risk of contamination. Given the close proximity of different farming practices in countries such as the UK, this may not be feasible. In this scenario, it might be possible to argue for 'organic-free zones' as well as 'GM-free zones', though the location of such sites would be heavily contested. The just person needs to recognize the wrong committed, admit to the injustice and endeavour to eradicate it. The problem in the case of organic farming is that both organic and non-organic farmers claim an equal right to practise farming according to particular principles, though an assessment of risk to organic farmers would seem to be prudent prior to approval of field trials.

The case of multinationals also crosses into a second area of justice, namely distributive justice, since this describes the relationship between those who have power and those who are in some sense 'delivered' to this power. Arguably, it might be contested that multinationals now have more power even than governments over the day-to-day working of the lives of ordinary peoples. Since biotechnology is governed largely by the work of multinationals and in some cases central government as well, the responsibility for just action is necessarily one of distributive justice. The difference is that whereas in the classic understanding of distributive justice, what belongs to an individual is a share in what belongs to everyone, for a multinational, apart from its relationship to its own employees or stakeholders, the individual has no share or part in its activities, except in so far as the flourishing of the company boosts the overall economy of the state as a whole.

Those who are guardians of the common weal calculate what is due to the individual in the case of distributive justice. For state-rendered compensation, particular subjects of particular grievances are taken into account in a way that is not true of commutative justice. Yet where those who are responsible do not exercise their powers justly, injustice reigns. Where the law of the state restrains multinationals to act responsibly towards individuals and the environment, one can expect some measure of justice to ensue. However, what happens in those situations where state law is less regulated? A good example is the relative lack of regulations on the safe use of chemicals, fertilizers and GM crops in the poorer nations of the world. The Nuffield Council on Bioethics report states that 'developing countries have less well developed regulatory structures and expertise to manage the introduction of GM crops appropriately'.[70] In this situation it relies on justice being exercised by the multinational companies towards the strangers, in this case those living in such nations. The parties to the Global Convention on Biodiversity (CBD) are seeking through difficult negotiations to adopt a Biosafety Protocol. However, while this may act like 'a first line of defence', it relies on members being part of this wider global community. In these instances, international bodies also contribute to the working out of justice and this raises the question as to what the common good might be.

As long as sufficient account is taken of prudence *in all its manifold aspects*, there may be examples where the introduction of GM foods *does* meet the requirements for justice. Clearly, justice would include access to the goods of biotechnology, but this is necessarily set in the context of wider social and environmental concern that varies from one place to the next.[71] What appears at first sight to be a good may turn out to be equally restricting for farmers in poorer parts of the world. As well as developing seeds that are sterile, an alternative possibility is the production of seeds without any need for fertilization or apomixis.[72] This strategy could allow seed to be used by farmers who are unable to purchase hybrid seed each year, though this depends on patents being granted that are likely to be beyond the means of such farmers. The products of any such crops could be used locally, but, ironically perhaps, could not be sold on a global international market if the patents that were developed in the West were infringed.

Biotechnology and Ecology

The ongoing task of attaining justice through prudence is likely to be a continuous process that is never fully completed. The significance of this is that the ordering according to justice, while it takes into account natural law, is always somewhat provisional, a tentative working towards the good that can never be perfect in this life. There will, in other words, always be wrongs that need to be corrected through the frame of justice outlined above, so that human relationships with each other and the natural world remain somewhat fluid in character, rather than being measured against a fixed and unalterable ordering in the world. This is an important aspect to stress, since interpretation of Aquinas has tended to emphasize the fixity in natural ordering in a way that has not given sufficient room for a more fluid and dynamic view of the natural world. In as much as this fixity exists, it needs to be recognized as culturally specific and bound; in as much as his views allow greater flexibility, then this needs to be welcomed and developed. Josef Pieper, writing about half a century ago, describes the task of the virtue of justice in the following way: 'the fundamental condition of man and his world is provisory, temporary, non-definitive, tentative, as is proved by the "patchwork" character of all historical activity; and that consequently, any claim to erect a definitive and unalterable order in the world must of necessity lead to something inhuman'.[73]

Such a view of justice is important, since it counters any romantic sense that there might be an ordered balance in the natural world to which human beings merely adjust accordingly. In chapter 2 I discussed the way values in ecological science have shifted away from the idea of ecosystems as stable equilibrium communities and more to a view that ecosystems are unstable, open to external influences, including that from humans, subject to numerous different controls and disturbance and only at times in an equilibrium state. The values presented in such a view of ecology cohere with the view of justice that I have just described. I am certainly not arguing that we derive our view of justice or the way to order reality from ecological considerations. Rather, in so far as justice *coheres* and is consistent with contemporary ecological science it could be said to reflect the scientific reality of interspecific relationships. It would be much more difficult to argue for a fixed ordering of justice according to a rigid description of natural law given the current understanding of ecology.

While I have suggested that ecological thinking has shifted compared with earlier models for ecology, this allows a more thorough appraisal of the values in biotechnology. Biotechnologists could counter the previous idea in ecology of fixed ecosystems in equilibrium as an overly romantic view of social relationships. The new model of ecology allows for some human influences; hence some biotechnology is justified. It is not simply ruled out of court because it is apparently against a predetermined 'order', or, to express it more theologically, against God's providential plan for existence. The idea that there might be an original divine order sanctioned through notions such as the Sabbath finds currency among those influenced by Barthian theology.[74] On the other hand, such a view can include a sense of God's purpose, or 'rule', where changes in creation are made on the basis of Christian eschatology, rather than simply according to what can be done through human ingenuity. Peter Scott has, rightly in my view, criticized those theologians who portray eschatology simply in terms of the narrow possibilities inherent in science, in particular, genetic engineering.[75] Yet decisions in biotechnology need to be made against the broadest considerations of the common good in human relationships with each other and the non-human world.

The ethical challenge is to convince biotechnologists and all those involved in its implementation of the need for broad discussion of the ethical and social consequences prior to the development of the new technology. Part of the difficulty in making such a change feasible and practicable is that scientists are by nature trained to think in terms of problem-solving for particularly difficult cases. Hence risk–benefit analysis is a logical extension of this kind of mindset, where rational appraisal of consequences mirrors the rational approach to problem-solving, in this case the difficulties of implementation. One way forward would be to acknowledge the ingenuity that is the basis for many biotechnological developments and to give credit where it is due for uncontested cases, such as examples where biotechnology can be used to manufacture drugs and other products for use in medicine and also for a whole host of research activities related to the biological sciences. I suggest that without some understanding of the contribution of biotechnology to the scientific enterprise, any criticism of its social or ecological consequences is likely to fall on deaf ears. On the other hand, the valid concerns of ecologists worried about the possible ecological effects of introducing new transgenic varieties need to be taken into account.[76]

I have argued throughout this chapter that a broader consideration of the virtues helps to move the debates beyond ethical issues couched simply in terms of costs and benefits. While consequences framed accordingly need to be taken into account, a focus on these issues alone leads to a form of gridlock.[77] Instead, the particular virtues associated with biotechnology, namely ingenuity and the use of knowledge, need to be placed in the context of their specific contribution to prudence as a whole, which is inclusive of other ways of knowing in addition to that described. Biotechnology tends to presume a way of relating to the natural world that emphasizes a desire to control the other. It is human manipulation writ large on the tapestry of the natural world. If we think of ourselves as part of a wider ecological community, which interventions are justified and which are not? I have suggested that prudence helps us to make such decisions, but there may be examples where prudential activity is particularly difficult to discern. One case is the use of animals in biotechnological experimental research. How far is this honouring ecological justice? Certainly, for animal rights campaigners, any genetic engineering of animals is equivalent to slavery.[78] On the other hand, those involved in the use of animals in research point to the advances in medicine that have been possible through the use of animals and argue that as long as animals are treated in a 'humane' way, then such experimentation is justified.[79] Ruth Bulger admits to giving 'inherent worth' to animals, but then retracts from making this part of policy as she considers that this is a matter for her own 'personal belief'.[80] It is not entirely obvious why this counts as a personal belief, while other principles such as the humane treatment of animals do not, though she suggests that this is because it is not 'common to all of society'. Yet is the humane treatment of animals necessarily common to all society in the way she suggests? The reduction and replacement of animals for use in experimental research are realistic goals in the context of animal experimental science, but does the goal of humane treatment necessarily limit such processes? The motivation for a move away from the use of animals in biological experimentation has to come from more than just a biocentric philosophy, which she suggests is leading to shifts in opinion among scientists.[81] It is more likely that this ideal of harmony that she labels as coming from the 'Greeks and Native Americans' actually encourages hostility from scientists, rather than change in orientation.

I suggest, instead, that if scientists are going to change their attitude to the treatment of animals in scientific research in general and biotechnology in particular, then a greater appreciation of the virtues of prudence and justice is required. Prudence will include ingenuity, but now it will be a way of countering some of the inhumane experiments that have taken place so far. None the less, credit needs to be given to biotechnologists for the way scientific developments can now take place through the use of tissue culture or other *in vitro* methods, without the need to use live animals.[82] One of the reasons for the shift may be the change in public opinion so that it is more sensitive to the treatment of animals. The animal rights lobby has also become increasingly influential in Britain, even though it has a history going back several hundred years.[83] One of the difficulties with the use of animals for experiments in biotechnology is that the effects of genetic changes, given the currently available techniques, are often indeterminate and unknown.[84] I will discuss the way animals have been used in experiments on cloning in the following chapter, since the ethical issues raised are worth exploring in some detail. I will raise the issue of how far such new innovations reflect an attitude of *curiositas*, and thereby intemperance.

Are there other virtues worth considering that cohere with ecological reality as a way of informing the development of appropriate attitudes to biotechnology? One virtue that is worth serious consideration that John Benson names as an environmental virtue is the ability to wonder.[85] Wonder is an appropriate attitude to foster, in that it encourages particular patterns of behaviour towards the non-human world. While there may be 'extravagantly spectacular' natural phenomena, such as a beautiful sunset, waterfall or rainbow, there are less obvious forms of wonder in the natural world, 'the astonishing variety of living things, the intricacy of their structures and complexity of their behaviour'.[86] An appropriate attitude of wonder does not come simply because we are unfamiliar with something, or through human ignorance of explanations.[87] Rather, wonder is appropriate when we see something for what it really is in itself. Unlike curiosity it is not possessive in nature, it is found in the quality of *giving attention* to something in and of itself. The philosopher Ronald Hepburn suggests that 'wonder does not deflect attention and concern away from the phenomenal world (the physical world as presented to experience) but on the contrary values and enjoys its diversity'.[88] He also, significantly, goes on to suggest that wonder is aligned with compassion, so that 'To respect and compassion, as moral correlates of wonder, we could add gentleness – a concern not to blunder into a damaging manipulation of another. . . . From a wondering recognition of forms of value proper to other beings, and a refusal to see them in terms of one's own utility purposes, there is only a short step to humility.'[89]

I suggest that Hepburn's way of making wonder necessarily prior to right relationships with nature is a secular counterpart to wisdom. The fact that the world exists at all is a source of wonder. However, while wonder on its own just leaves one with a sense of puzzlement at the enormous variety and complexity that, if Darwin's theory is accepted, has come about through a combination of chance and necessity, so wisdom points to the God who is the author of all such wonderment. Hence wonder and wisdom are related and linked, but only wisdom is directed to the ultimate Wisdom of God in the eternal law. In so far as wisdom is rooted in an understanding of God as creator of the world, wisdom fosters a similar sense of non-possessive attitudes to the natural world. Like wonder, wisdom is aligned with compassion, or more specifically charity.[90] Like wonder, wisdom is also aligned with gentleness and humility. Both wonder and wisdom lead to a sense of gratitude. For the non-theist this gratitude is directed to the earth, but for the theist the gratitude is directed to God as the author of such wonder and wisdom. Hepburn neither specifically mentions gratitude, nor tells us how to move on from attitudes such as wonder, gentleness and humility to particular actions. While he argues that wonder will prevent actions of abuse, such as putting a bullet through someone's brain, it has no frame of reference other than its own attitude of wondering. In so far as it is non-possessive it seems to have no way of allowing any human engagement with the natural world. We are simply left wondering, albeit in a gentle, humble contemplative way. It is hard to see how biotechnology could be reshaped through the pattern of wonder that he presents. It seems to lead to stasis in relationship with the world, even if it encourages respect for the other.

The secular idea of wonder is similar to the concept of the sublime that has been noted by other philosophers developing an environmental ethic, such as Bernard Williams.[91] Michael Banner has criticized the concept of the sublime, as he suggests that 'an experience of the sublime, with its associated feelings, does not seem to deliver what Williams and Wiggins were looking for, namely a basis for boundaries and limits in our handling of nature'.[92] Banner suggests that the Sabbath is a richer concept compared with the sublime, since the latter does not give us a basis for defining the limits of human interaction with nature. Exactly the same kind of criticism could be made of the idea of wonder, though I suggest that wonder is more akin to Christian understanding compared with the sublime, in that wonder also encourages compassion, rather than the 'holy dread' of Bernard Williams. I am also less convinced than Michael Banner that the idea of the Sabbath can move us to act in particular ways. What would it mean to develop a virtue focused on a sabbath theme? The practical outcomes are less clear, though it is true that the Sabbath is suggestive of themes of gift, rest and creation.

However, while wonder may suggest an ideal, and is important as one of the environmental virtues to hold to the fore when considering the relation between ecology and biotechnology, it seems to me that prudence as practical wisdom allows us to move from vision to reality. For prudence is concerned with practical questions and complex decision-making in the way that wonder is not. Wisdom, in encompassing prudence, permits contemplation and practical action to coexist. While wisdom, prudence and justice as virtues are necessarily focused on the character of the agent, this does not mean that no action flows from such attention. Rather, prudence necessitates particular courses of action in order to be counted as prudence. I suggest that while biotechnology may be challenged by wonder, in so far as it is focused on practical problem-solving, the concept of prudence is more likely to be heard by those committed to biotechnological change. One of the theological tasks is to fill out the meaning of prudence in particular ways in particular circumstances.

Conclusions

I began this chapter with a consideration of the overall place of technology in human society in general. Is biotechnology just one more stage in the inevitable 'progress' of technology and its grip on Western culture? While there are important insights in the critique of technology in the work of philosophers such as Heidegger and Ellul, finding positive ways forward is more problematic. The consideration of 'focal things' of Borgmann reminds us that technology is an ordinary human activity. How long will it take before biotechnological inventions become accepted as an ordinary part of our everyday existence? In so far as technology is unnoticed, it is also difficult to critique. However, while there have been significant cultural changes associated with biotechnology, I suggest that much of the impact of biotechnology, especially in the agricultural sphere, has yet to be realized. We are still at the debating stage of how far to integrate biotechnology into our lives; the rejection of GM tomato paste is a case in point. Hence it is still possible, perhaps remarkably, to consider that biotechnology will not lead to inevitable change in the way that more essentialist versions of technology imply. The possibility suggested by Feenberg, namely that there needs to be a democratization of technology, has to be taken seriously. Indeed, there are perhaps signs that this is taking place, through the interest in focus group work that attempts to uncover public attitudes to biotechnology funded by major multinational companies such as Unilever.[93]

In addition to social and political considerations, I have argued that in order to uncover the ethical significance of biotechnology we need to explore human attitudes and motivation. One attitude that is of particular significance is that of wisdom, for not only does it link with practical reason through prudence, but also from a theological perspective it links with understanding of the relationship between God, humanity and the world. Wisdom invites a theocentric perspective on ethics that does not exclude secular ethical considerations, but encompasses and critiques different secular alternatives. The different elements of prudence, in particular, are relevant when considering the ethical implications of specific cases in biotechnology. Yet the ethics of biotechnology is not simply about what is permissible for this or that organism and what are the limits of change, but also about the ways in which the information about biotechnology is presented by different groups, and the motivation for such change. Circumspection, foresight, memory as well as ingenuity and caution are all significant aspects of prudence when dealing with complex issues in biotechnology.

I have also dealt in some detail with different aspects of justice in relation to biotechnology. It seems to me that in view of the corporate nature of much biotechnological work, some sense of the way justice might work between individuals, corporations and governments is essential in an ethic of biotechnology. Given that I have argued for the cogency of a recovery of Aquinas's way of approaching ethics, his view of justice as a virtue is of particular importance. In discussion of the merits or otherwise of biotechnological change, justice between individuals and corporations is not simply defined in terms of breaking the law, such as that covering patents; instead, there are moral aspects of justice that make particular actions dishonourable. Yet justice requires prudential consideration of the alternatives before a claim can be made in the name of justice. In other words, the ability to see reality clearly that is the province of prudence leads to actions that affect human relationships with each other, which is the province of both prudence and justice. Justice also includes our relationship with the animals and wider ecological community. The ethics of biotechnology is, then, set in the context of this wider network of natural and social relationships.

Another question worth considering is how far the ethos of biotechnology might be compatible with that found in ecology, given the clash in values. I suggested that the new understanding of ecology is more compatible with at least some forms of biotechnology, in that it admits to the possibility of human involvement with the natural world in a way that purely equilibrium systems do not. I also suggested that the new ecology coheres with the way justice can be formulated, not so much in terms of a fixed ordering, but with movements in dynamic ongoing change, tending to equilibrium but never ultimately reaching a stable state. Are there other environmental virtues worth considering as a way of defining the task of biotechnology? The secular idea of wonder has some resemblance with wisdom, but on its own is insufficient, as it leads to a static appreciation of the other, rather than the possibility for involvement and change.

In what ways might human beings specifically alter the natural world in ways that are 'unnatural'? In order to discuss this issue more fully, it is necessary to explore an area that has become the subject of much heated public and political debate, namely that of cloning. Yet the focus on speculative consequences of cloning for humans has diverted attention away from the consequences with regard to the non-human world of animals. This is the subject of the chapter that follows.

Notes

1 See C. Deane-Drummond: *Theology and Biotechnology: Implications for a New Science* (London: Geoffrey Chapman, 1997), pp. 80–2.
2 A. Holland and A. Johnson: 'Introduction', in *Animal Biotechnology and Ethics* (London: Chapman and Hall, 1998), pp. 1–9.
3 J. Stewart: 'Re-ordering Means and Ends: Ellul and the New Genetics', in C. Deane-Drummond and B. Szerszynski, eds: *Re-Ordering Nature: Theology, Society and the New Genetics* (Edinburgh: T & T Clark/Continuum, 2002), p. 274.
4 Stewart: 'Re-ordering Means and Ends', p. 274.
5 Stewart, 'Re-ordering Means and Ends', p. 274.
6 See, for example, D. Bruce and A. Bruce, eds: *Engineering Genesis* (London: Earthscan, 1998); D. Bruce and D. Horrocks, eds: Evangelical Alliance Policy Commission Report, *Modifying Creation? GM Crops and Foods: A Christian Perspective* (Carlisle: Paternoster, 2002).
7 M. Banner chaired the following committee. Ministry of Agriculture, Fisheries and Food: *Report of the Committee to Consider the Ethical Implications of Emerging Technologies in the Breeding of Farm Animals* (London: HMSO, 1995). I discuss the Banner principles in relation to animal cloning in a later chapter.
8 See A. Linzey: *Animal Theology* (London: SCM Press, 1994), pp. 138–55.
9 C. Deane-Drummond: *Biology and Theology Today: Exploring the Boundaries* (London: SCM Press, 2001), pp. 128–31.
10 B. Dixon: 'Transgenic Ills and Otherwise: Review of *Redesigning Life? The Worldwide Challenge to Genetic Engineering*, Edited by Brian Toker', *Nature*, 412 (2001), p. 275.
11 This view was commonly held at a colloquium on theology, society and the new genetics. See Deane-Drummond and Szerszynski: *Re-ordering Nature*.
12 For an excellent discussion of the way ethical values inform practical environmental policy see M. Stenmark: *Environmental Ethics and Policy Making* (Aldershot: Ashgate, 2002).
13 C. Deane-Drummond: *Creation through Wisdom: Theology and the New Biology* (Edinburgh: T & T Clark, 2000), pp. 147–8, 219–20.
14 I am grateful to Peter Scott for pointing out this distinction. See P. Scott: 'Imaging God: Creatureliness and Technology', *New Blackfriars*, 79:928 (1998), pp. 260–74.
15 Peter Scott suggests that Heidegger's final comment that 'Only a god can still save us' reflects the deep pessimism that he held about the force of the 'Enframing' of the world as standing reserve, and while it might appear to open up the possibility of theological reflection, it is ultimately an appeal to romanticism rather than anything more theologically profound. Scott: 'Imaging God', pp. 263–5.
16 See R. J. Bernstein: *The New Constellation: The Ethical–Political Horizons of Modernity/ Postmodernity* (Cambridge: Polity Press, 1991), pp. 79–141.
17 J. Ellul: *The Technological Society* (New York: A. A. Knopf and Random House, 1964).
18 For commentary see Stewart: 'Re-ordering Means and Ends', pp. 257–74.

19 A. Borgmann: *Technology and the Character of Modern Life: A Philosophical Inquiry* (Chicago: University of Chicago Press, 1984).

20 Borgmann: *Technology and the Character of Modern Life*, p. 9.

21 Borgmann: *Technology and the Character of Modern Life*, p. 13.

22 Borgmann: *Technology and the Character of Modern Life*, p. 189.

23 Borgmann: *Technology and the Character of Modern Life*, p. 193.

24 See, for example, H. Rolston III: *Philosophy Gone Wild: Essays in Environmental Ethics* (Buffalo and New York: Prometheus Books, 1986). Richard Fern is similarly drawn to the wilderness ideal, but rejects the significance of the aesthetic component, see R. Fern: *Nature, God and Humanity: Envisioning an Ethics of Nature* (Cambridge: Cambridge University Press, 2002), pp. 12–14, 42–3.

25 Borgmann: *Technology and the Character of Modern Life*, p. 197.

26 P. Scott: 'Nature, Technology and the Rule of God: (En)countering the Disgracing of Nature', in Deane-Drummond and Szerszynski: *Re-ordering Nature*, pp. 287–8.

27 A. Feenberg: *Questioning Technology* (London: Routledge, 1999), p. viii.

28 Feenberg: *Questioning Technology*, p. 3.

29 Feenberg: *Questioning Technology*, p. 15.

30 Once technology becomes value-free it escapes from ethical analysis, but as I show below, this is a grossly oversimplified position to hold.

31 Borgmann: *Technology and the Character of Contemporary Life*, p. 10.

32 Borgmann: *Technology and the Character of Contemporary Life*, p. 30.

33 Borgmann: *Technology and the Character of Contemporary Life*, p. 31.

34 Deane-Drummond: *Biology and Theology Today*, pp. 25–47.

35 M. Midgley: *Wisdom, Information and Wonder: What is Knowledge For?* (London: Routledge, 1989), pp. 74–80.

36 Feenberg: *Questioning Technology*, pp. 131–47.

37 Feenberg: *Questioning Technology*, p. 134.

38 I recognize that this is a contested issue. For further discussion see Bruce and Horrocks: *Modifying Creation?*, pp. 108–39.

39 As Phillip Frossard points out: 'I have always had the uneasy feeling that the potential of a drug to treat human disease is a fortuitous side effect, a marketable commodity that helps win over media attention while the primary goal concerns two of the strongest motivating factors; greed and ambition.' P. Frossard: *The Lottery of Life: The New Genetics and the Future of Mankind* (London and New York, Bantam Press, 1991), p. 225.

40 Deane-Drummond: *Theology and Biotechnology*, pp. 91–92.

41 P. Scott: 'Nature, Technology and the Rule of God', p. 292.

42 Deane-Drummond: *Creation through Wisdom*, pp. 99–107; Deane-Drummond: 'Aquinas, Wisdom Ethics and the New Genetics' in Deane-Drummond and Szerszynski, eds: *Re-ordering Nature*, pp. 293–311.

43 See M. Csikszentmihalyi and K. Rathunde: 'The Psychology of Wisdom: An Evolutionary Interpretation', in R. J. Sternberg, ed.: *Wisdom: Its Nature, Origins and Development* (Cambridge: Cambridge University Press, 1990), pp. 25–51.

44 This 'terminator' technology is also associated with 'traitor' technologies where seeds require a chemical spray for normal growth. For discussion, see Bruce and Horrocks: *Modifying Creation?*, pp. 132–4.

45 Note that sham prudence includes two ways in which prudence may be distorted, in either substituting the goal of prudence for an end that is less than the good, or allowing deceitful means to attain a good (or partially good) end.

46   It seems to me that 'sham' prudence is an appropriate word to use in those instances where a company is making claims to serve the common good, but it is manifestly clear that this is not the case.

47   James Watson exemplifies this tendency in his latest book. J. D. Watson: *A Passion for DNA* (Oxford: oxford University Press, 2001).

48   See M. Northcott: 'Behold I Have Set the Land Before You (Deut. 1.8): Christian Ethics, GM Foods and the Culture of Modern Farming', in Deane-Drummond and Szerszynski, eds: *Re-ordering Nature*, pp. 85–106. For further discussion, see chapter on environmental ethics.

49   For further discussion see Stewart: 'Re-ordering Means and Ends', pp. 271–3.

50   This applies particularly to the UK Conservative Party's policy of selling off state-owned plant breeding to private industry, as I discovered from my own experience as an agricultural botanist in the 1980s, and also as noted by Professor John Beringar: 'Reply from John Beringar', *British Ecological Society Bulletin*, 31:2 (2000), p. 19, cited in Stewart: 'Re-ordering Means and Ends', p. 273. The ecologist D. Walton suggests that if the funding was supported by the state then there might be greater public acceptance that 'objectives were really feeding the hungry and not greater dividends, and that the control and oversight mechanisms were robust enough to ensure that health and the environment would be protected as far as possible'. Walton: 'Genetically Modified Futures?', Letters to the Editor, *British Ecological Society Bulletin*, 31:2 (2000), p. 15.

51   For discussion see Deane-Drummond: *Biology and Theology Today*, p. 65.

52   For discussion see B. Dixon: 'Transgenic Ills and Otherwise', *Nature*, 412, 19 July (2001), p. 275.

53   British Medical Association: *The Impact of Genetic Modification on Agriculture, Food and Health: An Interim Statement* (London: BMA, 1999), p. 17. There is a range of interpretations of the meaning of the precautionary principle, which is one of problems of its use. For discussion see D. Bruce: 'How Far Should We Take the Precautionary Principle?', Paper delivered to the British Ecology Society and the Linnaean Society, 26 April 2001, Burlington House, London.

54   For further discussion of the different elements of risk, see D. Bruce: 'Playing Dice with Creation: How Risky Should the New Genetics Be?', in Deane-Drummond and Szerszynski, eds: *Re-ordering Nature*, pp. 151–64.

55   Aquinas allowed for such adjustment of natural law in its secondary aspects where it is for the social good of a community. I suggest that this is the case for animals, since social goodness includes right relationships with all creatures under the eternal law.

56   Proverbs 8.16–17.

57   Onora O'Neill combines a Kantian approach with virtue ethics. See O. O'Neill: *Towards Justice and Virtue: A Constructive Account of Practical Reasoning* (Cambridge: Cambridge University Press, 1996).

58   Justice may include this aspect, but to eclipse all other considerations of justice in the interests of future generations is not particularly helpful. W. Beckerman and J. Pasek: *Justice, Posterity and the Environment* (Oxford: Oxford University Press, 2001), pp. 11–45.

59   Beckerman and Pasek: *Justice, Posterity and the Environment*, pp. 24–5.

60   Synderesis sets the outline of justice according to natural law, though positive laws are those which are formulated by a given community that cannot be set against what natural law requires.

61 It could be argued that wisdom also, as a theological category, moves away from virtue ethics in the manner understood by most philosophers. However, my intention is not simply to imitate virtue ethics, but to draw on these insights and incorporate them into a theocentric ethic of wisdom. Such a theocentric ethic is less alienating compared with other deontological theological positions, as it resonates with the language of virtues and orientates discussion around agents first, prior to consideration of particular theological principles.

62 Note that Aquinas did not use rights language, but it has become associated with the language of law and justice in liberal communities.

63 K. S. Jayaraman: 'Illicit Cotton Sparks Corporate Fury', *Nature*, 413 (2001), p. 555.

64 Bruce and Horrocks: *Modifying Creation?*, pp. 132–4. Vandana Shiva has called this kind of action 'piracy'. See V. Shiva: *Biopiracy* (London: Green Books, 1998); V. Shiva: *Stolen Harvest: The Hijacking of the Global Food Supply* (London: Zed Books, 2001).

65 I am drawing on the somewhat neglected work of the Roman Catholic philosopher, Josef Pieper. See J. Pieper: *The Four Cardinal Virtues* (Notre Dame, IN: University of Notre Dame Press, 1966).

66 Cited in Jayaraman: 'Illicit Cotton Sparks Corporate Fury', p. 555.

67 Pieper: *The Four Cardinal Virtues*, pp. 70–4.

68 Pieper: *The Four Cardinal Virtues*, pp. 73–4.

69 Pieper: *The Four Cardinal Virtues*, p. 79.

70 Nuffield Council on Bioethics: *Genetically Modified Crops: The Ethical and Social Issues* (London: Nuffield, 1999), p. 136.

71 See Deane-Drummond: *Theology and Biotechnology*, pp. 79–87; *Biology and Theology Today*, pp. 62–7.

72 Nuffield Council on Bioethics: *Genetically Modified Crops*, p. 77.

73 J. Pieper: *The Four Cardinal Virtues*, p. 80.

74 M. Banner, 'Burke, Barth and Biotechnology: On Preferring the Sabbath to the Sublime; Some Preliminary Thoughts', in Deane-Drummond and Szerszynski, eds: *Re-ordering Nature*, pp. 68–76. The idea of the Sabbath is a rich and fruitful concept to consider, though I would interpret it according to a more dynamic interpretation of human involvement with the natural world. This topic deserves more attention, but is outside the scope of this chapter.

75 Scott, 'Nature, Technology and the Rule of God', pp. 280–5.

76 As David Walton points out, 'we do not have an adequate ecological understanding of the complex interactions engendered by releasing GMOs even into semi-natural eco-systems'. D. Walton: 'Genetically Modified Futures?', p. 15.

77 Deane-Drummond: *Theology and Biology Today*, pp. 119–23.

78 See, for example, Linzey: *Animal Theology*, pp. 138–55.

79 R. E. Bulger: 'Use of Animals in Experimental Research: A Scientist's Perspective' in R. Bulger, E. Heitman and S. Reiser, eds: *The Ethical Dimension of the Biological Sciences* (Cambridge: Cambridge University Press, 1993).

80 Bulger: 'Use of Animals in Experimental Research', p. 193.

81 I compare biocentrism and anthropocentrism in an earlier chapter.

82 Sarah Andrew: Inaugural lecture, Chester College, 1999.

83 H. Kean: *Animal Rights: Political and Social Change in Britain since 1800* (London: Reaction Books, 1998).

84 See Deane-Drummond: *Theology and Biotechnology*, p. 86 and Deane-Drummond: *Biology and Theology Today*, p. 66.

85 John Benson names wonder as one of the environmental virtues. See J. Benson: *Environmental Ethics: An Introduction with Readings* (London: Routledge), pp. 71–5. Louke van Wensveen lists 189 virtues and 174 vices in environmental literature since the 1970s, and while wonder is listed in this collection, it does not receive separate treatment. L. van Wensveen: *Dirty Virtues: The Emergence of Ecological Virtue Ethics* (New York: Humanity Books, 2000), pp. 163–7.

86 Benson: *Environmental Ethics*, p. 72.

87 This is discussed by the philosopher Ronald Hepburn. See, R. W. Hepburn: 'Wonder', in Benson: *Environmental Ethics*, pp. 203–6.

88 Hepburn: 'Wonder', p. 205.

89 Hepburn: 'Wonder', p. 206.

90 Deane-Drummond: *Creation through Wisdom*, pp. 106–7.

91 B. Williams: 'Must a Concern for the Environment Be Centred on Human Beings?', in *Making Sense of Humanity and Other Philosophical Papers 1982–1993* (Cambridge: Cambridge University Press, 1995), pp. 233–40

92 M. Banner: 'Burke, Barth and Biotechnology', in Deane-Drummond and Szerszynski, eds: *Re-ordering Nature*, p. 74.

93 See R. Grove-White, P. Macnaghten, S. Mayer and B. Wynne: *Uncertain World: Genetically Modified Organisms, Food and Public Attitudes in Britain* (Lancaster: Centre for the Study of Environmental Change (CSEC), Lancaster University, 1997).

Chapter 5

The Ethics of Cloning

Cloning, of mammals at least, is one of those breakthroughs in scientific method that has become an overheated area of public debate, from both religious and secular perspectives. Books devoted specifically to the subject continue to be published, even five years after the initial flurry of responses.[1] One of the reasons for this is that we are still living in a period of what Ted Peters has called 'cloning shock', rooted as it is in the fear that perhaps one day we might be able to clone copies of ourselves, hence entailing anxieties about loss of human identity and family relationships.[2] The focus on possibilities for humans becomes obvious to all who read the available literature on the subject. In addition, the futuristic scenario of cloned babies, or reproductive cloning, slants the ethical and theological debate in particular ways. The debates surrounding human reproductive cloning are important, but deal with complex interrelated issues of human identity, sexuality and parenting, as well as socio-political issues to do with reproductive control.[3] There has been far less attention paid to what is a present reality, namely animal cloning and the use of therapeutic cloning techniques aligned with stem cell research in humans.[4] While the former is set in the context of animal experimentation, the latter is set in the context of human embryo research, which is, at present, legal in the UK up to the so-called 'primitive streak' stage of fourteen days after fertilization.[5] We also need to ask the question that Brian Wynne poses in relation to policy debates about the genetic modification of food, namely how far policy is merely 'set' by the science, rather than scientific understanding becoming a resource amid others.[6] The intention of this chapter is to explore more fully the ethics of animal cloning and other novel technologies, as well as the ethics of 'therapeutic' cloning and stem cell research in humans.[7] How far might the virtues of prudence, wisdom, charity, respect, justice and temperance inform ethical reflection on these novel processes?

The Ethics of Animal Experimentation

I suggest that just as genetic modification of crops needs to be set in the context of wider debates about the shift towards industrialized agriculture, so animal cloning needs to be set in the context of wider debates about animal experimentation. Our responses to the general question of how far and to what extent we can intervene in the lives of animals for human experimental purposes will influence our approach to animal cloning. Much of the ethical debate about how far and to what extent we might experiment on animals relies on the balancing of relative risks over benefits. More often than not the risks are couched in terms of the possible health risks to humans who might consume/use the products arising from manipulated animals, rather than the risk to the animals themselves. It is hardly surprising that campaign groups protesting animal rights arose in such a context. A rather different approach to the use of animals based on specific principles, and one that is gaining in currency, is that proposed by the Banner Committee in 1995. The Banner Principles stated that:

1   Harms of a certain degree or kind ought under no circumstances to be inflicted on an animal.
2   Any harm to an animal, even if not absolutely impermissible, none the less requires justification and must be outweighed by the good, which is realistically sought in so treating it.
3   Any harm that is justified by the second principle ought, however, to be minimized as far as it is reasonably possible.[8]

Some experimentalists have suggested that the principles are too restrictive.[9] Others reject all experimentation whatsoever as unwarranted speciesism.[10] These are more extreme views, and the majority would agree that the principles offer a level of protection of animals that would find support from a range of protagonists on the animal welfare/rights divide. The difficulty, none the less, is one of interpretation of the principles; in other words, what kind of harm is not allowed and what might be justified? Experimentation more often than not involves the death of an animal, yet for those who advocate animal welfare, this cannot be what the first principle has in mind. In other words, for them it is about the way animals are used for experiments, rather than a total ban on all experimentation. It seems, rather, that some suffering to animals is anticipated, but this is to be both minimized and justified. The question now becomes: what are the particular circumstances in which such harm might be justified? Animals have been legally protected against cruder forms of cruelty for some time in the UK. For example, when severe or lasting pain is anticipated in an experiment, then the Scientific Procedures Act (1986) demands that the animal be killed. The interpretation of the Banner principles might help in some situations, as, for example, if we ask if it is right to induce cancer routinely in mice through genetic engineering in order to model human disease. The consistency of the tumours induced through genetic manipulation violates the third principle of minimizing harm to a given population of mice, compared with other methods, such as chemically induced cancers. In this case the counter-argument could be that relatively more mice overall would be sacrificed if cancer was *not* induced through genetic means.[11] However, it is the intention that is important; knowingly causing the animal harm is the basis for rejection of oncomouse licensing, even if the medical research interest is advocated as the prime reason for such experimentation.

Deliberately inducing cancers in mice in a consistent way through genetic engineering could also lead to feelings of repugnance. Such feelings have also been highlighted when considering the possibility of human reproductive cloning. Leon Kass is one philosopher who has drawn attention to the importance of examining our instinctive reactions to cloning technologies.[12] However, while this might set up a temporary taboo on practice, a further elaboration of the *basis* of such negative reactions is called for. Moreover, as I will discuss later, it is important to examine and foster *positive* and habitual attitudes or virtues, rather than relying on temporary or 'gut' negative feelings that may be fleeting. The changing fashion for using animal leather and fur for coats among the bourgeoisie is a case in point. Are there any other ways in which it might be possible to consider when and in what circumstances it is justified to use animals for experimental research?

The Farm Animals Welfare Council Report (1998) on animal cloning has chosen to answer the question by *ruling out* certain practices, and these are:

1   If they inflict very severe or lasting pain on the animals concerned.
2   If they involve an unacceptable violation of the integrity of a living being.
3   If they are associated with the mixing of kinds of animals to the extent that is unacceptable.
4   If they generate living beings whose sentience has been reduced to the extent that they may be considered to be mere instruments or artefacts.[13]

In particular, the council was concerned about the possible 'instrumentalization' of animals for human use, simply as means to human ends and irrespective of animals' nature and welfare. However, it is not entirely obvious what might be meant by 'violation of integrity', since the meaning of integrity between species is itself a debatable issue.[14] This question is related to whether there are *any* circumstances in which kinds might be mixed, and what the idea of 'kinds' entails. Taken in its literal sense this would rule out genetic engineering altogether, though this is not what the committee had in mind. The question then becomes: how many genes can be transferred in arriving at a new kind?[15] I will return to this point again in discussion of the more recent novel technologies. This report is similar to others on animal welfare that stress what *must not* happen to animals, that they must not be allowed to suffer hunger, thirst, pain, disease, fear, distress.[16]

One of the more intriguing possible ways forward to the general question about what might be permissible in animal experimentation is that suggested by the philosopher Stephen Clark. He proposes a theory of just experimentation that takes its cue to some extent from just war theory. While the latter set limits to the extent of military violence, the former could act as a framework to guide experimentation on animals. Like other principled approaches it is about what, negatively, cannot be done to animals. It is significant, too, that he makes an analogy with just war arguments, for it implies that any killing is deeply regrettable and can only be accepted when violence is unavoidable as a last resort. The extension of the theory to the case of animals also, by implication, implies that animals do have a status that is, in some sense, comparable to humans, even if the idea of justice is used in a different context. None the less, there are clear differences between them; for example, no one would justify experimentation on neonates, regardless of the positive outcomes of the research in terms of wider human benefit. Clark suggests that the following are necessarily forbidden in relation to animal experimentation:

1   Invasive experimentation on the genome or the persons of any of the great apes.
2   The creation of human–animal hybrids.
3   Any work that can be expected to produce creatures who would suffer severe or lasting distress (including animals to be created as disease models unless there is clear evidence that the problems could be handled humanely).
4   The production at least of chimeras and of those hybrids which involve hybridization outside closely related taxa.
5   The creation or reduplication of toys, favourite 'pets' or fashion accessories.
6   Any work intended to strip organisms of their species-specific biograms, or render them incurably insentient.
7   Any unguided genetic modification that runs ahead of reasonable guesses about the function of particular genes, and the chance of managing any damaging effects.[17]

This list is relevant as a framework for guiding what might be permissible in animal cloning, since any of the above could be achievable through cloning technology, especially in combination with genetic engineering techniques.

Animal Experimentation and Virtue Ethics

Stephen Clark also points to the importance of attitude as an ethical ingredient in considering what might not be done in experimentation on animals. Indeed, if the motive for the proposed action is explored, it is easy to find fault with those who argue that cloning could be used to replace a much-loved pet.[18] However, he elaborates still further other faulty attitudes that lie behind the list of forbidden actions that he identifies in his just experimentation theory. As such the list is cast *negatively*, showing what should *not* be condoned. These express faulty motives of those who desire to carry out a particular invasive technique and are:

1 Doing it for fun.
2 Doing it simply for commercial goals.
3 Doing it just to expand the experimenter's portfolio.
4 Doing it for sentimental reasons.

Using this list it is possible to rule out certain courses of action as 'deplorable'; even a 'just' cause in the case of a 'just war' would be 'contaminated if the agents are moved by pride, hatred, boredom or blood-lust, and fight not to secure an honourable peace but to destroy or utterly humiliate their enemies'.[19] There are examples where animal cloning has been proposed simply for commercial reasons, such as the use of cloning in order to develop a uniform steak or better quality of wool.[20] Attempting to recreate a pet would fall into the fourth category. However, in many situations where animal cloning is proposed it becomes rather more difficult to identify purely negative attitudes for particular research. Few researchers would frankly admit to the first or third motives, yet in practice the level of excitement generated among those who conducted the first experiments on Dolly was palpable.[21] The research also clearly assisted the authors in building international reputations for their work. There were undoubtedly commercial benefits; a company that necessarily tailors its research within profit-making goals carried out the research. Yet the public justification for the work was cast in terms of noble, altruistic reasons, namely the desire to assist medical science through the development of drugs for the treatment of disease. In this case the ultimate intention was only really achieved through the second phase of the work, namely the arrival of Polly, who was genetically engineered so that she carried the human blood clotting factor gene IX. The question now becomes not simply whether faulty motivations were at work, but which, if any, were the overriding motivations or attitudes. This may be different from the motivations claimed by the scientists proposing the research. In this case there have to be some guards against false representations of the proposed benefits of particular research outcomes. Experimentation with animals can, for example, be given an altruistic 'medical' gloss, just as genetic experimentation with plants can be given an 'environmental' gloss in order to win public funds and support.[22] In these scenarios the scientists may be either deliberately presenting a particular claim in a certain way simply in order to attract funds, or deceiving themselves as to the likely benefits in order to justify to themselves the laborious and time-consuming nature of the research. It is hard to condemn the latter attitude, though the former needs to be identified and ruled out.

How might it be possible to adjudicate between the various claims for the basis of particular research on animals in these more complex situations? I suggest that the virtue of prudence is necessary for those making decisions about the approval or otherwise of particular research projects. This includes:

1 A realistic assessment of the likely motivation of those proposing the research in the light of their proposed intentions.
2 An assessment of the contribution of such research to the common good, not just the good of the individual researchers themselves.

3   Sensitivity to the way similar projects have contributed to the above in the past.
4   Taking time to deliberate in relation to social and political outcomes of the
     proposed research.

Aquinas has already defined these four aspects in his understanding of prudence
as encompassing: (1) circumspection; (2) foresight; (3) memory; and (4) caution.[23]
A Christian understanding of prudence also sees prudence as practical wisdom,
a virtue integrally connected with wisdom, rooted in the covenant of grace and
integral to an understanding of who God is.[24] The vocation of the Christian
towards wisdom is one where the theological virtues of faith, hope and charity are
implicit in any act. In this context of the Christian community the questions that
need to be asked are:

1   How far does this conform to the eternal wisdom of God, understood through
     reference to the divine covenant?
2   How far does this represent an act of charity towards God, neighbour and all of
     creation?
3   How far is this rooted in faith in God and hope in God's promises?

With reference to the first question the covenant God made with humanity
becomes inclusive of all creatures through the Noahic promise described in the
Genesis account.[25] Both the first and second questions reinforce the stipulations of
what might not be done according to Stephen Clark's just experimentation theory.
However, they also go further than this and imply that *active* means should be
sought to improve the lot of animals. For example, we need to ask the question of
whether research into genetic therapy of animal diseases is given sufficient priority,
taking account of the experimental process in arriving at such an end. In addition,
we need to ask ourselves how far and to what extent it is an act of charity to
conduct cloning experimentation on animals at all, aware of the negative outcomes
in terms of loss of life and multiple malformations of those that survive. In other
words, the positive attitude of charity, or in feminist terminology caring, would be
inclusive of the specific dangers to both animals and, in some cases, humans. Those
who conducted the experiments argue that cloning is more 'efficient' in terms of
success rate compared with other methods of genetic modification and is therefore
preferable to 'traditional' DNA insertion/injection methods. Some of the reasons
for this are as follows. In the case of cloning complete genetic change can succeed
in a given cell line, but alternative injection techniques used in genetic engineering
do not normally lead to compete integration of the new DNA in the first cell
cycle, resulting in a 'mosaic' embryo where some cells are transformed and some
are not.[26] The cell line used for the creation of Dolly was also a deliberate choice,
as mammary epithelial cells could be tested for their milk production potential at an
early stage and thereby provide an initial screen as to the animals most likely to
have high milk yields. Hence the eventual intention of 'pharming' drugs through
sheep's milk was designed into the cloning technology at the start. As with other

experimentation methods, the ends do not necessarily justify the means; for example, the question needs to be asked as to how much and to what extent animal suffering can be tolerated, even given positive intentions to work for good. Scientists claim that cloning is also more 'efficient' in terms of the total number of animals used compared with alternative injection methods for introducing new genes.[27] However, it is not clear if this 'efficiency' is related to the total number of abnormalities found in transgenic animals, or whether it simply reflects the laboriousness of the task at the initial stages. The question now becomes, what level of suffering and loss of life can be tolerated, given the outcomes? Cloning also needs to be set in the context of other transgenic methods currently proposed for a variety of applications, including biopharmaceuticals, modification of cow genes for milk production to enhance nutritional value, xenotransplantation of pig hearts, lungs, kidneys and pancreatic islets[28] and the use of animals as disease models.

In addition, the virtue of justice is relevant, as it helps to weigh up what might be required in those situations where there is a clash of interests. For example, is animal cloning always acceptable where the benefit is clearly for humans in order to treat debilitating diseases? The consensus among Christian as well as secular groups seems to be that cloning or genetic engineering of animals are acceptable where they lead to drugs for particularly horrific human diseases. Yet it is easy in this scenario, having approved such a development, just to let the research take its course. However, it seems to me that this represents a complacency that is unacceptable. Negatively, cloning necessitates, at least in the initial stages, causing considerable harm towards the animals themselves. Yet this was not taken into account sufficiently in decisions about whether to go ahead with animal cloning. For the business sector, the strongest practical argument against cloning animals seems to be that it still lacks the commercial viability that was promised in the early stages of its development. Positively, research needs to be encouraged using synthetic, bacterial or plant systems that develop alternative methods that do not require the use of live animals as 'pharms' for particular products. In addition, we need positively to encourage the virtue of temperance; that is, the ability to know what is appropriate to meet one's own specific needs without grasping for more.

Cloning and New and Exotic Technologies

It is worth asking at this juncture about the developments taking place in novel genetic technologies in the light of the above discussion on cloning and animal experimentation. It is also worth rehearsing the science of cloning briefly before considering other novel technologies. Cloning in mammals involves the removal of an egg cell nucleus, followed by replacement with another nucleus, from the embryo or some other body (somatic) tissue, then subjecting the cell to an electric charge in order to mimic fertilization. The cell divides rapidly into an undifferentiated clump of cells (blastocyst), generating cells known as stem cells, as each cell is pluripotent, which means it is capable of differentiation into any of the more specialized cells of the body. In some situations stem cells may be totipotent; that is, they have the capacity to become a new individual with the same genetic characteristics as the individual that contributed the donor nucleus. Scientific texts on cloning often describe the technique as cell nuclear replacement (CNR) or somatic nuclear transfer (SNT) rather than 'cloning', as the latter can bring with it an attitude of repugnance that many scientists prefer to set to one side. In addition, scientifically cloning is more commonly used just to mean replication of multiple copies, and habitually describes multiplication techniques used particularly in genetic engineering. Of course, it is possible to argue that scientists are ingenuous in making such a move to replace the loaded word 'cloning' with CNR or some such term, and a similar criticism could be made about the use of the term 'ovasome' instead of 'embryo' in order to describe an egg cell that has had its nucleus replaced. [29] Similarly, historically, scientists campaigning to persuade Parliament to legislate in favour of embryo research, and thereby remove it from the same ethical category as a human being, used the term 'pre-embryo' to describe the early embryo.[30] It seems to me that it is more likely that in the case of the 'ovasome' the scientists genuinely believe that a distinction can (should) be made between an embryo conceived through 'normal' fertilization and one conceived through asexual cloning methods. However, if this is the case, then it is odd that recommendations from the Donaldson Select Committee on human cloning suggested that there are no new ethical issues raised by CNR therapy for legislation already in place for embryo research.[31] The Church of Scotland and the Bioethics Group of the Conference of European Churches have criticized the Donaldson Report for this ethical failure to distinguish cloned eggs from fertilized eggs.[32]

The important point here is that the cloning method in mammals is a completely novel technique that does not have any known analogy in the natural world, at least at this level of evolutionary organization. It represents a change that was an enormous surprise to scientists. In the history of biology cloning was one of those developments that went against currently received dogma, entailing a significant paradigm shift.[33] There have been other surprising shifts in biology that are less well known outside the biological world. For example, early in the 1960s it was supposed that genes could not move between species, but by the end of the 1970s recombinant DNA technology had begun to mushroom, bringing with it a whole host of important possibilities for biotechnology. Cloning was, perhaps, a rather bigger surprise than some of the others, so scientists *qua* scientists are less concerned about the failure rate of cloning than the fact that it works at all. This has given some scientists the confidence to suggest that, given time, almost anything might be possible, barring that which might contravene the laws of physics. The zoologist turned philosopher Colin Tudge suggests:

We have all become members of each other's gene pools. More generally, the expression 'biologically impossible' must now be seen to be obsolete. Of course, some genuine biological impossibilities might arise in the future, but it would be cavalier to assume *a priori* that they will be so. The only safe assumption, now, is that any endeavour that does not break what Sir Peter Medawar called 'the bedrock laws of physics' must be considered do-able, not necessarily now, or next week, but in the fullness of time: in decades or centuries. There are no biological barriers, apart from those of physics, to prohibit the wildest of fantasies: nothing except our own sense of what is proper.[34]

Given this scenario, the debates about human reproductive cloning start to sound somewhat premature. He suggests that over the next fifty years or so reproductive cloning will already be obsolete, for 'By then it may well be possible to turn ordinary somatic [body] cells into gametes, and allow couples to mix their genes by *in vitro* fertilisation.'[35]

If he is right, then much of the agonized debate about detaching reproduction from sexuality in human reproductive cloning, which amounts to asexual reproduction, becomes somewhat superfluous.[36] So too is the debate about the psychological identity of the child *vis-à-vis* its parents. This also illustrates another dilemma. On the one hand it is important for ethicists to deliberate about what is likely to happen in the future so that decisions can be made that are ethically and socially responsible. On the other hand, the pace of change in novel technologies is such that today's new method is soon replaced by another even more ingenious solution to the problem. In order to assess how realistic such possibilities might be, it is worth considering the recent research in cloning animals itself, as well as other novel technologies.

Cloning to create replicas is still a fairly hit and miss affair. Abnormalities may develop early on, or they may appear later. The overall success rate is between 0.5 and 5 per cent development to term, with loss throughout gestation and birth. Research groups around the world have reported cloning in cattle, mice, goats and pigs in addition to sheep and monkeys from embryonic tissue, but at the time of writing it has yet to succeed at all in dogs, rats or horses.[37] Even following birth some more abnormalities are reported: excessive weight, premature ageing and arthritis.[38] One reason for the difficulties is that imprinted genes remain active in the cloned embryo. These are the genes that are normally suppressed in the embryo and are derived from the maternal or paternal genome.[39] Other difficulties appear to be related to the incomplete reprogramming of the genes following transfer to the enucleated egg cell; in other words, the differentiation process is not totally reversed.[40]

Given these difficulties with cloning, scientists are actively researching alternative methods of genetic manipulation. One that excited much media attention, given the difficulty of cloning monkeys, is the so-called parthenogenesis of monkey eggs reported in early 2002. Rather like cloning, parthenogenesis has so far only been observed in animals lower down the evolutionary scale, namely lizards and insects. The American company called Advanced Cell Technology conducted the research. The researchers chemically treated the nucleus of the monkey egg cell in order to mimic fertilization, though of course only a single genetic complement was present, rather than two sets as in fertilized eggs. Astonishingly, perhaps, the group was able to culture the resulting stem cells so that they went on to develop muscle, fat, heart and neuron cells, with the last of these even capable of producing dopamine, which is one of the chemicals active in brain cells.[41] It is a surprising result because these cells only have the genes from the mother. The scientists who conducted the experiment suggested that the technique would by-pass some of the ethical problems created by human therapeutic cloning. However, this is a very narrow instrumental way of viewing the issue; if the human eggs are induced through parthenogenesis and are non-viable one might doubt the effectiveness of the resulting stem cells themselves, especially for the treatment of males.[42] In addition, the creation of malformed human embryos could be called into question. It all depends on the relative status that these cells have: are they simply a collection of cells that can be used for particular purposes, or is there something intrinsically valuable about an embryo?

The creation of a hybrid between a human nucleus and a cow's egg that had the nucleus removed is also proposed as an alternative method for creating human stem cells. Such a cloned egg would not be viable (that is, the cells would not be totipotent), but could be stimulated to divide up to the blastocyst stage of division, when the stem cells would be removed and cultured as if they were human cells. There would be no guarantee that these cell lines would behave as expected. However, while seemingly solving the ethical dilemma of not creating a viable human embryo, such a mixture raises other intrinsic ethical problems about mixing human and animal kinds. If creating 'chimeras' between animals is objectionable on ethical grounds, as discussed above, then this stipulation also applies to chimeras between animals and humans. Of course, the status of the stem cells with respect to human personhood is crucial here: if stem cells are just a ball of cells, then chimeras at the initial stages are not problematic.

The use of cloning in the development of xenotransplantation of pig's hearts to humans is also being developed. PPL Therapeutics succeeded in cloning five piglets in 2000, in the hope that cloning will assist in the removal of pig genes responsible for creating one of the proteins that leads to an immunorejection response in humans. As discussed earlier, genetic modification is much easier through cloning methods, and in this case multiple gene changes are needed, in terms of both adding human genes and removing pig genes. The latter deletion or 'knockout' is more difficult technically. The successful removal of such genes in cloned animals was achieved just two years after the initial cloning experiment and was announced in January 2002.[43] There are, however, more problems to be resolved, including the possibility that pig retroviruses will escape into the human population and lead to a disease of epidemic proportions. At the moment there is a moratorium on clinical trials in the UK because of the possible risk to the human population. The government has reason to be cautious in the wake of public distrust over the BSE crisis and the possible animal origin of HIV. The ethical issue in this case is how far it is permissible to use a pig in this way as a resource for human organs. It represents a completely new use of animals compared with, say, food, clothing, transport and manure. In addition, the pigs would be kept in a highly sterile environment, leading to considerable distress for highly intelligent animals. The creation of laboratories of animals reared specifically for 'farming' of their organs through cloning methods that in themselves lead to considerable suffering and loss of life is not necessarily a sign of adequate respect for that animal. If we examine the reasons for doing the research, then this is the mismatch between the supply of donor human organs and the demand. In other words, xenotransplantation is just one of a number of options available, including the possibility of developing more effective artificial hearts.

The Society, Religion and Technology Project of the Church of Scotland adopts a characteristic intermediate approach to cloning pigs for xenotransplantation, suggesting that it could be justified in exceptional circumstances.[44] These include a long, high-quality life for the recipient. However, we might ask ourselves how realistic such a prospect is, given the difficulties already associated with the health of cloned animals, including complications such as reduced life expectancy.[45] The only way to find out would be to experiment on human subjects, and as longevity is called for this would effectively mean many years before the result was known. It is unlikely, in these circumstances, that the companies developing the research would be prepared to wait for such results before proceeding further, given the commercial pressure and the high cost of the research. It also seems to me to be problematic to endorse such procedures by giving out positive signals such as 'cautious welcome', for the message heard by scientists intent on such research will, overall, be one of approval. I am far less convinced of the ethical expediency of cloning for xenotransplantation from the perspective of animal welfare, as well as just distribution of research resources. In addition, the use of stem cell technologies that are likely to be developed over the next fifty years or so may obviate the need for whole organs altogether. Moreover, channelling resources into the promotion of pledges for organ donation immediately after death would reduce the pressure to find alternatives.

Another novel development is the use of cloning to resurrect the Tasmanian tiger by using a specimen that has been preserved for 153 years, or even to clone a mammoth from 20,000-year-old tissue discovered in Siberia. Such projects verge on wild speculation, since the DNA of such samples would be far too fragmented for success. Moreover, naked DNA is not enough: it would need to be implanted into a 'host' nucleus of another species. More realistic is the possibility of cloning endangered species where there are some surviving creatures, but again, close relatives would need to act as surrogate mothers. While the total number in a population might increase through this method, the lack of genetic diversity would put a question mark over the long-term viability of a species 'saved' by cloning technology.

Cloning technology in humans has also been proposed as a way of treating those with diseases inherited through mitochondrial DNA. Mitochondria are small organelles in the cytoplasm of all cells and contribute to the overall genetic make-up of an individual. Egg cells are responsible for passing down mitochondria from one generation to the next, which is why this form of genetic transfer is sometimes called maternal inheritance. CNR technology would be used, so that the nucleus of the egg with the faulty mitochondria was transplanted to another egg that had its nucleus removed prior to fertilization with sperm in the normal procedure for IVF. In the Lords Debate on cloning there was some concern by Lord Bishop Habgood that this might represent a form of 'back door' germ line therapy, since the genetic change would be inheritable from one generation to the next.[46] It clearly raises different issues from therapeutic cloning for stem cell research. Including this 'treatment' as a possible use for cloning technologies conflates cloning with inheritable genetic change in a way that seems to me to be ethically unacceptable. The law against germ line therapy would be violated, even if the outcome was a laudable one, namely the treatment of an incurable disease. The same could be said for germ line therapy of those with Parkinson's or Huntington's disease.[47]

The ethical difficulties facing scientists engaged in new technologies become apparent in the work of those who research at the interface of the two fields. Colin Tudge, for example, combines a number of seemingly incompatible positions. In the first place he argues that almost anything is possible for biological science within the limits of physics, and we are going to be living in a brave new world of designer organisms where exact specifications become plausible. On the other hand, he suggests that the level of scientific ignorance is unknown, so that even when we think we understand the science, 'a whole swatch of disasters might ensue'. Again, on the one hand he suggests that in some cases we need to move forward on the basis of the 'precautionary principle', understood in terms of risks and benefits, but then he claims that when it comes to assessment of the GMO debate over foods, 'risk–benefit arguments, as typically presented, are deeply flawed'.[48] He seems to want to affirm scientific progress understood from the perspective of scientists, but then counter this view by reference to wider social and philosophical issues in a somewhat incoherent way. However, more interesting, perhaps, is his conclusion, where he suggests that we need to return to ancient morality and develop the virtues of humility, respect and reverence, despite his earlier claim that any theological approach to ethical discussion 'simply embarrasses everybody else'.[49] He approaches virtues from a secular perspective, so that it is immaterial whether or not this is 'revealed truth'; instead, 'Pure pragmatism is enough to suggest that as general attitudes of mind they work.'[50] Yet he also recognizes that 'It is religion, rather than formal moral philosophy, that seeks directly to refine and cultivate the emotions on which the ethical arguments are based.'[51] When he applies these virtues to the question of human reproductive cloning it is rejected on the basis that such an action would show a lack of humility. However, he does not consider other novel genetic technologies. In particular, we might ask ourselves whether parthenogenetic technologies show an inappropriate lack of respect to the primates so manipulated.

Given the rich diversity of techniques becoming available it is worth asking how far these techniques are becoming a sign of intemperance, a compulsion that takes the search for knowledge too far, to the exclusion of other possibilities that nourish and support human life in all its richness. In this case what is needed is more awareness of the importance of the virtue of temperance. Temperance embraces other virtues and includes chastity, continence, humility, gentleness, mildness and *studiositas*, while forms of intemperance are unchastity, incontinence, pride, uninhibited wrath and *curiositas*. Once curiosity becomes *curiositas* it is a 'concupiscence of the eyes', leading to a form of obsessive addiction, a 'roaming unrest of spirit'. Has the stage been reached where the technology is becoming expressive of a desire for control and power over nature, cloaked in the language of human benefit, but more accurately disguising other less desirable attitudes?[52]

The use of cloning and other novel technologies in humans is much more restricted in many countries compared with its use in non-humans. The level of acceptance of such technologies in humans is worth pondering in the light of what is permissible in animal experimentation. While the legal framework on human cloning is inadequate as an ethical guide, it provides some degree of societal consensus on the issues to date, so that it is worth pausing briefly to consider such a framework before moving on to a discussion of the specific ethic issues involved in human 'therapeutic' and stem cell technologies.

Legal Aspects of Human Cloning

Laws and treaties on cloning have developed very quickly in some of those countries where strong public opinion has fuelled the debates. The Council of Europe's Convention on Human Rights and Biomedicine added an Additional Protocol in 1998 outlawing human reproductive cloning.[53] Germany and Switzerland ban all cloning technology in humans, including 'therapeutic' cloning, and Canada is set to follow suit. Greece and Ireland effectively ban cloning through general legislation against experimentation with human embryos. In the USA there is a bill in place to ban the creation of embryos for therapeutic purposes, and although existing cell lines can be used there is considerable debate about the extent of availability of embryonic stem cells for research.[54] In the UK there is now a law in place (2001) which prohibits reproductive cloning, but it is still possible to engage in therapeutic cloning as long as proper procedures are followed in terms of gaining a licence for the research through the Human Fertilisation and Embryology Authority (HFEA). In other countries, such as Israel and Russia, where there is a five-year moratorium on reproductive cloning, due time can be taken to deliberate the scientific, legal, ethical and social issues relating to cloning. In other nations, including in Africa, Asia and central and Eastern Europe, there is a legal vacuum, and no laws have been passed.

Maxime Tardu challenges the total ban on all forms of cloning as difficult to reconcile with Article 4 of the United Nations Covenant on Economic, Social and Cultural Rights, which states that scientific research may be subject 'only to such limitations as are determined by law only in so far as this may be compatible with the nature of these rights and solely for the purpose of promoting the general welfare in a democratic society'.[55] In this case it is a matter of interpretation how far therapeutic cloning represents a promotion of human welfare. In addition, if therapeutic cloning was available, would refusal of treatment amount to a lack of equal opportunity or discrimination? There have been a number of international resolutions banning reproductive cloning, such as the resolution of the World Health Organization General Assembly (WHOGA) and the UNESCO Declaration on the Human Genome and Human Rights. However, at world UN conferences such as those on population (Bucharest and Mexico) and gender equality (Nairobi and Beijing) there has been an increasing emphasis on freedom of procreative choice. Developing international law is therefore likely to be problematic, given the diversity of views held.

Once a policy is enshrined in law it tends to fix attitudes. Moreover, whether an action is legal or not seems to be the foundation for decision-making by bodies such as the HFEA in the UK.[56] The rush to make laws may actually be a disservice in the long term, in that the science is still in its infancy and there has been insufficient debate on the ethical and social aspects of cloning. One key concern from a legal perspective is how far anti-cloning law infringes the twin freedoms of scientists and couples wishing to have children. On the other hand, making cloning illegal has forced scientists to consider alternative ways of treating disease in a way that might not otherwise have been the case. Perhaps the level of public reaction to cloning was attuned to the lack of adequate ethical reflection on the issue. While a moratorium would have solved this problem, it is doubtful if this would have been sufficient to alleviate public fears.

The debate about patenting of animals and human stem cells also raises important issues at the legal/ethical interface. The Conference of European Churches argues that current patent law referring to the scope of biotechnological inventions blurs the distinction between living and non-living in a way that is unacceptable. A US patent has already been granted on 'cells that come from the early embryo and are totipotent', which amounts to monopolization of virtually all human embryonic stem cells. Of course, research on human embryos in the USA is still relatively restricted. The Working Group for the Conference argued that 'To grant a patent on any human body cells seems to us a violation of ethical norms, in that cells of the human body are common heritage of all people.'[57] A similar conclusion was reached in the case of patenting whole animals.[58]

The Ethics of 'Therapeutic' Cloning and Stem Cell Research

The storm over all forms of human cloning shows the extent to which, in the popular mind at least, humans are considered to be a very different moral category from animals. It seems to me that the exaggerated difference in reaction is unfortunate, both for the animals, as it seems to suggest that they do not deserve human respect, and for humanity, since consideration of procedures is ruled out before proper debate. While some secular philosophers, such as John Harris, argue that there are no good reasons why humans should not be allowed to clone themselves, most theologians argue against human reproductive cloning.[59] In addition to the more obvious risk factors in terms of health, the reasons for such a prohibition include, among others: the moral status of the early embryo; the infringement of the 'right' of the child not to be a commodity of its parents; respect for human dignity as being denied through asexual reproduction; the separation of sexuality from procreation and the integrity of family life; the desire to have biological children rarefied without proper consideration of other options such as adoption; using scientific knowledge inappropriately to grasp after an elusive power over nature; a false desire for perfection; a refusal to accept the reality of suffering; promoting still further an unjust system of health care that benefits an elite, and, finally, usurping the rightful place of God in the procreative process, where children are a 'gift'.

The case of therapeutic human cloning is, none the less, rather more ambiguous. Therapeutic cloning involves the same basic method of cell nuclear replacement of an unfertilized egg. However, in this case the cells harvested are at the stem cell stage in embryonic development. These cells have the capacity to develop into a number of different tissue types, depending on conditions. Such 'pluripotent' cells can also be harvested from a range of other tissues, including adult cells, umbilical cord blood, early embryos or foetuses. Given this diversity of source, why bother with cloned embryos? One important reason is that embryonic cells are far more effective in terms of their ability to regenerate other tissues compared with those derived from adult cells. In order to avoid immune rejection, an adult cell from the affected patient would have to be cloned and then harvested for stem cells, which would then be used for the treatment of disease.

The ethics of therapeutic cloning is related to the particular value afforded to the human early embryo. Legal approval of therapeutic cloning in the UK is consistent with approval of embryo research; even the creation of embryos up to fourteen days old for research purposes is legal.[60] Of course, the status of the early embryo is important in such debates; for example, at what 'stage' does the embryo attain 'personhood' and what particular protection should be afforded to such a living entity? The official Roman Catholic position is one that affords protection to the embryo immediately after conception, since although there is some debate about when the embryo acquires a 'personal' status, while this is unknown action should be on the basis of precaution, namely treating the early embryo *as if* it were personal. Scientific counter-arguments that show it is possible to divide up an early embryo to form a number of separate individuals miss the point, namely that such cells are not simply 'cells' but potential human beings. In this scenario the destruction and use of any embryonic tissue is a grave offence.[61] Such a stipulation would rule out research on embryos, harvesting stem cells from foetal tissue and 'therapeutic' cloning. At the other end of the scale, many scientists view the problem differently in terms of the agony of those facing debilitating diseases, and are generally aghast at the possibility of *not* using therapeutic cloning technology:

Is a microscopic cleaving egg, four days after fertilisation, really more important than curing your mother's Alzheimer's, your father's Parkinson's, or your son's diabetes? And before you answer, realise that the diseases I have mentioned are but the tip of the iceberg. Cloned human embryonic stem cells have the potential to cure, or assist in the discovery of a cure, for just about any degenerative disease or disorder that you can imagine. Pliable undifferentiated cloned cells, genetically identical to you, your salvation from the diseases that ail you. Therapeutic cloning is truly a modern day miracle.[62]

Yet before we come to the conclusion that it is ethically correct to proceed, drawn along by the powerful and emotive imaginary scenario just envisaged, it is important to reflect a little more on the ethical basis of such a choice. The argument is consequentialist, the good ends justify the means.[63] In this case the early embryonic stem cells are treated as simply a ball of cells that can be used for research purposes. The UK allows some limited research on early embryos, but the conflation of embryo research with cloning in the manner of the Donaldson report was somewhat unfortunate, for it implies that therapeutic cloning as such raises no new ethical issues at all other than those connected with the 'rights' of the early embryo.[64] There does, none the less, seem to be an ethical distinction between research on early embryos in order to understand normal developmental processes and stem cell research on cloned embryos or 'spare' embryos from IVF treatments, for the purpose of the research is notably distinct. Reprogramming early embryos (cloned or not) so that they become just bone, skin or nerve cells is clearly different from simply researching the development of an embryo in its 'normal', or possibly 'diseased', function. There is also a distinction between deliberately cloning an embryo for use in research and using embryo cells from aborted foetuses or embryos that are not used following IVF treatment. While the former involves the deliberate creation, then destruction, of life, the latter uses what already has a doomed existence in order to gain some benefits in terms of research. The Bioethics Working Group of the Church and Society Commission of the Conference of European Churches were well aware of this distinction, in that in therapeutic stem cell scenarios the embryo is becoming a means to an end. They pointed to the tighter regulation of animal cloning recommended by the UK Ministry of Agriculture Report in 1998, where animals should never become simply a 'means to an end'.[65] While this report did not cover experimentation on early embryos of animals, it is worth noting that adult animals seem to have more protection than early human embryos. In addition, creating a cloned life that has then to be destroyed because reproductive cloning is illegal seemed illogical to many of the working group participants, though of course the same could be said for any research on embryos created for research up to fourteen days old.

Is the instrumentalization of the embryo in therapeutic cloning a step too far in the direction of 'commodification' of potential human life? Even if we accept cloning technology can we really be sure that it will work? Even where animals have been 'used' as guinea pigs in preliminary trials, inevitably vulnerable and sick people will become the subjects of research. For example, there is no guarantee that the cloned stem cells will not turn cancerous and lead to even further problems.[66] Yet it is also worth considering in its favour the freedom of the scientist and the rights of the individual to the possible benefits of the research. Can particular religious and ethical concerns about cloning be imposed on the wider community? The freedom of the individual has to be balanced by the common good to the community as a whole. Who are the real beneficiaries of such cloning technology? Moreover, while the dignity of the early embryo is open to debate, one could argue that such technology facilitates the development of reproductive human cloning, otherwise known as the slippery slope argument.

A stalemate seems to be reached between those who argue that cloned embryos are not to be used and have a privileged status and those who argue that the potential benefits to treatment of disease outweigh such considerations. The European Working Party arrived at an intermediate position, suggesting that 'The creation and use of cloned embryos should not be allowed as a general therapeutic procedure. We urge, therefore, that priority should be put on nuclear transfer research which aims at avoiding use of embryos, by directly programming from one adult body type to another.'[67] Yet while this is an attractive possibility in many respects, considerable time would be needed for research before there was any possibility of clinical trials. In the situation where embryonic stem cells that had differentiated to become particular cell types proved effective for treatment of particular tissues, there would be considerable pressure to use this method rather than a less effective alternative.

Given the difficulties in formulating an ethical basis for human therapeutic cloning I suggest that an alternative approach is explored that relies more on virtue ethics. This would avoid crude ethical judgements that equate embryo research with murder of the innocents or see the embryo as having a total lack of ontological status.[68] In this case, given the particular virtues of charity, humility, justice, prudence, temperance, respect, love and wisdom, how might therapeutic cloning be judged? Clearly, charity demands that we respect views different from our own, but also show compassion for those who are sick. Humility requires that if such technology be used it is done with sensitivity towards the ontological status of the early embryo, even if it does not have an equivalent status to persons in a later stage of development.[69] In this scenario Stephen Clark's just experimentation theory might be helpful, for in the fight against diseases there may be occasions where we accept the risk of limited casualties for the greater good. Yet in the case of therapeutic cloning the relative number of early embryos lost would be considerable, with little guarantee of the benefits. If we adopt a sliding scale ethically through from conception of the early embryo to gestation and birth of the child, where it involves the deliberate creation and mass destruction and loss of life of such embryos for the purposes of possible extension of other lives this would be unwarranted.[70] Accordingly, the extent of loss of life needs to be evaluated very carefully in order to justify such an action. This position tentatively would support a very restricted use of already existing 'spare' IVF embryos in order to create a limited number of embryonic stem cell lines that are required for experimental research prior to the development of adult stem cells, while being much more cautious about the use of deliberate egg cloning to generate stem cells. Prudence also invites use of memory, as well as foresight. How far can we trust those conducting the research to show an appropriate attitude of respect towards the early embryo? It is very easy for early embryos or even foetal tissues to become 'just another cell line'; in fact, it would be almost impossible to do this research without such an attitude. James Keenan argues that the virtue concept of 'respect' is used simply negatively to mean what *cannot* be done to embryos, rather than positively in terms of the good, which is the true meaning of virtue.[71] This does not just apply to scientists. I am, quite frankly, astonished at the proposal for creating 'banks' of suitable tissues for use in transplants in the manner suggested by the ethicist Axel Kahn, who suggested that 'It is also perfectly feasible to create banks of human embryonic stem cells produced from tens of thousands of surplus embryos, frozen after *in vitro* fertilisation, which were not to be used for reproductive purposes and would otherwise be destroyed.'[72] Such an attitude does not, in my mind, show a proper attitude of respect towards what could have become a person, even if these cells would be destroyed anyway. Surely an additional ethical question is to ask *why* so many surplus fertilized eggs are being created, as well as why we should not use them if they were not going to live.[73]

Clear incentives need to be put in place in order to facilitate the shift towards alternative methods that do not involve use of embryos, cloned or not, such as stem cell generation from adult tissue, or genetic engineering of donor cell lines so that immune responses are no longer active in the recipient. Research suggests that this may become a reality in the not too distant future.[74] Those arguing that some limited research on cloned embryos is required since more specialized sources of stem cells are not as effective may seem to be suggesting a reasonable compromise, yet it has to be borne in mind that what was thought to be biologically difficult has been achieved in the past. A moratorium on deliberately creating cloned embryos for stem cells while alternative research possibilities are explored is not unreasonable given this scenario. The complaint of difficulty is surely not a licence for creating cloned embryos, given the ethical concerns associated with such practice.[75] Instead, research using alternative sources of stem cells or even other possible approaches needs to be actively encouraged. In addition, the practical difficulty of obtaining donor egg cells may make therapeutic cloning far less clinically viable than was first thought. The European Working Group predicted such a scenario, suggesting that 'It is very unlikely that enough donor human eggs could ever be provided in order to treat the millions of potential patients across Europe.'[76] There is also the possibility that vulnerable women will be exploited in order to buy their eggs, given the current shortage. Such a move would be reprehensible instrumentalization of women's bodies. Scientists entranced by the possibilities in therapeutic cloning clearly need to take into account these very practical restraints. Creating a chimera between a cow's egg and a human nucleus would also not solve the ethical problems; in fact the use of such intermixed cells would be morally abhorrent, as I discussed in the section above. It reflects an intemperance and desire for control that I raised earlier. In addition to the above, due account needs to be taken of the way cloning technologies are bound up with methods for genetic manipulation. Cloning methods, when combined with IVF, could pave the way for more effective methods for germ line therapy, at present illegal in the UK. We need to consider, then, whether therapeutic cloning would open a further Pandora's box of ethical issues and problems.

None the less, one could argue that the focus on human cloning in the public debate is symptomatic of a shift towards considering human persons simply in terms of our genetics. I have argued in this chapter that animal cloning also deserves serious consideration, not least as it demonstrates the ways in which our own attitude to the natural world is developing. I have suggested that while moves to restrict offensive practices need to take place, a greater sensitivity towards positive virtues of love, prudence, humility, respect, wisdom and temperance also needs to be fostered. Novel technologies are continuing to be developed, so that it is hard for ethics to keep pace with the science. Some have even suggested that policies have become enshrined in laws prior to proper public debate. While most religious leaders reject the idea of reproductive human cloning, that of therapeutic cloning is more ambiguous, bringing with it the promise of rich rewards in terms of treatment for disease. However, it would be prudent to be sanguine about the rhetoric of hope in such new technologies. We need to challenge two opposing mythologies. The first mythology is that living beings are just their genes, and cloning in this scenario represents a threat. The second mythology is that it does not really matter what manipulations are made, since living beings are more than their genes. An ethic of wisdom seeks to adjudicate when and if such changes can be made, given the context of developing an attitude of love and respect towards all creatures. Some distinctions can and must be made between humans and animals. Some limited cloning of animals may be acceptable, but such a technology needs to be a last resort, in awareness of the loss of life and suffering that this entails. It should never be undertaken simply in the interests of scientific curiosity alone. Therapeutic cloning is more difficult to discern. Yet given the way technologies are unfolding and what was once thought impossible is now possible, it does not seem unreasonable to expect scientists to find alternative ways of generating stem cells. We need to ask ourselves what the shift towards such technologies says about the way we are coming to make such decisions in the first place. How has our understanding of the workings of the mind through science influenced our understanding of our capacity for moral agency? We are living in a biological age where the expansion in biological knowledge is unravelling in such a way that the public are now turning to biologists rather than priests in order to understand how and why they behave in certain ways. How might this shift challenge or even inform the way we think about ethics? What implication might this have for an understanding of an ethics of nature orientated towards virtue? An attempt to explore some of these issues forms the subject of the chapter that follows.

Notes

1   See, for example, G. R. Pence, ed.: *Flesh of My Flesh: The Ethics of Cloning Humans* (Lanham, MD: Rowman and Littlefield, 1998); R. Cole-Turner, ed.: *Human Cloning* (Louisville, KY: Westminster John Knox Press, 1997); L. M. Silver: *Re-making Eden: Cloning, Genetic Engineering and the Future of Humankind* (London: Weidenfeld and Nicolson, 1998); J. Harris, *Clones, Genes and Immortality: Ethics and the Genetic Revolution* (Oxford: Oxford University Press, 1998); R. Cole-Turner: *Beyond Cloning: Religion and the Remaking of Humanity* (Harrisburg, PA: Trinity Press International, 2001); A. McLaren, ed.: *Ethical Eye: Cloning* (Strasbourg: Council of Europe Publishing, 2002); P. Lauritzen: *Cloning and the Future of Human Embryo Research* (Oxford: Oxford University Press, 2001); G. McGee: *The Perfect Baby: Parenthood in the New World of Cloning and Genetics*, 2nd edn (Lanham, MD: Rowman and Littlefield 2000); G. McGee, ed.: *The Human Cloning Debate* (Berkeley, CA: Berkeley Hills Books, 2002); J. A. Klotzko: *The Cloning Sourcebook* (Oxford: Oxford University Press, 2002); C. Raël: *Yes to Human Cloning: Immortality Thanks to Science* (Los Angeles: Tagman Press, 2001); M. C. Bannigan, ed.: *Ethical Issues in Human Cloning: Cross Disciplinary Perspectives* (New York: Seven Bridges Press, 2001); M. Ruse: *Cloning: Responsible Science or Technomadness* (Amherst, NY: Prometheus Books, 2001); B. Curran: *A Terrible Beauty is Born: Genes, Clones and the Future of Mankind* (London: Taylor and Francis, 2003).

2   Ted Peters: 'Cloning Shock: A Theological Reaction', in Cole-Turner: *Human Cloning*, pp. 12–24.

3   For a discussion of these issues from a Christian perspective see, for example, N. Messer: *The Ethics of Human Cloning* (Cambridge: Grove Books, 1991); B. Waters, *Reproductive Technology: Towards a Theology of Procreative Stewardship* (London: Darton, Longman and Todd, 2001); R. Song: *Human Genetics: Fabricating the Future* (London: Darton, Longman and Todd, 2002); Cole-Turner: *Human Cloning*; Cole-Turner: *Beyond Cloning*.

4   C. Deane-Drummond: *Biology and Theology Today: Exploring the Boundaries* (London: SCM Press, 2001), pp. 59–62, 109–17, 124–6. The Society, Religion and Technology Project is a notable exception to the trend; see D. Bruce and A. Bruce: *Engineering Genesis: The Ethics of Genetic Engineering in Non-human Species* (London: Earthscan, 1998). A new edition of this book is in the press at the time of writing. As this book goes to press a volume devoted specifically to religious responses to the issue of stem cell research in humans in the light of embryo research is about to be published. B. Waters and R. Cole-Turner, eds: *God and the Embryo: Religious Perspectives on the Debate Over Stem Cells and Cloning* (Washington, DC: Georgetown University Press, 2003).

5   Legislation in the UK was extended to apply to the production of human stem cells by nuclear transfer in 2001, the so-called Human Reproductive Cloning Act.

6   B. Wynne: 'Interpreting Concerns About GMOs – Questions of Meaning', in C. Deane-Drummond and B. Szerszynski, eds: *Re-ordering Nature; Theology, Society and the New Genetics* (Edinburgh: T & T Clark, 2002), pp. 221–48. Ron Cole-Turner suggests that the fourteen-day cut-off point is mostly due to practical and political expediency, though the fact that it coincides with the scientific marker for change is, it seems to me, significant. See R. Cole-Turner: 'Principles and Politics: Beyond the Impasse Over the Embryo', in Waters and Cole-Turner, eds: *God and the Embryo*.

7   A full discussion of the use of therapeutic cloning in humans requires a discussion of medical ethics and the ethics of human genetics, which is outside the scope of this book. It is, none the less, an area of increasing importance and public concern.

8   Ministry of Agriculture, Fisheries and Food: *Report of the Committee to Consider the Ethical Implications of Emerging Technologies in the Breeding of Farm Animals* (London: HMSO, 1995).

9   Stuart Darbyshire is one example; see *Living Marxism*, 115 (1998), cited in S. Clark: 'Thinking About Biotechnology; Towards Just Theory of Experimentation', in Deane-Drummond and Szerszynski, eds: *Re-ordering Nature*, p. 166.

10 For a definition and discussion of speciesism, see chapter 3.

11 The Society, Religion and Technology Project did not appear to take this into account in their discussion of the ethics of using animals as models for disease. See Bruce and Bruce: *Engineering Genesis*, p. 139.

12 Leon Kass, 'The Wisdom of Repugnance' in Pence, ed.: *Flesh of My Flesh*, pp. 13–38.

13 Farm Animal Welfare Council (FAWC): *Report on the Implications of Cloning for the Welfare of Farmed Lifestock* (FAWC, December 1998); see http://www.fawc.org.uk/clone/clonetoc.htm.

14 I discussed the idea of species integrity and the possibility of using this as a basis for environmental ethics in chapter 2.

15 For a discussion of the ethics of crossing over boundaries between species see Deane-Drummond: *Biology and Theology Today*, pp. 103–9 For a fuller discussion of the dilemmas in crossing the species boundary itself, see M. Reiss: 'Is it Right to Move Genes Between Species: A Theological Perspective', in Deane-Drummond and Szerszynski: *Re-ordering Nature*, pp. 138–50.

16 See, for example, F. W. Rogers Brambell: *Report of the Technical Committee to Enquire into the Welfare of Animals Kept under Intensive Livestock Husbandry Systems* (London: HMSO, 1965). This report also, significantly, recommended that animals ought to be allowed to express 'normal' behaviour, though again, while this would rule out the crudest of experiments, exactly what this might mean given the way animals have developed through husbandry and breeding is open for debate.

17 Clark: 'Thinking About Biotechnology', p. 176.

18 The proposal to use cloning to replace a pet cat 'Carbon Copy' announced on 15 February 2002, was roundly rejected by many ethicists; see SRT discussion on this, Society, Religion and Technology Project: 'Animal Welfare and Pet Cloning Ethics', 7 April 2002, accessed 12 August 2002 (http://www.srtp.org.uk/clonin84.htm).

19 Clark: 'Thinking About Biotechnology', p. 175.

20 Reference to steak in cloning, K. Campbell: 'Cloning Dolly', in McLaren, ed.: *Ethical Eye*, p. 62.

21 For a description of the process see Campbell: 'Cloning Dolly', pp. 55–67. As this book goes to press it has been announced that Dolly has died, her early death a salutary warning of the possible dangers of cloning.

22 It is worth noting that cloning animals is less commercially viable than was once supposed, so the impetus for this research has now dropped considerably.

23 For a discussion of these aspects of prudence see Introduction.

24 C. Deane-Drummond: *Creation through Wisdom: Theology and the New Biology* (Edinburgh: T & T Clark, 2000).

25 This first point could allow prudence to take its bearings from natural law, as it is participation in the eternal law. I have chosen in this particular context to relate

prudence to wisdom and covenant in order to reinforce the *theological* emphasis in the notion of wisdom that is rather more ambiguous when natural law becomes the axis of reflection.

26   See Campbell: 'Cloning Dolly', pp. 60–1.

27   See Campbell: 'Cloning Dolly', p. 61; A. E. Schnieke: 'Human Factor IX Transgenic Sheep Produced by Transfer of Nuclei from Transfected Foetal Fibroblasts', *Science*, 278 (1977), p. 2130. The supposed 'efficiency' of cloning has been called into question, given the relatively slow progress in refining cloning technology.

28   D. White: 'Xenografts from Livestock in Animal Breeding', in A. J. Clark, ed.: *Technology for the Twenty First Century* (Amsterdam: Harwood Academic Publishers, 1998), p. 229.

29   For a discussion of the introduction of the term 'ovasome' for cloned human embryos, see A. Kiessling: 'Correspondence', *Nature*, 413, 4 October (2001), p. 453.

30   M. Mulkay: *The Embryo Research Debate: Science and Politics of Reproduction* (Cambridge: Cambridge University Press, 1997).

31   L. Donaldson, chair: *Stem Cell Research: Medical Progress with Responsibility: A Report from the Chief Medical Officer's Expert Group Reviewing the Potential of Developments in Stem Cell Research and Cell Nuclear Replacement to Benefit Human Health* (London: Department of Health, 2000).

32   Bioethics Working Group of the Church and Society Commission Conference of European Churches: *Therapeutic Uses of Cloning and Embryonic Stem Cells: Discussion Document* (Strasbourg, September 2000).

33   See discussion by Colin Tudge: 'Cloning: Who has the Right to Do What and to Whom?', in McClaren, ed.: *Ethical Eye*, pp. 16–17.

34   Tudge: 'Cloning', p. 17.

35   Tudge: 'Cloning', p. 17.

36   I am not suggesting that this is a superfluous argument against reproductive cloning, but that novel biological techniques may circumvent this problem altogether. For a discussion of cloning and parenthood see Messer: *The Ethics of Human Cloning*; Waters: *Reproductive Technology*.

37   See J. Gurdon and J. Byrne: 'The History of Cloning' in McClaren, ed.: *Ethical Eye*, p. 44. The cloning of a horse was announced in August 2003 as this book was going to press.

38   Campbell: 'Cloning Dolly', p. 59.

39   Campbell: 'Cloning Dolly', p. 59.

40   Gurdon and Byrne: 'The History of Cloning', p. 46.

41   See BBC News report: 'Unfertilised Monkey Eggs Give Stem Cells', 31 January 2002, accessed 9 August 2002 (http://news.bbc.co.uk/1/hi/sci/tech/1794667.htm).

42   Donald Bruce argues against the use of parthenogenetic cells from an ethical perspective, and his concern seems to be arising from the unreliability of the science. The treatment would be ineffective for males because of imprinting; that is, specific genes switched on and off in male and female cell lines. As I mentioned above, in a normal embryo these genes are suppressed. See D. Bruce: 'Parthenogenic Stem Cells Don't Solve Embryo Ethical Problems', Press Release, Society, Religion and Technology Project, February 2002, accessed 9 August 2002 (http://www.srtp.org.uk/clonin79.htm).

43   PPL therapeutics press release, 2 January 2002.

44   See D. Bruce: 'Cautious Welcome for "Knockout" Pigs, but Ethical Doubts Remain' (http://www.srtp.org.uk/clonin71.htm).

45 See 'Mouse Clones Die Young', Society, Religion and Technology Project, Press Release (http://www.srtp.org.uk/clonin80.htm). Mice clones showed a significant early death due to shortening of the length of the telomeres at the end of chromosomes. SRTP used the results to argue that this should be further evidence against human cloning; however, I suggest that this also raises issues for animal welfare.

46 House of Lords Hansard, column 92/3, 22 January 2001.

47 A discussion of the ethics of genetic manipulation in humans is outside the scope of this chapter.

48 Tudge: 'Cloning', pp. 18–30.

49 Tudge: 'Cloning', p. 15.

50 Tudge: 'Cloning', p. 33.

51 Tudge: 'Cloning', p. 33.

52 Linda Woodhead contrasts desire for control in the 'power over nature' mythology that exists in genetic science with the equally false desire for security through an image of a totally static universe governed by a rigid conception of 'natural law'. See L. Woodhead: 'Human Genetics: A Theological Response', in I. Torrance, ed.: *Bioethics for the New Millennium* (Edinburgh: Board of Social Responsibility, Church of Scotland, St Andrew Press, 2000), pp. 82–96.

53 See 'The Council of Europe Additional Protocol to the Convention for the Protection of Human Rights and Dignity of the Human Being with Regard to the Application of Biology and Medicine, on the Prohibition of Cloning Human Beings', Appendix III in McClaren, ed.: *Ethical Eye*, pp. 187–90.

54 See P. Aldous: 'Can They Rebuild Us?', *Nature*, 410, 5 April (2001), pp. 622–5.

55 Cited in M. Tardu: 'Legal Responses', in McClaren, ed.: *Ethical Eye*, p. 153.

56 Ruth Deech: 'The Ethics of Embryo Selection', lecture delivered to workshop, The Meaning of the Person; Consciousness, Genetics and Evolutionary Biology, St Anne's College, Oxford University, 12 July 2002.

57 Discussion document prepared by Donald Bruce on behalf of the Working Group on Bioethics, Church and Society Commission, Conference of European Churches, 'Human Stem Cell Patents Would be Unethical', 16 November 2001 (http://www.srtp.org.uk/stempat1.htm).

58 See Bruce and Bruce: *Engineering Genesis*, pp. 211–44. A full discussion of patent law and its ethical implications is outside the scope of this chapter. For a brief discussion see Deane-Drummond: *Biology and Theology Today*, pp. 131–3.

59 See, for example, Cole-Turner, ed.: *Human Cloning*; Cole-Turner, ed.: *Beyond Cloning*: Messer: *Human Cloning*; Song: *Human Genetics*; Waters: *Reproductive Technologies*. For a survey of different possible religious responses see Waters and Cole-Turner, eds: *God and the Embryo*. For arguments for human cloning see Harris: *Clones, Genes and Immortality*. James Peterson is unusual in arguing for human reproductive cloning in some circumstances from a Christian perspective. J. Peterson: *Genetic Turning Points: The Ethics of Human Genetic Intervention* (Grand Rapids, MI and Cambridge: W. B. Eerdmans, 2001), pp. 299–301.

60 The UK is unusual in this respect; other European countries ban the specific creation of embryos for research purposes. See 'The Council of Europe's Position', in McClaren, ed.: *Ethical Eye*, p. 161.

61 For a discussion of the Vatican's position on therapeutic cloning see http://www.vatican.va/roman<us>curia/pontifical<us>academies/acdlife/documents/

rc<us>pa<us>acdlife<us>doc<us>20000824<us>cellule-staminali<us>en.html. For a
discussion of Roman Catholic responses to reproductive cloning see Deane-Drummond:
Biology and Theology Today, pp. 113–15.

62   G. Waite: 'Cloning Stem Cells and Infertility', 2001, (http://www.reproductivecloning.
net); cited with approval in Gurdon and Byrne: 'The History of Cloning', p. 48.

63   Ted Peters and Gaymon Bennett also take a consequentialist view in their stress
on beneficence, the good outcome of the stem cell technologies. See T. Peters and
G. Bennett: 'A Plea for Beneficence: Reframing the Embryo Debate', in Waters and
Cole-Turner, eds: *God and the Embryo*.

64   Donaldson, chair: *Stem Cell Research*. The edited collection by Waters and Cole-
Turner, *God and the Embryo*, also seems in many places to draw close parallels between
the ethics of therapeutic cloning/stem cell research and embryo research, and in some
cases even compares these with questions about abortion. While I agree that the status
of the embryo is an important consideration in ethical debates about all processes, it
is not the only consideration, and it can lead to an unfortunate conflation between
abortion, stem cell research, therapeutic cloning and embryo research.

65   Bioethics Working Group of the Church and Society Commission Conference of
European Churches: *Therapeutic Uses of Cloning*.

66   P. Cohen: 'Hold the Champagne', *New Scientist*, November (1998), p. 6. For further
discussion of this and the Report of the European Bioethics Working Group, see
D. Bruce: 'Ethics Keeping Pace with Technology', in Cole-Turner, ed.: *Beyond Cloning*,
pp. 34–49.

67   Bioethics Working Group of the Church and Society Commission Conference of
European Churches: *Therapeutic Uses of Cloning*.

68   In this I am going to be arguing for a more intermediate position, such as that taken by
Gene Outka. See G. Outka: 'The Ethics of Human Stem Cell Research', in Waters
and Cole-Turner, eds: *God and the Embryo*.

69   In this I am arguing for a gradualist approach to ontological status, while accepting that
the line for and against personhood is hard to draw. To give human life an equivalent
status from the moment of conception seems to me a mistake, as it would put sincere
researchers on the human embryo in the same ethical category as mass murderers. Yet
such early embryos still need to be afforded the respect due to them at this stage in
their development; that is, they cannot be treated simply as another resource that can
be used to benefit others.

70   Aquinas hinted at such a sliding scale in his view that in embryo development we find
a 'plant soul', followed by an 'animal soul' and then finally a human soul, implanted
by God. While full discussion of this issue is outside the scope of this chapter, it is
a matter that is worth developing in the future. See Aquinas: *Summa Theologiae*, 1a,
Qu. 76.3.

71   J. Keenan: 'Casuistry, Virtue and the Slippery Slope: Major Problems with Producing
Human Embryonic Life for Research Purposes', in Lauritzen, ed.: *Cloning and the
Future of Human Embryo Research*, pp. 67–81.

72   A. Kahn: 'Therapeutic Cloning and the Status of the Embryo' in McClaren, ed.:
Ethical Eye, p. 104.

73   Outka has used the 'Why not?' argument drawn from the work of Paul Ramsey
in order to defend the use of 'spare' *in vitro* fertilization (IVF) embryos, though it
seems to me that he does not take into account sufficiently the possible difficulties
of this approach in encouraging the creation of too many embryos. G. Outka: 'The

Ethics of Human Stem Cell Research', in Waters and Cole-Turner, eds: *God and the Embryo*.

74 Aldous: 'Can They Rebuild Us?'

75 I have allowed for a very restricted interim use of 'spare' IVF embryos that would otherwise be destroyed, allowing for the fact that extensive production of 'surplus' embryos through IVF is not acceptable either. See the discussion above.

76 Bioethics Working Group of the Church and Society Commission Conference of European Churches: *Therapeutic Uses of Cloning*. Rather like animal cloning, in the end commercial viability seems to set limits to the use of the technique, rather than ethical considerations as such.

Chapter 6

Psychology and Moral Agency

I have argued throughout this book for a recovery of ways of thinking that are aligned with virtue ethics, though situated in a broader framework of Wisdom theology, orientated towards the good understood in terms of the goodness of God. Aquinas used ways of thinking about the human mind that could not take into account the newer knowledge arising from contemporary psychological studies. It would be beyond the scope of this book to explore all areas of the vast spectrum of psychological knowledge in relation to the development of virtues. I have therefore chosen to focus the question in a specific way and ask in what sense trends in psychology challenge the possibility of moral agency that is presupposed in virtue ethics. In addition, I will consider how far contemporary psychological study actually *enlarges* the possibility for moral agency and development of the virtues, arising from a deeper knowledge of self and mental function. Prudence, in particular, involves a process from deliberation through to action, and hence moral agency is integral at all stages of prudential activity. What, for example, are the particular psychological predispositions needed for valuing the environment and how might they influence the development of virtues? Literature on Christian approaches to environmental ethics seems to have ignored this aspect, perhaps because of the shift away from anthropocentrism towards holism that I have discussed earlier and that I will elaborate further in the next chapter. However, I will argue in this chapter that it is vital to come to terms with the psychological aspects of human nature if we are to understand ways of fostering more responsible (virtuous) approaches to the natural world. In addition, moral agency is a far more important issue when considering ethics orientated towards virtues compared with other ethical approaches that focus more specifically on external duties or consequences of human action. Psychology, situated as it is on the border of neurobiology and social/cultural studies, can form a natural bridge between science and religion. It is also important to stress that while some psychologists are turning to neurobiological studies in order to help to elucidate human behaviour, others resist such a move as unwarranted reductionism. In this chapter I include scientific discussion of psychology from the more biological through to the more cultural end of the spectrum, without presuming any superiority of one over the other, but in order to open up the debate about our biological and psychological human nature and moral agency. However, while strides are being made to relate contemporary psychology to theology, it is disappointing how sparse is the attention being paid to the possible ethical implications from a Christian perspective.[1] Christian ethics is not alone in presuming the freedom of human agency. While it would be impossible to do this enormous field justice in such a short chapter, I intend to use illustrative examples of psychological literature in the light of philosophical discussion on the topics in order to ask what this might do to the elaboration of moral agency and thus the real possibility of the development of Christian virtues that I have been arguing for in this book. Of course, I could have explored what virtues mean from a psychological perspective. However, I suggest that taking this approach would merely *enlarge* our understanding of what it means, for example, to develop wisdom from a scientific point of view.[2] My intention is, instead, to probe those areas of psychology that are becoming increasingly popular and take on the form of a myth, in much the same way that genetics could be said to have acquired mythological status.[3] An ethics of nature needs to be robust enough to face this challenge and show how, far from reducing human behaviour to scientific analysis, contemporary movements in psychology can, instead, enliven the way we think about ourselves, our identity and who we are both in distinctiveness and in kinship relation to other creatures.

In preparing this chapter I became aware of the almost dizzy array of different approaches to psychology and the varied philosophical presuppositions adopted by different authors. Moral psychology is a vast field that can be approached from a philosophical perspective, or through a particular psychological school, or through more intermediate perspectives that try to do justice to both philosophical and psychological analysis.[4] It is also clear that within the field of moral psychology there have been heated debates about how moral development takes place, whether it is through socialization in society, the development of particular character traits or virtues, personal intention in reasoned moral judgment or, more probably, a combination of all three factors.[5] Another related issue is whether morality is learned and acquired through the reinforcement of particular habits, or whether it grows through more immediate transformation and change. A parallel question arises in consideration of the virtues according to the classical tradition, which envisages wisdom as learned but also given by God as gift, leading to personal transformation. Character formation, moral agency and virtue theory become important strands in moral psychology.[6] Within moral psychology there is also an interest in the extent to which we can explain moral (or immoral) behaviour through reference to particular brain states and neurological changes in the brain. There is also a growing popular appeal of all areas of neurobiology, parallel perhaps to the surge in interest in psychotherapy in the 1970s. I have already noted the allure of the gene myth that emerged towards the end of the twentieth century, particularly in Western culture, namely that everything can be explicable through genetics. Those working at the more biological end of the psychological spectrum are enjoying a similar, almost rival, popularity. This amounts to a reinforcement of the scientific naturalistic turn in philosophy.[7] Both genetics and psychology when absorbed into a popular frame of reference can become ways of excusing particular forms of behaviour. Yet from appraisal of the science itself it becomes clear that such a view is very limited in scope, even while being helpful in some cases to explain more bizarre behavioural patterns in those with genetic and/or mental health problems. The popular appeal of psychology can also lead to a negative reaction on the part of some philosophers, who reject naturalism and consider that purely psychological descriptions miss out crucial philosophical and historical factors shaping the way we think and behave. Trying to take all such views into account is itself a psychological task of some difficulty!

I intend to focus this chapter by beginning with a discussion of some psychological research on why, from a psychological perspective, we show complacency towards environmental concern. Are there psychological blocks that might prevent particular environmental virtues developing? How might we take into account psychological research in order to strengthen moral resolve for the good? Next I will ask if the concept of the unconscious excuses particular behaviour or not. Even if we admit that conscious decisions are possible, how do mind and brain contribute to moral agency? This question is critical for a response to the popular trend towards psychological determinism. Given the importance of the emotions to particular virtues, and in some cases their close identification, as in hope and love, for example, how far are such emotions instinctive or cognitive activities? This is particularly important when considering both our kinship with and our distinctiveness from non-human species. A virtue ethic approach gives primacy to the emotions in ethical discourse. However, more cognitive approaches to decision-making are also integral to some virtues, such as prudence and wisdom, and hence we need to consider psychological theories about cognition. While engagement is necessarily limited, my intention is first to clear away any misgiving that psychological explanations of behaviour preclude the possibility of moral agency and second to show how psychological understanding actually enlarges our perception on humanity as a virtuous agent in relation to the natural world.

The Psychology of Environmental Value

One of the questions that has received relatively little attention in either the psychological literature or the literature on environmental ethics is the underlying psychology of the way we think about the environment. In chapter 2 I suggested that environmental ethics needed to show an awareness of scientific ecology, as well as be informed by particular approaches to valuing the environment, including fostering virtues such as love, prudence/wisdom, temperance and justice and so on. This implies that if our attitude to the natural world were correct, then behavioural change would follow. However, psychological studies have shown that in Western cultures there is a considerable gap between generally positive attitudes to the environment and willingness to behave in ways that are ecologically friendly.[8] This suggests that prudence is incomplete; it has failed to lead to positive action according to deliberative intentions. How might we explain such discrepancy? In terms of practical policy, psychological research suggests that imposing particular environmental standards may encourage a 'no law against it' mentality that obscures the particular goal behind the standard, namely environmental protection.[9] Such research implies that ethics focused simply on what is legal according to rules is unhelpful psychologically when it comes to the treatment of nature. If attitudes towards specific practices, such as recycling, are measured, then there is less of a gap between stated attitude and behaviour.[10] In these cases, if a second use for a particular recyclable item is specifically identified, then people are more likely to make a decision to take action, since in general they resist the idea of wastefulness.[11] It also shows that if the common good is identified at the start, prudential decisions are easier to undertake. Policy-makers need to facilitate environmentally friendly decisions by making it psychologically easier to make such decisions. This is not social manipulation, but coherent with prudential and practical reasoning.

A further area worth discussion in the context of the present chapter is the way mental models have been constructed. For example, we might ask ourselves why the Northern elite mind is likely to be biased against community, the environment and a sustainable future.[12] The difficulties encountered in reaching mutual agreement during the Johannesburg Summit on Sustainable Development that took place in August 2002 seem to reinforce such an idea.[13] There are a number of related factors contributing to this problem. There are biological, worldview, contemporary and psychodynamic issues in the way thinking takes place in such cultures.[14] From a biological perspective it could be argued that neurobiological evolution took place under simpler, slower environmental conditions, so that the more automatic mental machinery is adapted to a very different world from the one humanity inhabits at present.

Gladwin et al., for example, suggest that biological evolution would tend to favour minds that could focus on one issue at a time, rather than complex systems, and that hence show a bias towards disconnection, rather than connection. This clearly does not apply in recent human history; for example, while Aquinas would have lived in an environment that was less subject to change compared with our own, he was clearly capable of synthetic and connective thinking to the highest degree. In addition, Gladwin et al. suggest that proximate effects would be more readily grasped, rather than long-term implications, and causes would be related to simple issues, rather than understood in their variegated complexity. In this scenario human perception would be generally ordered around certainties, rather than uncertainties. One of the difficulties of translating Aquinas's thinking into a contemporary context is his focus on certainties; however, he allows for uncertainty to an extent that has not always been given to his credit. Moreover, Gladwin et al. believe that reactions would be more rapid when a discrepancy is encountered;

while slowly developing and steadily compounding issues would elicit much weaker responses, even though the threat may be much greater. Modern examples of this might be the public overreaction to the cloning of Dolly the sheep, which disguises much broader and more general trends towards a biotechnological culture that is much harder to perceive.[15] As human minds interact other biological factors come into play that reinforce such mentality, including, for example, defensive routines, game playing and herd instincts, as well as 'social traps, prisoner's dilemmas and tragedies of common property at the societal level'.[16] Yet, given this scenario, it would be difficult to change the biological substrate given the overall time scale in which it has evolved.

Yet we can ask ourselves at this point whether 'the biological mind' really functions in the way suggested so far, given the difficulties of separating biological from social factors. The validity of this claim by Gladwin et al. depends on particular assumptions behind the relationship between mind and brain that I will return to in a section below. However, if we accept this analysis as the worst possible scenario, then given that we cannot change our biological substrate, other ways of thinking need to come into play in order to counter such biological trends. Gladwin et al. suggest that other ways of thinking currently in place may actually reinforce the difficulties; for example, current worldviews orientated towards atomism, mechanism, anthropocentrism, rationalism and individualism.[17] In addition, they argue that the contemporary mind is biased towards efficiency, growth, secularism, narcissism and techno–optimism, rather than social justice, spirituality and altruism. And as if this is not enough, they add the suggestion that the psychodynamic mind of today is biased towards repression, denial, projection, rationalization and insulation. It is worth considering each of these psychological factors in turn.

They argue in the first place that the fact that there might not be generations to follow because of impending environmental collapse can lead to considerable *angst*, so that repression follows; that is, the involuntary assignment of consciously repugnant ideas to the unconscious. The authors describe repression in the following way:

> Repression serves to hide information regarding potential threats to our livelihoods and the ways we view the world. With diminished attention or blank minds, we fall victims to forces of sociological and political propaganda. And because what is repressed from conscious memory is not deactivated, but remains unconsciously active, emotionally charged and potent, it tends to manifest itself in disguised symbolic form as generalised anxiety disorders.[18]

Denial, on the other hand, works to obliterate external reality, a way of blocking out the real pain of the world. Why, for example, did different nations find it so hard to agree on ways of dealing with the acute lack of clean water for millions of people worldwide at the Earth Summit in Johannesburg in 2002? One of the many factors involved is likely to be the denial of the reality of the problems at hand. Prudence includes a clear-sighted view of reality, facing the facts and being prepared to address the issue in realistic ways.

Projection is another form of psychological defence, where particular enemies are created as a way of avoiding facing up to personal responsibility. The tendency to blame other parties in issues of environmental concern is well known. Rationalization is a further, perhaps even more insidious, process, for it leads to complacency in the name of truth, so that 'with rationalisation, true, unworthy, and unconscious motives remain hidden, while reasonable, safe, and creditable (yet counterfeit) explanations are employed to account for one's practices or beliefs'.[19] The debates over GM foods and other claims and counter claims over a host of practices relating, for example, to issues over food safety in Britain in the past fifteen years or so give sufficient examples of such tendencies towards rationalization. The psychology of this process is the contemporary way of explaining what Aquinas described as sham prudence, using cunning as a means of attaining a goal or distorting the true goal in line with personal preferences. Finally, and importantly, there is the possibility of more generalized psychic numbing, whereby individuals acquire an armour of habitual mental routines that are defensive in reaction, displaying particular neurotic styles to ward off anxieties. Such insidious processes allow 'humans to do evil while believing that they are doing good'.[20] While Aquinas did not use modern psychological language, he rejected such behaviour as sinful, even while recognizing the need for taking counsel, listening to another in order to arrive at a clear perception of the truth.

When faced with the question of how to begin to change such deep-rooted attitudes there seems to be no answer for the psychologist, for 'How does one put an entire popular culture onto a therapeutic couch'?[21] Of course, what this research has shown is the subtlety of insidious tendencies in human thinking and behaviour. Yet it is just such attitudes that a virtue ethic seeks to address. More particularly, from a Christian point of view, alternative habits of mind can begin to take root as the Christian believer seeks to conform to 'the mind of Christ'.[22] Sinful behaviour can also be addressed by reliance not just on self, but also on the grace of God. Such a change is necessarily slow and perhaps painful if true honesty and integrity is to be reached. Yet is it also apparent that changes in attitude are not simply the work of isolated individuals, but the work of a community, a community of character, as Stanley Hauerwas would suggest.[23] As I have discussed the issues so far, a psychology of mind is indicative of the need for alternative ways of thinking to be embedded in social and cultural practice. However, we might ask ourselves how far human behaviour can ever be 'programmed', even in a weak sense, by biological modes of thinking. In order to discuss this further the crucial question of human agency comes to the fore.

Human Agency and the Unconscious

The possible identification of the biological processes involved in consciousness has become a fashionable topic in contemporary research, at both the popular and the more scholarly level.[24] In order to discover the meaning of the unconscious, it is instructive to define the different meanings of consciousness.[25] If an organism has sensory experience and can perform mental functions, then it is conscious at the most basic level. However, in addition to this, one can know that we know something, or have reflective self-consciousness. Finally, having feelings about something in an inner experience, or *qualia*, could also be said to be a conscious activity. I indicated above that repression to the unconscious was one response to environmental threat, and becoming conscious of such a threat is more likely to lead to change in behaviour.

If the Western world has repressed its concern for non-human nature, what does this mean in ethical terms? From a psychoanalytical stance the exploration of the unconscious is critical. It is even more important for ethics, since, as John Riker suggests, 'ethics is founded on a psychology which assumes that humans can come to know and master all their sources of motivation, while the psychology of the unconscious denies this fundamental assumption'.[26] While freedom is presupposed in ethical theory, including environmental ethics, psychology of the unconscious seems to challenge such a belief, and suggests that flawed developmental histories contribute to behaviour patterns (environmental vices?) that are outside the control of the persons concerned.[27] However, this is not exactly true of virtue ethics, especially that orientated on prudence in the manner I have discussed so far. Prudence is never simply isolated individual soul searching, even at the level of individual good, for although it includes a contemplative element, *taking counsel* is the first stage. There is, therefore, every reason to *include* psychological knowledge in this taking of counsel; indeed, I would suggest that in some circumstances it is *essential* to do so. Even having taken counsel the decision-making and judgement is that of an individual, so freedom of choice remains. Close analysis of the motivations of those involved can show claims for good intentions, but also more subtle and pervasive destructive tendencies that would not be obvious from bald self-descriptions of behaviour. This is analogous to what Aquinas has described as 'sham prudence'.

However, is such evil simply yet another narcissistic personality disorder, as some psychologists would have us believe? Riker argues that *maturity* is the point of intersection between psychologists' view of behaviour and ethical mandates for social responsibility. It is also a primary value in Aristotelian thought on the development of the virtues, though I would prefer to call this maturity prudence. One of the problems that Riker identifies is a lack of orientation towards the good in ethical debate; the classical notion of good in the Christian tradition is replaced by an individual liberal view of the good chosen on an autonomous basis. Indeed, the ideal of autonomy is embedded in practical psychoanalytic methods. Such prudence is, accordingly, *partial* when analysed in the light of the classic notion of good. Consequently, while psychology is helpful in identifying the underlying motivations for behaviour, it is less helpful in its teleology, for it assumes a limited autonomous good that is restrictive in scope. The crucial and critical task becomes one of drawing on the insights of psychology, without submitting to its underlying philosophy of individualism.

Riker also seems to be aware of the shift towards greater holism in environmental ethical perspectives, though he does not specifically refer to environmental concerns as such. He argues that such individualism needs to be replaced by a notion of 'ecological maturity' whereby selves 'can act autonomously while being connected to a role structure in the social order and deeply committed to intimate friendships, have a keen knowledge of their particular environment and wider interest in the world, are responsive to beauty and see the sacred as an essential part of life'.[28] While this seems an attractive possibility, namely an affirmation of the self in a healthy relationship to one's inner and outer identities, Riker seems to come close to a form of naturalism when he states that 'the ecological self balances freedom with fate'.[29] From the point of view of Christian virtue ethics that I have been elaborating, the goal of the goodness of God becomes primary, but it is set in the context of a social life, orientated with reference to the Christian community, but understood in the broadest sense as inclusive of both the wider human community and the community of creation. The idea of memory that is integral to the deliberative stage of practical wisdom (prudence) has to be enlarged to include the idea of *unconscious* memories. Those psychologically damaged by their own prior experience are in need of healing at a number of different levels. The virtue of love as informing all decision-making can serve to foster such healing. In addition, the virtue of patience is clearly essential, for those who have acquired negative habits of mind take considerable time to think in different ways.[30]

Moral Agency and Mind/Brain Questions

Of course, once we are conscious of particular thought processes, then it becomes impossible to deny the possibility, at least, of genuine moral agency. However, the way in which brain function relates to mental processes becomes critical for understanding the possible *extent* of human agency in different circumstances. The idea that we might be held responsible for our actions forces us to consider the distinction between biological reflexes and deliberate choices. The concept that we might act simply according to biological reflexes would seem to obviate any moral agency. In this scenario, is prudence feasible, given that it includes a unique capacity for human self-reflective reasoning? Biological reflexes could be used, for example, to excuse particular forms of immoral behaviour.[31] This needs to be qualified by the fact that we need to take into account the strong survival instinct of all species before coming to too hasty judgements on those who are environmentally irresponsible when faced with, for example, possible starvation or threats to their immediate families.

However, one of the distinctive characteristics of human nature is its ability to be self-reflective. Debates between scientists and philosophers on the way mind and brain relate are particularly useful in showing the real extent to which our actions, including moral actions, might or might not be 'conditioned' by brain function. Colin Blakemore comments that 'It seems to me to make no sense (in scientific terms) to try to distinguish sharply between acts that result from conscious intention and those that are pure reflexes or that are caused by disease or damage to the brain.'[32] However, from an ethical point of view making this distinction is *absolutely crucial*.[33] Midgley somewhat wryly points out that 'If a scientist were proved to have composed his article entirely by luck, merely by a series of muscular twitches as he sat at the keyboard without ever thinking the thoughts that seem to be expressed in it, he would not be considered responsible for that article and he would get no credit for it.'[34] This is where, perhaps, science begins to reach its limits, for Blackmore's denial of scientific validity in all probability reflects a genuine scientific difficulty in the study of consciousness, understood as higher order functions. As Midgley also suggests, the brain is just one part of us, an essential ingredient of mind, rather like one aspect of the way of perceiving human being. She suggests that we are like observers looking through one window in an aquarium or are living in a single world with many maps.[35]

Of course, the many maps model also has its problems, since it does not account for the fact that brain chemistry of some form is required for all higher mental activity, including consciousness, even if it is insufficient as an explanation of it. Midgley's stress is on the discontinuity of different ways of approaching mental activity. For her the ways we treat each other have been shaped by hard experience over many centuries, so that even to attempt to localize such actions in the brain is missing the point. There are other philosophers who have developed the notion of emergence as best explaining the relationship between brain and mind. According to this idea the mind *emerges* from brain function in a supervenient way, so that while it is rooted in brain function in one sense, it also acquires characteristics that are more than those simply explicable at the level of neural impulses.[36] While Nancy Murphy argues for the physicalist theory, the holistic form of the theory developed by Donald Davidson goes some way to responding to Midgley's critique of the levels approach, so that events are not just mental or physical, but a single, ontologically neutral class of entities.

Davidson's resistance to laws connecting brains and minds leads to his suggestion that there are differences in *type* between mental and physical activities (analogous to the two maps model for Midgley), so that for physical reality there is a law-like relationship with other physical phenomena, while for mental activity reasons, beliefs and intentions are all important.[37] Yet the connectivity between brain and mind is likely to be even looser at higher orders of consciousness than at lower levels. At the lowest level of consciousness some correlation exists between brain and mind, though this needs to be considered in terms of token–token relationships, rather than through type–type relationships.[38] Neils Gregerson, correctly in my view, doubts whether it will ever be possible to find physical determinism of any kind with respect to higher order consciousness. At this level it makes no sense to talk about individual neural firing in the individual brain, but much more sense to include considerations of social relationships and culture. This research shows that while mind and brain cannot be separated in a dualistic way, mental activity is more than just the neural firings in our brain. Behaviour cannot be reduced to brain function, any more than it can be reduced to genetics.

How might we take into account this more complex view of the relationship between mind and brain in order to evaluate human actions and moral agency? One possibility is Karl Popper's notion of three worlds to distinguish between different areas of human functioning.[39] He suggested that World 1 is that of physical states, World 2 that of states of consciousness and psychological dispositions, as well as unconscious states, and World 3 that of stories, myths, tools, scientific theories, social institutions, works of art and so on. Some areas of human activity belong to two worlds at once; for example, sculpture is both World 1 and World 3. He insists that perceptions are not as much 'given' to us as 'made' through human ingenuity. Popper seems to be unfashionable today, perhaps because he retained a dualistic understanding of mind and body that is no longer tenable.[40] The provisional conclusion is that while higher order mental functions, including ethical deliberations, require brains in some sense, the requirement is not causal in any rigid sense; rather, such thinking emerges through the complex interaction between individual minds set in a community of other minds who have developed patterns of thought over centuries of reflection. Such a view would cohere with the recovery of the classical sense of virtues, even if aspects need to be expanded in the light of what is currently known about mental function. Any fusion of deliberate choice with brain reflex function needs to be resisted, even if it is scientifically convenient to do so. Scientific research has failed to reduce consciousness to brain activity, leaving open the possibility of mind and human agency in free relationship with God, even while helping to enlarge ways of conceiving such a relationship at a neurobiological level.

The Emotions and Moral Agency

The intensive debates between philosophers and scientists on questions about the relationship between mind, brain and human agency are also reflected to some extent in more detailed work on the emotions. The emotions are also integral to virtue approaches to ethics and are intimately connected with the central theme of this chapter; that is, moral agency. In other words, virtues take emotions into account in deliberations over moral agency to a much greater extent than other ethical frameworks. Of course, some emotions are more relevant to the understanding of virtues than others and my discussion is illustrative, rather than including the whole gambit of emotional responses, such as grief, embarrassment, shame, guilt and so on.

Analysis of the emotions also illustrates a more modest role for psychology as intermediary between neurobiology and social/cultural value. This is also consistent with the idea that psychology inhabits Popper's World 2, though in this case World 2 includes an area of overlap between World 1 and World 3. The windows of Midgley's aquarium do, it seems to me, bridge into one another in interesting ways that this analogy finds difficult to portray. Luria's early work in neuroscience, for example, showed that learning new practices can actually reshape the brain and nervous system; in other words, our physical nature is plastic in its response to the demands made on it.[41] A study of the emotions bridges the gap between philosophy, cultural psychology and neuroscience. In general terms emotions are linked to the development of the virtues. But how might we link an Aristotelian understanding of virtue to modern conceptions about brain function? Gerrod Parrott and Rom Harré explain this succinctly in the following way:

> Certain emotions, such as shame and anger, also function to facilitate social control. This controlling function not only enforces norms but has a developmental purpose as well. By encouraging people to act in socially appropriate ways, the emotions of social control help to build the habits that constitute a virtuous character. For Aristotle, a person of good character is one whose mental functioning has been shaped by culture to function properly within that culture. His notion of character is defined by a person's perceptions and dispositions, the reactions that come naturally to a person. In modern terms, he considers the structure and function of the nervous system to be altered by the process of socialization. Aristotle's view that emotion is intimately involved with the development and display of character thus illustrates, as well as anything written since, our goal of linking the cognitive and cultural aspects of emotion with the somatic.[42]

We might want to ask in what way emotions are more precisely linked with bodily/brain function. Are they simply thoughtless natural energies, or is there some intelligence/mental activity involved? Martha Nussbaum has argued convincingly from a philosophical perspective that emotions are *intelligent*, as they are directed to someone or something in an intentional way. Hence, 'in fear one sees oneself or what one loves as seriously threatened. In hope one sees oneself or what one loves as in some uncertainty, but with a chance for a good outcome. In grief one sees an important object or person as lost; in love as invested with a special sort of radiance.'[43] The objects of emotions are not just 'tools' for individual satisfaction, even though they contribute to a person's flourishing; that is, they are eudaimonistic. She also suggests that beliefs are integral to the emotion itself, rather than simply a prerequisite for it. She resists a strict Aristotelian view on the emotions, as she believes he does not take sufficient account of individual preferences and conflicts of emotion; hence things I value cannot always be commended to others in an Aristotelian way. However, I suggest that while this may be true, from the point of view of an ethics of nature it is those things that are valuable to both individuals and communities for the common good that are worth the closest attention. Individual objects of emotional value that are not of general value to all are worth ethical consideration from the point of how that individual might live, but where these clash with community and social values they may need to be adjusted or discarded. For example, I may love my dog, but if this dog becomes vicious or threatens young children, then it can no longer be allowed to roam free and in more extreme cases may need to be 'put down'. Nussbaum also criticizes Aristotle for not taking into account the unconditional nature of love; for example, that common between parent and child. Aquinas's understanding of love does not suffer from this neglect, since it is rooted in an understanding of the unconditional and free love of God.

The importance of stressing that there is also a physiological component to emotion comes from Anthony Damasio's study of a patient called Elliot with a benign brain tumour, whose mental functioning seemed to be remarkably similar to that of the unfortunate individual Phineas Gage, a construction worker who had a bizarre accident in 1848, wherein an iron bar penetrated right through his skull into his brain, then out the other side.[44] In both cases knowledge and perception were unaltered, but there was no emotional quality to their lives. In the case of Elliot, Damasio was able to make a first-hand study of his psychology and found that his emotions and his capacity for making decisions and setting priorities were damaged. In other words, the goals or eudaimonistic sense was lacking in his life. While the results suggest that emotions have a physiological basis, they do not necessarily encourage the specific localization of the frontal lobe with emotional function: the capacity of the brain to remain plastic with regard to such function warns against such a conclusion.

Nussbaum also helpfully distinguishes between feelings and emotion: feelings are associated with emotion, but the extent of that feeling varies between individuals and cultures. She is somewhat sceptical about the possibility of *qualia*, which are feeling states that are universal across subjects. This is partly related to the nature of emotions as connected to imagination, so that 'what this means is that the emotions typically have a connection to imagination, and to the concrete picture of events in imagination, that differentiates them from other, more abstract judgmental states'.[45] Nussbaum's philosophy is consistent with the American psychologist James Averill's position. He argues that emotion has been falsely portrayed as primitive, impulsive, contrasted with reason, located in bodily function or lower brain areas and altogether more 'brutish'.[46] Such an attitude also has a long philosophical history, with David Hume suggesting that reason was not sufficient to motivate action, so that reason was the determination of means to ends supplied by our desires and emotions.[47] While there is still some debate about the possibility of explaining moral feeling and motivation as products of psychological processes that are independent of reason, the trend seems to be towards a more integrated view. Averill gives some support for this by suggesting that psychological evidence shows that human emotional life is far more complex and requires mental capacity beyond that of animals; not all human emotions are associated with physiological changes, lower brain areas require an integration into a larger, more complex system and, finally, emotions require appraisals of the world in order to appear. In addition, more specific neurobiological evidence shows a lack of correlation between emotions and neurochemistry, so that: 'Distinct emotions are not correlated with distinct physiological conditions, neither in the central nor in the automatic nervous system, nor in the associated neurochemistry of transmitters. There are very large individual differences in data, even though there is obviously a physiological underpinning to the display and experience of emotions.'[48]

The two-factor view that emotions are basically 'animalistic' and then adjusted by culture is now severely challenged. Moreover, it is difficult to distinguish social expression of emotion from that generated internally, since an imagined 'other' can always be present. The account of the emotions given so far might suggest that animals are not capable of emotion. However, there are animals that, to a greater or lesser degree, do have such a capacity, but it is important to note that in these cases as well the emotion is linked with rational activity. The emotion of fear, for example, has been studied in rats in terms of instinctive reactions, particular choices or actions and habitual patterns of action.[49] The idea that emotion involved 'some sort of judgement' can also be traced to Darwin's work on other species.[50] The range of emotion in animals is open to question, just as the degree of reasoning power in animals is less than that of humans.

Aquinas's discussion of emotions in animals and humans needs updating in the light of contemporary knowledge, though the fact that he recognized the capacity for animals to feel emotions is in itself significant. He also allowed for reasoning activity in animals, though perhaps not to a sufficient extent to take into account contemporary studies of primate behaviour. In both humans and animals emotions are appraisals of the world that relate to their sense of well-being. Animals' emotions must remain specific to the creature, rather than be projections on to those animals from human experience. However, those who have had close contact with animals and observed their behaviour have found that the valuation of dogs for their keepers, for example, outruns any simple instrumental interest in the requirement for food. The philosopher, George Pitcher, tells a moving narrative of how he won over the trust of a stray dog that had previously been seriously abused by humans.[51] He suggests that his dog was capable of a type of unguarded and unqualified 'love' that is not common among human relationships. The fact that animals are capable of showing emotion demonstrates that such emotions are not necessarily the result of reflexive self-consciousness.

The idea that altruism may have an evolutionary origin has been the subject of intense debate, especially among those who argue for forms of evolutionary ethics.[52] At first sight it seems that altruism is a corrective to the more competitive aspects of Darwinian theory. However, altruism understood in terms of biological fitness is also ultimately that which enables survival, normally understood in terms of inclusive fitness or reciprocal altruism. Elliott Sober and David Wilson argue for a form of group altruism that goes beyond kin interests and reciprocity in a group. Their views contribute to a discussion of whether genuine altruism exists that does not have a hidden self-serving aim, though as the survival of the group is thought to be enhanced by this process, their theory is still tied into an evolutionary perspective.[53] As applied to human behaviour, important insights include research on psychopaths who have impaired ability to show compassion or children who suffer from autism, and in both cases the behaviours are likely to be related to physiological changes.[54] This would help those who are recipients of such behaviour to show compassion towards those who are so afflicted. Other behavioural responses could also be investigated from the point of view of evolutionary ethics, though the focus so far has been almost exclusively on altruism.[55]

Robert Pluntchick has suggested that basic patterns found in animals have their counterparts in higher animals, including humans; for example, in protection, expressed eventually as fear, destruction as anger, incorporation as acceptance, rejection as disgust, reproduction as joy, reintegration as sadness, orientation as surprise and exploration as curiosity.[56] However, the problem with Pluntchick's account is that while it is capable of linking genetics with neurobiological function through to altruistic or other feelings, it can give the false impression that biological processes are somehow always hooked into social and cultural expressions in a way that seems to me to be quite unjustified. Rather more sophisticated research with human twins finds a genetic *component* to particular attitudes, values and religious consciousness, though the way genetic and social factors interact and the source of genetic variation is too complex to be clearly identified.[57] However, it is clear from this research alone that the effects of genes are not permanent or unchangeable, implying a flexibility or adaptation in given circumstances.

Colin Grant argues that altruism as biologically defined is very different compared with how it is understood according to the Christian tradition, for in the latter case it focuses on actions that are genuinely self-sacrificial in way that is difficult to explain in terms of genetic inheritance or Darwinian self-interest.[58] Grant discusses altruism in the light of the tendencies to see altruism in terms of self-interest. Deliberate behaviour implies, for Grant, a leaning towards self-righteousness, so he argues in favour of *indirection* in altruism. I suggest, in contrast, that deliberation is entirely appropriate for prudential activity, though in Aquinas's scheme charity infuses other virtues in a way that prevents the kind of distortion Grant proposes. Yet altruism in the Christian tradition is remarkably anthropocentric, and to extend it beyond the human community; that is, towards non-humans, in the particular way that Linzey attempts seems to me to be forced.[59] Instead, charity reorientated ethics is grounded in the love of God in a way that is impossible for secular altruism; hence the importance of charity as one of the three theological virtues and, for Aquinas, the mother of all virtues.

Once the love of God becomes the focus, then charity also lends itself to cross-species concern that is more difficult for altruistic love, which is most commonly defined in terms of unselfish behaviour towards other conspecifics. It is worth noting that evolutionary altruism is defined in terms of specific actions of an individual that, while decreasing its fitness, also increase the overall fitness of a group, compared with other groups. Psychological altruism, on the other hand, is focused on feelings that motivate behaviour, regardless of consequences.[60] Charity is more akin to the latter, though in comparison, does take account of consequences, rather than just being an emotional state.

Some emotions, such as hope, are not likely to be found in animals, at least in the sense that goes beyond simple anticipation. Hope is also commonly without bodily symptoms and varies enormously between different cultures, so that what we might hope for is clearly situated in the social context in which individuals are placed.[61] From a psychological point of view hope takes its specific cues from cultural and social constructions.[62] Hope, purpose and higher meaning can only emerge from science in a relatively superficial way, since science can never encompass the full breadth of human experience.[63] This is one of the reasons why evolutionary accounts resist teleological explanations, apart from those limited to short-term survival. The clash with Christian understanding becomes clear, for from the point of view of Christian theology hope is grounded in a particular story and narrative, namely the birth, death and resurrection of Jesus Christ. Hope is meaningful from a Christian point of view only within the bounds of faith, which is why Romanus Cessario names faith as the first virtue, since it grounds the theological life, leading to lives marked by hope and love.[64] Even from a secular point of view it is clear that an atmosphere of trust creates the climate in which human beings can thrive.[65] The philosopher Annette Baier argues that trust depends on goodwill towards another, for the truster risks abuse and so is vulnerable. Yet trust is situated in the context of a network of social trust, including distrust. Christian faith can include this element as well, since while it invites trust, it also cautions disciples to be on their guard towards those who might claim to be in positions of authority, namely the Pharisees.[66] This analysis suggests that while virtues such as hope become enlarged through an increase in psychological knowledge, where it serves to clash with the goal of the Christian life, namely hope in the goodness of God, it needs to be resisted.[67] In other words, secular hope cannot do the transformative work that is integral to a Christian understanding of hope, reaching as it does to the boundary beyond self to God as Other and resting on faith in the resurrection of Jesus Christ.

Another emotion worth mentioning in this context, as it is also an important virtue, especially in relation to environmental concern, is the capacity for wonder. Wonder is less introspective than many of the other emotions, since it looks out to the world and wonders about its beauty. It is also a virtue that is intimately linked with the virtue of wisdom, for wisdom sees creation in all of its wonderful complexity and diversity. Wonder causes us to move beyond our subjectivity to Being itself.[68] Nussbaum has suggested that wonder is frequently bound up with our ability to show compassion, so that where we see the natural world suffering or in pain, wonder helps to shape the conception of what it means to flourish.[69]

Moral Agency and Neurophysiological Science

A group of mental processes that are different, but also related to the emotions, are those processes classified under the term cognition, meaning remembering, deciding, reasoning, classifying, planning and so on. Cognitive developmental theories have largely replaced earlier behaviourist models that assumed that environmental triggers governed human agency.[70] An area of growing scientific research interest is the neurological basis for cognitive capacities. The combined study of neural and mental activity is known as cognitive neuroscience. Yet if the virtues are learned but also the 'gift' of God how might this be understood in terms of cognitive science? The latter relates to the issue of how to understand religious experience in general, and current attempts to locate religious activity in particular parts of the brain. Like Fraser Watts, I would be hesitant to read much into some of the research that claims to have identified 'God-spots' in the brain.[71] It is a false dichotomy to claim that we need to choose between religious experience being 'caused' by either the brain or God, since God relates to humanity as a psycho-somatic whole, mind, body and spirit. Trying to find an underlying causal 'agent' reflects a failure to understand the nature of mental activity and its multiple causal-ity, and the fact that the same brain or cognitive activity could take place as a result of many different experiences. Watts suggests that religious experience, like the emotional experience discussed above, is most likely to be concentrated in the frontal lobe region of the brain, but this does not prove that religion, or ethics for that matter, is simply the result of neural function.[72]

There have also been attempts to relate emotional life to cognitive theories that are somewhat more sophisticated than the two-factor view critiqued in the section above. Cognitive theories at this stage are not trying to relate mental events to neurological data; rather, they are attempts to organize different mental functions around different possible schemes. One of the more interesting cognitive theories is that of John Teasdale and Philip Barnard, known as interacting cognitive sub-systems (ICS).[73] ICS are separated into the propositional and implicational systems. The implicational system abstracts meanings from lower level subsystems and from these meanings emotion arises, eventually to be translated into more definite codes found in the propositional system. A propositional system becomes clear in particu-lar theories, including ethical theory. Fraser Watts suggests that the implicational system is especially significant for religious experience, which he likens in scope to emotional experience, prior to its formulation into particular language and codes. He also suggests that the ultimate aim would be to identify the neural substrate of the implicational system.[74] From the perspective of neuroscience there is the possi-bility that our perception of the brain as isolating processing units is too simple. Instead, the possibility for coordination between local processing systems seems to be expressed in neurological function, and in the theory of neuronal computation this is known as 'coherent informax'.[75] However, while this neurological experi-ence may be *analogous* in some sense to higher order coordinating functions, such as wisdom, it cannot be said that such neurological systems are the *basis* of such functions. It seems to me that ICS is an interesting theory that may have practical use for psychological analysis as a heuristic tool, but that is all that it is. In addition, for the purposes of virtue ethics there are some terms that range across both implicational and prepositional systems. Wisdom is a particularly good example: it is formulated in a language that cues into the experience of mystery in God as the God of wisdom; in the Hebrew Bible it uses metaphors, analogies and so on that are different from those in other literature that is more discursive and 'propositional' in tone. Having said this, wisdom also has prepositional elements within it, while resisting systematic definition. It is the ability of wisdom to bridge mystical experi-ence and theology, and encourage holistic thinking, rather than linear thinking, that makes it somewhat different from the kind of 'step' approach that is indicated by this two-system analysis. Seeking, in other words, to link aspects of ICS (Pop-per's World 2) with neurological data (World 1) misses the point when it comes to much religious experience.

Given the above discussion, it is worth considering the claims of Roger Sperry, who argues that science, especially neuroscience, can actually contribute to an understanding of human values. He begins with the practical issue that he sees at hand, namely the tendency to assume that science is insufficient in dealing with global problems, or even causative of them.[76] He also recognizes the power of values in helping to shape decisions and, thus, ultimately control world events. Those having different values will, consequently, behave differently when confronted with the same information. Distinguishing between different moral priorities becomes the task of a universalized science, so that problems in ethics become an area in which science contributes.[77] He suggests that possible dichotomies are resolved by seeing mind, brain and humanity in relation to nature in a holistic way. However, his 'holism' seems to be dependent on his attachment to psychological ways of thinking about how minds work. He suggests that:

> This shift from a causal determinacy that is purely physical to one that includes conscious subjective forces that supersede the physical – in other words the shift from a materialist, reductionist, mechanist paradigm to a holistic, mentalist paradigm – makes all the difference when it comes to using the 'truths' of science in building ethical values.[78]

Hence science in this revised form still becomes the arbiter of other forms of knowledge. Not only is psychological science seen as some universalizing category, sheltered as it were from the vagaries of culture, it is also given a prime role in adjudicating what is right in such culture. He avoids the reductionism characteristic of some scientists, while ending up with a view of holism that is remarkably monochrome in its orientation, for it still assumes that science understood in psychological terms has the greatest claim for ethics. He contrasts his view with that of sociobiology, where values are said to emerge from evolutionary origins. He believes that his view is superior to theirs, as the latter only accounts for more basic animalistic values, and overlooks the possibility of emergent mental processes. In addition, he believes that more traditional approaches to ethics now need to be superseded, as, he believes, they have failed to deliver the goods, for 'global conditions have reached a stage that demands value perspectives which transcend not only the innate biological drives but even traditional humanitarian guidelines that have been respected for centuries'[79] While I would agree with his view that global conditions need to move beyond values based on innate drives, his dismissal of the whole ethical framework in support of his own view is both arrogant and unfounded. Yet he cannot resist injecting something of the spiritual into his understanding of the way science might contribute to this process, for 'new, long-term, more godlike guidelines – of a kind that will ensure long-term survival and further progress in the quality of life – [should] be instituted very soon if humanity is to live again with a sense of hope, purpose or higher meaning'.[80]

His spiritualization of science, on the surface at least, might seem to be a welcome alternative to the rejection of all religious thinking by scientists caught up in reductionist philosophy. However, he seems to ignore the subtle relationship between World 1, World 2 and World 3 discussed by Popper. To assume that World 2 can become dominant, even while taking on some religious language normally characteristic of World 3, represents a move that might superficially seem to bridge the gap between science and values, but in practice simply reifies those values already imbedded in science. Hope, purpose and higher meaning can only emerge from science in a relatively superficial way, since it can never encompass the full breadth of human experience, what Karl Jaspers has called the Comprehensive.[81] As a Nobel laureate in brain research, Roger Sperry has devoted his life to the study of the brain and its functions. His concept of the emergence of different functions at different levels of activity has some merits, though the difficulties associated with the concept of levels when discussing diverse fields of thought have been noted already. His elaboration of the function of science in values serves to reinforce such difficulties still further, for it tends to lead to a linear, almost monochrome picture that does not take into account or value the diversity of human cultures and traditions.

Conclusions

Even allowing for the limited scope of this study, it is possible to come to the following provisional conclusions. First, consideration of the psychological aspects of human nature is important to take into account when unravelling how human beings relate to the natural world. Faced with the possibility of repression and denial of the importance of environmental issues, the initial path to responsible moral agency is through raising awareness that such factors are implicit in Western culture. Such awareness requires the virtues of courage and honesty in facing up to the real difficulties that are encountered, a reorientation so that human actions towards the environment are more closely governed by true prudence, rather than either sham or incomplete prudence. Second, given the popular trend towards psychological explanations of human behaviour, how far can such explanations be used as excuses for immoral action, including environmental vices? Such an issue includes consideration not just of the unconscious, but also of the relationship between actions that are instinctive and those that are consciously self-reflective. Neuroscience on its own cannot distinguish these two facets of human behaviour, however, so making this distinction is critical for ethical analysis of moral agency. Such a distinction draws on current philosophical discussion about the relationship between brain and mind. While complex, it is clear that attempts to reduce human behaviour to brain function are misguided; instead, brain science contributes to the overall picture of what it is to be a biological being. Third, the study of the emotions is also relevant to an ethic of nature for a number of reasons. In a direct sense emotions may in some cases be virtues, such as hope or love, and are motivating factors in defining moral agency.[82] Studies of emotions force twin consideration of both neurobiology and philosophy/cultural value and serve to place psychology in a more modest role of intermediary between both. In addition, studies of the emotions help to show kinship between, yet distinguish, human activity and that of higher animals. Prototypes of emotional responses can be found in non-human species, but this does not mean that emotions are thereby discounted as significant for ethics. Rather, emotion includes reasoned behaviour and hence links with more cognitive approaches to moral agency. Moral development schemes according to the classical models of Piaget and Kohlberg have been criticized because they fail to take into account more affective aspects of human behaviour.[83] A virtue ethic that is inclusive of non-human species, in that it focuses specifically on the quality of the relationships between human and non-human, is not deficient in this respect. A virtue ethic is also broad enough to include insights from cognitive theories, while qualifying their significance.[84] Throughout this chapter I have suggested that psychological studies, far from denying the possibility of moral agency, actually enlarge our understanding of its possibilities. They can also lead to compassion for those who are, for whatever reason, unable to take responsible choices. While recognizing our kinship with animals, psychology shows that moral agency is the province of human beings and as such should serve to enhance even further our sense of responsibility, rather than diminish it.

What might it mean to conform to the mind of Christ? Cognitive science suggests that human remembering and attention are very selective, while the mind of God would not have such limitations.[85] I have suggested elsewhere that the good life consists in orientating human decision-making towards the Wisdom of God; it is the telos that leads not only to flourishing but, as Aquinas has suggested, the beatific vision.[86] What might this mean given the differences between humanity and God? In the first place I suggest that the Wisdom of God as perceived by the minds of human beings is necessarily partial. In this sense it reinforces the apophatic tradition, as has already been noted by scholars immersed in Thomas's thought.[87] Second, it leads to deeper reflection on Christ as one who can be affirmed as having a human mind, but one whose whole life was orientated perfectly to the Wisdom of God. Reflection on Christ as the Wisdom of God is more practical in scope, in that it becomes possible to see more clearly what wisdom might mean in day-to-day existence. The Christological concentration of wisdom means that the vocation of the Christian is not as much to be conformed to this world, as 'transformed by the renewing of your mind'.[88] Such renewal can come about through the practice of contemplation, as Thomas Merton illustrates in his prose-poem Hagia Sophia:

> Sophia is the mercy of God in us. She is the tenderness with which the infinitely mysterious power of pardon turns the darkness of our sins into the light of grace. She is the inexhaustible fountain of kindness, and would almost seem to be, in herself, all mercy. So she does in us a greater work than that of Creation: the work of new being in grace, the work of pardon, the work of transformation from brightness to brightness *tamquam a Domini Spiritu* [as from the Spirit of the Lord]. She is in us the yielding and tender counterpart of the power, justice and creative dynamism of the Father.[89]

I would be less confident in attributing power, justice and creative dynamism to the Father, as that might imply that Sophia does not have such attributes, yet the overall thrust of this passage is clear enough, namely that it is through Sophia that humanity experiences inner transformation, in this sense in her capacity as Spirit-Sophia. Such a work cannot easily be translated into cognitive theory; indeed, if psychological or neurological changes accompanied such an experience it would be of scientific interest, but somewhat irrelevant to what it means to seek for wisdom.

   The kind of wisdom indicated above is wisdom as gift, though wisdom can also be learned, and it is here that cognitive science may contribute something towards what this might mean in practical terms. The repetition of certain actions can actually change the neurological chemical make-up of the brain, as I discussed earlier. Consequentially, envisaging wisdom as a habit of mind – that is, a virtue – could also lead to profound changes in mental functioning. In this sense the idea of renewal of one's mind takes on a rather different gloss, for it becomes possible to argue that our deliberate choices and actions, made repeatedly over the years, can actually transform us mentally and physically. In other words, the ability to have moral agency can change and develop. While this is within the limits of our own natural brain functioning, the possibility for change is built into our neural networks. One might even be able to argue that the ways neural networks connect with each other, and function as a unity, in themselves express a kind of analogous natural wisdom, but one that is holistic rather than reductionistic.[90] It is the possibility for such change that gives reason to hope that we are not simply forced to accept the repressive or negative approach to the natural world that seems to have emerged from psychological studies on Western elite communities. Rather, it is by transformation of our minds that new changes and new insights become possible, and moral agency is released, fuelled by religious desire to become conformed to the Wisdom of God.

Notes

1   Fraser Watts has mapped some important areas relating to theology and psychology in F. Watts: *Theology and Psychology* (Aldershot: Ashgate, 2002). Unfortunately, there is virtually no discussion of ethical issues that might pertain to this dialogue. An earlier comprehensive collection also failed to discuss ethical questions: R. J. Russell, N. Murphy, T. C. Meyering and M. A. Arbib, eds: *Neuroscience and the Person: Scientific Perspectives on Divine Action* (Vatican: Vatican Observatory Foundation, 1999).

2   An excellent book that does discuss wisdom from this perspective is R. Stenberg, ed.: *Wisdom: Its Nature, Origin and Development* (Cambridge: Cambridge University Press, 1990).

3   While behaviourism was popular in the 1970s – that is, the meaning of mental concepts could be ascribed entirely according to externally observed actions – a shift towards cognitive psychology includes attempts to examine brain science and model human cognitive processes.

4   Philosophical texts include N. J. H. Dent: *The Moral Psychology of the Virtues* (Cambridge: Cambridge University Press, 1984); T. E. Wren: *Caring About Morality: Philosophical Perspectives in Moral Psychology* (London: Routledge, 1991). A more empirically orientated study is D. Wright: *The Psychology of Moral Behaviour* (London: Penguin, 1971). O. Flanagan: *Varieties of Moral Personality: Ethics and Psychological Realism* (Cambridge, MA: Harvard University Press, 1991) tries to integrate both perspectives.

5   For discussion of these debates see H. Weinrich-Haste: 'Moral Development', in R. Harre and R. Lamb, eds: *The Encyclopaedic Dictionary of Psychology* (Oxford: Blackwell, 1983), pp. 398–400.

6   See, for example, O. Flanagan and O. Rorty, eds: *Identity, Character and Morality: Essays in Moral Psychology* (Cambridge, MA: MIT Press, 1993).

7   See, for example, W. A. Rottschaefer: *The Biology and Psychology of Moral Agency*, Cambridge Studies in Philosophy and Biology (Cambridge: Cambridge University Press, 1998).

8   A. E. Tenbrunsel, K. A. Wade-Benzoni, D. M. Messick and M. H. Bazerman: 'Introduction', in M. H. Bazerman, D. M. Messick, A. E. Tenbrunsel and K. A. Wade-Benzoni, eds: *Environment, Ethics and Behavior: The Psychology of Environmental Valuation and Degradation* (San Francisco: The New Lexicon Press, 1997), pp. 1–32.

9   A. E. Tenbrunsel, K. A. Wade-Benzoni, D. M. Messick and M. H. Bazerman: 'The Dysfunctional Aspects of Environmental Standards, in Bazerman et al., eds: *Environment, Ethics and Behavior*, pp. 105–21.

10 A. H. Eagly and P. Kulesa: 'Attitudes, Attitude Structure and Resistance to Change: Implications for Persuasion on Environmental Issues', in Bazerman et al., eds: *Environment, Ethics and Behavior*, pp. 122–53.

11 H. R. Arkes and L. Hutzel: 'Waste Heuristics: The Desire Not to Waste Versus the Desire for New Things', in Bazerman et al., eds: *Environment, Ethics and Behavior*, pp. 154–68.

12 T. H. Gladwin, W. E. Newburry and E. D. Reiskin: 'Why Is the Northern Elite Mind Biased against Community, the Environment and a Sustainable Future?', in Bazerman et al., eds: *Environment, Ethics and Behavior*, pp. 234–74.

13 See, for example, A. Browne: 'US Critics Jeer Powell as Summit Ends in Discord', *The Times*, 5 September (2002), p. 20.

14 I am drawing on Gladwin et al.: 'Why Is the Northern Elite Mind Biased against Community?' for this discussion.

15 This creeping culture has been dubbed 'post-human' as a way of indicating the change in the way humans perceive themselves. For a fascinating discussion, see, for example, E. Graham: *Representations of the Post/Human: Monsters, Aliens and Others in Popular Culture* (Manchester: Manchester University Press, 2002).

16 Gladwin et al.: 'Why Is the Northern Elite Mind Biased against Community?', p. 244.

17 The worldview suggested here is one that has received considerable critique from ecofeminists, as I will discuss in the next two chapters.

18 Gladwin et al.: 'Why Is the Northern Elite Mind Biased against Community?', p. 257.

19 Gladwin et al.: 'Why Is the Northern Elite Mind Biased against Community?', p. 258.

20 Gladwin et al.: 'Why Is the Northern Elite Mind Biased against Community?', p. 260.

21 Gladwin et al.: 'Why Is the Northern Elite Mind Biased against Community?', p. 265.

22 See, for example, Ephesians 4: 23-24, Philippians 4.8, Romans 12.2.

23 See S. Hauerwas: *A Community of Character: Towards a Constructive Christian Social Ethic* (Notre Dame, IN: University of Notre Dame Press, 1981).

24 See, for example, S. A. Greenfield: *Journey to the Centers of the Mind: Towards a Science of Consciousness* (New York: W. H. Freeman, 1995); J. Cornwell, ed.: *Consciousness and Human Identity* (Oxford: Oxford University Press, 1998); G. M. Edelman and G. Tononi: *Consciousness: How Matter Becomes Imagination* (London: Penguin Books, 2001).

25 I am using the typology suggested by Copeland in J. Copeland: *Artificial Intelligence: A Philosophical Introduction* (Oxford: Blackwell, 1993).

26 J. H. Riker: *Ethics and the Discovery of the Unconscious* (Albany: State University of New York Press, 1997), p. 1.

27 For a comprehensive list of possible environmental virtues and vices see L. van Wensveen: *Dirty Virtues: The Emergence of Ecological Virtue Ethics* (New York: Humanity Books, 2000), pp. 163–7.

28 Riker: *Ethics*, p. 216.

29 Riker: *Ethics*, p. 218.

30 Research on animals has shown that if they are unable to escape painful circumstances, there is little change in behaviour even when given the opportunity to escape. See M. E. P. Seligman: *Helplessness: On Depression, Development and Death* (New York: W. H. Freeman, 1975).

31 Aquinas suggests that humans, at their most immoral, become 'lower' than the beasts. Hence he seems to suggest that human behaviour that mirrors animals is associated with evil tendencies, while recognizing, through his notion of natural law, that all living creatures are in some sense oriented towards the good of their Creator.

32 C. Blakemore: *The Mind Machine* (London: BBC Books, 1988), p. 269.

33 Aquinas recognized this distinction in suggesting that the insane could not be held accountable for their behaviour, but that they would be given sufficiently of the gift of counsel as a grace, a 'settled endowment'. Hence 'The prudence of grace, however, is caused by God's imparting, and consequently baptized children who have not yet come to the use of reason have prudence as a settled endowment, though not as an activity; this is also the case with those out of their mind. Whereas in those who have their faculties it is also present as an activity concerning the things necessary for salvation'. *Summa Theologiae*, 2a2ae, Qu. 47.14.

34 Midgley: 'Consciousness, Fatalism and Science', in N. H. Gregerson, W. B. Drees and U. Gorman, eds: *The Human Person in Science and Theology*, Issues in Science and Theology Series, European Society for the Study of Science and Religion (Edinburgh: T & T Clark, 2000), p. 29.

35 She draws the analogy thus: 'A human being is, in fact, rather like a vast, ill lit aquarium containing a busy population of fish and plants which we can only observe through a number of windows spaced out round its outer wall. Observers at the different windows need to cooperate, rather than competing for sole dominion. The neurological window is important, but cannot tell the whole story.' Midgley: 'Consciousness, Fatalism and Science', p. 30.

36 For discussion, see N. Murphy: 'Supervenience and the Downward Efficacy of the Mental: A Nonreductive Physicalist Account of Human Action', in Russell et al., eds: *Neuroscience and the Person*, pp. 147–64. It is important to distinguish between a physicalist form of supervenience theory that suggests that physical states causally determine mental states, even though the language of physical states is not sufficient, and a holistic form of supervenience theory that argues in addition that we cannot reduce mental states in a nomological sense to physical states.

37   D. Davidson: *Essays on Actions and Events* (Oxford: Clarendon Press, 1980).

38   Type–type identity theory asserts that for every mental process, such as pain, this leads to identical neural fibres firing in the brain. Token–token theory, by contrast, asserts that events such as pain lead to neural fibres firing, but these will be different in different individuals, while consistent within one individual. Hence the coupling between brain and mental activity is much tighter in type–type theory. For an excellent discussion of this see K. J. Maslin: *An Introduction to the Philosophy of Mind* (Cambridge: Polity Press, 2001), pp. 71–104.

39   Popper's joint book with neuroscientist John Eccles is particularly instructive; see K. R. Popper and J. C. Eccles: *The Self and Its Brain* (Berlin: Springer Verlag, 1977). John Eccles's views have since been challenged by contemporary neuroscientists, but Popper's ideas can be accommodated as long as the strong dualism that he assumes is qualified.

40   It is worth noting that Popper is not even mentioned in Maslin's book *An Introduction to the Philosophy of Mind*. However, Gregerson suggests that it is possible to draw on Popper's understanding of three worlds in order to refine supervenience theory, while retaining an underlying monistic view of reality. Gregerson: 'God's Public Traffic: Holistic versus Physicalist Supervenience', in N. H. Gregerson, W. B. Drees and U. Gorman, eds: *The Human Person in Science and Theology*, Issues in Science and Theology Series, European Society for the Study of Science and Religion (Edinburgh: T & T Clark, 2000), pp. 175–85.

41   A. R. Luria: *Human Brain and Psychological Processes* (New York: Harper and Row, 1966).

42   W. G. Perrott and R. Harré: 'Chapter 1: Overview', in R. Harré and W. G. Perrott, eds: *The Emotions: Social, Cultural and Biological Dimensions* (London: Sage, 2000), p. 3.

43   M. Nussbaum: *Upheavals of Thought: The Intelligence of Emotions* (Cambridge: Cambridge University Press, 2001), p. 28.

44   A. R. Damasio: *Descartes' Error: Emotion, Reason and the Human Brain* (New York: Putman, 1994), pp. 11–51.

45   Nussbaum: *Upheavals of Thought*, p. 65.

46   J. R. Averill: 'An Analysis of Psychophysiological Symbolism and its Influence on Theories of Emotion', abridged version of article published in 1974 in Harré and Parrott, eds: *The Emotions*, pp. 204–28.

47   J. Deigh: 'Introduction' in J. Deigh, ed.: *Ethics and Personality: Essays in Moral Psychology* (Chicago: University of Chicago Press, 1992), p. 2. See also J. Deigh: *The Sources of Moral Agency: Essays in Moral Psychology and Freudian Theory* (Cambridge: Cambridge University Press, 1996).

48   Parrott and Harré: 'Overview', p. 15.

49   Joseph LeDoux's work in this area is well documented. See, for example, J. E. LeDoux: *The Emotional Brain* (New York: Simon and Schuster, 1996); J. E. LeDoux: 'Emotions; How I've Looked for Them in the Brain', in Russell et al., eds: *Neuroscience and the Person*, pp. 41–4. J. E. LeDoux: 'Emotions: A View through the Brain', in Russell et al., eds: *Neuroscience and the Person*, pp. 101–18.

50   Parrott and Harré: 'Overview', p. 18.

51   G. Pitcher: *The Dogs Who Came to Stay* (New York: Dutton, 1995).

52   S. G. Post, L. G. Underwood, J. P. Schloss and W. B. Hurlbut, 'General Introduction', in S. G. Post, L. G. Underwood, J. P. Schloss and W. B. Hurlbut, eds: *Altruism and Altruistic Love: Science, Philosophy and Religion in Dialogue* (Oxford: Oxford University Press, 2002), pp. 3–12.

53 E. Sober and D. Wilson: *Unto Others: The Evolution and Psychology of Unselfish Behavior* (Cambridge, MA: Harvard University Press, 1998).

54 See, for example, S. D Preston and F. B. M. de Waal: 'The Communication of Emotions and the Possibility of Empathy in Animals', in Post et al., eds: *Altruism and Altruistic Love*, pp. 284–328, esp. pp. 298–300.

55 See, for example, M. Ridley: *The Origins of Virtue* (Harmondsworth: Penguin, 1997).

56 R. Pluntchick: *Emotion: A Psychoevolutionary Synthesis* (New York: Harper and Row, 1980). Other work with primates suggests that they are capable of complex emotions that are both biologically and culturally conditioned and that have some parallels with human behaviour. See, for example, A. Jolly: *Lucy's Legacy: Sex and Intelligence in Human Evolution* (Cambridge, MA: Harvard University Press, 1999). This book also documents the primatologists' love towards primates, a 'love that does not expect anything in return but their tolerance of our presence and our curiosity'. It is love for 'the Other' and as such 'a trait of naturalists' (p. 141).

57 L. B. Eaves: 'Ought in a World that Just Is', in W. Drees, ed.: *Is Nature Ever Evil? Religion, Science and Value* (London: Routledge, 2003), pp. 284–309.

58 C. Grant: *Altruism and Christian Ethics* (Cambridge: Cambridge University Press, 2001). A full discussion of altruism is outside the scope of this chapter.

59 I am not denying that human beings are capable of showing great affection towards animals and other non-human creatures, or even nature itself, but this affection is in parallel with that shown in the human community, and thus we cannot give animals priority over children, as Linzey argues.

60 See, for example, definitions in Post et al., eds: *Altruism and Altruistic Love*, pp. 4, 52, 90–1, 265, 184–5.

61 For a discussion and comparison of American and Korean notions of hope see J. R. Averill: 'Intellectual Emotions', in Harré and Perrott, eds: *The Emotions*, pp. 24–38.

62 John Polkinghorne discusses the cultural and religious aspects of Christian hope drawing on belief in the faithfulness of God in comparison with the scientific understanding of the world's destiny as futility. See J. Polkinghorne: *The God of Hope and the End of the World* (London: SCM Press, 2002).

63 The philosopher Karl Jaspers has called this breadth of human experience the Comprehensive. Jaspers argues, correctly, that Being cannot be an object, the Comprehensive is that which involves the whole condition of humanity underlying the subject–object dichotomy. See 'The Existential Philosophy of Karl Jaspers: The Way to Wisdom', in T. R. Koenig, ed.: *Existentialism and Human Existence: An Account of Five Major Philosophies* (Malabar: Krieger, 1992), pp. 31–57. I am grateful to Andrew Hunt for pointing out this reference.

64 R. Cessario: *Christian Faith and the Theological Life* (Washington, DC: Catholic University of America Press, 1996).

65 A. Baier: 'Trust and Anti-trust', in J. Deigh, ed.: *Ethics and Personality: Essays in Moral Psychology* (Chicago: University of Chicago Press, 1992), pp. 11–40.

66 Matthew 16:5–12.

67 This is where I part company with James Gustafson, as I will discuss in the final chapter.

68 'The Existential Philosophy of Karl Jaspers: The Way to Wisdom', p. 38.

69 Nussbaum: *Upheavals of Thought*, p. 322.

70   See social cognitive bases of morality in W. A. Rottschaefer: *The Biology and Psychology of Moral Agency* (Cambridge: Cambridge University Press, 1998). Rottschaefer argues that while moral agency cannot be confined to psychology and biology, it still needs to rest on scientific research, and hence he argues for scientific naturalism. It seems to me that such confidence is misplaced; ethics can be consistent with science without being subject to its goals. Moreover, he does not take sufficient account of the clash between different sciences in arriving at his position.

71   For discussion of religious experience see Watts: *Theology and Psychology*, pp. 76–88.

72   While Watts resists being labelled as reductionist, the tendency of early researchers to allocate function to brain area is reductionist. The meaning found in a mental event has to be considered separately from the neurological events in the brain, even if there is a correlation between the two processes.

73   J. D. Teasdale and P. J. Barnard: *Affect, Cognition and Change* (Hillsdale, NJ: Lawrence Erlbaum, 1993).

74   Watts: *Theology and Psychology*, pp. 86–8. This would, of course, be the aim of a psychologist interested in neurological function. It would be impossible to 'codify' or contain religious insights through neurological function alone, even if a correlation is found between particular brain activity and particular religious experiences.

75   See W. A. Phillips and S. M. Silverstein: 'Convergence of Biological and Psychological Perspectives on Cognitive Coordination in Schizophrenia', *Behavioral and Brain Sciences*, 26:1 (2003), pp. 63–135.

76   R. Sperry: *Science and Moral Priority: Merging Mind, Brain and Human Values* (Oxford: Blackwell, 1983).

77   Sperry: *Science and Moral Priority*, pp. 111–12.

78   Sperry: *Science and Moral Priority*, p. 119

79   Sperry: *Science and Moral Priority*, p. 125

80   Sperry: *Science and Moral Priority*, p. 125 (italics in brackets added).

81   Jaspers argues, correctly, that Being cannot be an object, the Comprehensive is that which involves the whole condition of humanity underlying the subject-object dichotomy. See Koenig: 'The Existential Philosophy of Karl Jaspers', pp. 36–9.

82   Philosophically one can distinguish between motives, which relate to individual virtues, and motivation, which reflects the overall goal of human behaviour. For a discussion of different philosophical theories of motivation see J. Kennett: *Agency and Responsibility: A Common Sense Moral Psychology* (Oxford: Clarendon Press, 2001).

83   This criticism comes from those who are more conservative, such as Derek Wright, through to more radical feminist perspectives, such as Carol Gillingham. See Wright: *The Psychology of Moral Behaviour*, pp. 48–9; C. Gillingham, *In a Different Voice: Psychological Theory and Women's Development* (Cambridge, MA: Harvard University Press, 1982). Piaget has attempted to answer this criticism in J. Piaget: *Intelligence and Affectivity: Their Relationship During Child Development* (Palo Alto, CA: Annual Reviews, 1981). I will return to the issue of an ethic of care in chapter 8.

84   Sperry made the mistake of confusing scientific theory with ethics in his interpretation of neurobiological science as providing the criteria for ethics.

85   Watts has used this discrepancy to argue that Swinburne's argument for God's existence based on human consciousness cannot be correct. I am using this in a different way for practical purposes, namely ethical reflection. See Watts: *Theology and Psychology*, p. 43.

86   C. Deane-Drummond: *Creation through Wisdom: Theology and the New Biology* (Edinburgh: T & T Clark, 2000).

87 Josef Pieper's book *The Silence of St Thomas* illustrates this beautifully, especially his second essay entitled 'The Negative Element in the Philosophy of St Thomas Aquinas'. J. Pieper: *The Silence of St Thomas*, trans. D. O'Connor (London: Faber and Faber, 1957), pp. 51–75.

88 Romans 12.2, King James version.

89 T. Merton: 'Hagia Sophia', in L. S. Cunningham, ed.: *Thomas Merton: Spiritual Master. The Essential Writings* (New York: Paulist Press, 1987), pp. 258–64.

90 I am indebted to Professor William Phillips of Sterling University for this insight.

Chapter 7

Ethics and Gaia

I began this book with a chapter on environmental ethics in which I set out current proposals for alternative approaches to the environment. This chapter extends the discussion of more holistic alternatives by reference to the science of Gaia, proposed originally by James Lovelock.[1] I discuss, in particular, the way Gaian imagery continues to capture the imagination of prominent philosophers and theologians concerned about the way humanity relates to the natural world. It presents a strong alternative challenge to modernity but also a challenge to the position that I have been arguing for in this book, namely a recovery of virtue. It is therefore worth considering in detail as an alternative vision for science that might escape the problems associated with scientific reductionism. I will be asking if there are aspects to Gaian reflection as science that are worth retaining in the context of an emphasis on virtue ethics. In addition, Gaia could be seen as a further stage in a gradual resacralization of nature. This in turn is part of a wider cultural shift away from secularization and its associated framing of nature as an instrument for human use and manipulation.[2] Hence, for a theological understanding of virtue ethics to be convincing it has to take account of such a trend towards holism. The focus of the critique throughout this chapter is on how Gaia impinges on the way an ethic of nature develops; for example, how Gaia is used in different varieties of ecofeminist ethics, including the work of Rosemary Radford Ruether and Anne Primavesi. Chapter 8 will develop a much fuller discussion of the overall importance of ecofeminism for an ethics of nature.

In a general sense the idea of Gaia appeals to those seeking for alternative non-anthropocentric frameworks for an ethics of nature, as it is purportedly based on scientific understanding, yet challenges the purely reductionist methodology characteristic of classical experimental science. The Gaia hypothesis as originally developed by James Lovelock is a way of understanding the workings of the planet as an integrated whole, so that living organisms do not simply adapt to their environment, but also serve to keep external conditions constant. Of course, only limited, more local applications of Gaia can be 'proved' with any degree of certainty, so scientists will continue to debate the extent to which the Gaia hypothesis is valid as a model of the whole earth system. If one follows the postmodern/anti-realist critique of science then all scientific models are, to some extent, constructions of the human imagination. Hence, the question of actual scientific validity in the original sense of a testable hypothesis may not matter too much to those who insist that all scientific endeavour is a human construction and, as such, value-laden. Yet it seems to me that there is a difference between acknowledging the very human aspect of science and recognizing that the factual evidence gleaned through scientific experimentation does have some connection with the ontology of nature. In other words, scientists on the whole adhere to a form of critical realism. If scientists did not believe this to be the case, the motivation for science would cease. Of course, such results are always provisional, but even if it were 'proved' ethics emerging from Gaia would be another version of naturalistic ethics.[3] Yet, I suggest that current scientific knowledge does need to be taken into account. The premise of this book as a whole is that in the devising of ethical schemes knowledge gained through careful scientific analysis is valuable in so far as it gives us a way of perceiving the world that needs to be acknowledged.

The Science of Gaia

What is the science of Gaia? Lovelock's original hypothesis focused on the puzzle: why was the gaseous composition of the atmosphere and temperature of the earth ideal to support life compared with the other planets? His answer was attractive in its simplicity: it was not so much life that adapted to the environment, as the other way round, namely that it served to regulate the conditions experienced on planet earth. In other words, the sum total of all the different species on the planet act in concert in order to create the conditions needed for life as a whole to be sustained.

Scientific debates about the validity of this model are important, since they serve to highlight how far such a hypothesis can be grounded in scientific understanding.[4] An interpretation of Gaia as simply stating the interconnection between living forms and their environment is the one that makes the least number of assumptions. It is the basis behind the geological and biological recycling of nitrogen, carbon, sulphur and other nutrients that has been known for some time, since long before the idea of Gaia ever achieved prominence.

The second level, as it were, of appropriation of Gaia concerns the idea of homeostatic feedback, that all the different species living on planet earth communicate with each other in such a way that external conditions are brought back to preset norms. The difficulty here, of course, is identifying the sensor in a feedback system. Where might be such a device within the whole gamut of different creatures on the earth? If there is no such device, what might be the 'intelligence' for such a system? Of course, one way of by-passing this problem is to postulate that the feedback is automatic, it is simply a matter of autopoiesis. While biological life is certainly a necessary part of the process, the feedback mechanism is based on inorganic processes that can account for stability of environmental conditions. Hence 'life' need not be an integral aspect of the sensing process, though it certainly *contributes* to the changes taking place in, for example, the climate.[5] In other words, it is clear that the chemical reactions that are characteristic of life processes feed into the overall changes that are experienced. For example, the conversion of carbon dioxide into carbonate would be far too slow if it were not for the ability of plants and some microorganisms to fix carbon. Yet this does not mean that Gaia leads to the persistence of life; rather, according to this model, it is the persistence of stable conditions that may, or may not, be conducive to particular life forms. I suggest that this understanding of Gaia is crucial, since it challenges the idea that Gaia as science in and of itself promotes *cooperation*, for the processes will be automatic rather than 'chosen'.

What is the current status of Gaia in terms of science? Timothy Lenton's review article in the journal *Nature* focuses particularly on the nature of feedback systems and the struggle to try to define what these systems might be like.[6] From a biological perspective Gaia presents a problem: if Darwin's theory of natural selection is accepted as the basis for individual selection of species, how might this be compatible with planetary self-regulation?[7] The concept that the environment and the biota are coupled in some way with each other seems perfectly reasonable; it is the earlier suggestion that regulation is *by* the biota that is more problematic.[8] Lovelock has argued for Gaia as an automatic system, one that has no teleology in the classical sense of purpose. He uses a model of the earth as a collection of light or dark daisies that reflect or absorb light respectively as a way of showing that the temperature regulation of Gaia could work through automatic processes, rather than through teleological explanations.[9] How might this be compatible with the idea of Darwinian natural selection? It could be argued that those traits that indirectly stabilize favourable external environmental conditions for growth have a selective advantage, in other words they are favoured over other traits that do not lead to similarly positive environmental conditions. This is superimposed on the selection pressure working in the *opposite* direction of that particular environmental variable on a particular species; that is, the tendency for that species to adapt to environmental conditions according to classical Darwinian selection.

I suggest that as long as Gaian theory is suitably qualified in this way, then it seems entirely reasonable to suppose that *local* homeostatic Gaian systems may be operative such that some local environmental stabilizing takes place.[10] However, the difficulty still remains as to how to translate such localized explanations into a planetary model, for the kind of environmental conditions suitable for one species may not be suitable for another. Of course, it might be possible to argue that a particular collection of species on the planet are the ones that have the most influence on environmental conditions, and other life forms then contribute to or benefit from similar conditions and so thrive. If, alternatively, less influential life forms are not compatible with such conditions they would not be favoured in evolutionary terms. In fact this seems to be the case with the gaseous composition of the air, with microbes and algae providing the bulk of the stabilizing effects. Hence, rather than suggesting *cooperation* between all species, Gaian theory could equally support *competition*, with just one species or set of species 'dominating' at a planetary level. In this scenario only a few species do the 'work' of keeping external conditions appropriate for 'life', while other species then become more 'parasitic', gaining the advantages without any expense of energy. In the past the huge shift from anaerobic to aerobic conditions early in the history of the planet suggests that a sea change took place in the most dominant species at the time.[11]

However, Lovelock seems to go beyond the explanation that I have just suggested, as he claims that the directedness of Gaia operative at a planetary level is towards the *persistence of life*. Lenton suggests that since Lovelock first proposed his hypothesis, more and more evidence has accumulated in favour of planetary self-regulation. Yet this evidence most often takes the form of resistance of individual species to environmental perturbations.[12] Even if we envisage the coupling of the environment with living organisms in some sense, as I indicated above, the precise way the homeostatic processes works remains obscure. If the location of the 'sensor' for such a homeostatic system cannot be found easily in the living organisms, then if we reject the inorganic thesis that I have outlined above, the only other place to locate it is in the heart of Gaia herself, in other words to give to the earth system as a whole an identity, a 'life', so that she comes to resemble a giant organism. This seems to be exactly what Lovelock does in his Gaia hypothesis, even while claiming that it is non-teleological. While initially Lovelock was somewhat hesitant to identify with the religious and philosophical implications of Gaia, more recently he seems to have warmed to this suggestion.[13] Once Gaia takes on ideological and religious characteristics, she breaks the boundaries of what has been understood as classical science. Of course, there is no reason why a scientific hypothesis cannot have religious implications, but it is the way a version of the science is used to support a particular ideology that seems to me to be important.

Beyond Individualism

As I hinted above, for some philosophers Gaia is suggestive of an alternative, more holistic philosophy, one that puts emphasis on cooperation rather than competition.[14] Stephen Clark seems to be rather more cautious about using Gaia for an environmental philosophy now compared with his initial engagement with it.[15] Mary Midgley, by contrast, seems to have become progressively more attracted to the appeal of Gaia. Her work is worth considering in some detail in the light of the scientific understanding of Gaia outlined above, as she offers a philosophical argument for drawing on Gaia for an ethic of nature. Her earlier book *Utopias, Dolphins and Computers* welcomed Lovelock's Gaia hypothesis as an important imaginative leap currently needed to offset the fragmentation characteristic of modern science.[16] More recently she has expanded this argument further. John Holden, the editor of her book *Gaia: The Next Big Idea*, suggests that Gaia should be thought of on a par not just with Marxism, but also with Darwinism itself as the next 'big idea' about the way the world works.[17] While Midgley does not claim quite this status for Gaia in the text, she hints at such in her writing as a whole and by the title of the book.[18]

More importantly, perhaps, she suggests that it is the very fusion of science with religious insights that is of importance, for it is the reuniting of science with spirituality that leads to a more holistic interpretation of the world.[19] Like many others, she extrapolates the research demonstrating local recycling of nutrients as an argument in favour of planetary interpretations of Gaia.[20] She suggests that the later medical imagery of Gaia that Lovelock coined, where Gaia was envisaged as a damaged patient waiting for a doctor, was much more congenial for scientists than more 'scandalous' ideas about a female goddess.[21] Berry, rather oddly perhaps, is aware of the need to move beyond the balance of nature myth in ecology, yet welcomes Lovelock's approach as evidence for 'ordering' or design in nature.[22] Yet it is to Lovelock's credit, as far as Midgley is concerned, that he retained Gaia's religious aspect. She argues that those involved in the new physics have had no problem appropriating religious language into their explanations of the truth, so why should there be an issue over Gaia? Is it something to do with the fact that Gaia is a female goddess? It seems to me, contrary to Midgley, that it is far more likely that it is because Gaia is not really accepted as science; so including religious ideas merely increased suspicions about it. On the other hand, the new physics seemed to rest on 'surer' ground as far as the scientists were concerned, so that adding a religious gloss could not do it any harm; rather, it could only serve to widen its appeal. Midgley considers that wonder and awe are entirely appropriate if we believe that the earth as a whole has acted so as to contribute to stabilizing conditions on earth over millions of years. Of course, such awe and wonder at the earth could become virtues without accepting the Gaian explanation as to how such stabilizing conditions arose, though Midgley does not consider this option. Although Midgley has observed the way science has taken over religious language and used it for its own particular scientistic purposes, she suggests that the special place that science occupies in our lives needs to be taken into account.[23] Hence, while we do not necessarily accept all that science suggests, it can also help us to reformulate ideas in new and imaginative ways.

It is, indeed, precisely the lack of imaginative images that Midgley locates as one of the reasons why we have failed to develop adequate approaches to the environment. For she believes that the idea of the sacred has become restricted to humans alone and in this respect it becomes difficult to find ways of affirming the non-human world. It is this habit of individualism that she suggests needs to be addressed. Hence:

> Our habitual individualism uses a minimalist moral approach which already has diffi-
> culty in explaining why each one of us should be concerned about any individual
> other than our own self – why our value system should ever go beyond simple
> egotism. It answers this question in terms of the social contract which is supposed to
> make it worth while for each of us to secure the interests of fellow citizens.[24]

She suggests that thinking of our relationship with the earth in contractual terms is quite simply a misfit: it is impossible to envisage any sort of contractual relationship with the rain forest or Antarctic, for example. Rather, for her Gaia adds to the idea of a kinship with all creatures dependent on the earth. Given the discussion on Gaia that I outlined earlier I am far less convinced that Gaia leads to a sense of kinship with other creatures, or, if it does, it is only when it is severed from its scientific moorings. Such a severance would be incompatible with Midgley's own stated intentions for drawing on Gaian language. However, for Midgley the importance of Gaia is not simply a sense of sociability, which communitarians stress, nor is it just mutual dependence on other creatures, emphasized by ecologists. In both of the latter it is the *individual* that dominates, whereas Gaia reinstates the idea of holism, and this seems to be the 'added extra' that Midgley intends to emphasize. Instead of rational self-interest as a guide to ethics, she argues that we need the power of imaginative images to shift our thinking. But has the way Midgley portrayed Gaia moved into the realm of fantasy? In other words, has the holistic image of Gaia gone to the other extreme of weakening the sense of individual worth that is crucial for ethical understanding of nature?[25]

She is also particularly critical of the notion of prudence. Given the particular emphasis I have taken on reinstating the idea of prudence from a classical perspective, it is worth citing her misgivings in detail:

> When things go well, we simply don't believe in disasters. Long-term prudence, reaching beyond the routine precautions of everyday life, is an extraordinarily feeble motive. Human beings drive their cars wildly, climb mountains without proper maps and constantly run out of money. On a grander scale, the weakness of human foresight was pleasingly seen in the failure of the electronics industry to provide in advance against the Millennium Bug. For fifty years all these highly qualified, intelligent and well-funded people apparently assumed that the twentieth century would never come to an end. Although they got away with it on this occasion, this example is interesting because – as is the case of our own death – it was not doubtful that the emergency would arise. But prudence is supposed to operate on probabilities as well as certainties. And the increasing probability of environmental disaster has been well-attested for at least the last thirty years.[26]

Yet just because prudence has not captured the imagination of most people, does this necessarily mean that it is useless as an ethical guide in the way she seems to suggest? Perhaps she is correct to see that prudence alone is ineffective in motivating action, yet attention to virtue ethics forces us to look at the reasons behind our actions, and then respond accordingly. In other words, we need to ask *why* there is such an irrational response to known goods. The answer may well be a spiritual malaise that Midgley also seems to hint at through the notion of Gaia. However, for her Gaia is all-sufficient in providing the necessary energy to shift away from individualism. I will discuss the particular way Gaia intersects with religious ideas in more detail in the section below. However, it is first worth considering the premise of her argument, namely that duties to wholes differ from duties to individuals.

Midgley argues strongly against what she sees as a pervasive sense of individualism in sociobiological writings. Although authors like Richard Dawkins and E. O. Wilson qualify their statements by suggesting that this is simply metaphorical language, it seems to me that Midgley has identified an important trend in the language used by sociobiologists, the 'intensely individualistic ideology' along with the way 'unexamined moral and political ideas have become grafted into their scientific thinking'.[27] She suggests that the real ancestor to this kind of individualistic thinking is not so much Darwin as Herbert Spencer. The official purpose of sociobiology is to celebrate the oneness between humanity and the natural world, but she suggests that the language used to describe this is still cloaked in an individualistic philosophy. Sociobiology also takes on religious language in making claims for itself to be a fitting substitute for traditional religions. E. O. Wilson, for example, asks, 'Does a way exist to divert the power of religion into the great new enterprises that laid bare the source of that power?'[28] Such a new enterprise is, for Wilson, naturally enough, science, but it is shaped in such a way that it has 'deliberately affective appeal to the deepest needs of human nature, and kept strong by the blind hopes that the journey on which we are now embarked will be farther and better than the one just completed'.[29] For Midgley, Wilson is more aware than many scientists of the need for an imaginative vision, but there is no scientific reason why the future should be brighter than the past.

However, once we look at the details of the imagery, we find that the language used to cloak this sociobiological vision is the language of selfishness, spite, manipulation, investment, cheats, war games. This language, she suggests, simply reflects the naive social atomism of the late 1970s and 1980s, and could even be thought of as a type of biological Thatcherism![30] When it comes to a discussion of altruism and cooperative activities, these 'are treated as if they were all just devious stratagems to produce more descendents'.[31] In other words, the language of competition prevails. For writers like Richard Dawkins an even more profound sense of atomism emerges, in identifying the gene as the locus of conservation, and the individual a 'helpless puppet used to maximize the spread of its genes'.[32] While officially the word 'selfish' is intended to be a harmless technical term, she suggests that the ordinary sense of the word is so common that it cannot be dismissed, especially when Dawkins actually admits that we need to shake off our biological tendency to selfishness and learn to cooperate with each other. For Midgley any disclaimers by the authors that their words should not be taken literally 'have no more force than the tiny warnings on cigarette packets'.[33]

What might be an alternative? Not unexpectedly, Midgley believes that we need a counter vision to correct the bias towards social atomism, and this is where, for her, the Gaia hypothesis makes its most important contribution. Midgley correctly recognizes that there are other strands in biology that put emphasis on cooperation, including symbiotic relationships between different species. It is well known that organisms such as lichens combine a fungus with algae so that both can live in much harsher conditions than they would on their own.[34] Friendly bacteria living in mammalian guts are another well known example of biological cooperation. Virtually every animal cell contains mitochondria, which function as the powerhouse of each cell. Mitochondria are thought to have arisen originally from symbiotic bacterial ancestors, but are now routinely passed down to the next generation through the maternal egg cytoplasm. Much the same story could be told about plant cells containing chloroplasts. These are very significant organelles, since they contain the photosynthetic apparatus that is responsible for the conversion of carbon dioxide into fixed carbon through the energy of sunlight. These organelles are probably derived from algal ancestors originally living in symbiotic relationship with primitive plant cells. Biologists have known these facts for some time, but the language of cooperation has not taken hold in the same way as the language of selfishness. Midgley attributes this to cultural factors at the time when prominent books on sociobiology were published, a self-expressive and self-indulgent mood of the 1970s, turning into a more extreme version of competitive individualism in the 1980s. The biologist Brian Goodwin has suggested that it is time to move away from such destructive Darwinian metaphors towards putting emphasis on cooperative relationships that operate at different levels of our biological nature. He hints that such ideals are not romantic idealism, but grounded in science itself, namely the science of complexity.[35]

If the Gaia hypothesis does indeed help to shift us towards more cooperative ways of thinking about ourselves and other life forms, then it needs to be welcomed. However, from a scientific perspective it seems that the kind of cooperation, even where it is envisaged, is not one that lends itself to a ready translation into human social action. Does Gaia, in other words, really promote cooperation understood as mutual aid? For it seems that the stabilizing effects of biological species on the environment is less a *cooperative* strategy than a *survival* strategy. Damping down the environmental extremes to which living things are exposed will generally have a clear advantage in terms of survival. Species that alter their local environment so that it fluctuates far less than might be expected have particular advantages over other species that do not do this; hence, as I indicated above, the Darwinian competitive metaphor is still left intact. But there have been radical shifts in the chemical composition of the earth's atmosphere in the course of the history of life on earth, so that aerobic conditions replaced a predominantly anaerobic environment.[36] The point is that those species that favoured oxygenating conditions became the dominant ones. However, once we move to consider a planetary whole it becomes very difficult to envisage how species expending energy stabilizing the environment will have an advantage over others that simply rely on such stabilizing effects. Could altruism really work at such a planetary level, where those who benefit from a particular action are unknown and unrelated? The language of altruism or cooperation seems a misnomer in this context. Some writers have even pointed to the way humans are basically taking advantage of the work done by other species, especially microorganisms, in creating conditions appropriate for life; hence, according to Gaia, humans are more like *parasites* on the planet.[37] Midgley seems to be arguing that Gaia is needed in order to balance cooperation over competition, but I suggest that only one particular reading of Gaia will serve this function. Lovelock, in a manner rather similar to Richard Dawkins, suggests that we need to *learn* to be more cooperative, rather than less, in our dealings with the natural world. We need to be less like managers than shop stewards, speaking on behalf of those species that in fact serve our best interests.[38] Gaia by herself presents an image that is sterner than Midgley would have us believe, for, according to Lovelock, Gaia is unforgiving of those who ignore the stable system, even 'ruthless in her destruction of those who transgress'.[39]

Such language shows that Gaia language alone is incapable of shaking off metaphors of self-destruction. In one reading of Gaia we are still left with the image of competition or even parasitism, in another reading it is the language of the earth as a giant organism that is significant. It is the latter reading that Midgley prefers, but this too has its dangers, since it could equally be used to support the kind of rabid fascism that dominated the Nazi era.[40] It seems to me that using science to bolster particular ethical views is in itself problematic. Midgley suggests that we cannot escape from the way science dominates our cultural landscape, so we need to draw on helpful imaginative visions such as Gaia in order to foster particular behaviour. However, it seems to me that Gaia is far too ambiguous a metaphor to be used in this way. It is only a very *selective* reading of Gaia that serves the purpose Midgley intends, namely a move away from individualism to cooperation and holism.

An alternative philosophy that seeks to shift human thinking away from individualism and towards more holistic approaches is the classical notion of the common good. The common good has various meanings. It can mean the collective good of individuals, or the participation of minds and wills in the universal good, or the subsisting good that causes and transcends all the goods in the universe.[41] While Aquinas's discussion of political prudence would have a primary focus on the common good in the first sense, the other two senses are implied, and hence it is a way of pointing towards universal good without the shadow of competitiveness that remains when Gaian biological imagery is used.[42] In addition, general virtues, such as justice, direct the other moral virtues in order to serve the common good.[43] As Aquinas points out, 'justice is in the rational appetite, which is able to love good as a universal or unrestricted value, which the mind apprehends'.[44] This leads to a more morally grounded understanding of holism compared with Gaian imagery, and refuses to let go of the importance of the individual. In other words, I am suggesting that even though Midgley has tried to locate competitive metaphors in social models that are then transferred to biology, it is difficult to envisage a post-Darwinian biological model that does *not* include something of this tendency. In addition, even though the language used may be coloured by social context and shape the way particular scientific questions were asked, this does not mean that the insights gained were false.[45]

Theology as Embeddedness

Gaia has not only proved of interest to philosophers, it is also a source of inspiration to theologians.[46] I intend here to focus more particularly on the way Gaia has been used by the theologian Anne Primavesi in order to argue for a particular approach to theology and ethics. Primavesi's book *Sacred Gaia* shows that the image of Gaia is far from dormant among theologians seeking a more ecocentric way of approaching the natural world.[47] Primavesi's theology is in tune with the wider contemporary shift in understanding the natural world as sacred.[48] Lovelock is particularly enthusiastic about the way Primavesi has appropriated Gaia for theological ends, describing it as 'a splendid book', so much so that 'I now see why thoughts of Gaia are as much in the realms of theology as of science'.[49] He also identifies the theological strand in Gaia with a shift towards knowledge of wholes that he describes as emergent phenomena. For Lovelock, Gaia is not simply a shift in thinking away from reductionism, though it is certainly this, it also reflects the idea of emergence, in which a whole behaves differently from the sum of its parts.[50] For Primavesi the language of Gaia is useful in so far as it allows theology to become translated into a scientific language in a way that she believes will make theology accessible to a much wider audience.[51] I am in full agreement with her premise that constructive dialogue between science and theology can and must take place, with science providing insights into complex relationships with our environment and theology probing into the reasons why our lives are validated by our religious beliefs. While she attributes to Gaia theory the role of increasing awareness of dependence on other species, much the same could be said of ecology in general. Like Midgley, Primavesi sees in Gaia a means of shifting Western consciousness away from individual competition towards cooperation, though for Primavesi she identifies particularly with non-violent connectedness as normally associated with Buddhism. Yet Primavesi suggests that this particular interpretation of Gaia is not just significant ethically, for theology takes on the characteristics of Gaia and becomes 'another earth science'.[52] In particular, it is an *embedded theology*, for

> Whatever we may say about our environment, or about God, will relate God, ultimately, to every process and organism seen within the evolution of life on earth. Seeing myself embedded there will affect how I speak about God. But how should I perceive and describe myself within this evolutionary process?[53]

This challenge forms the basis for her ideas about human identity as situated concretely in different contexts. While Midgley viewed individualism as problematic, for Primavesi such individualism is also expressed in the particular Augustinian theological focus on the story of one individual, Adam, whose sin polluted the human race until the arrival of the one man Jesus Christ. In other words, she suggests that the story of the human race has been limited to the story of fall and redemption, focused on the death and resurrection in Christ.[54] It seems to me that Primavesi is correct to challenge Christian dogma that claims that human beings were either created in a state of perfection or did not evolve in the same way as other species.[55] However, does Christianity necessarily posit Jesus Christ as 'outside the flow of evolution' in the way she suggests? For her Christ is no more unique than any other human and in this sense he manifests the sacredness of all life. Yet just because theological tradition affirms the uniqueness of Christ's incarnation, that does not necessarily mean that it is *unable* to affirm the worth of all creatures in the manner that she quite correctly believes is necessary. In fact, I suggest that Christian theology's distinctiveness *needs* to be grounded in consideration of the incarnation of Christ as Logos/Sophia, even though Christology itself also needs to broaden its scope to consider non-human creation as well.[56] It is true that we must affirm all creatures as in some sense reflecting their Creator, yet the idea of humanity as the image of God can then become a way of describing a belief in human uniqueness. Although image bearing has commonly been interpreted in terms of human superiority, I suggest that the idea need not necessarily have such a connotation. Moreover, while we might challenge the pivotal role played by Adam, he is more often than not viewed theologically as a mythological rather than a historical figure in the same sense as Jesus Christ, so to suggest, as Primavesi does, that the two are of equivalent status in the tradition is a distorted caricature of that tradition.

It is clear, none the less, that Primavesi is anxious to set up a contrast between what she believes is a damaging interpretation of Christianity and her own view, which draws heavily on the idea of Gaia understood as connectedness. The language that she uses to describe our embeddedness is instructive. The particular boundaries around ourselves – that is, our body in relation to place, or our individual experience of coupling – is known as the *SelfScape*.[57] It represents personal subjectivity, a particular way of viewing things from one's own particular perspective. Next we have *SocialScape*, which, as the name implies, is suggestive of social interactions ranging from 'food to Internet access . . . and includes language, ritual, sex, education, play, culture and religion', which affirm the scope of SelfScape in some respects, but curtail it in others.[58] Our *EarthScape* reflects a more general interaction with our environment, but different objects may have a different purpose for those with a different EarthScape; for example, a stone may be used by a crab for shelter, but by a thrush to crack open a snail, or by humans as a missile.[59]

However, Primavesi includes another dimension as well, and this is the *PoieticScape*, the 'linguistic, poetic, intellectual, creative, imaginative and expressive dimension of our coevolutionary environment: the place where we "make" and remake our images of ourselves and of our relationships and express them through various media'.[60] It is significant that she describes this as a fourth dimension that goes beyond the Self, Social and EarthScapes, for it links up with the idea of autopoiesis, which literally means self-making, and which refers to a dynamic movement of self-renewal normally found within living organisms.[61] For Lovelock Gaia is an autopoietic system: namely there is a structural integrity between living organisms and their environment. For Primavesi theology understood in terms of PoieticScape corresponds to the link between belief and practice.[62] More importantly, perhaps, she suggests that the PoieticScape serves as a reminder of the partial theological perspectives that we all bring to a discussion.

While it is clear that Primavesi's particular definition of PoieticScape allows for diversity, it is only very loosely connected with the autopoiesis of Gaia through the ideas of both co-evolution and emergence, in the sense that we have somehow missed giving full recognition to this particular 'field' or fourth dimension emerging from our other embedded relationships. In much the same way as Midgley, Primavesi argues that a Gaian perspective moves us away from anthropocentrism to a more holistic understanding of our place from a co-evolutionary perspective.[63] However, for Primavesi autopoietic description is more than just cooperation, for she sees it as bringing together paradoxical ideas such as the fact that there is both connection and distinction between organisms and their environment. Importantly, she suggests that autopoietic language can serve to emphasize the paradoxical nature of relationality in terms of its competition/cooperation, as well as its autonomy/bonding, distinction/obliteration, dependence/separation and so on. This may be one reason why Primavesi can claim that PoieticScape allows for diversity, while at the same time suggesting that it draws on Gaian imagery. Yet despite such qualifications, it is the monistic tendency in Gaia understood as a single organism that may win through unless the metaphor is very carefully handled. In other words, we return to a question that has plagued environmental ethics: whether holistic valuing leads to an overemphasis on the whole at the expense of individuals.[64] How far we can really cross between linguistic codes in a way that is in excess of the original meaning of the terms in the manner that Primavesi suggests is a moot point.[65]

One of the themes that Primavesi translates from science to theology is the theme of emergence. Rather like biological systems, she suggests, theological language must emerge from a dynamic sense of becoming, with a 'very dim beginning and a very open future'.[66] Such a view implies a fluid concept of both theology and ethics. She also suggests that ideas such as natural selection, which emphasize the role of the particular species during the course of evolution, need suitable qualification. The concept of natural genetic drift puts much more stress on the importance of variations in the environment as a factor in shaping difference between species and the direction of evolution. This idea is important for Primavesi not only because she wants to get away from biological metaphors that imply a unidirectional goal-seeking, but also because it gives a good example of how to challenge previously held orthodoxies in much the same way as she believes theology must do today.[67] Moreover, it is the classical separation of the animal from the human and the sacred from the profane that she believes is responsible for the justification of negative human attitudes towards other species and the environment. In its place she argues for the recovery of a poetic imagination, but such imagination does more than just connect us to our immediate environment, for 'it can transcend this boundary too and connect us with the Gaian system, even though we can, literally, only imagine it in its magnitude'.[68]

Primavesi suggests that the appropriate theological response to a greater awareness of our embeddedness in the natural world is acceptance of life as a gift event, one that is sensitively aware of our creaturely dependence on all other life for our own existence, so that 'other species have not evaded or ignored the demands I make on them'.[69] The appropriate response becomes one of gratitude; sin is now violence against the earth community.[70] The idea of extending our obligation to the land is not new, as I discussed in an earlier chapter. Primavesi makes a distinctive contribution in the way she suggests that ethical outcomes, including ecological justice and interpersonal justice, are grounded in a particular view of the earth as sacred through the notion of Gaia. She insists that the unitary view of the earth as sacred counters the damaging theological apartheid that affirms the superiority of the human that she believes has contributed to environmental degradation.[71] Instead we see God as integral to the earth systems that she describes, but also, in a way that is not entirely clear, distinct from them as well. Hence, God is the 'God of the whole earth system: enchanting and terrible, giver of life and death, not separate from and not confused with the world and its sacred gift events'.[72] Yet how can God, especially God that draws on Gaian imagery, be 'not confused' or distinct from the world? Moreover, God as 'terrible', while being 'sacred', seems to deny not only the possibility of intimacy with God, but also the goodness of God, so that the future outcome of the God–human relationship is not secure. While I welcome her suggestion that humanity needs to be more aware of its biological and evolutionary origins, her conflation of God's being with the world seems to undermine her assertions about the real possibility for change. While process theologians can look to the promise of nature by exploring the cosmological context of evolution, such a dimension seems to be missing in Primavesi's version of sacred Gaia.[73] Her implication seems to be that God is a Gaian Goddess, though for some reason she resists making an explicit identification of one with the other in the same way as other ecofeminist writers, such as Rosemary Radford Ruether.[74]

An alternative to Gaian imagery, but one that still allows for the use of imagination in constructing the way we see ourselves in relation to the natural world, is wisdom.[75] Contrary, perhaps, to expectations, wisdom drawn from the classical tradition in theology can point to a more poetic way of perceiving the world, but one that also encourages the habit of paying attention to the relational aspects of existence. Wisdom can serve to fill the gap that Primavesi identifies in our relationship with the natural world, by becoming more conscious of the wisdom of God as the feminine face of God manifested in the intricate community of all creatures and our kinship with them. However, unlike PoieticScape, wisdom is not simply an emergent property *within* nature, but is also given as a gift from God, reflecting the Trinitarian community of persons, expressive of ultimate wisdom. Instead of seeing the earth as sacred, the perspective of wisdom encourages those with faith to find in creation the marks of Trinitarian love. Wisdom, in addition, is not a romantic idealism that ignores the suffering of creation, for wisdom includes the wisdom of the cross.[76] Aquinas, too, believed that creation is an expression of God's wisdom, for 'Just as the universe is governed by divine wisdom, so everything was made by God's wisdom, according to the Psalmist, *Thou has made all things in wisdom*'.[77] He also claims that 'God in the beginning made creatures different and unequal, according to his wisdom that the universe might be fully rounded. This he did without injustice and without presupposing a difference in merit in the things created.'[78] His own view of a hierarchical universe created through a chain of being needs some adjustment in the light of evolutionary biology; however, his notion that all life is expressive of divine Wisdom, but at the same time that 'divine wisdom is the cause of variety in things', serves to emphasize the embeddedness of the action of wisdom in the creative processes of the world.[79] He also believed that all creation expressed the divine goodness; indeed, it was the diversity of creaturely existence that allowed the single goodness of God to be 'in creatures multiple and scattered'. Given such affirmation of creaturely goodness, any violation of creatures would be sinful, and the place of humans is one of qualified responsibility due to particular powers given to humanity, rather than superiority.[80]

Gaia and Ecofeminism

It is worth noting that the scientist Lynn Margulis, who was one of the strongest proponents of Gaia, rejected the idea that Gaia has some sort of consciousness or is even an organism.[81] Other philosophers go as far as to suggest that Gaia has its own intelligence and its own power to act in certain ways.[82] Peter Russell even suggests that human consciousness is linked in some way to the emergence of Gaian consciousness, so that human civilization is in some sense analogous to the development of the individual brain. In this case the 'brain' of Gaia is the sum total of human development.[83] Clearly, this view is once more putting humanity in a crucial position *vis-à-vis* other creatures on earth, even if it is dependent on those creatures for its survival. In other words, such views seem to be once more championing a distorted view of consciousness, divorced from any social interaction, while being embedded in anthropocentrism.

Lawrence Osborn suggests that the next step after attributing consciousness to Gaia is for ecofeminists to attribute to her a religious identity.[84] There are certainly examples of ecofeminists using the language of Gaia to describe the earth as a goddess. Charlene Spretnak, for example, rejects the idea that transcendence is the 'sky God' of patriarchy; rather, she suggests that transcendence is the 'sacred whole' or the 'infinite complexity of the universe'.[85] The answer to the loneliness of fragmentation characteristic of modernity is to discover one's inner connectedness with all that exists, embracing both life and death, celebrating the erotic and sensual. While she seems to recognize that there are some difficulties in close identification between the earth and femaleness as such, she insists that the most important idea to retain is an understanding of the planet as a body, an organism. Yet this admission seems to contradict her call for a reinstatement of goddess spirituality.

However, not all ecofeminists use Gaia in order to imply a particular organism with a consciousness and thence goddess characteristics. Rosemary Radford Ruether, for example, while she accepts that Gaia behaves as a unified organism, resists the notion of a separate female goddess. For her Gaia cannot be seen as a focus for worship in the place of a male God, and she suggests 'that merely replacing a male transcendent God with an immanent female one is an insufficient answer to the "god-problem"'.[86] As with Primavesi, Gaia represents in Ruether's interpretation the interdependence of all life in a single living system. However, Ruether is also drawn to process thought and it is through this that she seems to arrive at some sense of a larger consciousness than a human one. Moreover, it is arrived at through a sense of compassion for all life:

> Compassion for all living things fills our spirits, breaking down the illusion of otherness. At this moment we can encounter the matrix of energy of the universe that sustains the dissolution and recomposition of matter as also a heart that knows us even as we are known. Is there also a consciousness that remembers and envisions and reconciles all things, as the Process theologians believe? Surely if we are kin to all things and offspring of the universe, then what has flowered in us as consciousness must also be reflected in that universe as well, in the ongoing creative Matrix of the whole.[87]

In other words, she seems to be looking for a sense of consciousness in the *universe*, rather than in the earth as such, and hence she seems to follow the critique of process thought that Gaia alone is too limited in its imagery of the divine, for it is restricted to planet earth.[88] That is not to say that Gaia does not have something to teach us about the divine nature. For her Gaia represents the sacramental dimension of the divine, as opposed to the covenantal: 'There is another voice, one that speaks from the intimate heart of matter. It has long been silenced by the masculine voice, but today is finding its own voice. This is the voice of Gaia. Her voice does not translate into laws or intellectual knowledge, but beckons us into communion'.[89]

Hence Ruether agrees that Gaia is associated with a female 'divine voice', without attributing to her characteristics of consciousness or the identity of an individual goddess. Anne Primavesi, whom I discussed in more detail earlier, also integrates her understanding of Gaia with her view of God, though she resists using the language of the goddess, or even suggesting that this is a 'female' voice of God. Primavesi is certainly aware of the patriarchal oppression of women identified by other ecofeminists.[90] However, her view of Gaia differs significantly from Ruether's in that it takes far more cognizance of the scientific understanding of the Gaia hypothesis and seeks to ground an understanding of theology in such science. Yet, as I indicated above, she feels free not to remain restricted to the language of science in reformulating theological models.

Osborn has suggested that one of the reasons why Gaia provokes such a strong reaction, either in its favour or against, is because it represents a particular archetype, which according to Jungian psychology 'tend to have irrational (or, perhaps more accurately, pre-rational) emotions associated with them – they tend to become objects of devotion or [vilification]'.[91] Ruether identifies religious narratives of apocalypse, as well as classical narratives of sin and evil, as taking hold of Western cultural heritage. Her alternative is to promote a sacramental and covenantal healing tradition, with Gaia *incorporated* into that vision. For her, as for Primavesi and other ecofeminists, the archetype of the earth as a machine needs to be replaced with the archetype of the world as an organism. However, it is only in some ecofeminist appropriations of Gaia that the *maternal* archetype appears in the manner Osborn suggests.[92]

Gaian Ethics

So far I have discussed the way particular philosophers and theologians have taken inspiration from Gaia in order to formulate a particular shift in either our philosophical or our theological understanding of the world. But how might this shift have a more direct bearing on our treatment of the natural world; in other words, what relevance has it for our treatment of nature as such?

Midgley believes that the way we treat the natural world is a direct outcome of our presuppositions about our place in it. Hence, she suggests that 'The message is not that we should value the health of the earth above human needs. It is that these are not alternatives. Without a healthy earth humans cannot survive anyway.'[93] For her, the priorities for environmental action take their cues from Lovelock himself, who suggests:

> We worry far more about some remote danger of harm from pesticide or unusual genes in food than we do about the grim inevitability of global warming and all the harm that it will bring. . . . Our priorities are all wrong. Our demons of nuclear radiation and carcinogens from chemical industry are thereby tiny and feeble compared with the monsters that endanger the earth and that we made. . . . We should fear the effects of removing natural habitats with their ability to serve as global and local regulators. . . . We should fear the consequences of changing the composition of the atmosphere.[94]

In other words, the shift away from individualism towards a Gaian view has direct practical consequences on priorities for environmental ethics.

Midgley is correct to point to the lack of proper clarity in seeing what are the most important priorities for humanity to consider in an ethical treatment of the natural world. Yet, as I indicated earlier, an alternative would be to reconsider the classical notion of the common good. If we view the loss of creaturely variety as a loss in goodness and a marring of universal goodness, if we accept, at least in principle, that there are important interrelationships between inorganic systems of climate change and life, then a higher priority will be given to environmental concern. A Gaian ethic, in other words, needs to be resituated in the context of the common good and suitably qualified as speculative science that gives us pause to think more clearly about how humanity engages with the whole of the natural world as planet earth.

Theologians drawing on Gaia are more likely to stress the claim for a new intimacy with the earth that comes from a reformulated Gaian perspective. Yet ethics does not simply arise from a description of physical processes. Rosemary Radford Ruether, for example, suggests that:

> human ethics can neither be reduced to a description of physical and biological processes, nor regarded as simply a negation of these processes derived from 'higher truths'. Since human conscience and consciousness arise from natural evolution, we

should regard these capacities in ourselves as reflecting the 'growing edge' of nature itself. Yet consciousness also allows us an element of volitional power that seeks to rearrange patterns in nature according to suit human demands. In doing so we are constrained by nature's ecologic system, but we can find in that system echoes of our ethical and spiritual aspirations.[95]

The ecological system that Ruether is referring to here is, of course, Gaia, so that a reshaping of nature 'is finally governed by the finite limits of the interdependence of all life in the living system that is Gaia'. She suggests further that: 'Ecological ethics is an uneasy synthesis of both these "laws": the laws of consciousness and kindness, which cause us to strain beyond what "is", and the laws of Gaia, which regulate what kinds of changes in "nature" are sustainable in the life system of which we are an inextricable part.'[96] Ruether seems to be suggesting here that Gaia as a system serves to restrain human activity, which has a net effect similar to that of Midgley, in that it serves to shape human priorities in relationship to the natural world. However, the above quotation implies that she does seem to allow for an element of human 'reshaping' of nature within these limits that appears to be missing from Midgley's account. On the other hand, as I indicated above, Ruether has also identified Gaia with the voice of the feminine divine, which implies that the function of Gaia goes beyond just biological restriction of human activities in the manner she suggests here. The divinization of Gaia implies that Ruether is naturalistic in her approach to Gaian ethics; that is, she derives an 'ought' from an 'is', or, more specifically, infers a spirituality from a system that is then used to endorse a particular ecological ethic.

Primavesi's view of theology as embeddedness in Gaia also has ethical implications. While she roots her ideas about theology in an understanding of Gaia as autopoeisis, it is the notion of connectedness that dominates. She also believes that Gaia supports non-violence and freedom from competition. While Ruether suggests that our attitude towards nature needs to be kindness, Primavesi argues that it should be gratuitousness for our awareness of our lives as a gift-event, reflected in a sense of deep dependence on the natural processes of the earth.[97] For Primavesi the ultimate basis for ethics is consideration of the system as a whole, rather than distinguishing ourselves from other species in order to sanction violence against them. Hence a Gaian ethic for Primavesi is also an ethic of non-violence:

> One of the tools the earth sciences give us is a different set of distinctions between life forms. These taxonomies . . . are based on the premise that the correct context for discriminating between one life form and another is the whole ecosystem and not merely the notionally demarcated species. Furthermore, the focus is secondarily on its use to us, and primarily on its relationships with other organisms within the ecosystem and therefore with the ecosystem itself. In Gaia science the correct context ultimately includes the planetary system and its life cycles, and within that, the relationship between an organism or species and its material environment, including other organisms.[98]

I have already suggested that characteristics such as cooperation do not automatically flow from an understanding of the earth system as interconnected. Moreover, once we place the system as a whole as an adjudicator of other interrelationships, a different problematic emerges, one that is associated with other forms of deep ecology as well. This is the tendency for holism to take on negative ethical dimensions, especially in terms of different individual species.[99] If a particular life form does not contribute to stabilization of the environmental or climatic conditions, what reasons could there be for conserving it? The loss of such a species, including humans, might not seem particularly problematic.[100] For all the rhetoric of interconnectedness, the preservation of a particular kind of biodiversity is all that seems to be required.

It is possible to use Gaia in such a way to support negative environmental action.[101] The robustness of the system is such that negative environmental consequences of industrial waste are a relatively minor player in the overall scheme of the earth's history as a whole. This could encourage an irresponsible attitude to human activity, rather than its opposite. Osborn suggests that Gaia can be put in its proper place by considering it as just one aspect of the created order. However, rather oddly perhaps, he assigns to Gaia a higher status than the rest of lowly creatures on earth, suggesting that Gaia is an angel.[102] He arrives at this curious, if novel, position by suggesting that heaven should be thought of as the inwardness of the world, so that the archetypes coming from this inwardness correspond more closely to angels or demons. Following Wink, angels become quasi-personal bearers of the mystery of God. Like other angels, angels of nature help to reorientate human beings so that they become participants in the natural world, rather than seeing it, as it were, from the outside as a closed system. In addition, they lead to praise of God. Osborn concludes: 'if in contemplating Gaia we see the hand of a caring God, Gaia will have performed the traditional angelic role of divine messenger'.[103]

While I find the idea of Gaia as expressive of angelic activity intriguing, I suggest that Gaia could equally be viewed as a demonic force, ruthlessly eliminating those who do not obey her. Given the freedom of all creaturely beings, what is to prevent Gaia from becoming the fallen angel, identified in Christian tradition with the serpent? Such language is not particularly helpful theologically or ethically. Osborn seems to want to give some expression to the fact that Gaia is taken up in a religious as well as a scientific way by her protagonists. However, it seems to me that however one might interpret heaven, to relocate Gaia in the spiritual realm of angels brings with it the cultural baggage of transcendence and difference. Furthermore, it excludes consideration of the fragility of individual ecosystems that I discussed in chapter 2, reinforcing the mythology of a stable balance of nature. In addition, it attributes to a particular view of science theological importance that seems unnecessary, though it is no doubt an attempt to mediate between the view of Gaia as a goddess and the view of Gaia as simply earth system science. Primavesi's interpretation in terms of PoieticScape is more effective in this respect.

Rather than an ethic of Gaia, I suggest that a true sensitivity to all life forms comes more through reflecting more closely on scientific developments at a local as well as a global level, and recognizing that fragility and capacity for change are as much part of the picture as the overall stabilizing effects. How far these stabilizing effects are coordinated at a planetary level is impossible to prove given the current status of scientific knowledge. It seems doubtful that any kind of conscious or unconscious organism can be read into these stabilizing effects, though I grant that such systems do include the biota as well as inorganic processes. Hence the only real ethical lesson to be learnt from Gaia is the importance of trying to understand the whole, rather than just focusing on the individual components. Yet the opposite danger must also be borne in mind: without close attention to individual species and creatures the point of environmental ethics soon vanishes. One way to include a concept of the whole that does not fall into the above difficulties is the notion of the common good, combined with an understanding of God and creation in terms of wisdom. Just as a refocus on wisdom will serve as a reminder of the importance of practical wisdom or prudence, orientated towards the common good, so prudence in itself as moral action 'is the door through which entry is made to the contemplation of wisdom'.[104]

Conclusions

I have suggested in this chapter that reflection on Gaia is important because of the way that it has been taken up and used by prominent philosophers and theologians in order to support a particular ecological ethic. However, I argued that the way Gaia is interpreted scientifically is also a necessary consideration if it is to be appropriated in order to develop an ethic of nature. It is fair to say that Gaia theory is not dismissed by scientists in the way it once was, perhaps, in the earliest years of its formulation.[105] However, even if we concede that Gaia represents environmental stabilizing tendencies on the planet as a whole, trying to understand the way Gaia works at a planetary level is still problematic from a scientific perspective. There is some evidence for the operation of local Gaian systems, but the way this interacts with natural selection in shaping the course of evolution is still being discussed.

From the perspective of an ethic of nature, Midgley has argued strongly that Gaia gives us the imaginative equipment we need in order to shift humanity out of its egocentric individualism. Of course, this is only true of a more positive interpretation of Gaia that views different species on an equal footing with humankind. However, as far as human treatment of the environment is concerned, Midgley seems to take ethical guidance from Lovelock's geophysiological science, so that ethical priorities are shaped by what is seen from this perspective to be good for the planet as such. Primavesi is also anxious to resituate theology in natural systems and allow a broad understanding of PoieticScape to emerge in human communities. She makes an imaginative connection between the science of Gaia, human language, religion, culture and ethics. Theologically this is a long way from traditional Christian interpretation, and deliberately so, for she believes that the paradox of

Adam/Christ narrows human history down to the significance of two individual lives. Her caricature of the Christian tradition puts her own view in a favourable light, but there are alternative ways of reading this tradition that are compatible with biological science. Ruether seems less dependent on Gaia as science in her reformulation of ecological ethics, though, as with Primavesi and Midgley, the move away from anthropocentrism is dominant.

I have suggested that such attempts to use Gaia to support an ecological ethic are fraught with difficulty, because of the ambiguous message of the science of Gaia itself. Certainly 'she' can remind us of the importance of interconnectedness, but not at the expense of the freedom of the individual and the value of biodiversity in all its richness, not just those species responsible for stabilizing the planet. I suggest, furthermore, that the claimed advantages of Gaia in terms of jolting humankind away from selfishness and egocentrism are not always apparent. It is clear from some New Age texts that Gaia can become another means of narcissistic self-help.[106] I have argued instead that an ecological reading of the common good can assist in reminding humanity to take due account of the interconnectedness of human life with all life processes. In addition, Wisdom can serve as a theological category that has the appeal of Gaia, but lacks Gaia's ambiguity in relation to human persons. Aquinas claimed that prudence is the door to wisdom, yet equally we might say that it is through wisdom that prudential decision-making becomes possible, prudence understood not just at the local particular and individual level, but at the social and political level as well. Yet does the shift in interest in Gaia among scientists reflect a wider interest in the idea of a more holistic method of science? Are there other aspects of feminism that are instructive in relation to the development of an ethics of nature? It is to these issues that I turn in the next chapter.

Notes

1   See J. Lovelock: *Gaia: A New Look at Life on Earth*, 2nd edn (Oxford University Press, Oxford, 1987).
2   For a fascinating discussion of this area, see B. Szerszynski: *The Sacralization of Nature: Nature and the Sacred in the Global Age* (Oxford: Blackwell, 2003).
3   Stephen Clark hints at this when he suggests, 'The Gaia hypothesis, any sensible biologist should admit, may well be true. But for that very reason it may not have the implications some environmentalists, including myself, have seen in it.' S. Clark: *How to Think about the Earth: Philosophical and Theological Models for Ecology* (London: Mowbray, 1993), p. 30. See also discussion in chapter 2 of the present volume.
4   See C. Deane-Drummond: 'Gaia as Science Made Myth; Implications for Environmental Ethics', *Studies in Christian Ethics*, Summer (1996), 1–15; C. Deane-Drummond: *Biology and Theology Today: Exploring the Boundaries* (London: SCM Press, 2001), pp. 144–64.
5   This model follows from chemical studies of Ilya Prigogine and others. See I. Prigogine: *From Being to Becoming* (San Francisco: W. H. Freeman, 1980); I. Prigogine and I. Stengers: *Order Out of Chaos* (London: Heinemann, 1984).

6   T. Lenton: 'Gaia and Natural Selection', *Nature*, 394 (1998), pp. 339–447.

7   Stephen Clark suggests that Gaia 'conflicts with no known evolutionary principle', but in fact trying to account for Darwinian natural selection directed towards adaptation of species to their environment through competition and that of Gaia towards species changing the conditions themselves requires further intellectual work, as Lenton's review demonstrates. Clark: *How to Think about the Earth*, p. 29.

8   Lovelock has shifted his views in this respect, his earlier suggestion that regulation is for the biota being replaced with the idea that both the biota and the environment work together as a whole. Compare Lovelock, *Gaia*, with J. E. Lovelock: 'Geophysiology: A New Look at Earth Science', *Bulletin of the American Meterological Society*, 67 (1986), pp. 392–7.

9   Deane-Drummond: *Biology and Theology Today*, pp. 148–9.

10 Even evidence for this is mixed in some respects. For discussion of sulphur cycling see Deane-Drummond:, *Biology and Theology Today*, pp. 156–8.

11 For commentary see Deane-Drummond: *Biology and Theology Today*, p. 151.

12 Lenton: 'Gaia and Natural Selection', p. 440.

13 In the preface to Primavesi's book, for example, he admits that his first book did not take into account religious ideas sufficiently, so that 'What I failed to see was that a theory of the Earth that sees it behaving like a living organism was inevitably theological as well as scientific.' A. Primavesi: *Sacred Gaia: Holistic Theology and Earth Systems Science* (London: Routledge, 2000), pp. xi–xii.

14 C. Deane-Drummond: *Theology and Biotechnology: Implications for a New Science* (London: Geoffrey Chapman, 1997), pp. 58–60.

15 Clark: *How to Think about the Earth*, pp. 26–31.

16 M. Midgley: *Utopias, Dolphins and Computers: Problems of Philosophical Plumbing* (London: Routledge, 1996), pp. 136–49. For brief comment, see Deane-Drummond: *Biology and Theology Today*, pp. 175–6.

17 John Holden, in M. Midgley: *Gaia: The Next Big Idea* (London: Demos, 2001), preface, p. 7.

18 It may be that she was not directly responsible for the title, for she refers to the book in a later publication as *Individualism and the Concept of Gaia*. See acknowledgements in M. Midgley: *Science and Poetry* (London: Routledge, 2001), p. ix. None the less, her agreement with it suggests that she finds such a thought conducive to her general line of argument.

19 Midgley: *Gaia*, p. 21.

20 Such extrapolation is invalid according to a classical understanding of scientific knowledge. Midgley: *Gaia*, pp. 16–17.

21 Midgley: *Gaia*, p. 24.

22 The incongruence is particularly marked in Berry's strong rejection of 'pantheist' and for that matter 'goddess' forms of religion, which he recognizes as implicit in Gaia. R. J. Berry: *God's Book of Works* (London: T & T Clark/Continuum), p. 121.

23 For commentary on the place of religious language in science see her earlier works, such as M. Midgley: *Evolution as a Religion* (London: Routledge, 1979); M. Midgley: *Science as Salvation: A Modern Myth and Its Meaning* (London: Routledge, 1992).

24 Midgley: *Gaia*, p. 25.

25 I will come back to the debate between individualism and holism later.

26 Midgley: *Gaia*, pp. 28–9. Also in Midgley: *Science and Poetry*, p. 188. It is noteworthy that Midgley removed the reference to the Millennium Bug in this version.

27 Midgley: *Gaia*, 32–3.

28 E. O. Wilson: *On Human Nature* (Cambridge: Harvard University Press, 1978), p. 193. A similar argument for using religion to promote ecological responsibility has been put forward by other scientists, such as Stephen Jay Gould. It is an ethically shallow reason for including religion in the discussion. I will return to this issue in the final chapter.

29 Wilson: *On Human Nature*, p. 209.

30 Midgley: *Gaia*, p. 35; also Midgley: *Science and Poetry*, p. 197.

31 Midgley: *Science and Poetry*, p. 195.

32 Midgley: *Science and Poetry*, p. 195.

33 Midgley: *Science and Poetry*, p. 195.

34 They are, none the less, very sensitive to environmental pollutants and so are used by environmentalists as pollution monitors. D. H. S. Richardson: *Pollution Monitoring with Lichens* (London: Richmond Publishing, 1992).

35 Brian Goodwin: *How the Leopard Changed Its Spots* (London: Orion, 1994), p. iv.

36 This is documented by Lovelock as the oxygen 'pollution' event. Lovelock suggests that this process was gradual, rather than sudden, reflecting a change in dominance of oxic organisms. See J. Lovelock: *The Ages of Gaia* (Oxford: Oxford University Press, 1988), p. 96.

37 The language of human parasitism is used by those who support Gaia. See, for example, J. Ravetz: 'Gaia and the Philosophy of Science', in P. Bunyard and E. Goldsmith (eds): *Gaia: The Thesis, Mechanism and Implications* (Wadebridge: Wadebridge Ecological Centre, 1989), p. 135. I will take up this point again in the final chapter.

38 J. Lovelock: 'Planetary Medicine: Stewards or Partners on Earth?', *The Times Literary Supplement*, 13 September (1991), pp. 7–8.

39 Lovelock: *The Ages of Gaia*, p. 212. For further commentary, see Deane-Drummond: *Biology and Theology Today*, pp. 181–3.

40 For discussion of eco-fascism see Clark: *How to Think About the Earth*, pp. 42–59.

41 T. Gilby: *Between Community and Society: A Philosophy and Theology of the State* (London: Longmans, Green, 1957), pp. 203–13. David Hollenbach has also applied the idea of the common good to environmental policy-making. D. Hollenbach: *The Common Good and Christian Ethics* (Cambridge: Cambridge University Press, 2002), pp. 42–61.

42 Aquinas suggests that 'prudence and justice, as belonging to man's rational part, are more closely engaged with the common good since the general or universal answers directly to the reason as the individual does to our sensitive part.' *Summa Theologiae, volume 36, Prudence*, trans. T. Gilby (Oxford: Blackfriars, 1974), 2a2ae, Qu. 47.10.

43 Aquinas: *Summa Theologiae, volume 37, Justice*, trans. T. Gilby (Oxford: Blackfriars, 1975), 2a2ae, Qu. 58.5.

44 Aquinas: *Summa Theologiae, volume 37*, 2a2ae, Qu. 58.5.

45 For further commentary on the way biological language shapes the way science is discussed, see E. Fox Keller: *Refiguring Life: Metaphors of Twentieth Century Biology* (New York: Columbia University Press, 1995).

46 See Deane-Drummond: *Biology and Theology Today*, pp. 165–72.

47 Primavesi: *Sacred Gaia*. Primavesi's book *Gaia's Gift* (London: Routledge, 2003) was published as this book went to press.

48 This cultural shift goes against the traditional sociological account of secularization aligned with the mechanization of nature. See Szerszynski: *The Sacralization of Nature*.

49   J. Lovelock, in Primavesi: *Sacred Gaia*, p. xi, xii. Mary Midgley also endorses this book enthusiastically, exclaiming, 'Here is a book really needed. Hurrah for it' (cover).

50   Such a view is also characteristic of ecology in general, see Deane-Drummond: *Biology and Theology Today*, pp. 45, 74.

51   Primavesi: *Sacred Gaia*, p. xii.

52   Primavesi: *Sacred Gaia*, p. xvii.

53   Primavesi: *Sacred Gaia*, p. xvii.

54   Primavesi: *Sacred Gaia*, pp. 37–8.

55   Primavesi: *Sacred Gaia*, p. 37.

56   C. Deane-Drummond: 'The Logos as Sophia: A Starting Point for a Sophianic Theology of Creation', in P. Clayton and A. Peacocke, eds: *In Whom we Live and Move and Have Our Being: Reflections on Panentheism in a Scientific Age* (New York: Eerdmans, 2003).

57   Primavesi: *Sacred Gaia*, p. 7.

58   Primavesi: *Sacred Gaia*, p. 8.

59   Primavesi: *Sacred Gaia*, p. 9.

60   Primavesi: *Sacred Gaia*, p. 9.

61   Deane-Drummond: *Biology and Theology Today*, p. 174.

62   Primavesi: *Sacred Gaia*, p. 10.

63   Primavesi: *Sacred Gaia*, pp. 15–23.

64   For further discussion about the problems associated with holistic environmentalism see D. E. Marietta: *For People and the Planet: Holism and Humanism in Environmental Ethics* (Philadelphia: Temple University Press, 1995), pp. 49–68. A similar problem was raised in chapter 3 of this book, although this time Singer's utilitarian calculus was compared with individual animal rights.

65   Primavesi: *Sacred Gaia*, p. 29. See also the discussion on p. 109. Evelyn Fox Keller has discussed the uses of biological language in her book *Re-figuring Life*.

66   Primavesi: *Sacred Gaia*, p. 45.

67   Primavesi: *Sacred Gaia*, p. 46–8.

68   Primavesi: *Sacred Gaia*, p. 65.

69   Primavesi: *Sacred Gaia*, p. 160.

70   Primavesi: *Sacred Gaia*, p. 166.

71   Primavesi: *Sacred Gaia*, p. 170–1.

72   Primavesi: *Sacred Gaia*, p. 179.

73   I will come back to a discussion of this issue in the final chapter.

74   R. Radford Ruether: *Gaia and God: An Ecofeminist Theology of Earth Healing* (London: SCM Press, 1993)

75   C. Deane-Drummond: *Creation through Wisdom: Theology and the New Biology* (Edinburgh: T & T Clark, 2000).

76   For further discussion, see Deane-Drummond: *Creation Through Wisdom*.

77   Aquinas cites Psalm 103.4.

78   Aquinas: *Summa Theologiae, volume 10, Cosmogony*, trans. W. A. Wallace (Oxford: Blackfriars, 1967), 1a, Qu. 65.2. Aquinas's insistence of equality of merit in creatures allows him to preserve a hierarchical view of the universe, while retaining an understanding of God's justice.

79   Aquinas: *Summa Theologiae, volume 8, Creation, Variety and Evil*, trans. T. Gilby (Oxford: Blackfriars, 1967), 1a, Qu. 47.1.

80   See earlier chapter for a discussion of the gap between Aquinas's own view of the
     ethical treatment of animals and his ontology.

81   Lyn Margulis, cited in R. Sheldrake: *The Re-birth of Nature: The Greening of Science and
     of God* (London: Century, 1990), p. 129.

82   Kit Pedler is a good example. See K. Pedler: *The Quest for Gaia* (London: HarperCollins,
     1991), p. 11.

83   P. Russell: *The Awakening Earth: Our Next Evolutionary Step* (London: Routledge and
     Kegan Paul, 1982).

84   L. Osborn: 'Archetypes, Angels and Gaia', *Ecotheology*, 10 (2001), p. 12.

85   C. Spretnak: *States of Grace: The Recovery of Meaning in a Post Modern Age* (New York:
     HarperCollins, 1993; 1st edn 1991), pp. 135–6. For further discussion see Deane-
     Drummond: *Biology and Theology Today*, pp. 169–70.

86   Ruether: *Gaia and God*, p. 4.

87   Ruether: *Gaia and God*, pp. 252–3.

88   D. R. Griffin: 'Introduction', in D. R. Griffin, ed.: *The Re-enchantment of Science*
     (New York: State University of New York Press, 1988), p. 21.

89   Ruether: *Gaia and God*, p. 254.

90   Primavesi: *Sacred Gaia*, pp. 121–36.

91   Osborn: 'Archetypes, Anglels and Gaia', p. 15.

92   Notably Charlene Spretnak, but also Carol Christ. See C. Deane-Drummond:
     'Creation', in S. Parsons, ed.: *Cambridge Companion to Feminist Theology* (Cambridge:
     Cambridge University Press, 2002).

93   Midgley: *Science and Poetry*, p. 206.

94   J. Lovelock: personal communication to Mary Midgley, 1999, cited in *Science and
     Poetry*, pp. 206–7.

95   Ruether: *Gaia and God*, pp. 47–8.

96   Ruether: *Gaia and God*, p. 31.

97   Primavesi: *Sacred Gaia*, p. 175.

98   Primavesi: *Sacred Gaia*, p. 22.

99   See Marietta: *For People and the Planet*, pp. 49–68.

100 Deane-Drummond: *Biology and Theology Today*, p. 180. It has also been observed by
     others. See Osborn: 'Archetypes, Angels and Gaia', p. 18.

101 Deane-Drummond: *Biology and Theology Today*, p. 179.

102 Osborn: 'Archetypes, Angels and Gaia', pp. 19–20.

103 Osborn: 'Archetypes, Angels and Gaia', pp. 20–1.

104 Aquinas: *Disputed Questions on Virtue*, trans. R. McInerny (South Bend, IN: St
     Augustine's Press, 1999); *Disputed Question on the Cardinal Virtue*, art. 1, ad. 4, p. 111.

105 For a comment by Lovelock see J. Lovelock: 'Hands Up for the Gaia Hypothesis',
     Nature, 344 (1990), pp. 100–2. He also documents his own personal account of the
     story of Gaia in Lovelock: *Ages of Gaia*, pp. xii–xx, 1–14.

106 See M. Pogacnik: *Daughter of Gaia: Re-birth of the Divine Feminine* (Forres: Findhorn
     Press, 2001). Pogacnik describes a series of exercises designed to connect with the
     feminine divine within each person and a means for spiritual inner growth.

Chapter 8

Feminism and the Ethics
of Nature

Charting the relationship between women and nature offers a rich labyrinth of possible avenues. The association of women with nature is ambiguous, with a variegated response among feminists, ranging from affirmation to rejection. Broadly, while some affirm an association of women and nature, others believe that such a link reinforces oppression of both. Historically women have been part of a range of activities associated with nature and the natural. For example, women have engaged with early progressive environmental conservation movements, and resisted androcentric ways of framing women's experience of pregnancy and childbirth.[1] Politically feminists have also embraced a range of perspectives, from liberal approaches through to more radical deep ecology positions. While it is possible to identify a spectrum of approaches among feminists, most ecofeminists adhere to the view that the dualism inherent in patriarchal cultures is in some sense responsible for the oppression of both women and nature.[2] Writers such as Rosemary Radford Ruether identify Judaeo-Christian religious traditions as fostering such dualism, while others such as Carolyn Merchant find the source of such dualism in mechanistic science. More radical still is the suggestion by authors such as Charlene Spretnak that it is the loss of the idea of the earth as sacred that is responsible for dualistic thinking.[3] Ecofeminism is sometimes known as the 'third wave' of feminism, though Merchant suggests that it needs to include the earlier varieties of feminism as well.[4] The purpose of this chapter is to examine ways in which feminist ethics of nature might be developed by critical examination of different feminist approaches to God and science, as well as a discussion of particular ways of developing ethics, in particular an ethic of care, including the care of animals. I also include discussion of how an ethic of care might be interpreted within ecological political frameworks. Aquinas's position on the place of women followed the patriarchal culture of the time, naming a wife as 'part of her husband', though he gave a wife a higher place in the domestic order than a slave or child.[5] Aquinas's particular views on women have generated hostile responses to his writing from many feminist authors.[6] Moreover, unlike his conception of animals, his view on the ontological status of women was in concert with his ethics, affording them lower status than men.[7] However, it is fair to suggest that more often than not he talks about rational creatures, rather than 'men', and hence for him the clearest division is between the rational and non-rational, rather than between male and female. In addition, he believed that both men and women share in the divine image and both have an intellectual nature.[8] I argue in this chapter that an ethic of care is a version of virtue ethics, though it is rarely named as such, and contrary to expectation Aquinas's development of the virtues has strands of commonality with a feminist ethic of care.[9]

Ecofeminism and the Language of God

Not all ecofeminists consider religious experience to be fundamental to their concerns, but those who do weave together ways of linking the transformation of religious language alongside a revisioning of how to treat the earth. In the chapter 7 I discussed in detail how Anne Primavesi envisaged the language of God through the lens of Gaia, identified with the earth as sacred Gaia. I argued that an account of God as feminine wisdom, impregnating the world from its beginning and continuously sustaining the world in its evolutionary history, was an alternative way to stress holistic interrelationships between God and creation. A feminist perspective, by arguing for a new way of thinking about God, seeks to uncover the language of oppression that has crept into God talk. Rebecca Chopp, for example, suggests that:

> It is possible to imagine a new relation to the body and to God, to creation and redemption, to law and to grace, not from a subjectivity that must destroy everything in its path to maintain and establish its identity, but from a subjectivity, a language and a politics that desires and embraces otherness, multiplicity and difference.[10]

In particular, she argues that it is from the *margins* that hope emerges, and visions of flourishing include corporality, so that this delivers not just an ethics of (eco)justice, but also a poetics of nature, itself pushing against the given order and transforming it.

The varied religious voices in ecofeminism include a range of religious beliefs, or more correctly, perhaps, a diversity of spiritualities, including Buddhist, Hindu, Jewish, Christian, Native American, post-Christian and Goddess.[11] Most of the authors in Carol Adam's anthology believe that some realignment of religious traditions with feminist concerns is necessary. Not all ecofeminists are convinced that spirituality or its recovery is beneficial for the central project of ecofeminism, namely to eliminate the oppression of women and nature. Smith, for example, suggests that drawing on the spirituality of Indian religious traditions trivializes the oppression of Indian women and makes spirituality just one isolated aspect that can somehow be extracted from its roots and used in a particular way.[12] Yet ecofeminists

who adhere to spiritual traditions do so because they have 'celebrated and conse-
crated our ties to the non-human world, reminding us of our delicate and inescap-
able partnership with air, land, water and fellow living beings'.[13] Gottlieb suggests
that the historically dominant meaning of classic texts of Judaism and Christianity
was the 'wise use' of the earth and its creatures, rather than celebration of the
inherent value of the earth as such.[14] However, rather than rejecting religion
altogether, he suggests that we need to incorporate religious ideas into contemporary politics if we are to find sources of social direction and personal inspiration.

Gottlieb is rather too dismissive of the possibilities inherent in Judaeo-Christian
tradition. The ecofeminist writer Mary Grey, for example, offers new ways of
reappropriating biblical prophetic themes so that they become sources of inspiration in what she calls an outrageous pursuit of hope.[15] The culture of consumerism
is of critical importance in fostering a culture where wants become needs, indirectly leading to exploitative attitudes towards the environment. Instead, she argues
for a prophetic vision taken from Isaiah as a vision of flourishing, one that is
inclusive of both people and planet, and one that does not split ecology from social
justice.[16] She also suggests that Isaiah fosters an ecological wisdom, embedded in a
liturgical context so that it becomes the source of change and renewal:

> The emphasis is on *Leitourgia*, the authentic work of the gathered community: a
> people who grieve, lament, give thanks, and at the same time work to free the land
> from the poison of pesticide, the long death of nuclear radiation and nuclear winter,
> and the injustice of being wrenched away from the ownership of indigenous peoples,
> with all the conflict and complexity that this means.[17]

The practical embeddedness of her writing is characteristic of other ecofeminist
theologians, namely that there can be no separation of religious belief and praxis.
Ecofeminist ethics is informed by religious views, but arises out of the concrete
concerns linking the devastation of the earth and the suffering of vulnerable people.
Grey also suggests that our failure to perceive our own entanglement in consumerism is a failure of wisdom. Embodied wisdom is deep connectedness to the earth
that, according to Grey, echoes the thought of Susan Griffin.[18]

My own notion of wisdom, while it also emphasizes connectedness, parts company with Griffin, as it seems to me that she displays an essentialist view of nature,
one where the earth and women are so closely identified that distinctions between
them are no longer clear. Stacy Alaimo has been strongly critical of such identification, for she suggests that while it sings of unity with nature, it unwittingly
widens still further the divide between nature and culture. To some extent I share
her reservations, for 'speaking for nature can be yet another form of silencing, as
nature is *blanketed in the human voice*. Even a feminist voice is nonetheless human:
representing cows as ruminating over the beauty of the mother–child bond no
doubt says more about cultural feminism than it does about cows.'[19]

Mary Grey is right to include within practical wisdom the idea that it is inseparable from the wisdom of ordinary experience, embodied in the lives of the poor

and uneducated. Knowing becomes a subversive form of knowing, celebrated in the Eucharist, the feast of wisdom.[20] This idea also both compares and contrasts with Freya Matthews's concept of the ecological self, though in this case the theme of holism seems to eclipse any sense of partnership. Matthews, for example, suggests: 'When the universe is viewed under the aspect of a self-realising system, then the relation in which it stands to me, when I am viewed as a self, is the equally holistic one of ecological connectedness: its selfhood contains mine, my selfhood conditions its.'[21] For Freya Matthews the only difference between humans and other creatures is that we are aware of the connectedness; the universe itself is a self, but rather oddly in view of Gaia theory, she suggests that lifeless objects are not part of the ecological order.[22] Matthews suggests that each organism has a self in as much as it has the power for self-realization. Her commitment to holism is apparent in her belief that all organisms have their place in the whole: 'Each organism, in fulfilling its conatus and achieving a state of flourishing, is helping to maintain the ecosystem further up the line, and each system, by maintaining itself in place, is preserving the conditions in which the organism can achieve self-realisation.'[23] It is not clear, according to this model, how far individuals take priority over whole systems, and if she leans more towards an ecocentric position then this would have clear practical implications for the treatment of animals.[24] Like Grey, Matthews is committed to the idea of flourishing as the goal, but her criteria for this are richness in emotional, imaginative, artistic, intellectual and spiritual life. The culture of interconnectedness leads to flourishing. Humans find meaning through their spiritual capacity, and it is this capacity that keeps 'the ecocosm on course, by teaching our hearts to practise affirmation, and by awakening our faculty of active, outreaching, world-directed love'.[25] Her notion of ecological self appears to be an overly romantic view of both humanity and the natural world.

Revisioning Science from a Feminist Perspective

How might the practice of scientific work change if it were to be informed by a feminist perspective? If an ethic of nature includes the context of how we treat the natural world through science, which I have argued is necessarily the case, then challenges to the way science is practised need to be taken into account. There have been claims of sexism in science at various levels: first, through male domination of practice and the historical exclusion of women; second, through presuming that males think in a superior way to females because of purported differences in brain chemistry; third, through sexism that seems to be inherent in research design; fourth, through domination of male ways of knowing to the exclusion of female ways of knowing; fifth, through the world view of science itself, which is about manipulation and detachment rather than caring. I will devote most attention to the last position, since it opens up an alternative approach to science and to nature generally; that is, through an ethic of care, which I will take up in more detail in the following section.

Historically the exclusion of women from science lends itself to cultural critique by feminist writers. Some argue that the exclusion of women followed cultural dualisms, the idea of the feminine being associated with emotion and passivity rather than reason and action.[26] Other theorists alight on the fact that those women who have, against the odds, made significant contributions to science are forgotten through the way history is recorded, a feminist critique then adjusts such a record and reinstates the importance of the contribution of women to science.[27] The fight for equal status for women in science is a strong strand in the liberal feminist tradition and one that most scientists would welcome today.

None the less, contemporary science still contains strands of essentialism, which are preconceived views about an ontological biological difference between males and females. Aquinas clearly held these views, though he used the story of Genesis as a means of supporting the ontology that he drew from Aristotle. I will argue later that his theology actually softened the more extreme essentialism found in Aristotelian philosophy, since both men and women were equally made in the image of God.[28] A good example of this essentialism still in existence today is to be found in contemporary discussions about neuroscience and gender, a heritage of the now discredited theory that women's brains are lighter and therefore inferior to men.[29] Ruth Bleier, who was a well established neuroscientist, strongly challenged the dominant contemporary paradigm of a biological basis for gender differences in cognitive abilities.[30] She suggests that the process whereby scientific research becomes accepted for publication fosters a closed system, where the prestige of the lead authors counts more than the quality of results. The dominant theory holds that males process visuospatial information with the right brain hemisphere, while females process it with both hemispheres, with the former processing assumed to be superior to the latter. This implies, indirectly, that human agency will also be gendered, for the minds of males and females will work in biologically different ways. She suggests that the quality of science arguing the case for the differentiation is weak, including basic flaws in design such as lack of controls for variables and lack of consensus in definition of what it means to have spatial ability. Moreover, the variation within each sex is far more than the variation between them; hence the whole concept of a biological basis for gender differences becomes problematic. The effect of sex hormones on cognitive abilities continues to be highly controversial, yet still popular, but Bleier points out that some studies show no effects at all of testosterone on brain function. Other research that claims that gender differences can be related to morphological differences in the particular part of the brain known as the splenum is also likely to be bordering on the fanciful. In particular, she suggests that scientists are not acknowledging sufficiently their lack of knowledge. Hence, 'in the light of the profound ignorance about the most basic elements of human cognition, it is utterly ludicrous to claim any particular cognitive significance whatsoever for any characteristics of the *corpus callosum*'. She goes on to suggest that the project as a whole contains 'an irreducible level of subjectivities', drawing on 'the naive hope that we can find something we can see and measure and it will explain everything. It is silly science and it serves us badly.'[31] She offered a similar critique of the supposed genetic basis for stereotypical views of women articulated by many sociobiologists.[32] The extrapolation from animal to human behaviour is particularly problematic, including the more extreme view that 'rape' is somehow the result of a 'natural instinct'.[33] It seems to me that while there is likely to be a biological component to human thinking and acting, much of the so-called 'science' seems to have been distorted through cultural lenses without adequate support.

A further, related example of how far gender differences have served to shape the way science is conducted comes through consideration of research design. Is the choice of male rats for experimental work purely the convenience of using the male sex, unhampered by biological processes such as menstrual bleeding, or does it reflect a particular bias in design? Evelyn Fox Keller suggests that such design issues imply a presumption that the male represents the species as a whole.[34] Other examples include the interpretation of animal behaviour, especially that of primates, according to male-dominated norms.[35] Much the same could be said of attempts, however well intentioned, to extend the human moral community to primates and other intelligent mammals by perceiving their culture in human categories, and thus making them morally responsible.[36]

Yet if we examine the way female primatologists describe their own work it is far less romantic than this view would suggest. Alison Jolly, for example, suggests that women's innate ability to be sensitive and patient with animals may account for the increasing interest in primatology among women scientists.[37] However, she draws back from any suggestion that this is necessarily simply biologically conditioned; it is more likely that an innate talent in women is then channelled by social expectations. In other words, women's interest in the great apes is not simply a substitute for maternal instincts. In addition, she suggests that 'the kind of woman who is likely to break for the wild wants to do science without being messed about herself by the controlling atmosphere of a hierarchical lab group'.[38] Hence, 'wild animals are wondrous to us precisely because they are wild'.[39] It is not so much a sentimental projection of an idealized nature, but nature as *raw nature* that women primatologists admire. So to rewrite primatology as simply emergent from rising cultural feminism in the way that Donna Haraway does in her book *Primate Visions* is, to female and male scientists alike, an offence.[40] Jolly insists that women primatologists genuinely observed something new, even if one of the reasons why they were prepared to notice such things arose from a mixture of gender, funding, family and national backgrounds. The three new areas identified primarily, though not exclusively, by women primatologists were the recognition of animal minds and personalities, the importance of females and female bonding in group structure and the increasing interest in wider social and political issues that impinge on the science, such as future evolutionary trends and biodiversity.[41] In addition, analysis of animal behaviour is becoming more and more sophisticated; for example, communication between primates and other animal species shows a level of complexity that is far greater than was once imagined.[42]

From the above it is clear that sexist attitudes have, to some extent, percolated into the way some science is designed and interpreted. None the less, feminist agendas may also influence the way science is perceived, so charges of sexism need to be treated with seriousness, but also a certain degree of caution. It is more likely that primatologist-ologists insist on *distorting* effects of gender, but from a primatologist's viewpoint (male or female), while they may be prepared to admit that the questions set are influenced by gender, and other social factors, the actual results themselves are 'real', rather than simply the result of social construction. The latter view of primatologists themselves seems to me to be the most honest interpretation. It is also clear that the harder 'sciences' such as mathematics and physics are less likely to be 'biased' in terms of content, though research programmes may well be influenced by male-dominated ideology. For example, the degree of funding for particle accelerators may well have been unacceptable had women become more heavily involved in this kind of work.[43]

Some ecofeminists, in particular, reject the scientific project as a whole, believing that the mechanistic attitude towards nature that is inherent in modern science betrays a dominating attitude towards the natural world that is wholly unacceptable. Carolyn Merchant, for example, is sharply critical of modern science and technology, especially those technologies that serve to dominate women and nature.[44] Examples include nuclear radiation damage to the human reproductive system and ecosystems, which, she suggests, is ignored by male technologists. However, she does not elaborate whether it might be possible to develop a science that is more sensitive to environmental issues, or cite examples where companies have started to move in the direction of greater awareness. *Forum for the Future*, for example, campaigns in the business sphere in order to introduce more sustainable practices within science.[45] In addition, to view mechanistic science as 'dead' and organicism as 'alive' is a very simplistic view of possibilities inherent in science. The Gaia hypothesis, for example, which I discussed in chapter 7, is good way of perceiving how science might be done from a more holistic perspective. However, the evidence for Gaia still relies on mechanistic interpretations of natural processes, such as sulphur cycling and the like. A simple organicism is virtually impossible in scientific practice, even though there may be ways of approaching science that give greater emphasis to whole systems, rather than the parts.

Standpoint theory is a more promising approach to revisioning science, since it suggests that while realism is possible in science, it needs to be considered from the perspective that acknowledges that knowledge is inevitably in some sense gendered. Sandra Harding, for example, argues that the experience of women needs to be included in revising scientific practice, hence avoiding the problem of essentialism associated with the close identification of women and nature.[46] How far this gendering of science could challenge more mechanistic images of the body inherent in scientific practice is open to debate.[47] None the less, the feminist writer Hilary Rose argues that once love becomes the critical factor in influencing a philosophy of science, then it becomes more responsive and responsible.[48] Above all, she suggests the requirement shared by feminists from different perspectives for an ethical science: 'They share a common wish to challenge the ethic of no ethic, the culture of no culture which lies at the universalizing core of modern science . . . and to rebuild the sciences as respectful and responsible.'[49] She is also highly critical of the philosophy embedded in Darwinism, which she believes betrays a dominating attitude to nature and women:

> I want to suggest that at a more profound level Darwinism (and the more I read of Darwin the less convincing is the distinction between social Darwinism and Darwinism) shored up the inheritance of the domination of Nature and of Woman which has long shaped the accounts of men and their relationship to both.[50]

Domination is expressed in various ways, such as the treatment of animals as if they were simply chemical reagents. Rose's longing grows for a form of knowledge that is not dependent on 'routine violence'. Significantly, she suggests that 'we can begin to see the possibility of new feminist philosophies of nature which do not abandon the task of making representations, of making scientific facts, but instead offer different approaches to the practice of science'.[51] This view is clearly more sophisticated than the simple anti-science propaganda adopted by more extreme radical ecofeminists. She acknowledges, for example, that it will still be possible to 'build defensible, objective accounts of the real, accepting that the real is always understood through historically, geographically, politically located and embodied subjects'.[52] In particular, she suggests that more account needs to be taken of the discourse between science and the public understanding of science, the construction of what counts as science and what does not count. Hence, she argues that more traditional interpretations of the sciences and humanities existing in two cultures are far too simplistic. For her the paradigm that must shape a new science is one of love, as evidenced in the various struggles, including that of the poorer communities of women in the third world, where the struggle for the protection of land is also one of survival. Hence for her, 'Within these examples we see feminism bringing love to knowledge and power. It is love, as caring respect for both people and nature that offers an ethic to reshape knowledge, and with it society.'[53] In what sense might caring be the privilege of women, rather than men? She is able to make such a suggestion by insisting that such a perspective on caring emerges from women's experience. In particular she suggests:

> a feminist epistemology which derives from women's lived experience is centred on the domains of interconnectedness and caring rationality, and emphasizes holism and harmonious relationships with nature, providing links to that other major social movement of our time, the ecological. At times the ecological movement also takes on gender and challenges new forms of imperialism.[54]

Rose avoids the difficulty of equating women with the earth in an essentialist way, yet links her own project of revisioning science to the ecological project. If ecology itself is found to be much more fluid than interpretations of balance and harmony suggest, then this association with ecology becomes more problematic in so far as it has less contact with ecology as science. She also suggests that the distinctive labour of women includes love, such that 'emotion is restored within work and within knowledge'.[55] Of course, such analysis assumes that science as practised does not portray love or emotion, and such a stereotypical view of science as coldly calculating may arise from a mistaken interpretation of the products or results of science, rather than listening to the experiences of scientists themselves. It seems to me that scientists have been hesitant to acknowledge the emotion in science, and this is perhaps the difficulty that needs to be challenged, rather than believing that injecting emotion into science will radically change the way it is done. As far as setting priorities for scientific research is concerned, a more holistic approach would be welcomed, but there is always a danger that individual worth will be lost in the process, as I discussed in chapter 7. How might an ethic of care make a difference in practice? She suggests that 'It is the admission of love, a recognition that the process of care shapes the product, which opens up the prospect of a feminist reconstruction of rationality itself as responsible rationality – responsible to people and the natural world.'[56]

Feminism and an Ethic of Care

How far might such admission to love influence ethics and become a basis for practice? In order to explore this possibility more fully it is worth considering in more detail examples of feminist writers who have developed an ethic based on the idea of caring. Such an ethic is important to consider, for it seems to me to align itself with virtue ethics and a corresponding focus on the individual character of the agents. Not all feminist writers who are seeking to develop an ethic of caring are ecofeminists. By drawing on a range of feminist thinking in this area, I hope to show how such an ethic of care might become translated into themes that are significant for an ethics of nature. It will therefore constitute an important element in the revision of Aquinas that I will discuss next, though he is less hostile to women than some of his critics have supposed. Carolyn Merchant suggests that most ecofeminists do advocate a version of an ethic of care, love and trust, as opposed to more traditional ethics based around rights, rules and utilities.[57] Peta Bowden has suggested that mothering is critical for understanding caring for a number of reasons.[58] First, she suggests that it is a privileged example of the possibility of human connectedness. Second, it represents an 'archetype of caring', such that the connection between the vulnerability of childhood and the potential responsiveness of mothers characterizes what caring is all about. Third, it serves to challenge the nature of the self as defined by conventional ethics; selfhood becomes a binary-unity, rather than a response to universal codifications. She argues, in particular, that whether we are actual mothers or not we are connected culturally and biologically to mothering practice.

Are there specific virtues that are called forth by mothering in the way that Sara Ruddick suggests?[59] These priorities and attitudes include preservative love, a hold-ing, one that minimizes risk and reconciles differences. This preservative love is expressed through the virtues of humility and cheerfulness. Cheerfulness, rather oddly perhaps, means the mid-point between the denial of limits and passive submission. Humility, on the other hand, is the mean between abandonment of control and domination. It is difficult from these definitions to see the distinction between cheerfulness and humility or how one might tell whether the mean is reached. I suggest that without the virtue of prudence, which sets the mean for the expression of other virtues, such talk about humility and cheerfulness is somewhat meaningless. Ruddick also argues that the blurring between self and other is part of the mothering process. Yet she does not seem to take sufficient account of the unequality in the relationship between mother and child. She also believes that mothering practices are not in themselves gendered, that is there is no *necessary* connection between mothering practices, birthing and pregnancy. Bowden rejects this view, even while insisting that we are all inevitably shaped one way or another by mothering practice. In this she lays herself open to the charge of essentialism. However, she tries to avoid this by using another illustrative example of the way mothering is socially conditioned. She contrasts Ruddick with Amy Rossiter's sense of mothering as being constrained primarily by social practice. In this scenario mothers no longer have a real sense of their own personhood, they are constrained by the social expectation of others and hence do not act out of their own needs. Rather than offering any way out of these contrasting views of what constitutes mothering, Bowden invites the reader to let such diversity stand. She concludes: 'while it has been the aim of the work to foreground the ethical values of caring and their implications for gender-sensitive enquiry, the conventional requirements for fixed definitions and determinate solutions to problems identified in both traditional and feminist ethics have been rejected'.[60]

How far might it be feasible to develop an ethic of care from such considerations of motherhood and mothering? It is clear that not all mothers develop the kind of qualities that Ruddick suggests are essential in an ethic of care. If they arise in the experience of only some women, in what sense could they become archetypal? Of course, Bowden invites the reader to consider a kaleidoscope in women's experience, rather than any universal principles. I suggest it is the only way to deal with such diversity. This leads, however, to a lack of clarity in what caring might mean, for if there are elements in it that are coercive through social restraint, then it becomes less desirable. Moreover, it is not obvious by what criteria we can distinguish such coercive elements from others that arise from the deliberate choice of women in their role as mothers. In addition, the link between caring and emotion is implicit, so that women are once more cast in the role of emotive, earth-bound and instinctive.[61] Yet there is another side to women that is often not acknowledged, namely the way women have mistreated others, including other women. Elisabeth Spelman suggests, correctly in my view, that a heavy focus on caring has diverted attention away from the less attractive histories of women who have shown lack of care.[62]

A less essentialist account of an ethic of care is found in the work of Joan Tronto.[63] She argues that the first step in the development of ethics is to recognize

that the powerless are omitted from the central concerns of society. Moral boundaries are set up to maintain the status quo. The idea of care is implicated in the
existing structures of power and inequality. She rejects the dyadic understanding
of care based on mother–child relationships as she suggests that it does not take
sufficient account of the social and political spheres of action. Instead, care is
defined culturally and is ongoing, it reaches out to something other than self and
will also lead to action. According to such a view there is no reason why women
are naturally disposed to be more caring than men. Hence:

> On the most general level we suggest that caring be viewed as a species activity that
> includes everything that we do to maintain, continue and repair our 'world', so that
> we can live in it as well as possible. That world includes our bodies, our selves and
> our environment, all of which we seek to interweave in a complex, life sustaining
> web.[64]

Such a view does not restrict the scope of caring to humans; it includes environmental concern, though this aspect is not specifically spelt out in her work. There
is no reason why it could not become extended to include human relationships
with animals as well as the wider questions about environmental issues. For Tronto
caring amounts to a virtue, it is both an activity and a disposition. She outlines five
aspects of caring that are particularly significant. In the first place it is *caring about*
something or someone; so recognition of the importance of the other is needed.
Caring includes being able *to take care of* someone or something; that is, taking
responsibility for an identified need and knowing how to respond. Third, caring is
concerned with *care giving*, it meets the particular need that is required of the carer.
Simply having the right attitude is not enough. Fourth, it is to do with *care receiving*;
that is, the objects of care will respond in an appropriate way to show that care is
received. Finally, care is a *practice*, so that 'producing an integrated, holistic way to
meet concrete needs is the ideal of care'.[65] She also recognizes that there might be
conflict between the different demands of care, though how to resolve such difficulties is left unanswered, except to say that some mediation is necessary. As one
might expect, she also insists that care is gendered, raced and classed; that is, the
way we think of care is subject to a number of sociopolitical framings, mostly
devaluing both those who do the caring and the caring process as such.

The four ethical elements of care arise from the four dimensions of care. I will
use the definitions suggested by Tronto and then show how these might be
extended to encompass human relationships with animals and environmental concern.[66] It seems to me that this is the most fruitful way that an ethic of care can be
applied: through extension to the non-human world. First there is *attentiveness*,
arising out of recognition of need. This concept echoes the thought of Simon
Weil's idea of *paying attention*. As applied to the non-human world the first step
would be to pay attention to what is happening to both animals and the environmental conditions of the planet, including a recognition of each species as in some
sense like us but also an Other.[67] Palmer also notes the importance of attentiveness

in her outline of an ethic of care towards animals.[68] Second, the idea of taking care of someone issues in the ethical premise to take responsibility for the Other, and as such requires constant evaluation. As applied to the non-human world, taking responsibility for what happens to animals and the planet becomes a crucial ethical component. The changing nature of human relationships with animals and environmental problems and issues means that such evaluation is continuously under review. Third, the idea of care giving leads to an outcome of competence, and as such includes an assessment of the consequences of particular actions. It is aligned with the idea of professional ethics. In relation to questions about animals and environmental concern this means that an ethics of nature is not just theoretical considerations about different priorities to be adopted, but a practice that leads to positive results for animals and the environment. It aligns with Palmer's insistence that there must be honesty about the way we perceive human relationships with animals, though she does not spell out how this might issue in both responsibility and competence in the way I have suggested here.[69] Fourth, care receiving engenders responsiveness, so that 'caring is by its very nature a challenge to the notion that individuals are entirely autonomous and self-supporting'.[70] The idea that the non-human world of animals or even other life forms in nature might be in some sense responsive in the relationship with humans is, perhaps, controversial. However, as long as any responsiveness is not cast in the same mode as that found in humans there is every reason to include it. Pitcher suggests that the faithfulness of his dogs exceeded what might even reasonably be expected of humans.[71] In becoming sensitive to the *response* of nature to human attempts to repair damage etc. the effectiveness of such action is monitored, as it were, from the perspective of species other than our own.

Tronto's ethic of care is not intended to be exclusive in the realm of ethics, for the 'injunction to care is not meant to serve as a total account of morality. It is not meant to overthrow such moral precepts as do not lie, do not break promises, avoid harm to others.'[72] Care provides a way of thinking about ethics in practical terms, rather than a set of rules or principles, so it is bound to take a more ambiguous form compared with rule-based accounts of the moral life. She suggests that 'it involves both particular acts of caring and a general "habit of mind" to care that should inform all aspects of a practitioners moral life'.[73] The concept of caring as a habit of mind bears close resemblance to that of virtue, though she does not specifically engage with the literature on virtue ethics. In fact she specifically rejects the idea that care is a social virtue and all other forms of virtue arise from it. None the less, she suggests that care is 'a crucial concept for an adequate theory of how we might make human societies more moral'.[74] It achieves this by serving as a critical standard and by putting moral ideas into action. Her idea that caring forms a critical standard sits somewhat uneasily with her insistence that it is not normative. In addition, she finds problems within caring itself, namely that it can become parochial and either reflect sublimated needs or be too detached. It is also not clear where the standard of care comes from, who decides what are the appropriate forms of care and so on.

She tries to alleviate some of these difficulties by joining her concept of care to justice. Without this the political will to value care and restructure institutions along these lines will stagnate. She concludes:

> care is a necessary, though not by itself a sufficient part of our account of the moral life. To address and correct the problems with care that we have noted requires a concept of justice, a democratic and open opportunity for discussion, and more equal access to power. An ethic of care remains incomplete without a political theory of care.[75]

She argues that since morality and politics are divided we are not aware of the restraints politics puts on our sense of morality and vice versa. Care might seem to be private and parochial because of the way we construct care, so that it only counts in these categories. She also suggests that because ethical analysis tends to be abstract, an ethic that starts with engagement with others and recognizes particularity may seem a secondary sort of moral concern. Tronto's account of an ethic of care shares with other feminist interpretations of ethics an attention to particularity in actual contexts, a sense of responsibility situated in a narrative and involving communication as a central activity.[76] Yet her inclusion of justice distinguishes her view from that of other feminists advocating a care ethic, such as Noddings, whom she criticizes as being too parochial, for it fails to address the social context in which care is shaped.[77]

How might such theories of care intersect with an ethic of nature? The dilemma in interpreting care as emerging from the experience of women or being shaped by social construction reflects the wider controversy among feminists relating to naturalism. According to the naturalist paradigm moral action 'contributes to the flourishing of the full human person by its making true in reality what is already there in nature'.[78] Those who adopt the maternal approach to caring would generally fall into this category, namely the suggestion that it is virtually unavoidable that what is biologically given affects the way we care. Those who support the naturalist paradigm are committed to the view that biological sex does, in some sense, shape gender.[79] On the other hand, those who reject naturalism might see any claim for particular feminine views of caring as colluding in the social oppression that has devalued women and their role in caring as such. Both versions of caring draw on experiences of women, but whereas in one case the sociopolitical boundaries shaping the meaning of caring are challenged, in the other the nature of caring itself can be discovered by close attention to unique characteristics of mothering. I am less convinced by developments of an ethic of care that draw on women's maternal experience, however powerful these may be as vehicles for inspiration and solidarity among women. Sarah Hoagland has similarly raised objections to the mother model as appropriate for female agency, since it relies on the primary experience of unequal relationship between mother and child.[80] She also suggests that when caring is modelled on mothering it is overly romantic, ignoring other aspects of mother–child relationships, such as resentment, along with tenderness. Instead, Tronto's inclusion of justice into an ethic of care serves to prevent caring becoming tied to a strong contextualist position associated with unequal and ambiguous relationships.

Those who identify the earth as Mother in ecofeminist discourse have also taken up the theme of mothering in a way that is problematic. I discussed the idea of Gaia as mother earth in chapter 7. What are the implications in relation to the above regarding a language of care? It is significant to consider this locus of care, as it shifts the source of care from individual humans to the earth. I will argue against such a move from feminist and ethical perspectives. Stacy Alaimo suggests that attempts by environmentalists to cast the earth in the role of mother remain one of the most persistent images linking women and nature.[81] Female figures linking the earth and nature have continued to proliferate, especially among environmental groups and campaign organizations. She argues convincingly that such a figure actually supports a domestic consumerism that severs environmentalism from public debate, becoming a domesticated version of our own mothers. Catherine Roach is similarly critical of the term, suggesting that:

> it is problematic because of our tendency to relate to our mothers as ambivalent love objects, expected to care for all our needs, and that for this reason, instead of achieving the desired result of encouraging us towards environmental soundness, this slogan has almost the opposite effect of helping to maintain exploitative patterns toward the earth and mother.[82]

Alaimo believes that the image of the earth as mother contributes to a domesticating discourse that harms both women and the environment. She finds portrayals of mother earth in media broadcasts in the USA as a sick victim of humanity's exploitation, only to be saved by consumerism and buying the right products, hence supporting a patriarchal and sexist interpretation of women, and putting most of the blame for environmental responsibility on women, as the consumer.[83] Industrial polluters are portrayed as 'unruly children'; hence the base shifts from the political to the domestic sphere, the blame coming home to roost with the mother who does the consuming. This somewhat bizarre appropriation of the image of mother earth illustrates its potential for harm from the perspective of ecofeminism. However, it is surprising how often this image is still invoked by those who are committed to ecofeminist ideas. She also criticizes the image of mothers as carers for the same reason, for discourses of nurturing can be used to bolster capitalism.[84] The counter to such dangers is a greater awareness of sociopolitical factors, as Curtin suggests that an 'ethic of care provides a very important beginning for an ecofeminist ethic, but it runs the risk of having its own aims turned against it unless it is regarded as part of a distinctively feminist political agenda that consciously attempts to expand the circle of caring for'.[85]

The possible way out of this dilemma of unhelpful domestication is to portray the image of nature as female in a way that breaks out of this cosy view of women. Gaia is described as a 'tough bitch', Mother Nature a 'butch' and a wild woman as a way of reacting against the domesticated versions of maternal feminine natures.

Hence 'these unruly heretical natures not only resist the domestication of Mother Earth, but they forge an alliance between feminism and environmentalism'.[86] Of course, those who align accounts of Mother Earth with religious ideas such as the goddess have to portray the divine as in some sense wild, or even in the case of Gaia as one who is unforgiving towards those who transgress her boundaries.[87] Such a view is totally incompatible with the Christian understanding of God as ultimate Goodness.

Ruether does not seem to appreciate this problem in her account of Gaia as the divine within nature. For her, while creativity includes risk, the earth is necessarily identified with the cosmic wisdom and goodness that is found in Christ. For 'The same wisdom and goodness underlies all other religious quests and has been manifest in many other symbolic expressions such as the Tao, the Buddha, the Great Spirit, and the Goddess.'[88] At death, she suggests we simply surrender to the earth, understood as mother of all creativity, so that 'Our final gesture, as we surrender ourself into the Matrix of life, then can become a prayer of ultimate trust: "Mother, into your hands I commend my spirit. Use me as you will in your infinite creativity".'[89] While this is perhaps less domestic compared with other views of mother earth, since it links in with the idea of the cosmic Christ, it still portrays unbounded connections between women and nature.

While Alaimo welcomes the undomesticated role of nature as cast in Susan Griffin's account of mother nature, as I mentioned above, she rejects her close identification of women and nature, which seems to brush aside the notion of nature as other. In addition, while she does acknowledge the critical role of such images of nature in resisting domesticated versions of the idea of woman and nature, she believes that the association of women and nature is itself problematic.[90] In the first place she suggests that the association of women and nature is pernicious, and, second, it confines nature to human categories. This aligns with Plumwood's argument for the otherness of nature, while recognizing a measure of continuity with it. Alaimo suggests that:

> the challenge, then, is to develop non-gendered tropes of nature that emphasize continuity between humans and nature while still respecting nature's difference, that have some sort of cultural potency while gesturing toward what cannot be encompassed by, controlled by, or even entirely known by human culture.[91]

One possible line of inquiry for Alaimo in response to this challenge is to explore the cyborg of Donna Haraway, for it invokes a connection with nature that does not raise problematic associations of women and nature. Instead of the earth as mother, Haraway suggests that it becomes a 'witty agent'.[92] Yet it is worth considering how far the androgenous category of cyborg really challenges the categories of sex and gender, since it is itself the product of technology that has been dominated by men. While the idea of the earth as a witty agent reminds us of the illusive character of nature, what other role might it perform from the perspective of feminist ethics?

The Politics of Feminist Ethics of Nature

So far I have discussed ways in which feminist writers have sought to argue for particular feminist agendas in relation to science and the natural world, articulating on the one hand equality between men and women, and on the other hand gendered difference through caring. The third possibility is one that is more explicitly political in orientation, seeking to challenge the social roots of gendered articulation of humanity's relationship with nature.[93] For the poorer nations of the world environmental issues are not just about saving the planet; rather, they are issues of survival.[94] In addition, the grassroots movements, which form around specific issues such as toxic waste management or nuclear power, are often associated with particular groups of women.[95]

Carolyn Merchant has argued consistently for something more than just critical analysis of the patriarchal presumptions behind social and political institutions. She suggests that the next step is to envisage new ways forward in developing alternative patterns of production, reproduction and consciousness. She also seems to welcome the idea of a spiritual ecology, like many writers refusing to draw up boundaries according to religious norms, while welcoming the possibility of the spiritual.[96] None the less, for Merchant ecofeminism is at its most characteristic when actively engaged in practical ecological protests of all kinds, such as planting trees in Kenya in order to restore degraded lands, or joining the Chipko movement in India in order to preserve resources and sustain livelihood, or in Sweden offering MPs a taste of jam made with berries that had been sprayed with herbicide. For her 'All these actions are examples of a world wide movement, increasingly known as "ecofeminism", dedicated to the continuation of life on earth.' She believes that an ethic of care is insufficient, as it tends towards essentialism. While this is not the case with more politically informed ethics of care, as discussed above, she prefers the idea of *partnership* with nature, one that is inclusive of both men and women. Yet her idea that this would allow humans to give non-human nature space and time so that it can reproduce and evolve, as well as respond to human actions, bears remarkable resemblance to the revised idea of an ethic of care based on Tronto's work that I suggested above.[97] She outlines what this would mean in the following way:

> In practice this would mean not cutting forests and damning rivers that make people and wildlife in floodplains more vulnerable to 'natural disasters', curtailing development in areas subject to volcanoes, earthquakes, hurricanes and tornados to allow room for unpredictable, chaotic, natural surprises; and exercising ethical constraint in introducing new technologies such as pesticides, genetically engineered organisms, and biological weapons into ecosystems.[98]

She recognizes that the idea of nature as a partner allows for personal and intimate relationship, though not necessarily in a spiritual sense, and for feelings of compassion towards animals as well as people who are sexually, racially and culturally different. Hence 'It avoids gendering nature as a nurturing mother or goddess and avoids the ecocentric dilemma that humans are only one of many equal parts of an ecological web and therefore morally equivalent to a bacterium or mosquito.'[99] Instead, she argues for a political basis for ecofeminism that asks sociopolitical questions such as: What is at stake for women and nature when production in traditional societies is disrupted by colonial development?; or What is at stake for women and nature when traditional norms of biological reproduction are disrupted by interventionist technologies, such as chemical methods of birth control, amniocentesis or chemical or nuclear pollutants in soil and water? In addition, she tries to envisage ecofeminist social transformation, in particular forms of socialist societies that take 'a healthy perspective' on men and women and environmental issues.[100]

In political terms this would mean that new forms of socialist ecology emerge that bring human reproduction and production into balance with that of the natural world, thus leading to global sustainability. Merchant takes up the issue of the tension between production and biological and social reproduction in subsequent work.[101] She calls once more for a radical revisioning of production, reproduction and consciousness. She also draws on Val Plumwood's idea of the relational self to envisage new definitions of reproduction in terms of creativity and knowledge that are in alliance with nature, rather than against it.[102]

Merchant does not assume that women are never in conflict with nature, or never manipulate nature for their own ends. However, it is not clear how such conflicts, when they arise, might be corrected. In any event, valuing remains ecocentric in orientation, moving out from the individual to include wider ecological identities in populations, species and ecosystems. Like many other ecofeminists she believes that the starting point is the physical and cultural experiences of women, rather than other approaches, such as transpersonal ecology or deep ecology, that seem to start outside women's experience. Her partnership ethic goes beyond the essentialist claims of those who identify women and nature, in that it is grounded in a concept of *relation*. It presumes, first, equality between human and non-human, moral consideration of human and non-human, respect for cultural diversity and biodiversity and inclusion of women, minorities and non-human nature in ethical considerations. While she argues for equality of status between human and non-human, she does admit to differences between them: 'It admits that humans are dependent on non-human nature and that non-human nature has preceded it and will post-date human nature. But it also recognizes that humans now have the power, knowledge and technology to destroy *life as we know it* today'.[103] Since the seventeenth century, she suggests, humanity has had the power to destroy nature in a way that was impossible in early millennia. Under the schema of partnership nature becomes an equal subject. She also suggests that even within science the idea that nature can be controlled is now challenged through chaos theory, so that: 'Science can no longer perform the God trick – imposing the view of everything associated with modernism, the Enlightenment and mechanistic science. The real world is both orderly and disorderly, predictable and unpredictable, controllable and uncontrollable, depending on context and situation.'[104] She recognizes that the idea that biodiversity led to ecological stability fostered the belief that species conservation could contribute to ecological health. However, chaos theory challenges fixed ideas about ecological stability, so that 'natural disturbances and mosaic patterns are the norm rather than the aberration'.[105]

Merchant's inclusion of ideas about chaos into her notion of ecology is particularly welcome. I discussed the shifts in ecological understanding earlier in this book. Her partnership motif is also a considerable improvement on an ethics of care that is simply bound up with notions of either women or the earth as mothers. I agree with her analysis that the latter fosters associations of women and nature that are damaging for both women and the environment. However, her ideal of partnership raises some important issues that are not fully addressed in her work. For example, if there is equality in moral status between human and non-human, how does one adjudicate between competing claims of one or the other, especially in the case of animals? It may be impossible in practice simply to align human activity to the natural processes in the way she suggests.[106] Further, if the natural world is not as ordered as we might have originally supposed, how does such reorientation of human goals work out? Does the idea of an ordered, natural world flounder in the face of a postmodern critique, and thus evacuate the concrete meaning of the natural as a means for establishing partnership?[107] Her partnership ethic, while suggestive in many respects, seems to fall short in terms of reworking a politics of relationship, which is one of her central concerns. She attempts to take into account postmodernity, in that her revisioning includes a reshaping of science so that 'a post classical, post modern science is a science of limited knowledge, of the primacy of process over parts, and of imbedded contexts within complex ecological systems'.[108] This sounds very interesting in theory, but how might such a science operate, given the particular ways in which science is set up and institutionalized within particular frameworks? She seems to assume that scientists will automatically be able to respond to the need for partnership, draw on their own theory of chaos and take into account the particular experience of women. It seems very doubtful that this will be the case, given entrenched attitudes that Merchant is keen to point out.

Other feminist theologians have, like Merchant, worked hard to combine ecological rationality with ecojustice themes. Gabriele Dietrich, for example, has taken up Sallie McFague's concept of the world as the body of God and used it as a metaphor for reflecting on the concerns of particular women's communities.[109] She includes the idea of God as mother, though the idea of God as lover or friend is also significant. These varied images avoid some of the problems associated with equating the earth, motherhood and God. None the less, while she includes the concept of the cross, which avoids the difficulty of more romantic images of cosmology, it is linked primarily with the theme of justice for women, rather than ecological connectedness. Injustices in the human community spill over into maltreatment of the earth. Val Plumwood, on the other hand, argues for an ecological rationality.[110] This form of rationality includes a form of prudential reasoning that is 'self-critical reason which scrutinizes the match or fit between an agent's choices, actions and effects and that agent's overall desires, interests and objectives as they require certain ecological conditions for their fulfillment'.[111] As with Merchant, the ultimate aim is partnership, though by including an intermediate step her proposals strike me as more realistic:

> Initially such an inquiry might aim at developing a balance between ecologically destructive capacities and corrective capacities, although a more sensible and ambitious objective would aim at phasing out destructive capacities and evolving a sympathetic partnership or communicative relationship with nature.[112]

The way such an ecological rationality might be introduced in practical terms is through a focus on local communities, where people have to live with the ecological consequences of their decisions, in contrast with political decision-making from remote centres. In addition, the social conditions of inequality foster this remoteness and associated ecological harm, so that:

> Inequality combines with geographic remoteness to generate conditions for epistemic remoteness, creating major barriers to knowledge and offering massive opportunities for redistributing ecoharms on to others in ways that elude the knowledge and responsibility of consumers and producers along with concern for ecological consequences.[113]

She also insists that while liberal democracy sounds promising, 'shallow forms' of such democracy provide only 'weak forms of ecological rationality'.[114] Part of the problem seems to be that if ecological concerns are just one of many 'interest groups', it does not pay sufficient attention to the fact that a healthy environment is the condition for most other interests. Another aspect of the problem relates to social equality. Those who are privileged, who also have the main role in social decision-making, can choose to live in areas remote from ecological damage, while consuming the greatest proportion of resources.[115] This leads her to suggest more radical or deliberative, participatory forms of democracy. Of particular importance is the idea that those who are marginalized are not only given the opportunity to participate: their voice is *actively solicited*. Hence the form in which communication takes place needs to be critically appraised so that everyone has the same opportunity to speak.

While Plumwood's analysis is suggestive in practical terms for new ways of thinking about how political ethics might take more account of both feminist and ecological issues, it lacks reference to spirituality. Those who are more in tune with spiritual issues may not take sufficient account of practical ways of transforming political processes. Even from a secular perspective it is worth asking how, in particular, it might be possible to motivate those who are dissatisfied with current liberal forms of democracy. From a theological perspective the inclusion of those marginalized from decision-making in society is not just a matter of theoretical interest, it is part and parcel of a Christian vocation. This seems to be behind what Parsons is saying in envisioning the recovery of the theological virtues of faith, hope and love beyond the fragmented and, at times, violent discourse emerging through feminist analysis.[116] Of course this would be global, not just local, drawing in voices from those societies that are different from our own. Rosemary Radford Ruether, in particular, has been particularly active in promoting the inclusion of views from different cultures and different religions.[117] While we might question how representative some of these voices are, given Plumwood's analysis, it is at least a start in the right direction. An ethic of wisdom can incorporate Plumwood's analysis in so far as it aligns itself with issues of justice and love, where justice is understood as providing opportunity for the least privileged in society to speak, rather than just redistribution according to those affiliated to the most privileged classes. In this respect Aquinas's understanding of redistributive justice, which I discussed in an earlier chapter, requires some modification.

Aquinas on Women

In this final section I will be addressing the question that immediately comes to mind when considering classical writings, namely Aquinas's supposedly hostile attitude to women. I argued in chapter 3 that while his ethical approach to animals was far from desirable, his ontology pointed in another direction. Aquinas drew on Aristotle for his view of women, which claimed that as a natural being a woman is a defective and 'manqué'. The biology of the time stated that a male seed was capable of self-propagation, but due to external influences such as a south wind the male's active power was affected, and this led to females. Aquinas, on the other hand, softened this very harsh approach towards women by claiming that as far as the human species as a whole is concerned, a woman is not manqué, for she is directed towards the important work of procreation. In addition, he argued that as both men and women shared in the divine image, both had rational natures, even though he, incorrectly, assumed that women were inferior to men in intellectual capacity.[118] He also distinguished clearly between a slave and master relationship and a male and female relationship, arguing that the former is for the service of the master, while men need to manage women for the latter's advantage.[119] Even though he believed, incorrectly, that men had a greater degree of rational discernment than women, he used Genesis texts to support his view that the role of man in relation to the woman was that of caring, of loving support; hence man is originator of woman 'in order to make the man love the woman more and to stick to her more inseparably, knowing that she had been brought forth from himself'.[120] He argued further that woman should never be despised, as otherwise she would have been made from a man's feet, nor should she have authority over a man, otherwise she would have been made from a man's head. Even more surprising, perhaps, given the Augustinian association of sin and sexuality, is his admission that just as ejaculation is pleasurable, so the process of making woman from man in the story of Genesis must also have been painless.[121] Finally, he counters the Aristotlean suggestion that females were born by an accident of nature by suggesting that 'just as variety in the grading of things contributes to the perfection of the universe, so variety of sex makes for the perfection of human nature'.[122] He also objects to the idea of women arising by an accident of nature, preferring the notion that they came about as a 'result of some strong mental impression', and so 'the sex of the progeny would have been settled by the decision of the progenitor'.[123] This study shows that Aquinas shifted the Aristotelian attitude towards women in a direction that was in favour of women by suggesting that they were capable of rational thought, the correct attitude of men to women was love not domination, they contribute to the perfection of humanity through adding to its variety and finally they are born by deliberate mental choice rather than an accident of nature. While Aquinas was restricted by the impartial knowledge of science of his time and he certainly was not a feminist in the contemporary understanding of the word, he did at least challenge the more extreme aspects of Aristotelian attitudes towards women.

Contrary to initial expectation, a modification of Aquinas's approach to the virtues that is more in touch with feminist thinking therefore resonates to some extent with the direction of his thought. Feminist writers have been sensitive to the implicit dangers in either extreme individualism or holism in our attitudes to the natural world. Caring is important, as it shifts the agenda away from principles and rules, which become guidelines rather than arbiters of human behaviour. In addition, caring, like the virtue approach, gives priority to relationships between persons and between persons and other creatures. A politically sensitive ethic of care seems to me to be the most convincing, as it includes the political sphere as well as the domestic sphere, but Aquinas's inclusion of prudence/wisdom, justice, temperance and fortitude is just as important as the virtue of charity, which is most closely aligned with caring.

Aquinas speaks about the commands to love immediately before the gift of wisdom. While the command to love God with all our heart holds primacy, he argues for a discriminatory love, so that those who are nearest and closest to us are loved more than those who are more remote in relationship.[124] In his discussion of whether virtues are equivalent, he is at pains to point out that the theological virtues are the foundation of the other virtues, and within the theological virtues charity has pride of place, so that 'charity is the greatest because it unites us more closely with God, and hope is greater than faith because hope moves the will to God, whereas by faith God is in a man by way of knowledge'. In the same passage he then goes on to say that 'Among all the other virtues prudence is the greatest because it governs the others, and after it comes justice by which a man is well ordered not only in himself, but also with respect to others.'[125] Indeed I would go as far as to suggest that without the concept of practical wisdom human charity/caring becomes detached from any specific moorings and no longer has the tools to tell us how to act, even if it does succeed in telling us what attitude to have in all our actions towards others.

It is clear that charity is fundamental for Aquinas's ethics, for 'charity is called a mother of the other virtues, because from the desire of the ultimate end it conceives their acts by charging them with life'.[126] Charity gives the energy needed to lead a life of virtue. Yet it is important to stress that it is the *wisdom* of God that directs charity aright, so that charity, while located in the human will, is 'ruled not by reason, as are the human virtues, but by the wisdom of God it goes beyond reason'.[127] In addition, charity's joy is about divine wisdom, so that 'this sort of joy is not mixed with sadness, for scripture says, *For companionship with her*, that is, with wisdom, *has no bitterness*'.[128] Such complete happiness is never possible in this world, for the movement of the divine in human persons is never ending, only in heaven the 'joy of the blessed is full'. It is for this reason that one might dare to call Aquinas's account of the virtues a *wisdom ethic*, for it is through the wisdom of God that charity, as mother of all virtues, is rooted in the human heart. As a theocentric ethic it parts company with the feminist ethic of care in as much as it seeks to move beyond what is possible through human nature alone, urging a participation in God that is only dimly perceived in this life.

Of course, prudential decision-making also takes account of natural law, and just as I have argued that the traditional concept of natural law needs some adjustment in order to take into account biological insights about animals, it can also be adjusted according to feminist ethics.[129] Yet the purpose of natural law is most marked at the beginning, where 'to regulate human life according to divine norms is in fact the work of wisdom, and the first indications of this ought to be reverence for God and subjection to him, with the consequence that in all things whatsoever a person will shape his life in reference to God'.[130] Yet such 'fear of the Lord' is the beginning of wisdom, 'while the last stage is like the end wherein everything is brought back to its right order. And that belongs to the nature of peace'.[131] Aquinas's sense of order in nature was related to his particular under-standing of cosmology and biology. In the light of current scientific knowledge it is more appropriate to see such ordering in more fluid terms, so that dynamic growth and the possibility for transformation is built into the structure of living things. In addition, Aquinas presupposes the importance of charity, so that the ability to receive the gift of wisdom is rooted in charity, even though its action is essentially rational.[132] Aquinas admits that charity leads to a 'sympathy or co-naturality with divine things', so that following contemplative union with God, action in accordance with 'the divine reasons' becomes possible in such a way that the 'bitter becomes sweet and the toil a rest'.[133] Wisdom is, therefore, both con-templative and practical. Given the scope of divine goodness in all creation, it makes more sense to suggest that caring needs to expand to include not only animals, but the wider ecological community as well.[134] Such a cosmic community is not fixed, but labile, subject to disturbance and inclusive of the human commu-nity. The way our attitude to such community might evolve through an ethic of wisdom is the subject of the final chapter, which follows.

Notes

1   See S. Alaimo: *Undomesticated Ground: Recasting Nature as Feminist Space* (New York: Cornell University Press, 2000).

2   For a survey of these views see Carol Adams: 'Introduction', in C. Adams, ed.: *Ecofeminism and the Sacred* (New York: Continuum, 1993), pp. 1–9.

3   See, for example, C. Merchant: *The Death of Nature: Women, Ecology and the Scientific Revolution* (New York: Harper and Row, 1980); J. Plant, ed.: *Healing the Wounds: The Promise of Ecofeminism* (Philadelphia: New Society Publishers, 1989); R. Radford Ruether: *New Woman: New Earth: Sexist Ideologies and Human Liberation* (New York: Seabury, 1975). See also R. Radford Ruether: *Women and Redemption: A Theological History* (London: SCM Press, 1998); C. Spretnak: *States of Grace: The Recovery of Meaning in a Postmodern Age* (San Francisco: HarperCollins, 1991).

4   See C. Deane-Drummond: 'Creation', in S. Parsons, ed.: *Cambridge Companion to Feminist Theology* (Cambridge: Cambridge University Press, 2002).

5   Aquinas uses Ephesians 5.28 in order to support the belief that a wife is part of her husband, but Aristotle in order to support the view that her right is greater than that of slave or child relative to parent. Aquinas: *Summa Theologiae, volume 37, Justice*, trans. T. Gilby (Oxford: Blackfriars, 1975), 2a2ae, Qu. 57.4.

6   Esther Reed has put this graphically by her suggestion that 'Vast tracts of Aquinas' writings . . . are texts of horror which perpetuated misogynism.' E. Reed: 'Pornography and the End of Morality?', *Studies in Christian Ethics*, 7:2 (1994), p. 86.

7   See, for example, Aquinas: *Summa Theologiae, volume 12, Human Intelligence*, trans. and ed. Paul T. Durbin (London: Blackfriars, 1968), Qu. 92.1–92.4.

8   Of course, Aquinas held that women were in some sense deficient in their reasoning powers. For further discussion see J. Porter: *The Recovery of Virtue* (London: SPCK, 1990), pp. 138–40.

9   Diana Cates has also noted the promising elements in Thomistic thought from a feminist perspective, though she uses Aquinas in a way that reinforces the idea of *human* friendship as virtue, rather than as applied to non-human creatures. The concept of friendship would be worth developing further, especially in relation to its application to creatures other than humans. D. Cates: *Choosing to Feel: Virtue, Friendship and Compassion for Friends* (Notre Dame, IN: University of Notre Dame Press, 1996).

10 R. Chopp: *The Power to Speak: Feminism, Language and God* (New York: Crossroad, 1992), p. 122.

11 For an anthology see Adams, ed.: *Ecofeminism and the Sacred*.

12 A. Smith: 'For All Those Who Were Indian in a Former Life', in Adams: *Ecofeminism and the Sacred*, pp. 168–71.

13 R. S. Gottlieb: 'Introduction', in R. S. Gottlieb, ed.: *This Sacred Earth: Religion, Nature, Environment* (London and New York: Routledge, 1996), p. 9.

14 Gottlieb: 'Introduction', p. 9.

15 M. Grey: *The Outrageous Pursuit of Hope: Prophetic Dreams for the Twenty First Century* (London: Darton, Longman and Todd, 2000).

16 Grey: *Outrageous Pursuit*, p. 49.

17 Grey: *Outrageous Pursuit*, p. 57.

18 Grey: *Outrageous Pursuit*, p. 87.

19 Alaimo: *Undomesticated Ground*, p. 182 (italics added).

20 Grey: *Outrageous Pursuit*, pp. 93–8. See also C. Deane-Drummond: 'Come to the Banquet', *Ecotheology*, 9, July (2000), pp. 27–37.

21 F. Matthews: *The Ecological Self* (London: Routledge, 1991), p. 149.

22 Matthews: *Ecological Self*, p. 155.

23   Matthews: *Ecological Self*, p. 156.

24   For a discussion of the relationship between environmental ethics and policy-making see M. Stenmark: *Environmental Ethics and Policy Making* (Basingstoke: Ashgate, 2002).

25   Matthews: *Ecological Self*, p. 160.

26   Linda Schiebinger believes that dualistic compatibility theories at the end of the eighteenth century were particularly significant. None the less, the concept of the female as passive and the male as active and rational has a long history, from Aristotle through to Aquinas and beyond. L. Schiebinger: *The Mind Has No Sex: Women in the Origin of Modern Science* (Cambridge, MA: Harvard University Press, 1989); for discussion see C. Deane-Drummond, *Biology and Theology Today: Exploring the Boundaries* (London: SCM Press, 2001), pp. 185–7.

27   See, for example, G. Kass-Simon and P. Farnes: *Women of Science: Righting the Record* (Bloomington: Indiana University Press, 1993).

28   See, for example, Aquinas: *Summa Theologiae, volume 8, Creation, Variety and Evil* (Oxford: Blackfriars, 1967), 1a, Qu. 45; *Summa Theologiae, volume 10, Cosmogony*, trans. W. Wallace (Oxford: Blackfriars, 1967), Qu. 72.

29   The theory was proposed originally by Paul Broca in 1860, but he failed to take into account variables about height and age, and thus his results were finally discredited. The fact that it took over a century for this to be challenged reflects the social bias against women and strongly embedded essentialist ideas.

30   R. Bleier: 'Science and the Construction of Meanings in the Neurosciences' in S. V. Rosser, ed.: *Feminism within the Science and Health Care Professions: Overcoming Resistance* (New York: Pergamon Press, 1988), pp. 91–104. For further discussion on the ethical issues associated with neuroscience see chapter 6 of this volume.

31   Bleier: 'Science and the Construction of Meanings', p. 98.

32   Deane-Drummond: *Biology and Theology Today*, pp. 190–1.

33   See chapter 7 for a further critique of sociobiological models of human behaviour.

34   E. Fox Keller: 'Feminism and Science', in E. Fox Keller and H. E. Longino, eds: *Feminism and Science* (Oxford: Oxford University Press, 1996), pp. 29–30.

35   Deane-Drummond: *Biology and Theology Today*, p. 194.

36   Michael Northcott, for example, argues that higher animals, such as primates, that show some evidence of similarity in behavioural characteristics to humans need to be considered as moral agents, capable of sharing in the human moral community. See discussion in chapter 3.

37   A. Jolly: *Lucy's Legacy: Sex and Intelligence in Human Evolution* (Cambridge, MA: Harvard University Press, 1999), pp. 140–1.

38   Jolly: *Lucy's Legacy*, p. 141.

39   Jolly: *Lucy's Legacy*, p. 141.

40   See Jolly: *Lucy's Legacy*, pp. 146–7; D. Haraway: *Primate Visions: Gender, Race and Nature in the World of Modern Science* (London: Routledge, 1989).

41   Jolly: *Lucy's Legacy*, pp. 147–53.

42   For discussion of 'language' and intelligence in non-humans, see S. T. Parker and K. R. Gibson: *'Language' and Intelligence in Monkeys and Apes* (Cambridge: Cambridge University Press, 1990).

43   See Margaret Wertheim for a fascinating discussion of this issue. M. Wertheim: *Pythagoras's Trousers: God, Physics and the Gender Wars* (London: Fourth Estate, 1996).

44   Merchant: *The Death of Nature*.

45   This UK-based organization is led by green activist Jonathon Porritt.

46   S. Harding: *Whose Science, Whose Knowledge? Thinking from Women's Lives* (Ithaca, NY: Cornell University Press, 1991); see also Deane-Drummond: *Biology and Theology Today*, pp. 201–2.

47   It is also worth noting that much of the language used in biology has been the language of physics, even though there are more women in biology compared with a minority in physics, thus predisposing the natural world to be thought of in physical ways. For a fascinating discussion of the role of language in biology and the influence of information technology see E. Fox Keller: *Re-figuring Life: Metaphors of Twentieth Century Biology* (New York: Columbia University Press, 1995).

48   H. Rose: *Love, Power and Knowledge: Towards a Feminist Transformation of the Sciences* (Cambridge: Polity Press, 1994).

49   Rose: *Love, Power and Knowledge*, pp. 230–1.

50   Rose: *Love, Power and Knowledge*, p. 231.

51   Rose: *Love, Power and Knowledge*, p. 233.

52   Rose: *Love, Power and Knowledge*, p. 233.

53   Rose: *Love, Power and Knowledge*, p. 238.

54   Rose: *Love, Power and Knowledge*, p. 33.

55   Rose: *Love, Power and Knowledge*, p. 58.

56   Rose: *Love, Power and Knowledge*, p. 50.

57   C. Merchant: *Radical Ecology: The Search for a Liveable World* (New York and London: Routledge, 1992), p. 185. I also mentioned this in chapter 3.

58   P. Bowden: *Caring: Gender Sensitive Ethics* (London: Routledge, 1997), p. 21.

59   S. Ruddick: *Maternal Thinking: Towards a Politics of Peace* (Boston: Beacon Press, 1989).

60   Bowden: *Caring*, p. 186.

61   For further discussion of the relationship between virtues and the emotions see chapter 6 of this volume.

62   E. Spelman: 'The Virtue of Feeling and the Feeling of Virtue', in C. Card, ed.: *Feminist Ethics* (Lawrence: University Press of Kansas, 1991), pp. 213–32.

63   J. Tronto: *Moral Boundaries: A Political Argument for an Ethics of Care* (London and New York: Routledge, 1993).

64   B. Fisher and J. Tronto: 'Towards a Feminist Theory of Care', in E. Abel and M. Nielson, eds: *Circles of Care: Work and Identity in Women's Lives* (Albany: State University of New York Press, 1991), p. 40.

65   Tronto: *Moral Boundaries*, p. 109.

66   I am deliberately distinguishing ethical concern about animals and that about the wider environment, though it seems to me that the ethical dimensions of care can be applied to both, albeit in rather different ways.

67   This idea is taken up in L. Larkin: 'Turning: Face to Face with *Limobius mixtus*', *Ecotheology*, 7:1 (2002), pp. 30–44. I will also be discussing 'other' animal ethics in the following chapter. It is important to note that otherness implies distinction, but this need not preclude recognition of similarity as well.

68   C. Palmer: 'Animals in Christian Ethics: Developing a Christian Approach', *Ecotheology*, 7:2 (2003), p. 182.

69   See Palmer: 'Animals in Christian Ethics', p. 182.

70   Tronto: *Moral Boundaries*, p. 134.

71   In chapter 6 I commented on the way his dogs expressed loyalty that was more than a simple desire for nourishment. However, it would be too crude to suggest that such

emotions are identical experiences to those found in human society. See G. Pitcher: *The Dogs Who Came to Stay* (New York: Dutton, 1995).

72 Tronto: *Moral Boundaries*, p. 126.

73 Tronto: *Moral Boundaries*, p. 127.

74 Tronto: *Moral Boundaries*, p. 154.

75 Tronto: *Moral Boundaries*, p. 155.

76 M. U. Walker: 'Moral Understandings: Alternative Epistemology for a Feminist Ethics', in E. Browning Cole and S. Coultrap McQuin, eds: *Explorations in Feminist Ethics: Theory and Practice* (Bloomington: Indiana University Press, 1992), pp. 165–75.

77 Tronto: *Moral Boundaries*, p. 209, n22. See N. Noddings: *Caring: A Feminine Approach to Ethics and Moral Education* (Berkeley: University of California Press, 1984).

78 S. Parsons: *Feminism and Christian Ethics* (Cambridge: Cambridge University Press, 1996), p. 123.

79 Parsons: *Feminism and Christian Ethics*, p. 124.

80 She compares this unequal relationship with the male egotistical model. Both are faulty because both are reliant on relationships that are unequal in terms of power. See S. Hoagland: 'Some Thoughts about Caring', in C. Card, ed.: *Feminist Ethics* (Lawrence: University of Kansas Press, 1991), pp. 246–63.

81 Alaimo: *Undomesticated Ground*, p. 172.

82 C. Roach: 'Loving Your Mother. On the Woman : Nature Relation', *Hypatia*, 6:1 (1991), p. 56.

83 Alaimo: *Undomesticated Ground*, pp. 173–4.

84 Alaimo: *Undomesticated Ground*, pp. 174–5.

85 D. Curtin: 'Toward an Ecological Ethic of Care', *Hypatia*, 6:1 (1991), p. 71.

86 Alaimo: *Undomesticated Ground*, p. 180.

87 See, for example, J. Lovelock: *The Ages of Gaia* (Oxford: Oxford University Press, 1988), p. 212.

88 Rosemary Radford Ruether: *God and Gaia: An Ecofeminist Theology of Earth Healing* (London: SCM Press, 1993), p. 241.

89 Ruether: *God and Gaia*, p. 253.

90 Alaimo: *Undomesticated Ground*, p. 183.

91 Alaimo: *Undomesticated Ground*, p. 183.

92 See D. Haraway: *Simians, Cyborgs and Women: The Reinvention of Nature* (New York: Routledge, 1991).

93 The categories I have suggested here are similar to Susan Parson's typology of feminism in relation to the question of an ethics of gender, focused specifically on equality, difference and liberation. See S. F. Parsons: *The Ethics of Gender* (Oxford: Blackwell, 2002), pp. 25–42.

94 D. Rocheleau, B. Thomas-Slayter and E. Wangari, eds: *Feminist Political Ecology* (New York: Routledge, 1996).

95 For example, see J. Opocensk: 'Nuclear Energy Protests: A Story from Southern Bohemia', Lifestyle, *Ecotheology*, 7:1 (2002), pp. 88–90.

96 Merchant: *Radical Ecology*, pp. 110–31. Sallie McFague has also integrated economic and spiritual concerns in *Life Abundant: Rethinking Theology and Economy for a Planet in Peril* (Philadelphia: Fortress, 2000).

97 Merchant: *Radical Ecology*, p. 188.

98 Merchant: *Radical Ecology*, p. 188.

99 Merchant: *Radical Ecology*, p. 188.

100   Merchant: *Radical Ecology*, pp. 196–8.

101   Merchant: *Earthcare: Women and the Environment* (London: Routledge, 1995), pp. 186–8.

102   Merchant: *Earthcare*, pp. 203–4.

103   Merchant: *Earthcare*, p. 217.

104   Merchant: *Earthcare*, p. 220.

105   Merchant: *Earthcare*, p. 220.

106   A similar problematic exists in Lisa Cowell Cahill's revaluation of nature as a way of understanding the ethics of gender. See L. Cowell Cahill: *Sex, Gender and Christian Ethics* (Cambridge: Cambridge University Press, 1996).

107   The problems raised by postmodernity in the context of a range of different feminist writers, including Cahill, are discussed in Parsons: *The Ethics of Gender*, pp. 124–30.

108   Merchant: *Earthcare*, p. 221.

109   G. Dietrich: 'The World as the Body of God', *Ecotheology*, 5:6 (1999), pp. 25–50.

110   V. Plumwood: 'Inequality, Ecojustice and Ecological Rationality', *Ecotheology*, 5:6 (1999), pp. 185–218.

111   Plumwood: 'Inequality', p. 189.

112   Plumwood: 'Inequality', p. 189.

113   Plumwood: 'Inequality', p. 199.

114   Plumwood: 'Inequality', p. 200.

115   Plumwood: 'Inequality', pp. 203–4. As this book went to press a significant book by Mary Grey was published on issues in globalization and ecology. M. Grey: *Sacred Longings: Ecofeminist Theology and Globalization* (London: SCM Press, 2003).

116   Parsons: *The Ethics of Gender*, pp. 151–87.

117   See, for example, Rosemary Radford Ruether: *Women Healing Earth: Third World Women on Ecology, Feminism and Religion* (London: SCM Press, 1996).

118   Aquinas: *Summa Theologiae, volume 13, Man Made to God's Image* (London: Blackfriars, 1964), 1a, Qu. 93.4.

119   Aquinas: *Summa Theologiae, volume 13*, 1a, Qu. 92.1.

120   Aquinas: *Summa Theologiae, volume 13*, 1a, Qu. 92.2.

121   Here he claims that 'Just as seed pertains to the male's perfection as procreator, and is pleasurably released by a natural process. Much more then by an act of divine power could the woman's body be formed from man's rib without pain.' Aquinas: *Summa Theologiae, volume 13*, 1a, Qu. 92.3.

122   Aquinas: *Summa Theologiae, volume 13*, 1a, Qu. 99.2.

123   Aquinas: *Summa Theologiae, volume 13*, 1a, Qu. 99.2

124   Aquinas: *Summa Theologiae, volume 45, Consequences of Charity*, trans. T. R. Heath (Oxford: Blackfriars, 1972), 2a2ae, Qu. 45.3.

125   Aquinas: *Disputed Questions on Virtue*, trans. R. McInerny (South Bend, IN: St Augustine's Press, 1999), *Disputed Question on the Cardinal Virtue*, art. 3, p. 130.

126   Aquinas: *Summa Theologiae, volume 34, Charity*, trans. R. J. Batten (Oxford: Blackfriars, 1975), 2a2ae, Qu. 23.8.

127   Aquinas cites Ephesians 3.19 in this context. Aquinas: *Summa Theologiae, volume 34*, 2a2ae, Qu. 24.1.

128   Aquinas: *Summa Theologiae, volume 34*, 2a2ae, Qu. 28.2.

129   A discussion of feminist ethics and natural law is outside the scope of this chapter, which was concerned to focus primarily on an ethic of care. For further analysis of this issue, see Parsons: *Feminism and Christian Ethics*, pp. 237–41; C. Traina: *Feminist*

Ethics and Natural Law: The End of Anathemas (Washington, DC: Georgetown University Press, 1999). Traina does not specifically consider the impact of 'feminist' natural law on treatment of the natural world as such. It is worth noting that Traina's incorporation of natural law into feminist ethic allows her to affirm the natural as an important basis for flourishing, while denying that natural desires are inevitably good in a normative sense (p. 334).

130   Aquinas: *Summa Theologiae, volume 33, Hope*, trans. W. J. Hill (Oxford: Blackfriars, 1966), 2a2ae, Qu. 19.7.

131   Aquinas, *Summa Theologiae, volume 35, Consequences of Charity*, trans. T. R. Heath (Oxford: Blackfriars, 1972), 2a2ae, Qu. 45.6.

132   Aquinas, *Summa Theologiae, volume 35*, 2a2ae, Qu. 45.2.

133   Aquinas, *Summa Theologiae, volume 35*, 2a2ae, Qu. 45.3.

134   Aquinas restricted caring and friendship to humans, though he did suggest that one ought to be kind to animals as a way of reinforcing the habit of kindness. I argued in an earlier chapter that his ontology pointed more in the direction of caring for creation, even though his more specific ethical statements were counter to this and encouraged a view that animals were simply instruments for human use. This is where I part company with Diana Cates, who confined caring to the human community; see D. Cates: *Choosing to Feel*.

Chapter 9

Towards an Ethic of Wisdom

In this final chapter I address the way in which the variegated strands in the discussion on an ethics of nature drawing on the motif of wisdom are related and connected. I begin by contrasting the theological basis for developing an ethics that draws particularly on the notion of wisdom with alternatives that are particularly committed to addressing the ethics of nature. In the introduction to this book I highlighted practical wisdom as *virtue* and showed the sense in which a virtue ethic, as applied to the natural world, could offer a distinctive Christian approach compared with other alternatives; for example, those that take their bearings from Barthian neo-Orthodoxy or secular renditions of natural law. In this chapter I focus the lens of the discussion a little more sharply on the distinctive contribution of wisdom as integrated into an understanding of *God*, especially in the light of Darwinian science. I will start by considering in more detail John Haught's approach to an ethics of nature that takes its inspiration from process theology. Does an ethic of wisdom that draws extensively on Aquinas in the way that I have elaborated so far necessarily become obsolete in the light of contemporary science? Has, for example, Charles Darwin's theory of evolution evacuated a sense of purpose from the natural world? I will next clarify what I mean when I describe wisdom in theological language, God as wisdom, before comparing this approach with that of the Protestant writer James Gustafson who has also argued for a theocentric ethic, but one that draws on a rather different understanding of God. Finally, I will weave the different aspects of the book together, showing how an ethic of wisdom can properly be understood as relating to different facets of the way we relate to both our human nature and the non-human world.

Stanley Hauerwas's monumental contribution to the rediscovery of virtues as relevant for ethical reflection has so far failed to grapple with environmental questions and issues concerned with human relationships with the non-human world. His Gifford lectures are revealing as to why he has not considered this question in detail, insisting that it is the revelation of God in Christ that needs to be proclaimed as witness to the cross, it is this witness that shows up most fully 'the grain of the universe'.[1] Yet we can ask ourselves whether a concern for social and political justice and peacemaking, as exemplified by writers such as John Howard Yoder, can ever really be detached from environmental problems in the way that Hauerwas seems to assume.[2] He argues from the position of witnesses to a story, namely the story of Christian community, but now that the human community and ecological community are so closely bound together, how can we consider one without the other? In particular, I have argued throughout this book that our ethical reflection can no longer afford to be myopically confined to narrowly defined anthropocentric concerns. Paul Santmire tells of his meeting with Karl Barth, where Barth scolded the younger man for his interest in nature.[3] But the legacy of Nazi Germany's attraction to distorted versions of natural theology shows clearly that vices and not virtues were at the heart of this deplorable regime. Such distortions need not prevent Christian theologians taking a serious look at issues surrounding an ethics of nature. Santmire proposes a theological ethics that celebrates martyrdom and that coheres somewhat with the vocation to fortitude that I have discussed in this book. Similarly, he suggests that we need to cooperate with nature righteously, in a manner that is analogous to the idea of temperance, not trying to gain more of the goods of the natural world than we really need for human life. He also suggests that we need to care for nature sensitively, which again leads to actions that are prudential in orientation. His final suggestions are that we should care for nature with the eye of wonder, while anticipating the reign of God joyfully, in a way that echoes the position I have elucidated here, namely the development of the virtues of love and charity, celebrating wisdom as the reign of God inclusive of all creation.

Nature as Promise?

John Haught, like many writers devoted to developing an eco-theology, is passionate about the need to develop an adequate environmental ethics.[4] He is also equally concerned that theologians come to terms with contemporary science, in particular, Darwinian theories of evolution.[5] Although scientists have recognized that religion may be very useful in stirring up a sense of environmental responsibility, he rejects this basis for inclusion of religion as too shallow. He argues, instead, correctly in my view, that unless religion is at the root of our concern, simply giving environmentalism a religious gloss will not work. But if we look carefully at the logical outcome of Darwin's theory of evolution, it becomes clear that there is fundamentally no purpose to evolution at all, in the end everything is perishable. Why then, he asks, are scientists also keen environmentalists?[6] Is it because they find it hard to accept the cosmic homelessness that is ultimately the outcome of modern cosmology and science?

Our sense of homelessness contrasts with the cosmology of the medieval period when the Great Chain of Being provided a sense of stability and security, and every creature knew its place. I have argued in a previous chapter that while the Chain of Being is naive in the way it views a linear progression from one level to the next, there is more room for a dynamic interchange between the different aspects of creation in this model than most modern writers, including Haught, seem to suppose. None the less, I suggest that any residual notions of 'fixity' of levels between different species need to be called into question and transformed in the light of Darwinian science. Jean Porter suggests that Aquinas's belief in the intelligibility of specific kinds is still compatible with different interpretations of classification of creaturely existence, otherwise known as the incommensurability thesis.[7] In other words, there is universal agreement that there are broad categories of inanimate objects, plants and animals. Aquinas accepted the possibility of change in a species; though he did not have the knowledge to appreciate that evolutionary process is integral to the living history of the world. The theological challenge becomes one of retaining a dynamic sense of fluidity in the created world, as put forward by contemporary science, while resisting the idea of purposelessness that stems from science's commitment to materialist philosophy.

Haught's way out of the dilemma of wanting to affirm science, yet render it ultimately invalid as a basis for ethics, is to turn to process thought. He finds in the natural world beauty, but it is beauty that provides an alternative to scientific materialism.[8] In his more recent book he also includes discussion of scientific concepts of information, which are the realm of possibility.[9] While one might infer that information and beauty are integrally related, it is disappointing that he does not spell out the connection between them. Information, as understood in contemporary scientific cosmology, works by integrating particulars into wholes; hence it goes against scientific reductionism and provides an alternative approach from within science itself. Haught suggests that 'the origin of information and its integrating capacity resides in some other logical space than that of the atomic and historical particulars that natural science appeals to in its modern ideal of explanation'.[10] Significantly, unlike many other writers in science and religion who are committed to the idea of emergence, he argues that complex levels in evolution do not simply emerge; this, he suggests, is merely a *description* of what happens, rather than an *explanation* of what happens. This is where he believes that the idea of information is particularly significant in facilitating the process of increasing complexity in evolution. He argues, in addition, that information is not simply an abstraction; rather, it is concretely 'real', even though it cannot be identified as such by standard scientific procedures. While he does not claim to be challenging Darwinian biology, he seems to be remarkably close to radical alternative approaches to the biological evolution of complexity, such as that proposed by Brian Goodwin.[11] Hence, by making information theory drawn from contemporary discussions of cosmology an integral part of biological natural evolution, he seems to be challenging one of the premises of Darwinian science: that the evolution of the natural biological world is based on a combination of chance and necessity. While information language has dominated genetic theory in the past, whether contemporary biologists working in neo-Darwinian science will accept this terminology is a matter for debate.[12] Yet Haught's way out of the eschatological difficulties implicit in evolutionary science is not necessarily the only way to come to terms with Darwin's theory from a Christian perspective. Alternative ways of relating Christianity to a more strictly Darwinian understanding of the natural world have been usefully summarized by Michael Ruse.[13]

How might wisdom connect with Haught's idea of beauty and scientific information? Haught suggests that 'Beauty is a delicate synthesis of unity and complexity, stability and motion, form and dynamics.'[14] Wisdom is also at the border of order and chaos, is inclusive of the idea of beauty, though understood in a theological sense it is like a whisper to the world in its becoming, perhaps on a different plane of reality than that discovered by science.[15] So far such a description of wisdom might seem to be remarkably close to the Whiteheadian notion of beauty adopted by Haught. The difference is that, as I will show below, the idea of wisdom working in the created world is not simply the emergent God of Beauty of process thought, but wisdom as created, working alongside, or even at joyful play with, Divine Wisdom, who is integral to the ontological being of the three persons of the Trinity, distinct from, yet closely related to, the created world.[16] I would also be reluctant to render the idea of information concrete in the way Haught has proposed, or necessarily identify wisdom with this information.

This difference is crucial to the way an ethics of nature is constructed in Haught compared with my own position. In Haught an ethics emerges from nature, through tuning into this beauty/information in the world; it is an ethics *of nature* that is at one with the cosmological purpose of the universe. Critically, he suggests that information (beauty?) is concretely *real*, which is controversial for many scientists, who see information merely as an abstraction. Hence, while he is more sophisticated than simple scientific naturalism, ultimately his view of ethics is one that emerges from the natural world, though in his understanding God and nature coalesce here, so that it is impossible to distinguish one from the other. Thus he suggests that 'it is to this deep and ageless evolutionary straining towards an intensification of beauty that we may link our own sense of meaning and morality. It is thanks to the evolutionary picture of the universe, and not in spite of it, that we gain this significant moral perspective.'[17] By resituating the idea of evolution within a *cosmic* universe, he escapes the purposeless element of Darwinian theory. However, in a wider cosmological perspective we can find similar notions of ultimate hopelessness.[18] Haught rejects ultimate cosmic pessimism, which is characteristic of future cosmological predictions about the fate of the universe, but seems to be less concerned about the long-term future of the earth as long as some sense of purpose can be found within natural evolution.

Carolyn King appears to come down more firmly on the side of evolutionary theory as a basis for her ethics of nature in her suggestion that it is biological 'grounding' that is the fundamental arbiter in thinking through moral claims.[19] While this view is understandable from a biologist's perspective, it shows a tendency to assume that all language is *necessarily* related to the biological in a way that is not justified. She is, none the less, right to point to alternative understandings of human nature emerging from evolutionary biology. It is not simply raw individu-alism that seems to be encouraged by neo-Darwinism, there is an 'ingrained habit of fitting in with, and looking out for, one's own closest group'.[20] This reflects her sense of wanting to see the positive in evolutionary processes, including, for exam-ple, symbiotic and cooperative relationships, rather than being worried by its more ruthless aspects, for 'We do not need to let the ruthlessness of natural selection detract us from the wonders that it has produced.'[21] Haught, by comparison, views the ruthless aspects of creation as acceptable only in the light of an eschatological promise of the future yet to be unfolded. From the perspective of wisdom the raw suffering of creation is tragic in as much as it can never be totally 'explained' by reference to a positive future in a Hegelian sense. Rather, creaturely suffering and pain is identified with the wisdom of the cross and is thus ultimately redeemable, but wisdom also takes the form of human responsibility to take due account of that suffering where it comes from human activities.

If we simply accept wonder as the outcome of the evolutionary process, we are left without a clear sense of what to do with that wonderment.[22] I agree that wonder is an important ingredient in developing environmental virtues, but on its own it does not take us very far. King seems to be aware of this when she argues for what she terms 'God's realm of no selection', which appears to be superior to either natural or cultural selection.[23] Consequently, she believes that divine grace, while working with nature, takes it 'into another stage unattainable by selection processes'.[24] The idea that grace perfects nature is of course not a new one, though her argument is not rooted in historical or contemporary discussion of nature and grace. This omission may be related to her own distain of doctrine, which for her is like a hermit crab shell that can be shed in new environments.[25] Her view on grace is also somewhat inconsistent with her earlier suggestion that ethics needs to be grounded in evolutionary biology. The ways in which grace might intersect with the natural world, which also provide criteria for moral value, seem rather ambiguous. Haught, like King, wishes to put more emphasis on the grace-laden aspect of the relationship between God and the world, though for him it is rooted in an understanding of God as process and promise. Haught portrays grace as 'letting creation be itself', and while King would also endorse this suggestion, she seems to go beyond this in her idea that grace takes nature into 'another stage'. While the language of grace is helpful, I have generally preferred to use the language of love and charity in describing the milieu in which God creates the world. Grace has the advantage of putting emphasis on the freedom and generosity of God's action, while love and charity are expressive of the warmth and enfolding of God's movement in creation.

While Haught has successfully reclaimed the ground for theology without losing sight of Darwinian science, it becomes more difficult in practice to envisage how his ethics of nature might work in situations where there are competing claims for priority. Like many other ecological writers, he resists situating humanity as in any sense having priority over other creatures, though the goal of enrichment and beauty is more readily seen in human activities, which implies anthropocentrism, at least with respect to other creatures presently resident on earth. He qualifies this by suggesting that the future of the earth may not include humanity if there were other ways of achieving greater beauty and flourishing. While we may hope in a world not yet actualized, if such hope is part of the promise of nature it becomes hard to know what to do in practical situations where the outcome is uncertainly related to that promise. In other words, the *content* of the promise is vague in relation to what humanity needs to do, apart from more obvious restraint with respect to environmental destruction and despoliation of the earth. The advantage of such a view is that it is flexible in its expectation of the future, and there is no fixity as to what the outcome of the earth's future might be, including the future of humanity. However, I have my doubts if the motive to care for the earth is such that we would be prepared to tolerate the idea of a world without humanity in the way that Haught indicates.[26]

By contrast, virtues that specifically focus on wisdom show in more specific ways how to behave, especially where the virtue of wisdom is rooted in charity and combined with the four cardinal virtues of prudence, justice, temperance and fortitude in the manner I have suggested in this book. Haught does acknowledge in passing that the evolutionary ethic that he proposes can include the practice of virtue, but for him virtues have to be related to the purpose of intensifying cosmic beauty.[27] I agree that a cosmological perspective is important, for wisdom is situated within an understanding of God as wisdom that takes its bearings from classical theism. While resisting a strong dualism implicit in classical theistic views, an approach to ethics through wisdom acknowledges the difference between God and creation, even while stressing the immanence of God in creation.

God as Wisdom

Wisdom is described in Proverbs 8 as God's creation, rather like a little child, engaging playfully with God in the creation of the world.[28] However, as the literature of the Hebrew Bible develops, wisdom also becomes a theological term, one that points not just to human behaviour, but also to a figure of Wisdom, a divine personification reflecting the character of God as such. Evidence for such a figure in biblical literature can be found in, for example, Ben Sira, Proverbs and the books of Wisdom. Wisdom, according to the book of Wisdom, is 'intelligent, holy unique, manifold, subtle, active, incisive, unsullied, lucid, invulnerable, benevolent, sharp, irresistible, beneficent, loving to man, steadfast, dependable, unperturbed, almighty, all-surveying'.[29] It could even be said that some wisdom books, such as the book of Ecclesiastes, echo to some extent the approach adopted by contemporary philosophers advocating virtue ethics.[30]

Wisdom in the Hebrew Bible is also something that is learnt in the human community, through experience in practical decision-making in family life, education and observation of the natural world. What are the possible ways to find wisdom? The book of Proverbs invites its readers to 'Go to the ant, you sluggard,

See its ways and be wise.'[31] The seeing is not so much simple observation of information about the ants as *perceiving* the inner distinctive core of what it is to be an ant.[32] In other places in wisdom literature the word 'to discern' (*bin*) is used, often following the act of seeing, to describe the *process* of becoming wise. Hence discernment is integral to what it means to gain wisdom. Discernment considers a range of options, but ultimately lights on 'the way', understood not just as the alternative between two paths, but also as the inner driving characteristic of something. This, it seems to me, is particularly important, as it locates discernment as that which correctly identifies the inner core of something, that itself is expressive of wisdom.

Significantly, in the book of Job 28 the characteristic of finding wisdom *also* applies to God, as God 'sees' the different components of creation. On this basis it is possible that Proverbs 8.22 means not that God created wisdom, but, in the more common understanding of the word *qana*, God *acquired* wisdom. This reinforces the suggestion that an essential characteristic of God is that of wisdom.[33] Moreover, there appears to be a dialectical relationship between God and the world in the creative process. God creates through wisdom, but God also *discovers* wisdom in its turn in the created order. This does not preclude the primary focus of the Christian tradition on God relating to the world through overflowing love. Rather, creation is in love, but through wisdom. This sapiential understanding of God's relationship to the world has common ground with some other religious traditions and serves to challenge the individualistic way we think about ourselves and in its place situate humanity in the wider cosmic community of life.[34]

In addition, we find wisdom taken up in the New Testament to refer to the action of God in Christ, through the wisdom of the cross, as well as more obliquely in the Logos language of John, showing significant parallels with motifs of wisdom found in the Old Testament. James Dunn is one biblical scholar who has pointed consistently to the wisdom Christology emerging from the New Testament accounts.[35] Wisdom language is also used to describe the actions of the Spirit of God, indicative of a pneumological interpretation of wisdom.[36]

Given the biblical framing of wisdom as an important ingredient in our language about God, it is hardly surprising that early theological traditions, including the Augustinian tradition, used wisdom vocabulary to describe God.[37] However, the extent to which such language has been taken up subsequently in Christian tradition is somewhat patchy.[38] I suggest that the full flowering of a Sophianic theology emerged in the work of the Russian Orthodox sophiologists, including Vladimir Solovyov and Sergii Bulgakov. Bulgakov, in particular, argued against any idea that Sophia represented a quaternary in God. Instead, he suggested that wisdom was an integral part of the *ousia* or being of God.[39] Bulgakov distinguished between divine wisdom and creaturely wisdom, though he argued that they were interconnected with each other. Of course, traditional Orthodoxy would resist any claim that we can say anything specific about God's being; rather, it is only the energies of God that can be described.[40]

Feminist thinkers, who find in wisdom an image that is more specifically feminist in orientation, have also taken up the language of wisdom to describe God.[41]

Wisdom is like the feminine face of God, reflected in all three persons of the Trinity.[42] Elisabeth Johnson, similarly, also argues for the recovery of wisdom in our thinking about God, although she prefers to use Mother to describe the third person of the Trinity.[43] This seems to me to denote a Trinitarian view that is matriarchal, rather than patriarchal. Instead, I suggest that we should think of both mother and father as integral to imaging God. It is in this sense that wisdom serves to remind us of the feminine face of God. In addition, the importance of wisdom as a motif is that she no longer isolates God from creation: wisdom is integral to the creative and redemptive processes, and hence God and nature are now considered not separately but through relationship.

Gustafson's Theocentric Ethic

Given the suggestion above that God is in one sense wisdom, how might this influence the development of ethics, in particular an ethics of nature? Following Bulgakov, we can distinguish divine from creaturely wisdom rooted in the natural world, yet such a definition of the relationship between creaturely and divine wisdom points to a particular way of conceiving ethics. Hence wisdom can serve to set the broad framework for ethical decision-making, an ethos in which particular actions can begin to take shape.

In order to delineate this view more clearly, I will take up a discussion with James Gustafson, who has also argued consistently for a theocentric approach to ethics.[44] Perhaps unusually, in his major work on environmental ethics he identifies the concern coming from threats to our own survival or the survival of biodiversity with an instrumental approach to nature.[45] He suggests that the idea of intrinsic beauty in nature cannot connect with the desires and ends of non-human creatures such as squirrels or red headed woodpeckers, so that for him theological ideas rooted in the beauty of nature are not sufficiently persuasive.[46] Such a view echoes what Peter Scheers has described as a 'benevolent interpreter'; that is, being willing to find meaning and excellence in non-human others, without 'humanizing' that other.[47] Yet is such connectivity necessarily incompatible with aesthetic appreciation of the value of nature? Haught's concept of beauty is rather more cogent, since it is much more than simply human aesthetic appreciation, as I discussed above. Instead, Gustafson's own view is that we need to recover a *sense of the divine* that is hinted at in some writing, such as in Midgley's idea about the sense of wonder in nature. He also draws on more traditional Reformed sources, citing Calvin as one who pointed to creation as the theatre of God's glory.[48]

However, Gustafson's view of God is heavily influenced by a Schleiermachian emphasis on dependence, so that his theocentric approach amounts to 'a sense of dependence, a sense of gratitude, a sense of accountability which properly on occasions evokes a sense of remorse and even guilt, and a sense of the possibility to intervene for justifiable ends'.[49] This contrasts strikingly with Haught, who suggests that 'A world given lease to become more and more autonomous, even to help create itself and eventually attain the status of human consciousness and freedom has much more integrity and value than any conceivable world determined in every respect by an external "divine designer".'[50] The idea of justifiable ends in Gustafson is particularly interesting, since he rejects the idea that we can have any clear sense of theological telos. But unlike the target of Haught's critique, he resists a clearly defined purpose as intrinsic to natural ecology. Instead, he seems to be more aware of the contingencies of nature, which, he suggests, cohere well with his understanding of God in terms of dependence:

> The contingencies as well as ordering of the natural world, the elements of conflict, and perhaps even chaos within it, as well as the elements of harmony thrust me, and perhaps others, into a sense of ultimate dependence upon the powers, and (if it be a leap of faith so be it) the power of God.[51]

Importantly, the final outcome of the divine processes in the natural world for Gustafson is not necessarily good, so that he cannot ultimately affirm what he calls the triumph of the good, or, as it could be said in Haught's language, the promise of nature. It is here that his views are radically divergent from Aquinas's under-standing of the teleology of the universe towards the good, a view that he explic-itly rejects as being impossible because of the discoveries of modern science.[52] Instead, 'the source and power and order of all of nature is not always beneficent in its outcomes for the diversity of life and for the well-being of humans as part of that'.[53] However, despite this view regarding ultimate outcomes, he also affirms the human capacity to have revulsion towards evil. It seems, then, that through a theocentric perspective we become more conscious of effects:

> which can be judged by humans to be undesirable, deleterious, or even evil in both the very natural ordering of things and our participation in nature. It makes us conscious of the potentiality for benefits through our justifiable interventions, but at the same time conscious of our limits to control all the outcomes in accord with our praiseworthy intentions.[54]

Overall, he offers us no reprieve from ambiguity and risk, not even a future promise.[55] Instead, fired by a sense of the divine, moral decisions are made *despite* moral ambiguity. He suggests, then, that there is 'no clear overriding telos, or end, which unambiguously orders the priorities of nature and human participation in it so that one has a perfect moral justification for all human interventions'.[56] Hence, while God is the source of human good, for Gustafson, God does not guarantee it. The theme that predominates for Gustafson is one of human participation in nature, which, he suggests, is premised in observations about all of life supported by the natural sciences. At the same time, Aquinas was aware that there are ambiguities at the level of decision-making, so Gustafson's implied assumption, that a goal-directed ethic necessarily obliterates all ambiguity, does not apply in Aquinas's scheme.[57]

How might a theocentric approach drawing on the wisdom motif compare with Gustafson's sense of the divine? There are some areas of convergence. In the first place I welcome the idea that we need to listen to a range of alternative understandings of nature, including the one presented by science. Haught, by contrast, while resisting scientific materialism, still seems to want to give science priority, as evidenced by his commitment to the concept of information drawn from theories about the cosmos. Gustafson's appreciation of natural contingencies as an inherent part of ecology shows a greater degree of listening to scientists than does the 'balance of nature' or 'equilibrium' view common in discussions about environmental ethics.[58] Gustafson likens science to just one of the barrels we need in constructing a raft, the other being human experience, philosophical judgements and the heritage of Christianity and Judaism. I also appreciate the idea of *participation in* nature; wisdom as inherent in all creaturely being can form the basis for developing a sense of divine in nature as well as ourselves.

Yet wisdom has more affinity with the idea of beauty than Gustafson's vaguer sense of the divine. I suggest that if beauty is defined through wisdom, in the way that Bulgakov suggests, it need not be as narrowly 'anthropocentric' in the way that Gustafson seems to indicate is the case for Aquinas's position. Aquinas also related human wisdom to the Wisdom of God, and it is this Wisdom in the mind of God that serves to orientate human decision-making. It is therefore a misnomer to label Aquinas 'anthropocentric' in the way Gustafson does in order to reinforce his own supposedly theocentric position. It seems to me that Gustafson is actually far less theocentric than he claims to be, as for him God is merely contained within the fragile and ambiguous ordering of this world, there is no room for immortality and he rejects the notion of a good end on the basis of *human* discoveries from science.[59] On the other hand, while he accurately notes the themes of grace in Aquinas, and the goodness of God, Aquinas's theocentric focus is swallowed up in Gustafson's interpretation because of the offence he takes towards Aquinas's understanding of a hierarchical ordering of being, which Gustafson believes is the root cause of his 'anthropocentrism'.

In addition, as I argued in the first chapter, there is a sense in which it is entirely right to look to the human condition as a prerequisite to thinking about an ethics of nature. Even Gustafson admits that humankind must do the best in can in *discerning* God's purposes for creation, acting out of 'piety' that he takes from the Calvinist tradition.[60] He argues that discernment is an essential human quality in the moral life, but it is discernment in relation to God's purposes that are detached from any overriding confidence in the good end of creation. There are aspects of his notion of discernment that have some parallels with Aquinas's notion of practical wisdom or prudence, but because it is no longer directed to the ultimate good, as for Gustafson such a belief is impossible, it would be what Aquinas would term a version of 'sham prudence', for it is directed to the wrong end. While drawing on Calvin, for it is cast in the *language* of God's glory and Christian piety, Gustafson's understanding of discernment assumes that this glory is not expressed in goodness as the final end for creation. Porter suggests that Gustafson is inconsistent in his rejection of anthropocentrism, for he 'gives us no examples of a situation in which the appropriate response to God's purposes would call upon us to disregard or act against any and all forms of human good, including that of the species'.[61] He also does not show how such discernment of God's purposes for creation might be achieved, given that he denies that the ultimate purpose of God for creation is towards goodness.

I suggest that the opposite extreme that Gustafson presents, namely an unambiguous and rigid ordering through hierarchical structures in traditional theology, is not necessarily the only alternative to his own more ambiguous position towards teleology.[62] In the first place, Aquinas's understanding of species is one that allowed for their *mutability*, even though order is still present; that is, 'every creature that now exists, did exist, or will exist belongs to some species'.[63] Rather, we can still *hope* for a good end, without presuming that our decision-making is always in perfect alignment with it. While admitting to ambiguities in human perception, unlike Gustafson I suggest that it is vitally important to affirm faith in the goodness of God as the ultimate purpose for creation. This does not narrow the scope of ethics in the sense that it is true for the Christian community and no one else, so that 'the fact that it is developed from within a particular historical framework does not necessarily invalidate its claims for truth'.[64] Once the idea that God's purpose for creation is good is lost then the motivation for transformation becomes much weaker. I would also like to suggest that the hope for the ultimate good purpose in creation is a uniquely human attribute, bringing with it both a unique promise and responsibility.

Aquinas viewed natural law as a natural orientation towards goodness and avoidance of evil inherent in natural processes, common to all living creatures. Is such a view tenable in the light of current understanding of the ambiguity or even 'evil' present in the natural world, including humankind? One of the difficulties that Gustafson faces, as does any writer who draws on natural theology, is the 'evil' and ambiguity in natural processes. The difficult question as to how far nature is itself 'evil' in contemporary debate echoes that of the Manichean controversy that Augustine and Aquinas so vigorously resisted.[65] None the less, the extent of evolutionary 'waste' and the raw suffering in nature remain a challenge to those who affirm belief in the goodness of God and creation. Yet to allow the eschatology of science to set the agenda for theological and ethical reflection seems to me to be misguided, for it undermines the very basis for belief in God and God's goodness. In the light of scientific knowledge either the scope of theodicy enlarges, or the understanding of God is adjusted, a route that Gustafson seems to prefer. Ambiguity seems, for him, to be inherent in his understanding of God. Instead, in the approach delineated by wisdom, the ambiguity of suffering is taken up and challenged by the Christological referent of the wisdom of the cross.[66] Gustafson's vaguer sense of the divine cannot include this, so we are simply left in a sea of unknowing. It is for this reason that some critics have accused Gustafson of not being Christian in his theological ethics.[67] However, Gustafson's insistence that his view takes account of science in the way that traditional ethics does not presumes that incorporating science into ethics is necessarily *incompatible* with more traditional ethical formulations.

While the processes of natural selection seem aimless, bringing good as readily as evil, the overall path is towards a decrease in entropy, leading to the conservation of more complex kinds. Hence 'complexity must be situated between order and disorder, or "at the edge of chaos", or we might say "on the edge of evil" on either side'.[68] Such a fine balance between order and chaos can also be given the term 'wisdom', though as wisdom and natural law include participation in the eternal law, there remains an important distinction between God and the emergent processes of the world, including human beings and consciousness. Even Thomas Aquinas's understanding of natural law allowed for ambiguity in human perception about the natural law. Aquinas believed that in matters of practical reason there is room for ambiguity, so that 'the more we get down to particular cases the more we can be mistaken'; hence 'practical truth and goodwill are not the same for everybody with respect to particular decisions'.[69] Wisdom, I suggest, gives a better outline of the ethics of decision-making compared with simply a sense of dependence, or for that matter Haught's view that the natural world simply grows towards autonomy. For wisdom, while being theological, is also philosophical and practical, since it links with practical wisdom or prudence.

Like Gustafson I agree that environmental decision-making is difficult and complex. However, unlike Gustafson I suggest that we *can* hope for an ultimate good end that in its turn serves to orientate decisions. Such decision-making is rooted in the knowledge of the Wisdom of God, while remaining conscious that this knowledge can only be partial and never complete. Gustafson admits that he presents us with a 'fractal image' in ethics, one that consists of a series of arcs, rather than a 'closing of the circle' in order to stress the difficulties in moral decision-making. To some extent a wisdom ethic would also include a measure of modesty about our ability to have certainty in decisions, especially in environmental decision-making.[70] God can never be fully known, nor can perfection ever be reached in this life, due to sin. However, I suggest that Gustafson's sense of divine does not go far enough in filling out how such decisions will be made.

Wisdom, Virtue and an Ethic of Nature

The premise of this book is that the recovery of virtue is a helpful way of approaching difficult ethical questions arising from consideration of the natural world. Virtue, in its primary focus on agents, forces a degree of self-reflection that is not always achievable if the problems are identified as external or alien to ordinary human lives. Instead, as Cessario has reminded us, virtue is about Christian discipleship alongside the three theological virtues of faith, hope and charity, with an emphasis on the last as the mother of all virtues. I have argued that it is against the background of such theological virtues that wisdom becomes articulated.

Louke van Wensveen believes that virtues and vices need to be taken out of the original dualistic context in which they were envisaged, as in, for example, Aquinas's scheme where the flourishing of higher creatures is assumed to promote in an automatic way that of the creatures 'lower' in the Chain of Being.[71] Aquinas was clearly unaware of the possible ecological devastation caused by human activity, so his assumptions in this respect do need to be challenged. However, virtue ethics that draws on Aristotelian and Thomistic understanding can become interpreted in more holistic ways so that creatures are valued alongside the human community in the manner I suggested in earlier chapters. At the same time, we still need to be realistic about the 'natural' desire to give greater priority to one's own family, friends, tribe, species and so forth. In other words, I suggest that a holistic orientation needs to be tempered by the wisdom that can distinguish between different species in giving priority to one rather than another. Such choices are inevitably fraught with difficulty, but conservationists have to make such choices as a matter of common policy. Van Wensveen is also highly critical of traditional interpretations of the virtues where they seem to suppress the 'animal inside us', as if natural desire is inevitably evil. She argues that such suppression goes hand in hand with the oppression of nature.[72] While she is correct to worry about the rejection of the emotions that such a view might imply, I suggest that even holistic virtues when considered in opposition to vices will inevitably involve some form of rational self-control and ascetic behaviour. In an earlier chapter I suggested that we needed to affirm human emotions and see them as cognitive, rather than simple reflex reactions. Animals, too, are capable of a level of sophisticated reasoning and emotion that challenges the characterization of vices as in any way related to 'animal' behaviour.

I agree with van Wensveen that virtue needs to be situated in the context of a network of being, rather than in a rigid hierarchy. She argues in particular for the virtue of *attunement with* the natural world instead of *mastery over* the natural world. This relates to the focus on alignment with the natural world that has become characteristic of much ecofeminist thought, as I discussed in chapter 8. Ultimately, van Wensveen suggests that the measure through which we can assess whether an action is virtuous or not is whether it is in harmony with sustainability of the earth.[73] This takes us considerably further than just finding virtues in the literature on environmental ethics, for it links up with a particular way of shaping environmental policy. However, sustainability can be interpreted in different ways, though van Wensveen would be more favourably disposed towards a biocentric rather than an anthropocentric position. I suggest that the virtues that I have argued for in this book, namely wisdom, prudence, justice, temperance and fortitude, are helpful in clarifying what it might mean to adopt a sustainable approach. The meaning of prudence, justice, temperance and fortitude will be different if anthropocentrism is adopted rather than biocentrism, or biocentrism rather than ecocentrism.[74] The theocentric approach drawing on wisdom is in one sense anthropocentric in as much as it begins with human persons and where they are in relation to the natural world. Bernard Lonergan was well aware of this when he commented on wisdom in Aquinas, suggesting that 'our knowledge of truth is not to be accounted for by any vision or contact or confrontation with the other, however lofty and sublime. The ultimate ground of our knowing is indeed God, the eternal Light, but the reason why we know is within us.'[75]

However, a wisdom ethic also challenges any false sense of human mastery, viewing all creatures as having intrinsic value, given that they, too, are reflective of God's wisdom in a different way. Moreover, the earth itself as a whole system is valuable, though it cannot act as a final arbiter of value in the way that those who are fundamentally attracted to the Gaia hypothesis suggest. Hence a prudential approach that is more holistic compared with the traditional understanding of prudence will take due account of the needs of non-human creatures, while discerning where and how to act in particular ways for the good of the individual and the good of the community, including the ecological community. The ultimate reference point, according to the wisdom approach that I have been enunciating, is not sustainability as such, but the God who is the author of Wisdom and in whom we live and move and have our being.

In what sense might animals have 'rights', or is this merely an extension of anthropocentric attitudes? Other ways of arguing for including animals within the moral community as moral agents are commonly based on the increasing recognition of the intelligence and communication skills of non-humans. Alternative approaches to animal ethics that stress the difference between animals and humans are beginning to come into vogue in discussions about environmental ethics.[76] Such demand for difference could be seen as in some sense reflecting the parallel trend from viewing women as like men, then turning to a celebration of difference.[77] Elisa Aaltola argues that 'other animal ethics' may not help those who are concerned for animal welfare, for it is not clear how we might go from a sense of otherness to a sense of moral value. To put it bluntly, why should we value something just because it is different from us? For those who support animal otherness the process of mutual becoming is all that is needed in order to find connections with those creatures unlike ourselves. In this scenario feelings of being bound to the natural world replace subject–object approaches that are orientated more towards analysis than understanding. But Aaltola is correct to ask what such interconnectedness does in terms of moral attitude; a symbiotic relationship does not necessarily lead to respect for that creature in and of itself, but only arises because of mutual need. She asks pointedly, in addition, what might be the criterion for wonder; if it is sentience then we have already created an anthropocentric attitude that 'other animal' ethics is trying to undermine.

Aaltola argues instead for viewing animals not so much as those simply different from humans, but in their wholeness as *both* like and unlike us. Instead, she suggests that 'we need to have a point of reference to tell us what similarities are important', and one such cause for identification is consciousness, to be a being that is capable of having experiences. By acknowledging this facet of animal life, she suggests that we begin to be able to enter into another animal's world. From the perspective of wisdom that I have been elaborating, this turn to phenomenological consciousness in other creatures is realistic. Yet to take the next step and argue that animals are then equivalent members in the moral community seems to me to be a mistake. However, while consciousness studies may act as a guide in discerning which creatures to give the greatest value, it tends to exclude the ecocentric dimension that looks to the intricate connection between all creatures, even those without any particular sense of an experiencing self. In other words, I would want to widen the circle of care so that it is more conscious of the *web* of creation in which we are situated, the concept that all creatures, however humble, have an important place in the overall workings of the planet.[78] As such, we need to be acutely aware that the wisdom of God is greater than the wisdom of humanity, that our judgements as to the worth or otherwise of non-human creatures need to be provisional in the light of discoveries about the way the lives of different creatures intersect and interact.

The ethics of nature is also broader than just simply looking at particular cases of the way humanity behaves towards animals or ecosystems, for it is situated in a cultural context in which technology has increasingly split humanity apart from its engagement with the natural world. The technological ideal of working with the grain of the universe has, quite simply, dropped out of consideration in the desire for human flourishing. The relationship between humanity and technology is therefore the backdrop against which environmental problems surface. In addition, the particular way we use biological systems and animals in biotechnology forces the issue still further, for now the natural world itself has become integrated into technological processes. It is not just a matter of humanity and their machines, but nature itself becomes mechanized for human uses and production. If technology is an alien essentialist force to be reckoned with, then there is little hope for change – only accommodation is possible. On the other hand, if technology is about ordinary decisions in everyday life, then it becomes feasible to counter negative elements in technology by alternative modes of being and acting. Such alternatives can come to expression, for example, in the life of a community, specifically in the liturgical life of the church. Wisdom, once it is seen as integral to the liturgical life of the earliest Christian communities, can serve in this way to help to build up an alternative ethos to the one dominated by technological progress. Biotechnology itself can become scrutinized through prudential decision-making, taking its cues from a wisdom ethic, and in the light of justice and temperance. Such decision-making is never easy, for it involves balancing the needs of individuals and groups with the wider concerns of the human community and the non-human community.

The relative lack of discussion of animal cloning exemplifies the paucity in reflection on the ethics of nature aside from specifically human interests. Christian theologians have broadly followed this trend, taking up the debate in terms of human reproductive cloning, while giving far less attention to the implications for animal welfare and animal ethics. Stephen Clark's just experimentation theory is helpful in this respect, for it can be applied to cloning in order to show those situations where it might be justified and where it is arbitrary and neglectful of concern for animals. Other novel technologies related to cloning are proliferating in animal experimentation. The question becomes whether all such practices should be tolerated, or whether there are limits that need to be set prior to experimentation taking place. I suggest that a wisdom ethic cannot endorse limitless research; rather, due attention needs to be paid to the particular attitudes of the agents, as well as the outcomes of the research. Difficult decisions are also called for when considering the permissibility of therapeutic cloning and stem cell research. Quite apart from the fraught discussions about the status of the embryo from the moment of conception, cloning for therapeutic purposes introduces an additional dimension, namely the instrumental use of human life in order to extend another human life. I suggested that while some restricted research on embryos that had already been created is permissible, deliberate creation of embryos for stem cell research or therapeutic cloning is not. By drawing such a boundary in stem cell research I am taking into account the possibility of using cloning for reproductive purposes in the future, which seems to me to be ethically abhorrent.

In as much as an ethic of nature needs to take into account human nature, expressed through the virtues, what might science say about human agency? Can, for example, human behaviour simply be explained through particular genetic and environmental influences expressed eventually in psychological language? I have argued in this book that in Western culture there has been a tendency to repress environmental concern, since facing with honesty the extent of the problem is too traumatic. However, even though such a realization might help explain apathetic reactions to environmental issues, this cannot be used to obviate moral responsibility. Psychology, in its turn, has come to rely increasingly on biological interpretations of human behaviour in terms of neurological function. Given the premise of this book that virtues need to be developed and vices avoided, how far might psychological forces that are ultimately biological in origin determine our human nature? Has an ethics of nature drawing on virtue ultimately come back to evolutionary psychology, so that it is still, ironically, an ethics emergent from nature? In order to tease out this question more fully I considered the relationships between the philosophy of mind and brain science, concluding that while brain chemistry is important in setting the limits of mental activity, the philosophy of mind could not be reduced to neurological function. One of the claims of virtue ethics is that it is inclusive of human emotions, and in discussion of such emotions it became clear that emotions are cognitive, rather than simple reflex reactions. Such a study blurs the boundaries between human and other mammalian species, but also shows the distinctive development of human self-conscious reflective activity. Wisdom, in particular, relies on the capacity for discernment. While such capacity could be analysed from a psychological perspective, scientific analysis does not rule out the possibility of both learning and receiving wisdom in the manner I have suggested, any more than it rules out the possibility of other religious experiences. An ethic of nature drawing particularly on wisdom is therefore consistent with contemporary understanding of the psychology of moral agency, while parting company with it where it claims to provide the moral basis for ethics, as in, for example, Roger Sperry's interpretation of neurobiology.

While there are scientific challenges to the understanding of an ethics of nature from an investigation of human psychology, there are also challenges from the perspective of holistic science. By holistic science I am referring to James Lovelock's Gaia hypothesis. Lovelock has argued consistently for a new way of looking at life on earth, so that living things and their environment are considered integral to each other. At one level this hypothesis is singularly attractive for ethics, for it seemingly tunes into the cooperative elements in the natural world that together form a stable, viable and flourishing system. Has Darwinian theory forgotten symbiosis and cooperation in the natural world and thereby opened up a space for Gaia as a more conducive way of looking at the geo-biological evolution of life? I argued that while it is possible to combine Darwinian science with Gaia, generally speaking philosophers such as Mary Midgley and theologians such as Anne Primavesi have preferred to draw on what they perceive as cooperative elements in Gaia. Of course, how far Gaia really is a cooperative system is a mute point, given that one could argue that one dominant species sets the environmental agenda, and other species simply adapt so that these conditions are stabilized. In this system humanity could even be viewed as parasitic on the planet. Karoly Henrich uses this model to conceptual advantage by claiming that understanding the damaging relationship between humans and the natural world in terms of predator over prey in a master over slave hierarchical relationship is too simplistic; instead, humanity is much more like a cancerous tumour invading its host.[79] She argues that such a picture of humanity, while being true, needs to be replaced with that of co-evolution, so that humanity develops in cooperation with the earth, rather than through parasitic dependence on it, which is ultimately self-destructive. Few would wish to prevent calls for greater cooperation with the earth. Few, in addition, would not feel inspired by reflecting on the inherent wisdom that is characteristic of symbiotic and cooperative processes that are integral to the way the natural world has evolved. However, ultimately the natural order, even that defined by Gaia, is highly ambiguous, and so cannot act as a basis for ethics in the way that Gaian philosophers and theologians would have us believe. In as much as Gaia helps us to break out of individualism and human self-centredness, then it can be welcomed. However, I have my doubts whether it can ever achieve this function, as its mixed messages ultimately lead to an ambiguous ethic and might even promote complacency in as much as Gaia as system is capable of considerable resilience and self-regeneration.

The turn to more holistic concepts of the natural world is the hallmark of much eco-feminist literature. Such literature is important, since it not only raises possible connections between human abuse of nature and women, but also moves the ethical agenda into social and political discourse. A growing voice in eco-feminist literature is that of caring. I suggested that an ethic of care that drew simply on women's experience of mothering was unlikely to find widespread support, as it tended to assume a link between gender and biology that is at the root of the feminist concern about environmental abuse. Instead, an ethic of care that is rooted more firmly in political and social discourse can help to prevent an overly romantic notion of the relationship between humanity and nature. Caring is significant, in that it affirms a virtue that has some important ethical consequences in relation to the natural world. It is analogous to the virtue of charity that is the context in which wisdom grows. One might even suggest that it is in caring that it becomes possible for the virtue of wisdom to flourish, for it draws on human family experiences in the manner hinted at in the Hebrew Bible. However, I prefer to situate caring within a teleological goal of the caring of God for creation, orientated towards the common good. By this I am not suggesting that God is oppressive in such care; rather, it is a caring that comes from attunement and knowledge of what is created, while giving such creation freedom to be itself. The delicate balance between nature's autonomy, preferred by Haught, and dependence, preferred by Gustafson, comes to expression in the Wisdom of God, who allows creation to unfold according to God's eternal purposes. Such purposes are not rigid, in the sense of a single pre-ordained reality, but serve to encourage development that works for good, for both the individual and the community.

Finally, an ethics of wisdom points in a theological direction in a way that prudence, justice, temperance and fortitude do not, namely towards a future beatitude in God.[80] While Aquinas's thought is consistent with the turn to virtue ethics, it also presents a challenge to think theologically about the ultimate goal of human life, expressed through the notion of beatitude and the good understood as the face-to-face vision of God. In filling the human heart completely with goodness, God satisfies the longing of human endeavour, and though this is given by grace, it leads to profound joy. Aquinas situated such beatitude within the heart and minds of humans alone and thereby excluded 'brute beasts'. Given the greater scientific awareness of conscious powers within non-human creatures, such exclusion is no longer warranted. Moreover, once we understand Christology as having a much broader soteriological scope, the beatific destiny of creaturely existence is much broader than Thomas envisaged. It is not possible to know precisely how many creatures will share in the divine life; such knowledge is beyond human reasoning. The promise, then, is not so much the promise of nature in the way that Haught suggests, but the promise of God for nature and nature's beatification. To assume that divinization of human beings is inclusive of all creatures simply because we share in their nature seems to be condescending towards the particular life that is theirs. It is the problem associated with more Orthodox conceptions of humanity as microcosm of the macrocosm.

Thomas, unlike Barth, wished to point to God as Creator as a means of fostering the ethical life. In creation we can find hints of the wisdom of God, even though such wisdom needs to be tested against the eternal law. The suffering and cruelty evident in the natural world echoes a dilemma that has plagued Christian thought throughout the centuries, namely how to affirm the goodness of God despite human evil and suffering. Theodicy needs to become more inclusive of ecological suffering, and while I have hinted at how this might be achieved through reference to the wisdom of the cross, it requires further elaboration.[81] The ethic of nature that I have been developing here is one step on the path to alleviation of that suffering where it is the result of human activity. Yet it is more than just simple alleviation of pain, for it points to creaturely flourishing and beatitude, as I have just indicated above. While our individual actions may seem insignificant, a theological ethics grounded in Christian hope gives reasons to persevere. Much of the clamour of world news would give us pause to doubt that such a task is feasible.

Yet where brokenness persists a deeper understanding of the wisdom of the cross can lead ultimately to renewed faith in the resurrection. Such anticipated joy is what Aquinas longed for in the beatific vision and is the ultimate ground on which any theological ethic needs to rest. For such grounding can turn despair into hope, frustration into fulfilment and anxiety into peace. We will know, then, a little more what Aquinas meant when he claimed that the beatitude most clearly associated with wisdom was peacemaking, so that 'Accordingly spiritual peace and the resulting joy correspond directly to the Gift of wisdom'.[82] Let us hope that the Christian community, at least, will be moved to begin such a task towards an ethics of nature.

Notes

1 S. Hauerwas: *With the Grain of the Universe* (London: SCM Press, 2001), p. 225.

2 A good example of a book that does take the political dimension of ecology with utmost seriousness is P. Scott: *A Political Theology of Nature* (Cambridge: Cambridge University Press, 2003).

3 H. P. Santmire: *Nature Reborn: The Ecological and Cosmic Promise of Christian Theology* (Minneapolis: Fortress Press, 2000), pp. 115–28.

4 J. Haught: *The Promise of Nature: Ecology and Cosmic Purpose* (Mahwah, NJ: Paulist Press, 1993).

5 J. Haught: *God after Darwin: A Theology of Evolution* (Boulder, CO: Westview Press, 2000).

6 Haught: *Promise of Nature*, pp. 22–31.

7 J. Porter: *The Recovery of Virtue* (London: SPCK, 1990), pp. 54–7.

8 Haught: *Promise of Nature*, pp. 31–4.

9 Haught: *God after Darwin*, pp. 69–80.

10 Haught: *God after Darwin*, p. 76.

11 B. Goodwin: *How the Leopard Changed his Spots: The Evolution of Complexity* (London: Phoenix, 1997).

12 None the less, Evelyn Fox Keller has charted the way information language has influenced the way genetic science developed and the subsequent responses to this trend in E. F. Keller: *Re-figuring Life* (New York: Columbia University Press, 1995).

13 M. Ruse: *Can a Darwinian be a Christian? The Relationship between Science and Religion* (Cambridge: Cambridge University Press, 2001).

14 Haught: *God after Darwin*, p. 131; see also Haught, *Promise of Nature*, pp. 27–36. Other writers have taken up the idea of beauty as significant for an ecological theology. See, for example, S. Bouma-Prediger: *For the Beauty of the Earth* (New York: Eerdmans, 2001).

15 C. Deane-Drummond: *Creation through Wisdom: Theology and the New Biology* (Edinburgh: T & T Clark, 2000), pp. 87, 107, 149, 245.

16 Note that I do not argue that Wisdom is a separate hypostasis in God in the manner suggested by some Russian sophiologists such as Vladimir Solovyov. Deane-Drummond: *Creation through Wisdom*, pp. 78–92.

17 Haught: *God After Darwin*, p. 133.

18 Polkinghorne has noted this clash between Christian eschatology and ultimate cosmic despair, though for him such cosmic hopelessness needs to be challenged by a traditional

Christian understanding of eschatology. For discussion see J. Polkinghorne: *The God of Hope and the End of the World* (London: SPCK, 2002).

19 C. King: *Habitat of Grace: Biology, Christianity and the Global Environmental Crisis* (Hindmarsh: Australian Theological Forum, 2002). Susan Bratton's discussion of environmental ethics is similarly rooted in reflection on environmental issues. See S. Bratton: *Christianity, Wilderness and Wildlife* (Scranton, NJ: University of Scranton Press, 1993).

20 King: *Habitat of Grace*, p. 95.

21 King: *Habitat of Grace*, p. 118.

22 E. Aaltola: 'Other Animal Ethics and the Demand for Difference', *Environmental Ethics*, 11 (2002), pp. 193–209.

23 King: *Habitat of Grace*, p. 119.

24 King: *Habitat of Grace*, p. 153.

25 See earlier discussion in King: *Habitat of Grace*, pp. 9–14.

26 Haught: *God after Darwin*, pp. 159–60.

27 Haught: *God after Darwin*, pp. 133–4.

28 Deane-Drummond: *Creation through Wisdom*, pp. 15–27.

29 Wisdom 7:22–3.

30 E. Christianson: 'The Ethics of Narrative Wisdom: A Test Case', in W. Brown, ed.: *The Character of Scripture: Moral Formation, Identity, and Ethics in the Bible.* (New York: Eerdmans, 2002).

31 Proverbs 6:6.

32 N. Habel: 'The Book of Job: Suffering and Cognition in Context', Paper delivered to the Colloquium of the Royal Netherlands Academy of Arts and Sciences, 22–23 April 2002.

33 Deane-Drummond: *Creation through Wisdom*, pp. 131–7.

34 Nasr also criticises the West for its focus on environmental ethics; for him a religious understanding of the order of nature needs to have a higher priority. I suggest that a shift in understanding of ordering is commensurate with a new ethical approach. S. Nasr: *Religion and the Order of Nature* (Oxford: Oxford University Press, 1996). John Haught has reviewed Nasr's contribution to the science and religion debate in more detail. See Haught: *God after Darwin*, pp. 65–8, 187–8.

35 J. Dunn: 'Jesus: Teacher of Wisdom or Wisdom Incarnate', in S. Barton, ed.: *Where Shall Wisdom be Found?* (Edinburgh: T & T Clark, 1999), pp. 75–92.

36 For a discussion of biblical texts see Deane-Drummond: *Creation through Wisdom*, pp. 121–4.

37 A discussion of the particular way Augustine used wisdom language is outside the scope of this book. It is sufficient to note here that he used the term Wisdom when speaking of all three persons of the Trinity.

38 Tracing this development is outside the scope of this paper. See R. Williams: *Sergii Bulgakov: Towards a Russian Political Theology* (Edinburgh: T & T Clark, 1999), pp. 113–31.

39 The novelty and controversy of Bulgakov's writings comes from his insistence that Wisdom is integral to God's being. See Barbara Newman: 'Sergius Bulgakov and the Theology of Divine Wisdom', *St Vladimir's Theological Quarterly*, 22 (1978) pp. 39–73.

40 V. Lossky argued against Bulgakov for this reason. See V. L. Lossky: *The Mystical Theology of the Eastern Church*, trans. The Fellowship of St Alban and St Sergius (London: J. Clark, 1957), pp. 79–80.

41 See, for example, the special issue on wisdom of *Feminist Theology*, 16 (1997).

42 Deane-Drummond: *Creation through Wisdom*, pp. 124–31. See also 'Sophia: The Feminine Face of God as a Metaphor for an Ecotheology', *Feminist Theology*, 16 (1997), pp. 11–31.

43 E. Johnson: *She Who Is: The Mystery of God in Feminist Theological Discourse* (New York: Crossroad, 1992).

44 I am grateful to Michael Allsopp for pointing out the need to engage more fully with Gustafson in my work. See M. Allsopp: 'Review of *Creation through Wisdom*', *Studies in Christian Ethics*, 14:2 (2001), pp. 135–8.

45 J. M. Gustafson: *A Sense of the Divine: The Natural Environment from a Theocentric Perspective* (Edinburgh: T & T Clark, 1994), pp. 30–6. Normally an instrumental view is narrowly defined to mean specific benefits, rather than long-term considerations of the needs of future generations. Mary Midgley, for example, argues that in consideration of environmental issues our own survival is at stake, but she suggests that the shift to realizing the importance of environmental concern cannot come from rational threats such as these. See chapter 7 in this volume and M. Midgley: *Gaia: The Next Big Idea* (London: Demos, 2001), pp. 28–30.

46 Gustafson: *A Sense of the Divine*, p. 30.

47 P. Scheers: 'Human Interpretation and Animal Excellence', in W. B. Drees, ed.: *Is Nature Ever Evil? Religion, Science and Value* (London: Routledge, 2003), pp. 56–64.

48 Gustafson: *A Sense of the Divine*, p. 41.

49 Gustafson: *A Sense of the Divine*, p. 73. This idea has been developed more fully in his two earlier major works, setting out his theological position in relation to ethics in J. Gustafson: *Theology and Ethics* (Oxford: Blackwell, 1981) and *Ethics from a Theocentric Perspective. Volume 2, Ethics and Theology* (London: University of Chicago Press, 1984).

50 Haught: *God after Darwin*, p. 41.

51 Gustafson: *A Sense of the Divine*, p. 47.

52 Gustafson: *Theology and Ethics*, p. 83; *Ethics and Theology*, pp. 44–5.

53 Gustafson: *A Sense of the Divine*, p. 47.

54 Gustafson: *A Sense of the Divine*, p. 48.

55 F. E. Blumer: 'Foreword', in Gustafson: *A Sense of the Divine*, p. viii.

56 Gustafson: *A Sense of the Divine*, p. 72.

57 For a discussion of discernment in Gustafson's ethics see Gustafson: *Theology and Ethics*, pp. 347–52.

58 For a discussion of the shifts in ecological science from the equilibrium to the non-equilibrium view see C. Deane-Drummond: *Biology and Theology Today* (London: SCM Press, 2001), pp. 42–6.

59 For his rejection of human immortality see Gustafson: *Ethics and Theology*, p. 55; *Theology and Ethics*, pp. 182–3.

60 Gustafson: *Theology and Ethics*, pp. 347–52.

61 Porter: *The Recovery of Virtue*, p. 28. In this respect it could be said that Gustafson is rather more 'anthropocentric' than he claims.

62 It is fair to note that Gustafson was also aware that Aquinas did not believe in a totally static conception of nature, but even so, Gustafson argues that his views about nature have to be dispensed with in the light of modern science. I have argued earlier in this book that Aquinas's understanding needs adjustment in the light of modern evolutionary science and ecology. Although Aquinas's understanding of a chain of being works to some extent as a simple description of lack of reproductive compatibility between species, even contemporary ecologists argue for the existence of ecological hierarchy in

their understanding of observation sets, related to time and scale. Hence, the idea of 'levels of being' is not totally foreign to contemporary biological science. See R. V. O'Neill, D. L. De Angelis, J. B. Waide and T. E. Allen: *A Hierarchical Concept of Eco-systems* (Princeton, NJ: Princeton University Press, 1986).

63   Porter argues that Gustafson has failed to take this into account in his critique of Aquinas. Porter: *The Recovery of Virtue*, pp. 52–3.

64   Porter: *The Recovery of Virtue*, p. 57.

65   Drees, ed.: *Is Nature Ever Evil?*

66   See Deane-Drummond: *Creation through Wisdom*, chapter 3. This bears some resem-blance to Holmes Rolston's idea of nature as 'cruciform'. Rolston, similarly, resists the idea of nature as in some sense 'morally evil', in the strong sense of morally depraved. However, unlike Rolston, I would also see 'perfection' in the natural world as being a future hope, rather than present reality, and I am not reading into the world an understanding of God through a physico-theology, a possible criticism of Rolston's position. See Holmes Rolston: 'Naturalizing and Systematizing Evil', in Drees, ed.: *Is Nature Ever Evil?*, pp. 67–86.

67   See, for example, R. A. McCormick: 'Gustafson's God: Who? What? Where? (Etc.)', *Journal of Religious Ethics*, 13:1 (1985), pp. 53–70; G. Meilaender: 'Review of *Ethics from a Theocentric perspective, Volumes One and Two*', *Religious Studies Review* 12:1 (1986), pp. 11–16.

68   Rolston: 'Naturalizing and Systematizing Evil', p. 71.

69   Aquinas: *Summa Theologiae, volume 28, Law and Political Theory*, trans. T. Gilby (Lon-don: Blackfriars, 1966), 1a2ae, Qu. 94.4.

70   C. Deane-Drummond: 'Wisdom, Justice and Environmental Decision-making in an Age of Biotechnology', Paper presented to Consultation on Environmental Decision Making in an Age of Technology conference, Windsor Castle, 12–14 April 2002; published as C. Deane-Drummond: 'Wisdom with Justice', *Ethics in Science and Envir-onmental Politics*, ESEP (2002), pp. 65–74 (http://www.int-res.com).

71   L. van Wensveen: *Dirty Virtues: The Emergence of Ecological Virtue Ethics* (New York: Humanity Books, 2000), pp. 28–31.

72   van Wensveen: *Dirty Virtues*, pp. 28–9.

73   L. van Wensveen: 'Ecosystem Sustainability as a Criterion for Genuine Virtue', *Envir-onmental Ethics*, 23 (2001), pp. 229–41.

74   Stenmark has helpfully shown how these three different philosophical approaches make a difference in policy-making on the environment. See M. Stenmark: *Environmental Ethics and Policy Making* (Aldershot: Ashgate, 2002). Susan Bratton has also approached environmental ethics from a starting point of particular problems and policies. See S. Bratton: *Six Billion More: Human Population Regulation and Environmental Ethics* (Louisville, KY: Westminster John Knox Press, 1992).

75   B. J. Lonergan: *Verbum: Word and Idea in Aquinas*, ed. D. Burrell (London: Darton, Longman and Todd, 1968), pp. 73–4.

76   For discussion, see, for example, Aaltola: 'Other Animal Ethics'.

77   E. Graham: *Making the Difference: Gender, Personhood and Theology* (London: Cassell, 1995).

78   For a discussion of this from a theological perspective see R. Page: *God and the Web of Creation* (London: SCM Press, 1996).

79   K. Henrich: 'Gaia Infiltrata: The Anthroposphere as Complex Autoparasitic System', *Environmental Values*, 11 (2002), pp. 489–507.

80   Fergus Kerr suggests that Aquinas's moral considerations in the *Summa Theologiae* should not be as virtue ethics, or divine command ethics, but an ethics of divine beatitude. F. Kerr: *After Aquinas: Versions of Thomism* (Oxford: Blackwell, 2002), pp. 114–33.

81   Christopher Southgate argues that a distinctive ecological theodicy is now required, given the extent of loss and suffering in evolution. See C. Southgate: 'God and Evolutionary Evil: Theodicy in the Light of Darwinism', *Zygon* 37:4 (2002), pp. 803–24.

82   Aquinas: *Summa Theologiae, volume 32, Consequences of Faith* (London: Blackfriars, 1975), 2a2ae, Qu. 9.4.

Select Bibliography

Aaltola, E. 'Other Animal Ethics and the Demand for Difference', *Environmental Ethics*, 11 (2002), pp. 193–209.

Abel, E. and M. Nielson, eds. *Circles of Care: Work and Identity in Women's Lives*. Albany: State University of New York Press, 1991.

Adams, C. ed. *Ecofeminism and the Sacred*. New York: Continuum, 1993.

Alaimo, S. *Undomesticated Ground: Recasting Nature as Feminist Space*. New York: Cornell University Press, 2000.

Aquinas. *Summa Contra Gentiles, Book Two, Creation*, trans. J. F. Anderson. Notre Dame, IN: University of Notre Dame Press, 1975.

——. *Summa Theologiae, volume 1, Christian Theology*, trans. T. Gilby. London: Blackfriars, 1964.

——. *Summa Theologiae, volume 11, Man*, trans. T. Suttor. London: Blackfriars, 1970.

——. *Summa Theologiae, volume 16, Purpose and Happiness*, trans. T. Gilby. London: Blackfriars, 1969.

——. *Summa Theologiae, volume 21, Fear and Anger*, trans. J. P. Reid. London: Blackfriars, 1965.

——. *Summa Theologiae, volume 23, Virtue*, trans. W. D. Hughes. London: Blackfriars, 1969.

——. *Summa Theologiae, volume 24, The Gifts of the Spirit*, trans. E. D. O'Connor. London: Blackfriars, 1974.

——. *Summa Theologiae, volume 28, Law and Political Theory*, trans. T. Gilby. London: Blackfriars, 1966.

——. *Summa Theologiae, volume 32, Consequences of Faith*. London: Blackfriars, 1975.

——. *Summa Theologiae, volume 33, Hope*, trans. W. J. Hill. London: Blackfriars, 1966.

——. *Summa Theologiae, volume 34, Charity*, trans. R. J. Batten. London: Blackfriars, 1975.

——. *Summa Theologiae, volume 35, Consequences of Charity*, trans. T. R. Heath. London: Blackfriars, 1972.

——. *Summa Theologiae, volume 35, The Gospel of Grace*, trans. C. Ernst. London: Blackfriars, 1971.

——. *Summa Theologiae, volume 36, Prudence*, trans. T Gilby. London: Blackfriars, 1973.

——. *Summa Theologiae, volume 37, Justice*, trans. T. Gilby. London: Blackfriars, 1974.

——. *Summa Theologiae, volume 39, The Grace of Christ,* trans. L. G. Walsh. London: Blackfriars, 1973.

Attfield, R. *The Ethics of the Global Environment.* Edinburgh: Edinburgh University Press, 1999.

Ball, I. M. Goodall, C. Palmer and J. Reader, eds.. *The Earth Beneath: A Critical Guide to Green Theology.* London: SPCK, 1992.

Banner, M. *Christian Ethics and Contemporary Moral Problems.* Cambridge: Cambridge University Press, 1999.

Barad, J. *Aquinas on the Nature and the Treatment of Animals.* San Francisco: International Scholars Publications, 1995.

Barton, S. ed. *Where Shall Wisdom be Found?* Edinburgh: T & T Clark, 1999.

Bauckham, R. 'Joining Creation's Praise', *Ecotheology,* 7:1 (2002), pp. 45–59.

Bazerman, M. H. D. M. Messick, A. E. Tenbrunsel and K. A. Wade-Benzoni, eds. *Environment, Ethics and Behavior: The Psychology of Environmental Valuation and Degradation.* San Francisco: The New Lexicon Press, 1997.

Beckerman, W., and J. Pasek. 2001. *Justice, Posterity and the Environment.* Oxford: Oxford University Press, 2001.

Benson, J. *Environmental Ethics: An Introduction with Readings.* London: Routledge, 2000.

Berkoff, M. ed. *Encyclopedia of Animal Rights and Animal Welfare.* London: Fitzroy Dearborn, 1998, pp. 280, 361–2.

Bernstein, R. J. *The New Constellation: The Ethical–Political Horizons of Modernity/Postmodernity.* Cambridge: Polity Press, 1991.

Berry, R. J. *God's Book of Works: The Nature and Theology of Nature. London:* T & T Clark/ Continuum, 2003.

Biggar, N., and R. Black, eds. *The Revival of Natural Law: Philosophical, Theological and Ethical Responses to the Finnis–Grisez School.* Aldershot: Ashgate, 2000.

Bioethics Working Group of the Church and Society Commission Conference of European Churches. *Therapeutic Uses of Cloning and Embryonic Stem Cells: Discussion Document.* Strasbourg: BWGC and SCCEC, 2000.

Blakemore, C. *The Mind Machine.* London: BBC Books, 1988.

Bonting, S. *Chaos Theology: A Revised Creation Theology.* Toronto: Novalis/Saint Paul University, 2002.

Borgmann, A. *Technology and the Character of Modern Life: A Philosophical Inquiry.* Chicago: University of Chicago Press, 1984.

Bowden, S. *Caring: Gender Sensitive Ethics.* London: Routledge, 1997.

Brannigan, M., ed. *Ethical Issues in Human Cloning: Cross Disciplinary Perspectives.* New York: Seven Bridges Press, 2001.

Bratton, S. *Christianity, Wilderness and Wildlife.* Scranton, NJ: University of Scranton Press, 1993.

——. *Six Billion More: Human Population Regulation and Environmental Ethics.* Louisville, KY: Westminster John Knox Press, 1992.

Brennan, A., ed. *The Ethics of the Environment.* Brookfield: Dartmouth Publishing, 1995.

British Medical Association. *The Impact of Genetic Modification on Agriculture, Food and Health: An Interim Statement.* London: BMA, 1999.

Brooke, J., and G. Cantor. *Reconstructing Nature: The Engagement of Science and Religion.* Edinburgh: T & T Clark, 1997.

Bruce, D., and A. Bruce, eds. *Engineering Genesis.* London: Earthscan, 1998.

——, and D. Horrocks, eds. *Modifying Creation? GM Crops and Foods: A Christian Perspective.* Evangelical Alliance Policy Commission Report. Carlisle: Paternoster, 2002.

Bulger, R., E. Heitman and S. Reiser, eds. *The Ethical Dimension of the Biological Sciences*. Cambridge: Cambridge University Press, 1993.

Bunyard, P. and E. Goldsmith, eds. *Gaia: The Thesis, Mechanism and Implications* (Wadebridge: Wadebridge Ecological Centre, 1989.

Cahill, L. Cowill. *Sex, Gender and Christian Ethics*. Cambridge: Cambridge University Press, 1996.

Caputo, J. D. *Heidegger and Aquinas: An Essay on Overcoming Metaphysics*. New York: Fordham University Press, New York, 1982.

Card, C. *Feminist Ethics*. Lawrence: University Press of Kansas, 1991.

Cessario, R. *Christian Faith and the Theological Life*. Washington, DC: The Catholic University of America Press, 1996.

Chopp, R. *The Power to Speak: Feminism Language and God*. New York: Crossroad, 1992.

Christianson, E. 'The Ethics of Narrative Wisdom: A Test Case', in W. Brown, ed. *The Character of Scripture: Moral Formation, Identity, and Ethics in the Bible*. New York: Eerdmans, 2002, pp. 202–10.

Clark, A.J., ed. *Technology for the Twenty First Century*. Amsterdam: Harwood Academic Publishers, 1998.

Clark, S. *Animals and Their Moral Standing*. London: Routledge, 1997.

——. *Biology and Christian Ethics*. Cambridge: Cambridge University Press, Cambridge, 2000.

——. *The Political Animal*. London: Routledge, 1999.

——. *How to Think about the Earth: Philosophical and Theological Models for Ecology*. London: Mowbray, 1993.

Clarke, P., and A. Linzey, eds. *Dictionary of Ethics, Theology and Society*. London: Routledge, 1996.

Clayton, P., and A. Peacocke, eds. *In Whom we Live and Move and Have Our Being: Reflections on Panentheism in a Scientific Age*. New York: Eerdmans, 2003), in press.

Cole, E. Browning, and S. Coultrap McQuin. *Explorations in Feminist Ethics: Theory and Practice*. Bloomington: Indiana University Press, 1992.

Cole-Turner, R., ed. *Human Cloning*. Louisville, KY: Westminster John Knox Press, 1997.

——, ed. *Beyond Cloning: Religion and the ReMaking of Humanity*. Harrisburg, PA: Trinity Press International, 2001.

Cooper, D. E., and J. A. Palmer, eds. *Spirit of the Environment: Religion, Value and Environmental Concern*. London: Routledge, 1998.

Copeland, J. *Artificial Intelligence: A Philosophical Introduction*. Oxford: Blackwell, 1993.

Crisp, R., ed. *How Should One Live? Essays on the Virtues* (Clarendon Press, Oxford, 1996.

——, and M. Slote, eds. *Virtue Ethics*. Oxford: Oxford University Press, 1997.

Cunningham, L. S., ed. *Thomas Merton: Spiritual Master: The Essential Writings*. New York: Paulist Press, 1987.

Curran, B. *A Terrible Beauty Is Born: Genes, Clones and the Future of Mankind*. London: Taylor and Francis, 2003.

Damasio, A. R. *Descartes' Error: Emotion, Reason and the Human Brain*. New York: Putman, 1994.

de Waal, F. *Good Natured: The Origins of Right and Wrong in Humans and Other Animals*. Cambridge, MA: Harvard University Press, 1996.

Deane-Drummond, C. *Theology and Biotechnology: Implications for a New Science*. London: Geoffrey Chapman, 1997.

——. *Creation through Wisdom: Theology and the New Biology*. Edinburgh: T & T Clark, 2000.

——. *Biology and Theology Today: Exploring the Boundaries*. London: SCM Press, 2001.

——, and B. Szerszynski, eds. *Re-ordering Nature: Theology, Society and the New Genetics*. Edinburgh: T & T Clark, 2002.

Deigh, J., ed. *Ethics and Personality: Essays in Moral Psychology*. Chicago: University of Chicago Press, 1992.

——. *The Sources of Moral Agency: Essays in Moral Psychology and Freudian Theory*. Cambridge: Cambridge University Press, 1996.

Dent, N. J. H. *The Moral Psychology of the Virtues*. Cambridge: Cambridge University Press, 1984.

Donaldson, L., chair. *Stem Cell Research: Medical Progress with Responsibility*. A Report from the Chief Medical Officer's Expert Group Reviewing the Potential of Developments in Stem Cell Research and Cell Nuclear Replacement to Benefit Human Health. London: Department of Health, 2000.

Elliot, R., ed. *Environmental Ethics*. Oxford: Oxford University Press, 1995.

Ellul, J. *The Technological Society*. New York: A.A. Knopf and Random House, 1964.

Farm Animal Welfare Council (FAWC). *Report on the Implications of Cloning for the Welfare of Farmed Lifestock*. London: FAWC, 1998 (http://www.fawc.org.uk/clone/clonetoc.htm).

Feenberg, A. *Questioning Technology*. London: Routledge, 1999.

Fern, R. *Nature, God and Humanity: Envisioning an Ethics of Nature*. Cambridge: Cambridge University Press, 2002.

Flanagan, O. *Varieties of Moral Personality: Ethics and Psychological Realism*. Cambridge, MA: Harvard University Press, 1991.

——, and O. Rorty, eds. *Identity, Character and Morality: Essays in Moral Psychology*. Cambridge, MA: MIT Press, 1993.

Francione, G. L. *Animals, Property and the Law*. Philadelphia: Temple University Press, 1995.

George, K. 'Should feminists be vegetarians?', *Signs: Journal of Women in Culture and Society*, 19:1 (1994), pp. 405–34.

Gillingham, C. *In a Different Voice: Psychological Theory and Women's Development*. Cambridge, MA: Harvard University Press, 1982.

Goodwin, B. *How the Leopard Changed Its Spots: The Evolution of Complexity*. London: Phoenix, 1997.

Gottlieb, R., ed. *The Ecological Community*. London: Routledge, 1997.

Graham, E. *Making the Difference: Gender, Personhood and Theology*. London: Cassell, 1995.

Greenfield, S. A. *Journey to the Centers of the Mind: Towards a Science of Consciousness*. New York: W. H. Freeman, 1995.

Grey, M. *The Outrageous Pursuit of Hope: Prophetic Dreams for the Twenty First Century*. London: Darton, Longman and Todd, 2000.

Griffin, D. R., ed. *The Re-enchantment of Science*. New York: State University of New York Press, 1988.

Grove-White, R., P. Macnaghten, S. Mayer and B. Wynne. *Uncertain World: Genetically Modified Organisms, Food and Public Attitudes in Britain*. Lancaster: Centre for the Study of Environmental Change (CSEC), Lancaster University, 1997.

Gustafson, J. M. *Theology and Ethics*. Oxford: Blackwell, 1981.

——. *Ethics from a Theocentric Perspective. Volume 2: Ethics and Theology*. London: University of Chicago Press, 1984.

——. *A Sense of the Divine: The Natural Environment from a Theocentric Perspective*. Edinburgh: T & T Clark, 1994.

Habel, N. 'The Book of Job: Suffering and Cognition in Context', Paper delivered to the Colloquium of the Royal Netherlands Academy of Arts and Sciences, 22–23 April 2002.

Habgood, J. *The Concept of Nature*. London: Darton, Longman and Todd, 2002.

Haraway, D. *Simians, Cyborgs and Women: The Reinvention of Nature*. New York: Routledge, 1991.

Harding, S. *Whose Science, Whose Knowledge? Thinking from Women's Lives*. Ithaca, NY: Cornell University Press, 1991.

Harré, R., and R. Lamb, eds. *The Encyclopaedic Dictionary of Psychology*. Oxford: Blackwell, 1983.

——, and W. G. Perrott, eds. *The Emotions: Social, Cultural and Biological Dimensions*. London: Sage, 2000.

Harris, J. *Clones, Genes and Immortality: Ethics and the Genetic Revolution*. Oxford: Oxford University Press, 1998.

Hauerwas, S. *A Community of Character: Towards a Constructive Christian Social Ethic*. Notre Dame, IN: University of Notre Dame Press, 1981.

——. *The Peaceable Kingdom*. Notre Dame, IN: University of Notre Dame Press, 1983.

——. *With the Grain of the Universe*. London: SCM Press, 2001.

——, and C. Pinches, *Christians among the Virtues: Theological Conversations with Ancient and Modern Ethics*. Notre Dame, IN: University of Notre Dame Press, 1997.

Haught, J. *The Promise of Nature: Ecology and Cosmic Purpose*. Mahwah, NJ: Paulist Press, 1993.

——. *God after Darwin: A Theology of Evolution*. Boulder, CO: Westview Press, 2000.

Henrich, K. 'Gaia Infiltrata: The Anthroposphere as Complex Autoparasitic System', *Environmental Values*, 11 (2002), pp. 489–507.

Holland, A., and A. Johnson. *Animal Biotechnology and Ethics*. London: Chapman and Hall, 1997.

Hursthouse, R. *On Virtue Ethics*. Oxford: Oxford University Press, 1999.

Hursthouse, R. *Ethics, Humans and Other Animals: An Introduction with Readings*. London: Routledge, 2000.

Johnson, E. *She Who Is: The Mystery of God in Feminist Theological Discourse*. New York: Crossroad, 1992.

Kass-Simon, G., and P. Farnes. *Women of Science: Righting the Record*. Bloomington: Indiana University Press, 1993.

Katz, E. *Nature as Subject: Human Obligation and Natural Community*. Lanham, MD: Rowman and Littlefield, 1997.

Kean, H. *Animal Rights: Political and Social Change in Britain since 1800*. London: Reaction Books, 1998.

Keller, E. F. *Refiguring Life: Metaphors of Twentieth Century Biology*. New York: Columbia University Press, 1995.

——, and H. E. Longino, eds. *Feminism and Science*. Oxford: Oxford University Press, 1996.

Kennett, J. *Agency and Responsibility: A Common Sense Moral Psychology*. Oxford: Clarendon Press, 2001.

Kerr, F. *After Aquinas: Versions of Thomism*. Oxford: Blackwell, 2002.

King, C. *Habitat of Grace: Biology, Christianity and the Global Environmental Crisis*. Hindmarsh: Australian Theological Forum, 2002.

Klotzko, J. A. *The Cloning Sourcebook*. Oxford: Oxford University Press, 2002.

Kotva, J. *The Christian Case for Virtue Ethics*. Washington, DC: Georgetown University Press, 1996.

Larkin, L. 'Turning: Face to Face with *Limobius mixtus*', *Ecotheology*, 7:1 (2002), pp. 30–44.

Lauritzen, P. *Cloning and the Future of Human Embryo Research*. Oxford: Oxford University Press, 2001.

LeDoux, J. E. *The Emotional Brain*. New York: Simon and Schuster, 1996.

Lenton, T. 'Gaia and Natural Selection', *Nature*, 394 (1998), pp. 339–447.

Leopold, A. *A Sand County Almanac and Sketches Here and There*. New York: Oxford University Press, 1968 (first published 1949).

Linzey, A. *Christianity and the Rights of Animals*. London: SPCK, 1987.

——. *Animal Theology*. London: SCM Press, 1994.

——. *Animal Rites: Liturgies of Animal Care*. London: SPCK, 1999.

——, and T. Regan, eds. *Animals and Christianity*. London: SPCK, 1989.

Lossky, V. L. *The Mystical Theology of the Eastern Church*, trans. The Fellowship of St Alban and St Sergius. London: J. Clark, 1957.

Loughlin, G. *The Bible as Narrative*. Cambridge: Cambridge University Press, 1999.

Lovelock, J. *Gaia: A New Look at Life on Earth*, 2nd edn. Oxford: Oxford University Press, 1987.

——. *The Ages of Gaia*. Oxford: Oxford University Press, 1988.

Low, N., and B. Gleeson. *Justice, Society and Nature: An Exploration of Political Ecology*. London: Routledge, 1998.

Luria, A. H. *Human Brain and Psychological Processes*. New York: Harper and Row, 1966.

McGee, G. *The Perfect Baby: Parenthood in the New World of Cloning and Genetics*, 2nd edn. Lanham, MD: Rowman and Littlefield, 2000.

——, ed. *The Human Cloning Debate*. Berkeley, CA: Berkeley Hills Books, 2002.

MacIntyre, A. *After Virtue: A Study in Moral Theory*, 2nd edn. London: Duckworth, 1985.

——. *Whose Justice? Which Rationality?* London: Duckworth, 1988.

——. *Dependent Rational Animals: Why Human Beings Need the Virtues*. London: Duckworth, 1999.

McLaren, A., ed. *Ethical Eye: Cloning*. Strasbourg: Council of Europe Publishing, 2002.

Maslin, K. J. *An Introduction to the Philosophy of Mind*. Cambridge: Polity Press, 2001.

Matthews, F. *The Ecological Self*. London: Routledge, 1991.

Meilaender, G. *The Theory and Practice of Virtue*. Notre Dame, IN: University of Notre Dame Press, 1984.

Merchant, C. *The Death of Nature: Women, Ecology and the Scientific Revolution*. New York: Harper and Row, 1980.

——. *Radical Ecology: The Search for Liveable World*. New York and London: Routledge, 1992.

——. *Earthcare: Women and the Environment*. London: Routledge, 1995.

Messer, N. *The Ethics of Human Cloning*. Cambridge: Grove Books, 1991.

Midgley, M. *Animals and Why They Matter*. London: Penguin, 1983.

——. *Wisdom, Information and Wonder: What Is Knowledge For?* London: Routledge, 1989.

——. *Utopias, Dolphins and Computers: Problems of Philosophical Plumbing*. London: Routledge, 1996.

——. *Gaia: The Next Big Idea*. London: Demos, 2001.

——. *Science and Poetry*. London: Routledge, 2001.

Ministry of Agriculture, Fisheries and Food. *Report of the Committee to Consider the Ethical Implications of Emerging Technologies in the Breeding of Farm Animals*. London: HMSO, 1995.

Mulkay, M. *The Embryo Research Debate: Science and Politics of Reproduction*. Cambridge: Cambridge University Press, 1997.

Nasr, S. *Religion and the Order of Nature*. Oxford: Oxford University Press, 1996.

Newman, B. 'Sergius Bulgakov and the Theology of Divine Wisdom', *St Vladimir's Theological Quarterly*, 22 (1978), pp. 39–73.

Noddings, N. *Caring: A Feminine Approach to Ethics and Moral Education*. Berkeley: University of California Press, 1984.

Northcott, M. *Christianity and Environmental Ethics*. Cambridge: Cambridge University Press, 1996.

Nuffield Council on Bioethics. *Genetically Modified Crops: The Ethical and Social Issues*. London: Nuffield, 1999.

Nussbaum, M. *Upheavals of Thought: The Intelligence of Emotions*. Cambridge: Cambridge University Press, 2001.

O'Neill, J. *Ecology, Policy and Politics: Human Well Being and the Natural World*. London: Routledge, 1993.

O'Neill, O. *Towards Justice and Virtue: A Constructive Account of Practical Reasoning*. Cambridge: Cambridge University Press, 1996.

Osborn, L. 'Archtypes, Angels and Gaia', *Ecotheology*, 10 (2001), p. 12.

Page, R. *God and the Web of Creation*. London: SCM Press, 1996.

Palmer, C. 'Animals in Christian Ethics: Developing a Christian Approach', *Ecotheology*, 7:2 (2003), p. 182.

Park, C. *Environment: Principles and Applications*, 2nd edn. London: Routledge, 2001.

Parsons, S. *The Ethics of Gender*. Oxford: Blackwell, 2002.

——, ed. *Cambridge Companion to Feminist Theology*. Cambridge: Cambridge University Press, 2002.

Pedler, K. *The Quest for Gaia*. London: HarperCollins, 1991.

Pence, G. R., ed. *Flesh of My Flesh: The Ethics of Cloning Humans*. Lanham, MD: Rowman and Littlefield, 1998.

Pickett, S. T. A., J. Kolasa and C. G. Jones. *Ecological Understanding: The Nature of Theory and the Theory of Nature*. London: Academic Press, 1994.

Pieper, J. *The Silence of St Thomas*, trans. D. O'Connor. London: Faber and Faber, 1957.

——. *The Four Cardinal Virtues*. Notre Dame, IN: University of Notre Dame Press, 1966.

Pinches, C., and J. Mcdaniel, eds. *Good News for Animals? Christian Approaches to Animal Wellbeing*. Maryknoll, NY: Orbis Books, 1993.

Pitcher, G. *The Dogs Who Came to Stay*. New York: Dutton, 1995.

Plant, J., ed. *Healing the Wounds: The Promise of Ecofeminism*. Philadelphia: New Society Publishers, 1989.

Plumwood, V. 'Inequality, Ecojustice and Ecological Rationality', *Ecotheology*, 5:6 (1999), pp. 185–218.

Pluntchick, R. *Emotion: A Psychoevolutionary Synthesis*. New York: Harper and Row, 1980.

Pogacnik, M. *Daughter of Gaia: Re-birth of the Divine Feminine* (Forres: Findhorn Press, 2001).

Polkinghorne, J., ed. *The Work of Love: Creation as Kenosis*. London: SPCK, 2001.

——. *The God of Hope and the End of the World*. London: SCM Press, 2002.

Popper, K. R., and J. C. Eccles. *The Self and Its Brain*. Berlin: Springer Verlag, 1977.

Porter, J. *Moral Action and Christian Ethics*. Cambridge: Cambridge University Press, 1995.

——. *The Recovery of Virtue*. London: SPCK, 1994.

Post, S. G., L. G. Underwood, J. P. Schloss and W. B. Hurlbut, eds. *Altruism and Altruistic Love: Science, Philosophy and Religion in Dialogue*. Oxford: Oxford University Press, 2002.

Primavesi, A. *Sacred Gaia: Holistic Theology and earth Systems Science*. London: Routledge, 2000.

Radford Ruether, R. *Gaia and God: An Ecofeminist Theology of Earth Healing*. London: SCM Press, 1993.

Ramsey, P. *Basic Christian Ethics*. Louisville, KY: Westminster John Knox Press, 1950.

Reed, E. *The Genesis of Ethics: On the Authority of God as the Origin of Christian Ethics*. London: Darton, Longman and Todd, 2000.

Regan, T. *The Case for Animal Rights*. Berkeley: University of California Press, 1984; reprinted London: Routledge, 1988.

Richardson, D. H. S. *Pollution Monitoring with Lichens*. London: Richmond Publishing, 1992.

Ridley, M. *The Origins of Virtue*. Harmondsworth: Penguin, 1997.

Riker, J. H. *Ethics and the Discovery of the Unconscious*. Albany: State University of New York Press, 1997.

Rocheleau, D., B. Thomas-Slayter and E. Wangari, eds. *Feminist Political Ecology*. New York: Routledge, 1996.

Rolston, H. III. *Philosophy Gone Wild: Essays in Environmental Ethics*. Buffalo and New York: Prometheus Books, 1986.

——. *Environmental Ethics: Duties to and Values in the Natural World*. Philadelphia: Temple University Press, 1988.

——. *Genes, Genesis and God: Values and Their Origins in Natural and Human History*. Cambridge: Cambridge University Press, 1999.

Rose, H. *Love, Power and Knowledge: Towards a Feminist Transformation of the Sciences*. Cambridge: Polity Press, 1994.

Rosser, S. V., ed. *Feminism within the Science and Health Care Professions: Overcoming Resistance*. New York: Pergamon Press, 1988.

Rottschaefer, W. A. *The Biology and Psychology of Moral Agency*. Cambridge: Cambridge University Press, 1998.

Rowlands, M. *Animal Rights: A Philosophical Defence*. Basingstoke: Macmillan Press, 1998.

Rudd, R. *Biology, Ethics and Animals*. New York: Oxford University Press, 1990.

Ruddick, S. *Maternal Thinking: Towards a Politics of Peace*. Boston: Beacon Press, 1989.

Ruether, R. *New Woman: New Earth. Sexist Ideologies and Human Liberation*. New York: Seabury, 1975.

——. *Women Healing Earth: Third World Women on Ecology, Feminism and Religion*. London: SCM Press, 1996.

——. *Women and Redemption: A Theological History*. London: SCM Press, 1998.

Ruse, M. *Can a Darwinian be a Christian? The Relationship Between Science and Religion*. Cambridge: Cambridge University Press, 2001.

——. *Cloning*. Buffalo and New York: Prometheus Books, 2001.

Russell, P. *The Awakening Earth: Our Next Evolutionary Step*. London: Routledge and Kegan Paul, 1982.

Russell, R., J. N. Murphy, T. C. Meyering and M. A. Arbib, eds. *Neuroscience and the Person: Scientific Perspectives on Divine Action*. Vatican City: Vatican Observatory Foundation, 1999.

Santmire, H. P. *Nature Reborn: The Ecological and Cosmic Promise of Christian Theology*. Minneapolis: Fortress Press, 2000.

Schiebinger, L. *The Mind Has No Sex: Women in the Origin of Modern Science*. Cambridge (USA): Harvard University Press, 1989.

Schrage, W. *The Ethics of the New Testament*, trans. D. Green. Philadelphia: Fortress Press, 1988.

Scott, P. 'Imaging God: Creatureliness and Technology', *New Blackfriars*, 79:928 (1998), pp. 260–74.

——. *A Political Theology of Nature*. Cambridge: Cambridge University Press, 2003.

Seligman, M. E. P. *Helplessness: On Depression, Development and Death*. New York: W. H. Freeman, 1975.

Sheldrake, R. *The Re-birth of Nature: The Greening of Science and of God*. London: Century, 1990.

Shiva, V. *Stolen Harvest: The Hijacking of the Global Food Supply*. London: Zed Books, 2001.

Shiva, V. *Biopiracy*. London: Green Books, 1998.

Silver, L. M. *Re-making Eden: Cloning, Genetic Engineering and the Future of Humankind*. London: Weidenfeld and Nicolson, 1998.

Singer, P. *Animal Liberation*. London: Pimlico, 1990.

Sober, E., and D. Wilson, *Unto Others: The Evolution and Psychology of Unselfish Behavior*. Cambridge, MA: Harvard University Press, 1998.

Song, R. *Human Genetics: Fabricating the Future*. London: Darton, Longman and Todd, 2002.

Southgate, C. 'God and Evolutionary Evil: Theodicy in the Light of Darwinism', *Zygon*, 37:4 (2002), pp. 803–24.

Sperry, R. *Science and Moral Priority: Merging Mind, Brain and Human Values*. Oxford: Blackwell, 1983.

Spretnak, C. *States of Grace: The Recovery of Meaning in a Post Modern Age*. New York: HarperCollins, 1993.

Statman, D., ed. *Virtue Ethics: A Critical Reader*. Edinburgh: Edinburgh University Press, 1997.

Stenmark, M. *Environmental Ethics and Policy Making*. Aldershot: Ashgate, 2002.

Sternberg, R. J., ed. *Wisdom: Its Nature, Origins and Development*. Cambridge: Cambridge University Press, 1990.

Szerszynski, B. *The Sacralization of Nature: Nature and the Sacred in the Global Age*. Oxford: Blackwell, 2003.

Taylor, R. *Ethics, Faith and Reason*. Englewood Cliffs, NJ: Prentice Hall, 1985.

Thiselton, A. *The Two Horizons: New Testament Hermeneutics and Philosophical Description*, 2nd edn. Grand Rapids, MI: Eerdmans, 1993.

Torrance, I., ed. *Bio-ethics for the New Millenium*. Edinburgh: Board of Social Responsibility, Church of Scotland, St Andrew Press, 2000.

Tronto, J. *Moral Boundaries: A Political Argument for an Ethics of Care*. London and New York: Routledge, 1993.

United Nations Environment Programme. *Global Environment Outlook 3: Past, Present and Future Perspectives*. London: Earthscan, 2002.

van de Veer, D., and C. Pierce, eds. *People, Penguins and Plastic Trees: Basic Issues in Environmental Ethics*. Belmont, CA: Wadsworth, 1986.

van Wensveen, L. 'Ecosystem Sustainability as a Criterion for Genuine Virtue', *Environmental Ethics*, 23 (2001), pp. 229–41.

——. *Dirty Virtues: The Emergence of Ecological Virtue Ethics*. New York: Humanity Books, 2000.

Warren, M. *Moral Status: Obligations to Persons and Other Living Things*. Oxford: Oxford University Press, 1997.

Waters, B. *Reproductive Technology: Towards a Theology of Procreative Stewardship*. London: Darton, Longman and Todd, 2001.

——, and R. Cole-Turner. *God and the Embryo: Religious Perspectives on the Debate over Stem Cells and Cloning*. Washington, DC: Georgetown University Press, 2003.

Watts, F. *Theology and Psychology*. Aldershot: Ashgate, 2002.

Wenz, P. S. *Environmental Ethics Today*. Oxford: Oxford University Press, 2001.

Wertheim, M. *Pythagoras's Trousers: God, Physics and the Gender Wars*. London: Fourth Estate, 1996.

Westra, L. *Living in Integrity: A Global Ethic to Restore a Fragmented Earth*. Lanham, MD: Rowman and Littlefield, 1998.

White, L. 'The Historic Roots of our Ecological Crisis', *Science*, 145 (1967), pp. 1203–7.

Williams, B. *Making Sense of Humanity and Other Philosophical Papers 1982–1993*. Cambridge: Cambridge University Press, 1995.

Williams, R. *Sergii Bulgakov: Towards a Russian Political Theology*. Edinburgh: T & T Clark, 1999.

Wilson, E. O. *On Human Nature*. Cambridge, MA: Harvard University Press, 1978.

Wren, T. E. *Caring about Morality: Philosophical Perspectives in Moral Psychology*. London: Routledge, 1991.

Wright, D. *The Psychology of Moral Behaviour*. London: Penguin, 1971.

Index

DATE DUE

MAY 0 1 2018			

Made in the USA
San Bernardino, CA
14 September 2014